D1518233

Jewish Renaissance in the Russian Revolution

Jewish Renaissance
in the
Russian Revolution

Kenneth B. Moss

Harvard University Press

Cambridge, Massachusetts

London, England

2009

Library of Congress Cataloging-in-Publication Data

Moss, Kenneth B.
Jewish renaissance in the Russian revolution / Kenneth B. Moss.
p.   cm.
Includes bibliographical references and index.
ISBN 978-0-674-03510-2 (cloth : alk. paper)
1. Jews—Russia—Intellectual life—20th century.   2. Hebrew language—Social aspects—Russia—History—20th century.   3. Yiddish language—Social aspects—Russia—History—20th century.   4. Russia—Intellectual life—20th century.   5. Language and culture.   I. Title.
DS134.82.M67 2009
305.892′404709041—dc22   2009008220

For Anne, Itsik-Leyb, and Arn-Volf

Khane'n, mit libe un dankshaft,
un mayne kinder Itsik-Leyb un Arn-Volf:
"in shpil fun friyorike shtraln,
derher ikh dem reynem gepilder fun kinder"
—un davke af a loshn an eygenem!

Contents

Illustrations follow page 172.

Note on Transliteration and Translation

Because most of the sources for this study are in Hebrew, Russian, Yiddish, and in a very few cases Ukrainian, I have had to transliterate extensively. For Yiddish sources, I have transliterated according to the guidelines of the YIVO Institute. Note that the transliterations remain true to the spelling in the Yiddish originals, however, which often deviates from YIVO standards, because this is relevant historical information for those interested in the development of the language and its culture. For Hebrew, Russian, and Ukrainian sources, I have generally followed Library of Congress rules. I have tried to keep diacritical marks to a minimum, but have chosen to use ḥ for the Hebrew *(k)het* in the titles of Hebrew publications and the names of Hebraist organizations. I have transliterated Hebrew in accordance with contemporary standards of pronunciation rather than seeking to approximate the Ashkenazi pronunciation that most of the historical actors would have used, except where that approximation provides relevant historical information; thus, I refer to the Jewish Enlightenment as the *haskalah* rather than the *haskole*. By the same token, transliterating Yiddish according to the YIVO standard means that I do not seek to approximate the diverse regional dialects of the historical actors themselves. For all languages, I have sometimes deviated from these transliteration rules when dealing with personal names relatively familiar to English-language readers (for example, Sholem Aleichem rather than Sholem Aleykhem).

Some of the history related in this book took place at sites characterized by extensive ethnolinguistic mixing. When discussing towns and regions that substantial numbers of Jews called by a particular name, I have used that name rather than the Ukrainian, Polish, Lithuanian, Belorussian, or Russian equivalent, except in cases where the location has a familiar name in English (for example, Warsaw instead of Varshe). Given that there is no linguistically (or politically) neutral choice in such matters when one is writing the history of this once-multiethnic region, and given that this book is mostly about people who understood themselves as Jews in linguistic terms above all, this seemed the fairest choice.

All translations are mine, and all italics in quotations are from the original works, unless otherwise noted.

Introduction

To create among Jews a broad, comprehensive modern culture
with all of its colors and nuances, with all of its achievements and
searching—that is [our] great task.
—"VOS IZ DI KULTUR-LIGE," 1921

The February Revolution brought down Russia's sclerotic autocracy and
unleashed an extraordinary wave of public celebration among the diverse
subjects-turned-citizens of the war-ravaged empire. It also unleashed numerous wildly ambitious visions of societal transformation, many of
which proved wholly irreconcilable. Over the course of 1917, these
conflicting visions, coupled with a welter of social crises, dragged the fragile revolutionary society toward open conflict. On July 3 and 4, the streets
of Petrograd were convulsed by violent confrontation between masses of
armed radical demonstrators and forces loyal to Russia's rickety coalition
government of statist liberals and more moderate socialists. In the wake of
what came to be known as the July Days, the veteran Russian-Jewish newspaperman Ben-Tsion Katz abandoned his work in Hebrew publishing to
take part, as he put it, in the political fight against Bolshevism.[1] What precisely he meant by this is unclear. Perhaps he authored political pamphlets
for Russia's liberal-statist Kadets against social revolution, or for Russia's
burgeoning Zionist movement, urging Russian Jews not to place their faith
in revolution as a solution to their predicament; or perhaps he devoted
himself to the municipal midyear political campaigns in Moscow, where
he, along with tens of thousands of Russian Jewish refugees, had migrated
during the war.[2] In any event, Katz's trajectory would seem to typify the essential dimension of life in Russia between 1917 and 1921: the primacy of
political struggle. Not only in Petrograd and Moscow, but across Russia's
disintegrating empire, 1917 compelled numerous actors—not only socialists, liberals, and White restorationists, but also nationalists of a dozen

1

varieties, anarchists, peasant guerrillas, and a host of others—to participate in an increasingly violent political struggle to decide the fate of Russia,
the Revolution, or their own village, city, region, or ethnos.

Highly literate, disproportionately urban, and deeply politicized by years
of state abuse, popular violence, and a fraught debate over their place in
Russian (and Polish, and Ukrainian) society, the 3.5 million Jews remaining in Russia's war-reduced borders were especially primed to take part in
these struggles. Most Jews in Russia and Ukraine no doubt spent the years
of the Revolution and Civil War merely struggling to survive, like most
of their countrymen. But a disproportionately large minority participated
in revolutionary Russia's tumultuous political life. Most famously, many
played important roles across the spectrum of Russian radical and liberal
politics. At the same time, in both Russia and the Jewish demographic
heartland of Ukraine, a self-declared Jewish nationalist intelligentsia seized
on the freedoms briefly afforded by 1917 to pursue self-determination for
what they dubbed the Russian Jewish "nation."[3] Bitterly divided between
Zionists and diaspora autonomists and between liberal nationalists and
those who combined their nationalism with revolutionary socialism, this
national intelligentsia shared the belief that February heralded both unprecedented danger and unprecedented possibility for Russia's Jews—both
of which had to be confronted through a collective Jewish politics.[4]

Yet for a significant cohort of intellectuals, writers, artists, patrons, publicists, teachers, and activists embedded in this national intelligentsia, February also bore a second imperative. Even as they mobilized themselves
(into opposing camps) for a desperately pressing political struggle, these
figures—among them some of Russian Jewry's most talented men and
women—also threw themselves into efforts of unprecedented scale and intensity to create what they called a "new Jewish culture." Between February
1917 and the consolidation of Bolshevik power in 1919–1920, European
Russia and Ukraine became the sites of the most ambitious programs
of Jewish cultural formation that Eastern Europe had yet seen or, indeed, would see again. With wholly unprecedented support from private
patrons, mass organizations, and even public authorities, Hebrew and Yiddish literati in Moscow, Kiev, and Odessa organized omnibus literary
journals, avant-garde anthologies, *Gesamtkunstwerk* projects and massive
collective programs of literary translation through some dozen publishing
houses, each of which vied, as one put it, to "be *the* cultural institution to
build our literary cultural work and chart a path!"[5] At this moment there

emerged the first serious efforts to carve out distinct realms of Jewish plastic art, orchestral music, and theater—a Jewish culture spanning the full Renaissance "system of the arts."[6] The Ha-Bimah Hebrew troupe and Moscow Yiddish Chamber Theater, which would astonish Soviet and European audiences in the 1920s with their audacious modernist performances and sets, took shape amid a range of now forgotten parallels, from an avant-garde Yiddish theater initiative in Kiev to a Hebrew opera company in Odessa. Organizations devoted to broad ideas of "Jewish art" staged exhibitions in Petrograd, Moscow, and Kiev that brought together the work of academy painters like Leonid Pasternak and avant-garde figures like Marc Chagall and El Lissitzky.[7] This period was marked by the birth of Yiddish literary modernism, the high point of Hebrew literature's belated Romanticism, and the writing of some of the most intellectually significant reflections on the question of Jewish culture itself.

While some of the Russian-Jewish literati, visual artists, and composers who took part in this burst of Jewish cultural creativity understood it only as a particular idiom to be explored within the framework of Russian metropolitan culture, most conceived their individual aesthetic, intellectual, and institutional activities as part of a collective effort to create a separate, encompassing Jewish high culture—a *tarbut ivrit, evreiskaia kul'tura,* or *naye yidishe kultur* in the Hebrew, Russian, and Yiddish languages of this endeavor.[8] Tellingly, the figures who sought to shape this new Jewish culture—whom I will call "Jewish culturists" to capture the programmatic valence of their efforts—sought also to disseminate their culture-in-the-making among the Jews of the old empire and beyond.[9] Jewish cultural activists initiated adult education programs both for the "folk-strata" or "masses" and for the Russified middle class and youth whom they hoped to retrieve for Jewish culture. They created hundreds of Jewish schools with curricula framed by their conceptions of Jewish culture, and recruited the finest Hebrew and Yiddish writers to create, virtually overnight, rich Hebrew and Yiddish literatures for children. In Moscow and Kiev, competing camps of Hebraists and Yiddishists forged overarching cultural organizations of unprecedented scale and resources, the Hebrew Tarbut (Culture) and the Yiddish Kultur-Lige, which founded hundreds of branches in even the smallest Jewish towns despite the chaos of the era, and planned Jewish museums for ethnography and art, traveling theaters, and mobile exhibitions to bring the new culture to the provinces.

This book explores why so many felt compelled to pursue the seemingly rarified endeavor of *kultur/tarbut/kul'tura* in the fraught years of the Russian Revolution and Civil War. Three striking aspects of this endeavor frame my investigation. First, these culturists were in no way insensible to the fraught nature of the moment they were living through; most were politically active. Yet they were convinced that the creation of a new "Jewish culture" was a matter of utmost importance that could no more brook delay than politics.

Second, Jewish culturists were by no means deaf to the claims of historical rupture and new beginnings that the Revolution promised (or threatened). Many of them were themselves revolutionaries. Some shared the modernist convictions of the pan-European avant-garde, which saw wholesale cultural and psychic reinvention as essential to the creation of a new world. But as they themselves were quite aware, the conception of "culture" that even the more avant-garde among them sought to realize was deeply old-fashioned, rooted both institutionally and intellectually in nineteenth-century conceptions of "high culture." Even those Jewish culturists who hoped that February would be followed by a more total sociopolitical revolution were convinced that true cultural revolution in Russian Jewish life and consciousness demanded the realization of a pre-revolutionary cultural vision.

Finally, these culturists were almost by definition cultural nationalists (whether left or liberal, autonomist or Zionist) in that they saw their bid for Jewish culture as service to a secular Jewish "nation" in the making. Yet they did not conceive or create their culture in accordance with the instrumental, identitarian, and collectivist terms that such a stance would seem to dictate. As I shall demonstrate, the Jewish cultural sphere unfettered by February was marked by both the conviction that "culture" was essential to Jewish political mobilization and a powerful commitment to the separation of what contemporaries called "culture" from what they called "politics." In their relationship to the larger Jewish society, culturists initiated grandiose projects of cultural dissemination, yet they bridled at any notion of directly instrumentalizing culture for the sake of national mobilization. With regard to the content of Jewish culture itself, many of the era's leading figures vociferously rejected the idea that their new culture had to be framed by some essential Jewishness; instead, they dreamed of a Hebrew- or Yiddish-language culture characterized by universality of theme and individuality of expression. It was no accident that the young Hebraists of the era idolized the once-marginalized "pagan" poet Shaul

Tchernikhovsky. Translator of Finnish, Babylonian, and ancient Greek epics, and himself a seductive, vitalistic Romantic poet, he mixed a deep Jewish nationalism with a dizzying cultural universalism:

> I fathomed an age's sorrow, each nation's song bewitched me.
> The dream of On's soothsayers inscribed upon a wall,
> This inscription of Druids inscribed in chalkstone,
> Amulet on parchment, magician's song, the poor man's stutter.[10]

In a larger sense, culturists' conviction that "culture" was the essential site of national reconstruction and renascence coexisted with a commitment to art, aesthetic experience, and the cultivation of individuality as exalted ends in themselves. Most intriguingly, not only the former but also the latter stances were defended and even defined in terms of the needs of the "nation."

The revolutionary-era cultural trajectory of the Kievan Yiddish writer Dovid Bergelson provides a first elaboration of these claims. In 1917, at age thirty-three, Bergelson was already a leading author in a Yiddish literary sphere that had begun to develop among Russian and Polish Jews in the late 1880s. He was also committed to a radical politics that synthesized revolutionary socialism and Jewish diaspora nationalism. The party to which he adhered, the United Jewish Socialist Labor Party (Fareynikte), preached maximal political autonomy for a supposedly secular Yiddish-speaking Jewish nation within the framework of a revolution that would sweep away class distinctions. In 1917, Bergelson propagandized these views among the Jewish intelligentsia and workers of Ukraine's cities through the party's Kiev newspaper and talks at party-affiliated workers' clubs.[11]

Yet between 1917 and 1920, when he left the Soviet Union, Bergelson lived a second life that was both intimately linked to his political activism yet profoundly different from it—even opposed to it. In the name of "Jewish culture," Bergelson devoted himself to practices that did not serve any direct political ends and even clashed with his own political views and the imperatives of the Revolution itself at critical junctures. As a writer, he refused to bend his own literary work to either Jewish national or revolutionary socialist ends. Thus, in 1918–1919, even as he took part in a Yiddish cultural journal called, symptomatically, *Oyfgang* (Sunrise, Ascent)—with the "ascent" being simultaneously nationalist, socialist, and cultural—he continued to work on his dark magnum opus *Opgang* (Descent, Decay). Dense and formally complex, with an approach that moves subtly between the perspectives of individual characters within the framework of a seemingly omniscient narration à la Henry James, *Opgang* explored the psychic and social degeneration of prerevolutionary small-town Jewish life with no concessions to the revolutionary present. In its forbidding style and dark themes, Bergelson's writing confounded nationalist and socialist expectations alike, infuriating both those who demanded that the writer serve as a creator of national ideals and those who demanded clear slogans and "positive heroes" in the service of revolution.[12]

Bergelson's literary choices do not merely bespeak the innate formal tendency of artistic texts to "exceed their ideological brief." Rather, his literary practice was integrally linked to a larger ideological conception of Jewish culture. As mentor to a cohort of talented young Yiddish writers who gathered in Kiev in 1917–1918, Bergelson urged others to a similar complexity of voice and defended their work from demands for revolutionary "relevance" even after Kiev's Yiddish cultural sphere was folded into the Bolshevik order in 1919.[13] Furthermore, he enacted similar views in his capacity as editor and public cultural activist. Bergelson played a central role in the Yiddish cultural institutions that sprang up in Kiev in 1918 (in the context of promises of unprecedented formal cultural autonomy by short-lived Ukrainian nationalist governments). As a literary editor in several publishing houses, literary adviser to an experimental drama troupe, and leading voice in the Yiddish Kultur-Lige organization, Bergelson hewed a path away from the model of culture-as-politics-by-other-means that is generally deemed the hallmark of all East European nationalist and socialist intelligentsias.

Thus it was not his socialism but his Yiddishism—his belief that all other forms of Jewish cultural life should give way to a new, monolingually Yiddish secular culture—that most consistently structured his cultural practice. Indeed, in the name of the development of a Yiddish high culture, he was willing to work both with "class enemies" and political opponents.[14] Despite his socialist politics, he served as a literary editor for a Yiddishist publishing house founded by non- and antisocialist Yiddishists. He even reached out to literary figures identified with Zionist politics and with Hebraism, a vision of Jewish cultural formation that accorded the birthright to classical Hebrew rather than vernacular Yiddish—that is, to figures in the Jewish political and cultural camps with whom he should have been locked in bitter conflict. In 1918, he and his compatriots in another Kiev Yiddish publishing house, this one nominally socialist and radically

Yiddishist, even turned to the great Hebrew poet and Zionist thinker Haim Nahman Bialik in the hopes that he would contribute to their growing list of Yiddish children's literature. Bergelson and his compatriots had long-standing personal ties with Bialik, but tellingly, although their solicitation appealed to these personal ties, it also acknowledged their political differences and posited a realm of culture beyond politics: "From the publications [already sent], you have already seen that our press is a *purely literary* press, and thus your participation is not only possible but desired."[15]

By the same token, Bergelson made no concession to cultural populism as editor, activist, or writer. Thus, he followed a lecture on "The Role of the Jewish Worker in Further Cultural Creation" at his party's Odessa workers' club with a reading from his own work, generally regarded as the most difficult prose in Yiddish literature.[16] Bergelson was the presiding figure in the Kiev literary circle that, between 1917 and 1919, ushered Yiddish poetry simultaneously into aesthetic maturity and daring modernism; when he edited the 1918 Yiddish literary anthology *Eygns* (One's Own), published by a press nominally connected to his party, he again made no concessions to accessibility. Judged against the crude binary of highbrow/lowbrow, Bergelson was certainly an "elitist"; but his elitism consisted in the view that everyone, including the masses, should, and could, master the habitus of the intellectual.

As of 1917, the well-respected Bergelson had, in the terms of Pierre Bourdieu, a large amount of cultural and literary capital in this emerging Jewish "cultural field." No doubt this currency gave him greater latitude than most. Yet the sensibilities he represented did not merely appear here and there, a deviation from some mainstream practice of Jewish culture-as-politics. Rather, they pervaded the era's discourse of Jewish culture, structured the agendas of its main institutions, strongly framed most of its artistic creativity, and manifested themselves in the thought and practice of numerous Jewish culturists both minor and major. The study that follows might be said to spring from the question: What was "Jewish culture" that it could have shaped such stances in this age of total revolution and ideological politics?

In seeking to answer that question, this book is on one level a history of the fate of this ideal in the years that followed 1917. In part, that means a history of the fragility of this ideal in an "age of enormity." In 1917, the thirty-year-old Hebraist and Zionist literary critic and journalist Natan Grinblat (later Goren) participated in the strange year-long transforma-

tion of Russian Orthodox Moscow into the world center of modern Hebrew culture. In mid-1918, Jewish socialists invested with the power of the
new regime destroyed everything he had helped build. By 1919, Grinblat
found himself in a small Jewish town in Ukraine just as the region de-
scended into civil war and a bewildering array of armies unleashed a wave
of atrocities against Jewish communities. Father to an infant son, the former literary critic put aside dreams of culture to organize local defenses
and was badly wounded while repelling would-be pogromists.[17]

As the foregoing discussion suggests, however, the history of Jewish culture at the revolutionary watershed was not merely one of tragic erasure.
Quite the contrary, one of the most fascinating aspects of this cultural
endeavor—as with so many programmatic endeavors undertaken in the
midst of revolutionary upheaval—was the coexistence of extremes of violence and deprivation with extremes of ambition and creativity. The history of Jewish culturist efforts at the 1917 juncture is one of actors, texts,
and institutions of pivotal importance in modern Jewish history yet largely
unknown even to scholars of East European Jewry. The story of how Jewish culturists negotiated the relationship between their endeavor and the
institutions that bounded it—the market, political parties, the state, other
ethnolinguistic cultures—speaks to central questions of Russian history
yet is largely invisible to historians of Russia for linguistic reasons.

In part, this is also a history of how one group of participants in the
Russian Revolution understood the Revolution in relation to an ideal of
Jewish culture—and what the Revolution and its executors, the Bolshevik
party, ultimately meant for the Jewish cultural project. The Bolshevik regime assumed no meaningful presence in the Jewish cultural life of Moscow and Petrograd until mid-1918, and did not take and hold Kiev and
Odessa until 1919. In 1919, the incorporation of the Jewish cultural project
into the Bolshevik order began in earnest. As several historical studies have
recently reminded us, this incorporation was not simply a matter of suppression.[18] But, as I will argue later, it did utterly transform the Jewish cultural project. While some culturists sought to defend the prerogatives of
Jewish culture both as a national endeavor and as an autonomous realm
into the 1920s, others (especially some of the Yiddishists favored by the
new regime) obediently began to remake their culture—and themselves—
in accordance with the Revolution's ideological imperatives. Even many of
those who first resisted eventually acceded to the logic of the Revolution

and placed themselves "in harness," as a recent work puts it; indeed this would be the fate of Bergelson, who first coined that phrase.[19]

Yet although it might seem self-evident that the Sovietization of the Jewish cultural sphere along with Russian Jewry itself is the story of lasting significance, while the moment of cultural possibility ushered in by the February Revolution was a moment without issue, this is not so, for two reasons. The endeavor of Jewish culture taken up in 1917 actually continued in its original form *outside* Soviet space: among the Jews of interwar Poland and the other East European successor states, in the United States to some degree, and above all in Palestine and then Israel. Indeed, in its secular Israeli incarnation, the East European Jewish cultural project has outlived the Soviet experiment itself.

Furthermore, the efforts to create a new Jewish culture in 1917 were not inventions of the revolutionary era but in all essentials represented the unfettering, culmination, and fullest expression of an ideological program born long before the Revolution. Beginning in the late 1880s, Jewish literati in the imperial capital Petersburg and in urban centers of East European Jewish life such as Warsaw, Odessa, Vilna, and Kiev began to posit the need for Jewish creativity in all the arts. By the 1890s, they had begun to articulate the idea of a separate and encompassing Jewish culture in dialectical relationship to the Russian *kul'tura,* German *Kultur,* and Polish *kultura* in which they were steeped.[20] The turn of the century brought the first Hebrew and Yiddish journals devoted explicitly to "Jewish culture," and the relaxation of government restrictions on Jewish cultural life after the 1905 Revolution allowed more formal institutions to develop.[21] Alongside a burgeoning sphere of Jewish print culture in Hebrew, Russian, and increasingly, Yiddish, there appeared the first shoots of sustained Jewish endeavor in the other arts. The venture of Jewish culture began to attract ever-widening circles beyond the still-narrow stratum of Jewish creative intelligentsia.[22]

The havoc of World War I demolished the organizational framework of the prewar cultural sphere, but did surprisingly little to undermine the intellectual, ideological, and aesthetic principles that had powered it.[23] Rather than marking a break, the February Revolution meant that the intellectuals, activists, and writers who had collectively shaped the contours of post-traditional Jewish culture within the narrow legal, political, and discursive bounds of tsarist Russia could now articulate and act on their visions of Jewish culture without constraint. The new centers that sprang up in Moscow and Kiev (cities partially closed to Jews before 1914) were direct outgrowths of prewar efforts in Warsaw, Vilna, and Odessa, organized by veterans of those earlier ventures. Even the new conditions ushered in by February—the freedom to organize on a mass scale, the enhanced openness of the Jewish population as a whole to the new culture, and the glittering possibility of state support in a federal Russia or an independent Ukraine—initially served not to alter but to reinforce prewar cultural visions.

Despite the terrible chaos of the era, then, the 1917 watershed offers the historian of Jewish culture a twofold clarity. The events of 1919–1921 comprise a history in miniature of how the cultural project was violently altered by the most extreme forms of twentieth-century sociopolitics and revolutionary socialism. But the brief interlude of 1917–1919 offers historians something more interesting still. Because the conditions of that moment both allowed and compelled the champions of Jewish culture to articulate and enact their long-developing conceptions of culture as they never had before and would not do again until the formation of Israel, 1917–1919 provides the ideal framework within which to address questions of larger scope and import concerning the Jewish search for a modern culture, the nature of Jewish nationalism, and the relationship between ideals of culture and ideals of nationhood in the modern world.

Nation and Culture

The bid for Jewish culture at the 1917–1921 juncture, especially the seemingly orphaned moment of 1917–1919, offers, first, an especially suitable context in which to think about Jewish culture as an idea and undertaking from its beginnings long before 1917 and its development beyond Soviet borders long after. This issue is in itself decisive for the study of Jewish history as a whole. The idea of a full-fledged, separate Jewish version of the pan-European institution of culture was peculiar to East European Jewish modernity. In Western and Central Europe, Jews were offered an emancipatory contract that they essentially fulfilled: societal and cultural integration as individuals in exchange for the dissolution of all Jewish corporate identity other than the confessional.[24] In the Ottoman Empire and the Arab world, modernization within the framework of European domination reoriented Jews en masse toward metropolitan European culture.[25]

In Eastern Europe, by contrast, mutually reinforcing factors such as the ethnic discriminations of the tsarist state, the ethnopolitics of coterritorial Polish and Ukrainian nationalism, and the persistence of separate Jewish language and associational patterns on a mass scale ensured that Jewishness remained a powerful axis of group mobilization and individual self-identity for millions of Russia's Jews, even as its meaning became ever more contentious. Under the twin conditions of the radical unsettling of traditional norms and the reinforcement of Jewish identification and collectivity, it was logical that some East European Jews rejected—or simply never considered—the notion that the price of modernity was the erasure of their Jewishness, and sought instead a modernity of their own making. As historians have long recognized, the concept of "Jewish culture" stood at the center of this search.[26]

Investigating the concept of "Jewish culture" in Eastern Europe is not only essential to an understanding of modern Jewish history. It also offers a prism through which to advance our understanding of the tangled relationships among culture as a general ideal of modernity; modern conceptions of language, art, and selfhood; and two of the ideologies that have so decisively shaped the modern world, nationalism and socialism. "Culture" is perhaps the strangest and most self-contradictory of Western modernity's defining concepts-cum-institutions. The concept—in some views a mere discourse—was born out of parallel quests by early nineteenth-century German and English Romantic intellectuals for a new form of creativity and experience that could realize two exalted and crucial ends. Early champions of culture, who were witnesses to the bloody birth of modern politics in the French Revolution and the rise of market society with all its attendant material and psychic woes, hoped to chart a third realm that might somehow rise above these fallen ones while helping to resolve their constituent problems. Heirs to the Enlightenment who accepted (however reluctantly) the dictates of secularity and of individual autonomy, these intellectuals also hoped to find a means to cultivate a creative, psychically whole individuality in a disenchanted age. They staked their hopes above all on art and aesthetic experience.[27]

The idea that culture is inherently liberating, a handmaiden of individual autonomy, can be criticized from many points of view. Through the lens of a critical history of ideas, the concept of culture can seem inherently self-defeating because it posits an impossible union of the ideal of individual autonomy through reason with an irrationalist faith in the transformative power of aesthetic creativity and experience. Indeed, it is not hard to cite evidence from the career of the arts over the past two centuries that shows art's affinity with extremes of disintegrative skepticism, its hostility to claims and slogans of self-determination or even its embrace of mythic, anti-rational visions of self and society.[28] If the concept of culture can appear heteronomous to defenders of the Enlightenment, it can seem merely a pseudo-activity to certain traditions of critical social thought. Skepticism concerning culture as a practice can be found among historians and social scientists for whom such an "immaterial" discourse seems a mere mask, epiphenomenal to more concrete interests, commitments, and social conflicts. Though classically associated with base-superstructure models in the Marxist tradition, this suspicion has, ironically, only grown within the human sciences since the post-Marxist interdisciplinary rediscovery of culture in the broader anthropological or discursive sense ("the cultural turn"). Whereas a previous generation tended to ask about the social and material interests represented by the activities of high or elite culture, many historians now readily approach high culture—when they deal with it at all—in terms of the "politics" of "underlying" exclusions, prejudices, and desires that it is seen as ultimately serving. Finally, scholars associated with schools of critical sensibility such as cultural studies and postcolonial analysis have come to see in "culture" a real power in its own right—but an especially insidious one, which robs those on the periphery of power, non-elites and subalterns at home and abroad, of voice and subjectivity precisely through its claims to disinterestedness, transcendence, and the sovereignty of the creative individual.[29]

All of these approaches have added depth to our critical understanding of culture, but collectively they can lead us to ignore the powerful generative implications of culture's own claims. Historically, under certain circumstances, these claims have achieved real social purchase and generated real and profound effects in human society. In particular settings and to varying degrees, "culture" has manifestly become a real historical power—an institution, both in the macrosociological sense of a distinct sphere of actors and organizations with its own interests and rules, and in the microsociological sense of an ensemble of beliefs, repertoires, and stakes that become givens for some actors, guide their behavior, and operate with some independence from other ideological determinations.[30] Put in different terms, whatever else it became over the course of the nineteenth century, culture also sometimes came to serve as "an ethos that guarantee[d]," or at least provoked and justified, "the free play of ideas and the individual exercise of imagination."[31] This ethos of culture helped to shape rich European cultural spheres marked by continuous negotiation of the relations between individual and collective expression, innovation and tradition, art and ideology, creativity and the market, intellectual freedom and engagement.

This recognition suggests the value of what we might call a neo-institutionalist approach to culture, one that takes culture as a real activity performed by real individuals who related to its claims with a mix of critical distance and true belief, who valued it both instrumentally and for its own sake, and who sought to obey its dictates even as they sought to use culture to suit their other ends. Attention to the generative power of culture as concept and institution, however, tends to fade as scholars look east, beyond the cultural spheres of Western and Central Europe. Multiple scholarly literatures laden with a variety of assumptions have bequeathed us an enduring image of the profound differences between culture West and East, metropolitan and non-metropolitan, pivoting around such oppositions as cosmopolitan versus parochial (or authentic), universal versus particular, individual versus collective, and culture as end versus culture as instrument. The sociologist Zygmunt Bauman puts it particularly baldly:

> The intellectual idiom as embraced in the East knew no division of labor between political and cultural leaders, between body politic and "civil society," between the rights of the legislator and the duties of spiritual leadership. The separation between intellectual work and professionalized politics, the retreat of intellectuals into distinctly cultural institutions, the growing preoccupation of intellectuals with the autonomy of culture . . . all these processes which had been set in motion in the West soon after the Napoleonic wars and by the end of the nineteenth century reached their completion encapsulated in Weber's idea of *Wertfreiheit*—made little progress in East-Central Europe.[32]

Even bodies of work that do not wholly subscribe to Bauman's grim depiction of a "model which—unlike the pattern which inspired it—is absolutist, fundamentalist, and totalistic in its long-term aspirations and middle-range program" show the pervasive influence of such assumptions. The theoretical literature on nationalism tends either to treat the cultural spheres created by nonmetropolitan nationalists as mere extensions of nationalist politics, created to reshape and mobilize the "folk" (and to secure a kind of power for frustrated provincial intellectuals) or as sites of authentic but wholly reactive cultural "resistance" to metropolitan cultures. In each case, essential differences between "reactive"/"provincial" cultures and metropolitan cultures are basically assumed.[33]

A similar suspicion about culture is now growing, if not already dominant, in Russian and East European studies. Inspired by Gramscian and Foucaultian approaches, Russianists and East Europeanists are beginning to lay bare the authoritarian dimensions inherent in the "uplift" projects of the region's nationalist, socialist, and liberal intelligentsias alike.[34] Already suspect as an "elitist" category, *kul'tura* has not been excluded from this reevaluation. Jeffrey Brooks's groundbreaking 1985 study of reading practices in Russia, which drew attention to the regulatory and censorial sensibilities shared across the Russian intelligentsia from right to left, has been joined by works that conceive deviation from intelligentsia categories of culture as a kind of popular resistance to elitist, nationalist, statist, and Communist modernities alike.[35] While these works are alive to the complexity of intelligentsia commitments, the larger intellectual shift they represent threatens to paint all political and cultural projects in the region as fundamentally similar authoritarian efforts to "legislate" modernity or even as mere bids for power by *ressentiment*-filled intelligentsias.

In some respects, the search for a modern Jewish culture in Eastern Europe was unusual. It took shape in dialectical tension with a still-potent religious tradition that permeated the everyday life of East European Jews far more pervasively than did the religions of their urban neighbors; many of its creators were themselves renegades from the traditional elite steeped in Judaism's most abstruse texts. It was atypical in its multilinguality, counterposing to the languages of the metropoles (German, Russian, Polish) not one but two ethnic languages, high Hebrew and vernacular Yiddish. It was politically unique, not because it had no state—a typical feature of the region's cultural spheres—but because its fund of myths was partly rooted in a distant territory and a mythic history that had happened elsewhere. And it was socioculturally unique because its creators were not the classically educated gentlemen-poets who had given birth to the region's other modern cultures, but the children of merchants, shopkeepers, artisans, and religious scholars belonging to a pariah community that lived almost wholly outside the post-Renaissance Western cultural tradition.[36]

But in other respects, the Jewish cultural project was typical of the nonmetropolitan cultural projects that sprang up in the nineteenth century across Eurasia. Most importantly, it was bound to a typical sort of East European nationalism. Granted, this nationalism was inflected by the strange territorial and sociological features of Jewish life; its political forms ranged from Zionism to various diaspora-nationalist visions of a separate Jewish national life in a reconstructed, federal Russia, both crosscut by socialism. But it shared the most decisive feature of all the nationalisms born in Eastern Europe's distinctive environment of multiethnicity and empire: it was not merely a political ideology, but a social vision centered around questions of cultural and psychic reformation as well as questions of political self-determination and statehood.[37]

Equally typical for Eastern Europe, this project was borne by a self-declared "Jewish intelligentsia"—a Jewish version of that self-constituted social group, so particular and central to East European history, that imagined itself as both the servitor and avant-garde of a larger unformed "society" or "folk." Like other regional intelligentsias, the Jewish national intelligentsia was in some ways deeply at odds with the posited collective it sought to lead. During the late nineteenth century, an ever-widening flow of hundreds of thousands of Russian Jews streamed into metropolitan centers as a concomitant flow of new ideas, values, texts, and commodities made its way into even the most remote Jewish *shtetlekh* (towns); many of these towns even sported makeshift movie theaters by World War I.[38] A market-driven Yiddish mass culture emerged that shared the sorts of pulp literature, theater, and "yellow" press common to all European mass cultures. At the same time, changing economic needs and cultural opportunities stimulated rapid assimilation. Although 97 percent of the empire's Jews declared Yiddish their mother tongue in the 1897 census, Russification, and in certain regions Polonization, were clearly accelerating, reaching ever lower strata of Jewish society and ever more young people.[39]

The bid for a new Jewish culture was born of these same developments sociologically, but ideologically it cast itself against them. The champions of Jewish culture sought more than the overthrow of tradition. Themselves steeped in Russian, Polish, or German literary culture, they sought to carve out a Jewish culture that could hold its own. At the same time, these culturists were true believers in the virtues of high culture, and loathed the emerging Yiddish popular culture of Eastern Europe and New York as shameful and debilitating. The Jewish cultural project was shot through with the antimarket convictions that have led other scholars of the region to speak in Lukács's terms of "Romantic anti-capitalism."[40]

In short, the Jewish cultural project as it took shape in the decades before 1917 might reasonably be analyzed through the optic of culture as nationalist myth and intelligentsia dreams of power. A recent monograph by Olga Litvak casts the Jewish intelligentsia's practice of Jewish culture in the 1890s as a fundamentally conservative effort to "mobiliz[e] the reserves of Jewish conscience for the preservation of collective discipline in a world where Jewish social institutions ceased to have a commanding presence over the conduct of Jewish men and women."[41] As for the Jewish cultural project in 1917, given what we know both about 1914–1921 and the weight of emphasis in the relevant scholarship, we should expect the reemergent Jewish cultural sphere to have been dominated by the most essentialist visions of Jewish culture and the most instrumentalist sociopolitical conceptions of its uses. From Jewish cultural producers, 1917 should have elicited the most unabashed, confident, and assertive efforts to date to use secular cultural means to shape a new Jewish collective identity and mythic consciousness.[42] We might expect the means to that end to have been conceived in essentially hierarchical terms: the cultural tutelage of the masses by secular intellectuals claiming the mantle of a new priesthood. For those who sought to organize Jewish culture institutionally, the goal should have been to yoke the cultural sphere to political mobilization as closely as possible. And there certainly seems little reason to expect much discursive and institutional space for such selfishly individualist (and old-fashioned) notions of culture as a sphere of self-cultivation and self-expression.

These expectations and this sort of approach might seem especially well-suited to the era of the Russian Revolution, moreover. Going not only beyond the classic narrative of Reds and Whites but also beyond social history's search for what "society" really wanted, many historians are now rethinking 1917–1921 as a moment defined by the efforts of small groups of intelligentsia seeking to realize very particular projects (and interests) in the name of vast collectives that they in fact sought to bring into existence and to discipline through productive violence. This characterization would seem to apply not only to revolutionaries but indeed even to Russia's liberals, and certainly to the nationalists of the borderlands like the Jewish culturists.[43]

And there is indeed much about the project of developing Jewish culture at the revolutionary conjuncture that fits this composite profile. Grand ambitions and plays for power among Jewish culturists occurred not only during 1919–1921 but also prior to the Revolution's transformative impact. February propelled culturists into a bitter open struggle for hegemony over the terms of Jewish culture itself. Competing Hebraist and Yiddishist camps moved to remake the complex polyglot reality of the new Jewish culture in accordance with radical, uncompromising monolingualisms. Jewish culturists also seized 1917 as the moment to project their culture to the whole of Jewish society, not least with the power of the state.

But in key respects, the Jewish cultural project taken up in 1917 differed profoundly from such a picture. Although all of the tendencies sketched earlier were to be found, they were by no means triumphant or even dominant. Rather, as this study demonstrates, they stood in tension with surprisingly powerful countervailing imperatives of cultural experimentalism and anti-essentialism, a paradoxical will to cultural egalitarianism and self-abnegation on the part of culturist intelligentsia, a widespread resistance to the instrumentalization of culture, and obdurate defenses of the distinct prerogatives of art and self-cultivation—all within the framework of Jewish cultural nationalism.

In Chapters 1–5, I reconstruct the surprising ways in which contemporaries conceived the "new Jewish culture" itself. Both the Hebrew and Yiddish cultural milieus of the era resounded with calls for an outright revolt against the idea that a modern Jewish culture had to be based on indigenous national traditions. The Hebraists of Moscow and Odessa listened with respect to the demands of the great Hebrew poet Bialik that the new Jewish culture return to tradition, cease imitating Europe, and live up to its "national tasks." But they took their intellectual cues instead from once-maverick "Europeanizers" like the critic and translator David Frishman, Hebrew literature's most unapologetic aesthete, whose decades-long campaign to render Hebrew literature "European" now became the watchword of the day.

Locked in an increasingly zero-sum battle with these Hebraists over the language and politics of the new Jewish culture, Yiddishists in this period nevertheless paralleled their will to cultural de-Judaization, and even boasted of their superior achievements on this score. While some Yiddishists adhered to the idea that their new Jewish culture had to grow directly out of the aesthetics and ethos of East European Jewish folk culture, many insisted instead that Yiddish culture now needed to grow beyond that culture, make room for the individual voice, and incorporate into its canons "the fundamental motifs and moods, visions and images, symbols and figures, legends and myths of the world poetry of all generations, peoples, and languages."[44] Many of the intellectuals, writers, and cultural publishers in both camps devoted special energy in this period not to ethnography or the recuperation of classical Hebrew texts, but to ambitious projects for the systematic translation of the European canon into Hebrew or Yiddish.

Similar complexities abound when we turn our gaze from the content of culture to plans for its dissemination to the larger Jewish population. These plans were pervaded both by ideas of culture as a means of political mobilization and by a dream of cultural power—not only to overcome cultural assimilation, but also to erase the hybrid forms of actual Jewish cultural life with "high culture." Yet as I will demonstrate, Jewish culturists proved strikingly reluctant to create cultural products and fora specially suited to propagandizing popular audiences. Like Bergelson, leading individual and organizational voices of the Jewish cultural milieu actually explicitly rejected such a strategy. Spokesmen for the Kultur-Lige, one of the mass cultural organizations mentioned earlier, defined their organization in part by its efforts to provide "in all realms of its work . . . not cheap merchandise but rather products of fundamental cultural worth. The activists of the Kultur-Lige have kept in mind that popular does not mean vulgar, that bringing culture to the masses does not mean giving them something which would not be acceptable to oneself."[45] The elitism of the Jewish cultural project expressed itself in a paradoxical form. Rather than seeking to establish themselves as a stratum of "priests" or mandarins, many Jewish culturists entertained the strange conviction that everyone could share their categories of cultural value.

Furthermore, in an era when the political stakes for Jews could not have been higher, culturists took surprising pains to assert a robust distance between what they called culture and what they called politics. Many Jewish culturists were willing and even eager to use whatever institutional means available to them to impose their idea of Jewish culture. In fact, some, particularly (and ironically) the very socialist diasporists who attacked the idea of the nation-state as reactionary, proved open to the seductions of using state power—legal, infrastructural, consecratory, and coercive—in the cultural sphere. But at the same time, Jewish culturists of every stripe insisted on the vital importance of insulating what they designated as distinctly "cultural" institutions and practices from the dictates of party politics. They did so despite the fact that virtually all of them were politically engaged persons who shared the typical Zionist or socialist-diasporist political views of the nationalist intelligentsia as a whole—that is, they sought to insulate their cultural practice from their own politics.

More broadly, efforts to employ culture as a means of national mobilization and identity formation were surprisingly modest, and opposition to them was surprisingly robust. During this period the expectation that Jewish culture should serve the task of nation-formation directly was widely flouted, and countervailing if halting articulations of the irreducible prerogatives of art and self in culture emerged. This defense of the cultural prerogatives of the individual was not merely the stock in trade of modernist writers like Bergelson. It pervaded the Jewish cultural sphere, shaped cultural institutions, and even made its way into Jewish nationalist pedagogy.

Beginning essentially in 1919, the Jewish cultural sphere had to adjust to the demands of the Revolution. Chapters 6 and 7 trace the process of this "adjustment"—complete with acts of outright suppression directed against Hebrew culture—as it took place first in revolutionary Moscow in late 1918, then in Bolshevik Kiev in 1919 in the midst of the Civil War, and finally in 1920–1921, the years of revolutionary terror and victory. Whereas the first five chapters highlight imperatives toward a wide-ranging autonomy for Jewish culture from the other commitments of culturists themselves, especially nationalism in the narrow sense, the book's closing chapters investigate how, when, and why these imperatives were subordinated to encompassing ideals of Revolution, psychosocial engineering, and utopia. Here the surprising power of an ostensibly abstract concept like "culture" to shape the intelligentsia's practice even under duress is shown to have its limits. In dialogue with recent revisionist work on early Soviet Jewish culture, I argue that the root-and-branch reshaping of the Jewish cultural project by the Revolution began much earlier than the late 1920s, and was in fact visible in all its particulars by 1919–1920. I suggest a model of Sovietization that takes into account not only explicit institutional dictates and repressions—under which standard Soviet Yiddish culture might be deemed to have been largely free to develop as its makers wished until Stalin—but also the influence of the idea of an essentially limitless revolution on the actors' own conceptions of culture and culture's autonomy.

For it was only in the Soviet context that these conceptions of autonomy disappeared. Admittedly, in the 1917–1919 period and beyond, these ideas about culture's autonomy were unstable and stood in tension with the continuing significance of the more familiar face of Jewish culture as an instrument of nation-formation and the like. Indeed, instrumentalism and essentialism alike would prove resurgent—though never monolithically so—in the Jewish cultural spheres of interwar Poland and Palestine.[46] But despite the weight of circumstance and their own contradictions, these forms of autonomous cultural practice remained potent throughout the interwar period everywhere except the Soviet Union.

The Power of Culture

As scholars of Jewish culture will immediately recognize, all of the modes of cultural practice to be examined in this study had pre-revolutionary roots: all were found in one form or another in the pre-revolutionary East European Jewish cultural sphere. This fact is important not only because it reminds us in advance that the practice of Jewish culture in 1917 does not need to be explained by invoking the revolutionary break itself.[47] It is also important because it suggests how the history of Jewish culture at the 1917 juncture might be read in relation to a larger history that many scholars of the Russian and East European Jewish past have begun to rewrite.

Over the past few decades, even as the nationalist intelligentsia model sketched earlier has remained central to how scholars think about Russian Jewish history (while switching its valence from positive to negative for a new generation of postnationalist Jewish historians), the findings of many scholars have provided a growing mass of exceptions to its assumptions. Students of history increasingly find that the links between Jewish cultural life and Jewish nationalist political movements were far more tension-ridden and often far more tenuous than we had imagined.[48] Literary scholars such as Dan Miron and Chone Shmeruk have elaborated a new history of the relationship between Jewish literature and political projects of nation-formation, one defined not by easy consonance but rather by tensions over the tasks of Jewish literature vis-à-vis the nation, society, and the self that began in the 1890s and intensified at the turn of the century.[49] Seth Wolitz, Yaacov Shavit, and Iris Parush have turned their attention to a vast body of cultural creativity born within the ideological and institutional framework of "Jewish culture" that did not seek to mobilize traditional forms, motifs, and narratives to modern ends, but instead insisted on the importance of bringing "Hellenic," "European," and "universal" aesthetic and intellectual dimensions into the emerging Hebrew and Yiddish cultural spheres.[50] Marcus Moseley's magisterial study of the autobiographical mode in Hebrew and Yiddish literature captures the agonizing but irre-pressible power of the impulse to express individuality among modern East European Jewish writers and intellectuals. His work suggests that the anarchic impulses concerning freedom of self-expression and self-making articulated at the turn of the century by the Hebrew-Yiddish-German writer and Zionist intellectual Micha Yosef Berdichevsky (which were condemned by many older contemporaries in the Jewish national and Hebraist movements as dangerous Nietzschean heresies) enjoyed ever-broadening resonance in Jewish cultural life.[51]

The work of these scholars does not simply establish that individual Jewish cultural producers were affected by the intellectual and aesthetic trends common to the European fin-de-siècle. Rather, it paints a picture of transition within the space of "Jewish culture" from a project of iden-tity formation to something much more complicated, in which the sover-eign value of art and selfhood became a fundamental postulate of Jewish culturist ideology.[52] Given these findings, it bears asking whether these de-velopments should be seen not as a deviation from the project of creating a new Jewish culture, but as inherent in the very idea of culture itself.[53]

Because I focus on the revolutionary period yet reject any simple expla-nation in terms of revolutionary break or immediate cultural influence, this book does not claim to offer a full account of why and how this ideal of Jewish culture emerged as it did. But a study of the 1917 period does suggest not only the power of these trends in cultural practice, but also the power of culture itself as a guiding idea and institution in the life of the Jewish nationalist intelligentsia. For this intelligentsia, "culture" was not merely a discourse to be filled with whatever content one wished, as it was for the Russian revolutionary left.[54] Rather, it was conceived to be a complex institution with its own laws of development, its own rules, and its own ends. Devotion to culture as a vocation was not mere mimicry of metropolitan intellectuals by Jewish provincials but reflected deep faith in vague but powerful promises concerning art and selfhood in a secular age. It is telling that many of the actors encountered in the study that fol-lows were personally conflicted about the tensions between their cultural commitments and other imperatives—political goals, nationalist ideals, in many cases socialist dreams. Yet they insisted on the prerogatives of culture relative to these other intelligentsia duties. And this insistence marked not merely the calculated moves of intelligentsia seeking to defend their inter-ests against properly political actors, but obedience to what they themselves experienced as necessity—often in ways that made them distinctly uncomfortable and wracked them with feelings of irresponsibility. By 1917, I will suggest, these culturists had come to have an interest—better, an investment that was simultaneously a deep belief—in the idea of culture that could inflect, refract, even lead them to resist what would seem to be the obvious dictates of their nationalist and often socialist commitments.[55]

Finally, the rhetoric and practice of Jewish culture at the 1917 conjuncture suggests more than just the substantial autonomy of cultural ideology and practice from culturists' nationalist commitments. Culturists gropingly but insistently argued that their defense of culture's sovereign prerogatives was not a betrayal of the nation, but in fact represented true service to the nation—that it was a nationalist act in the truest sense. Natan Grinblat, the Hebrew literary critic introduced earlier, was a firm Zionist in his politics. Yet in 1918, he asserted as a matter of course that formulaically Zionist poetry could not be considered by any "lover of poetry and person of good taste . . . as [poetry] at all." By contrast, he argued, the very act of writing good poetry in Hebrew—good by European literary standards and the standards of the sophisticated, modern individual's aesthetic experience—was itself true cultural nationalism: "literary revival in its true meaning means the renewal and elevation of creativity, and each one who has enriched the literature . . ., each who has plowed the earth, renewed form and content . . . behold, it is he who has revived the literature, the spirit of the people, and prepared hearts for redemption."[56]

However paradoxical they might seem, these sort of sentiments did not remain in the realm of rhetoric. Much about the practice of "culture" by Jewish nationalist intelligentsia at the revolutionary juncture can best be understood as evidence of a powerful, reflexive conviction that culture had to be made "properly" if it was to realize the promise of both modern selfhood and nationhood—and that a culture improperly trammeled by other demands would in fact be fatally crippled as a national culture. On this basis, I argue for a different understanding of the relationship between culturist commitments and cultural nationalism itself, in which nationalism came to be not only a justification for the cultivation of an autonomous, metropolitan, and fundamentally free cultural sphere, but also one of the chief ideological motors driving that endeavor.

— 1 —

The Time for Words Has Passed

All those questions which in the years before the war and the Russian Revolution seemed for the most part "matters undecidable until the days of the Messiah" have now become questions of the moment that brook no delay.

—MOSHE KLEINMAN, "SHALOSH VE'IDOT," 1917

In the immediate wake of the February Revolution, the Hebraist patron Hillel Zlatopolsky and his daughter Shoshana Persits summoned Russia's leading Hebrew writers, pedagogues, and publicists to gather in Moscow: "The recent revolution in Russia reveals before us a wide perspective for cultural-national-Hebraist work [*avodah tarbutit-le'umit-'ivrit*]. Now all the external obstacles on the path of our work have been cleared away; now we can gather all our powers and organize them."[1]

As the letter's language of obstacles cleared and paths reopened suggests, these two Hebraists experienced February not as a rupture but as a consummation. The magnate Zlatopolsky had long dreamed of transforming Jews into a Hebrew-speaking nation possessed of a Hebrew national culture both in a Jewish state and in Eastern Europe. Neither the February Revolution (which he welcomed) nor the October Revolution (which he did not) altered his goals, only his sense of what was possible. Within the tight strictures of the tsarist administrative regime, he had confined himself to quiet support of modern Hebrew-language schooling, teacher training, and publishing. Only in his own home had he been able to pursue the Hebrew cultural revolution that he desired: with magisterial indifference to gender expectations and the bruising secularist-religious *Kulturkampf* in Jewish life, he had educated his daughter Shoshana in Jewish religious texts, Russian and German culture, and modern Hebrew literature. Now February seemed to bring "the hegemony of Hebrew culture in [Russian-Jewish] life" within reach—to make possible the extension of this same

23

synthesis to the whole of Russian Jewry. In the two years that followed, first in Russia and then in Ukraine, Zlatopolsky would devote vast personal resources to creating a Hebraist movement of national scope, founded on a network of publicly recognized schools, kindergartens, and gymnasia and linked to a Hebrew cultural sphere that he and like-minded activists sought to render independent of the market through organized communal funding.[2]

For her part, Persits (later a member of the State of Israel's Knesset) shared her father's Hebraist and Zionist commitments from an early age. Married at age eighteen, she devoted herself thereafter exclusively to activism on behalf of both Zionism and a passionate Hebraism that led her to conduct her home life in Hebrew.[3] For her, February meant a chance to disseminate the ideals inscribed in her education to the nation as a whole. At age twenty-three, she founded a Hebrew publishing house in the heart of Russian Orthodox Moscow and, drawing her staff from Hebrew writers and students among the city's swelling population of Jewish war refugees, embarked on an ambitious publishing program. Her publishing house, Omanut (Hebrew for "art"), devoted special effort to producing a "European" Hebrew children's literature, illustrated by the best Russian Jewish artists and built around translations of the best European writing for children. The death of her four-year-old son Gamliel did nothing to undermine her commitment; it was rooted in a larger programmatic will to see "Hebrew culture in all of its forms attain equal footing at least with the cultures of the great peoples."[4]

A similar sense of consummation characterized the roiling Jewish political life of the 1917–1918 conjuncture. After February, a half-dozen Jewish political parties defined by nationalist and often socialist principles re-emerged after a decade of semi-underground existence, convinced that the moment had come to realize longstanding political programs. Above all, they hoped to achieve their shared goal of formal autonomy for the Jewish "nation" in a federal Russia—whether as a step toward Jewish statehood in Palestine, a pendant to revolutionary transformation as the Jewish socialist parties wished, or as the true end of Jewish politics in the eyes of a small contingent of nonsocialist diaspora nationalists. As ethnonationalism became an axial principle of political identity and everyday life across the region, the divided Jewish nationalist movement achieved unprecedented political success.[5] Membership in nationalist parties swelled to unheard-of levels. By May 1917, Russian Zionism could claim between 100,000 and

140,000 members, while the most powerful socialist-nationalist synthesis party, the Bund, had 40,000 by the end of 1917; in urban centers like Kiev and Odessa, these movements could call thousands into the streets. Locked in an increasingly bitter struggle with each other, these various Jewish nationalist groups worked together to build new institutions of Jewish communal self-rule defined by nationalist principles: a democratic *kehillah* (community council) in every Jewish population center and a Russian Jewish Congress to represent the will of the nation to the Russian state. This long-planned bid for a political revolution in Jewish life was rendered moot in European Russia by the Bolshevik takeover, but taken up again in independent Ukraine in late 1917 and again in late 1918; it expired only in 1919, after bloody pogroms and the Bolshevik conquest of Ukraine.[6]

Ironically, Jewish nationalist politics drew strength from the terrible devastation that the preceding years of war had wrought in Russian Jewish life. For two years, the front had ground back and forth across the Jewish demographic centers of the Russian-Polish borderlands. East European Jewry had been caught up in the maelstrom of Europe's first total war in all the ways common to the era: hundreds of thousands of Jewish men were drafted into opposing armies; the civilian population was "mobilized" and exploited by Russian, German, and Austro-Hungarian military governments; and desperate people flowed out of the shtetl into both the countryside and the cities, succumbed to starvation and disease, and turned to smuggling and prostitution. In addition to their share of the common suffering and degradation, East European Jews were subjected to special abuse by both the Russian and Austro-Hungarian armies. Viewed as potential traitors by leading Russian generals, thousands of Russian Jews were expelled by their own army (ironically, they were sent eastward, into the heart of Russia previously forbidden to most Jews). Under these circumstances, representatives of the Jewish national movement in its various forms (especially its more radical variants) had collectively won unprecedented authority and respect in the broader community through their service as relief workers, teachers, and intercessors for communities and refugees seemingly abandoned by more traditional leaderships. More broadly, the war experience greatly bolstered Jewish popular support for nationalist formulations.[7]

But if wartime devastation and ethnically marked suffering strengthened the appeal of nationalist political logic, it hardly seemed propitious for cultural renaissance. Indeed, on the face of it, the war had been a disaster for Jewish culture. Many of those to whom Zlatopolsky and Persits had addressed their letter were themselves refugees from the Russian-Polish borderlands now living hand-to-mouth in Odessa, Kharkov, or Moscow. The German conquests early in the war had completely disrupted cultural life in the centers of Hebrew and Yiddish culture, Warsaw and Vilna; these cities, along with 40 percent of the prewar empire's Jewish population, remained largely cut off after February as well. During the war, Russian government and military leaders in the grip of wide-eyed fantasies about Jewish collective treason had outlawed all written expression in Yiddish and Hebrew (private letters included) in an expansively defined war zone. The prewar Hebrew and Yiddish journals and publishing houses of Warsaw, Vilna, and Odessa had been suppressed or had collapsed. Even Russian-language Jewish print culture, though not banned, had been reduced, in the words of one contemporary, to "newspapers and pamphlets [instead of] the Jewish book in Russian."[8]

Thus while some culturists like Zlatopolsky and Persits exulted over prospects for the new Jewish culture after February, others entered the new world of 1917 bearing a darker vision. The Hebrew poet Haim Nahman Bialik, commonly accorded the status of the "Jewish national poet" even by his political and cultural opponents, welcomed the fall of the pathologically anti-Semitic tsarist regime with the same fervent relief as other Russian Jews. But the Revolution did nothing to reverse his long-deepening doubts about the future of Jewish culture in the diaspora and even of a Jewish collectivity as such. Well before the war, this icon of the new Jewish culture had already become the most trenchant internal critic of many of the cultural project's assumptions, even as he continued to play a central cultural role as an editor, publisher, and literary authority. Now, when the young Hebraists who regarded themselves as Bialik's acolytes opened his anthology *Kneset* in April 1917, they were confronted by a brutal essay—Bialik's most famous theoretical statement, "Halakhah and Aggadah" (Law and Legend)—which accused them of having created a literature as empty of national value "as a pool without fish" and cast doubt on the very possibility of a secular Jewish culture.[9]

Nevertheless, for all Bialik's deepening doubts about the cultural project, he shared Zlatopolsky's and Persits's sense that February had inaugurated a decisive moment in the decades-old effort to forge a modern Jewish culture. As the guest of honor at the Hebraist conference that convened in April 1917 in response to Persits's and Zlatopolsky's call, he subjected the assembled Hebraists, "the true believers in renascence and the ingathering of the exiles," to his familiar grim diagnosis of Jewish modernity as one long process of national-cultural disintegration. But this gloomy assessment brought him to the same practical conclusions as Zlatopolsky's optimism: "Gentlemen! The time for words has passed and the time for deeds has come . . . Gather the remnant of our spiritual powers and begin organized and well-planned work. The time is now, let us not delay. Let us not increase our national disgrace."[10]

Not optimism but urgency drove Bialik: a sense that February marked the last chance for Jewish culturists to shape a new cultural order in place of the religious self-delusion, assimilationism, and degraded, patchwork popular culture he saw around him. In the Jewish cultural milieu of 1917, intoxicated hopes and dread-tinged historical urgency actually flowed seamlessly together. Indeed, many culturists oscillated between both stances; Zlatopolsky's drive to organize a Hebraist cultural revolution was not only a vaunted end in itself but also a reflection of his view that the "spiritual liberation" of the nation was a precondition for the fulfillment of Zionist political hopes, which had never been more pressing.[11] Yiddishists, those who had dreamed for a decade of a culture wherein Yiddish rather than Hebrew would have hegemony, shared this urgency. For the many revolutionary socialists among them, the idea that the current moment was both pregnant with unprecedented possibility and threatened by unprecedented disaster was an article of revolutionary faith.

Zlatopolsky, Persits, and Bialik were thus not alone in their perception of February's significance as a moment of possibility and truth for their longstanding dreams of Jewish cultural formation. Throughout 1917, the divided cohort of Jewish intellectuals, writers, and activists who had sought to build the new Jewish culture before the war renewed their efforts under the sign of this dual conviction. Moreover, veteran culturists were joined by swelling ranks of clamorous new arrivals: young would-be Hebrew and Yiddish poets and teachers from the provinces, artists and composers from Russia's cultural capitols suddenly interested in the idea of a Jewish culture, wealthy persons suddenly eager to patronize culture in Hebrew, and even in perennially low-status Yiddish.

Of course, these would-be creators of Jewish culture—"dreamers of dreams and planners of plans" as one participant later put it—were not insensible to the war's utter devastation of the Jewish cultural sphere or to the brute material obstacles to cultural renascence in hungry, chaotic Russia.[12] Nor were Jewish culturists unaware of or indifferent to the Revolution. The new revolutionary realities taking shape in the larger society were also at work within Russian Jewry. Internal social conflicts erupted into full-fledged challenges to the Jewish community's economic and institutional order, the Jewish population learned the ritual vocabulary of mass demonstration, disenfranchised elements of Jewish society reconstrued long-standing grievances through the new revolutionary rhetoric of *demokratiia* and class, and many Jewish intellectuals embraced the possibilities of revolutionary experimentation.

Yet many in the Jewish intelligentsia nevertheless reacted to the events of 1917 by reasserting pre-revolutionary agendas for Jewish cultural formation. The Revolution did not undermine the values, commitments, and assumptions regarding culture that had compelled them to seek to create a modern Jewish culture in the first place. Rather, amid the devastation and chaos of 1917, a variety of political, social, and cultural factors convinced them that the moment had come to realize their longstanding plans for cultural formation and reformation.

Reviving the Cultural Sphere

In material terms, the war seemed to have set the endeavor of Jewish culture back thirty years. The sense of this devastation can be gleaned from comments by Bialik regarding one of the few wartime efforts to publish Jewish literary work. As Odessa filled up with refugee writers from Warsaw and Lodz in late 1915, Bialik and his collaborator Y. H. Ravnitsky had raised funds for Hebrew and Yiddish anthologies, *Kneset* and *Untervegs,* which they had hoped (futilely) to get past the censor. When *Kneset* could finally appear in 1917, Bialik characterized his wartime mindset thus: "I had no grand pretensions and I formulated no 'program.' There was only one goal before my eyes: to furnish the remnant of our writers with a place of gathering for the time being, a place where they might sound a *voice,* whatever it might be, just so that they might ease a bit the terror of silence."[13]

Even after the fall of the regime, the practical implications of wartime events remained grim. As of February, many of the leading Jewish cultural producers were concentrated in Odessa, Moscow, Kiev, and Petrograd. But many of the other factors necessary for the revival of cultural life were in short supply in those cities—for instance, Hebrew and Yiddish typeface and printers trained to work with it, both of which proved extraordinarily hard to secure. Moreover, if many would-be creators of Jewish culture were resettled in central cultural locations by February, others were far from them. As of February, the Kiev Yiddish literary critic Nahman Mayzl was working in a military factory in Perm. The Yiddish poet Oysher Shvartsman served part of 1917 in a cavalry division that was transferred to Petrograd in the midst of the bloody July Days. The Hebrew writer M. Z. Valpovsky and Peretz Markish, who would soon emerge from nowhere to become the boldest poet of the Yiddish avant-garde, were still at the front. Problems of communication, travel, and transport limited contact among Russia's cities. Deteriorating industry, inflation, and a worsening transportation crisis disproportionately affected the Russian Jewish community, which was heavily dependent on trade and crafts.[14]

Furthermore, the Jewish culturist intelligentsia entered 1917 sharply divided into two increasingly irreconcilable Hebraist and Yiddishist camps, each of which claimed to represent Jewish national culture and sought to win East European Jewry (or at least the "masses") over to their side. This division had been long in the making: before the war a growing valorization of Yiddish by a portion of the Jewish intelligentsia, coupled with the belated but rapid upsurge in Yiddish cultural production, had compelled those who had always taken for granted the cultural primacy of Hebrew to elevate that view to a programmatic stance as well.[15] Several factors ushered in by February sharpened this split into often-ferocious conflict. In particular, the ever-closer identification between Hebraism and Zionism on the one hand and Yiddishism and Jewish socialism on the other ensured that the Hebraist-Yiddishist division would be especially fierce in 1917, when the long-simmering struggle between Zionism and socialist diaspora nationalism flared into open conflict with real stakes.

Throughout 1917–1918, Jewish culturists moved toward an ever-firmer embrace of exclusivist Hebraism or Yiddishism not only in matters of dissemination or education, but also in the more rarified domains of cultural production and consumption. Many literati who had worked bilingually before the war ceased to participate in the forums of the other Jewish language (though they often continued to write "for the desk"). Hebraist and Yiddishist intellectuals even moved to excise creativity in the other Jewish language from their cultural memory. The death in November 1917 of Sh. Y. Abramovitsh (Mendele Moykher Sforim), the nineteenth-century founder of modern Yiddish and Hebrew prose, touched off a wave of critical essays claiming that the "true" Mendele was to be found in one or the other language.[16]

A few resisted this process. Aging figures like the literary critic Isidor

Eliashev (Baal-Makhshoves) in Petrograd and the cultural activist Ravnitsky in Odessa continued to insist that respect toward both Jewish languages followed from proper nationalist principles.[17] A variety of Jewish civic and arts organizations founded by Russified but ethnically engaged Jewish circles in Petersburg adhered to a policy of linguistic neutrality or a principled trilingualism with Russian at the center. But neutrality found no institutional purchase and trilingualism collapsed. The half-century-old Obshchestvo dlia Rasprostraneniia Prosveshcheniia mezhdu Evreiiami v Rossii (Society for the Promotion of Enlightenment among the Jews of Russia) or OPE, the empire's decisive institutional actor in nontraditional Jewish educational and cultural institutions like popular libraries, had made trilingualism a policy of sorts during the interrevolutionary decade. But in mid-1917, the organization essentially evaporated. After an explosive split between Yiddishist and Hebraist delegates at its teachers' conference in June 1917, its entire rank-and-file of Jewish teachers and activists abandoned it for radically Hebraist and Yiddishist successor organizations.[18]

Thus almost all the Jewish cultural activity reemergent in 1917 was either radically Hebraist or radically Yiddishist. In every locale, no matter how small, two mutually opposed camps of Hebraists and Yiddishists emerged. Almost all the new cultural organizations created in the course of the year—teachers' unions, publishing houses, and the great umbrella cultural organizations Tarbut and the Kultur-Lige—articulated exclusively Hebraist or Yiddishist policies. When the Jewish educational activist and historian Ben-Tsion Dinaburg (later Dinur) arrived in Kiev in mid-1918, he found two separate Hebraist and Yiddishist cultural spheres with absolutely no formal connection, bound only by fraying ties of friendship between a few former comrades. His own respect for both cultural movements generated suspicion from both sides.[19]

For these reasons and others, actual activity by culturists in the first postrevolutionary months was spotty and mostly small-scale. Many of these efforts took place in cities that had no significant tradition of secular Jewish culture but were now home to large Jewish refugee populations. In the southern Russian industrial center of Kharkov, for example, a small Yiddishist publishing house and Hebrew and Yiddish theater troupes were created, but these did not amount to much.[20]

The resumption of cultural endeavors was halting even in established centers. In Odessa, a perennial center of Hebrew literary culture and a popular Zionist movement, the lifting of what Bialik called the old regime's "iron yoke" allowed the reemergence of a substantial literary sphere. Bialik's own Moriah publishing house, the premiere Hebrew publishing house of the prewar decade, resumed its work despite severe local material problems. A steady stream of original and translated literary work flowed from the press in 1917, including writer-critic David Frishman's translation of the Grimms' tales and many children's books.[21] In June, the preeminent Hebrew "thick journal" *Ha-Shiloah* reappeared after a year and a half of closure. Guided by its editor, critic and cultural historian Yosef Klausner, *Ha-Shiloah* resumed its prewar role as a clearing house for both Zionist thought and Hebrew-language literature and scholarship that often bore no particular relationship to Zionist agendas. Until it was closed by the Bolsheviks in 1919, *Ha-Shiloah* served as the primary forum for aesthetic and canonical debate among Russian Hebraists, a particularly pressing matter at a moment that Hebrew writers themselves saw as one of demographic, thematic, and formal transition. But more ramified cultural initiatives lagged behind, perhaps because leading figures like the preeminent Odessa Zionist leader Menahem Ussishkin were then locked in a bitter electoral contest between a Zionist-led liberal bloc and a Bolshevik-dominated socialist bloc for control of the city administration.[22]

Petrograd should have been an even more robust center of renewed Jewish culturist activity. During the war, the imperial capitol had been the seat of a thickly intertwined network of Jewish aid organizations devoted to relief work among Jewish refugees. After February, the activists in these organizations flowed out into the various Jewish parties that vied to speak for Russian Jewry (or its "democratic masses"). Throughout 1917, Petrograd was the center of Jewish public life in a nationalist key, awash in political activists and public meetings. The "question of culture" loomed large at the national conferences convened by the reemergent Jewish political parties. Yet actual cultural activity in Petrograd remained limited even before the chaotic Bolshevik takeover and the miserable winter of 1917–1918. An Evreiskoe Teatral'noe Obshchestvo (Jewish Theater Society) founded during the war to foster the development of Yiddish theater was derailed for some months after February. The chief branch of the Evreiskoe Obshchestvo Pooshchreniia Khudozhestv (Jewish Society for the Encouragement of Art), founded in late 1915 by a group of Russian Jewish art patrons and artists, mounted an impressive art exhibition in 1916 but did little thereafter. Jewish newspapers proliferated in the city, but most were

Russian-language party publications. Cultural matters found a bit of space only in those newspapers with a more ambitious brief like *Der petrograder togblat,* a Yiddish newspaper with Zionist leanings founded in May.[23]

As the case of Petrograd suggests, the presence of a Jewish nationalist political milieu, even a large one, was no guarantee of cultural revival. Kiev, though a major Zionist center and home to a rapidly swelling Jewish population of 87,000 (some 20 percent of the population in mid-1917), had no significant Hebrew cultural institutions throughout the year. When flight from Bolshevik repressions brought a wave of Hebraists from Moscow to Kiev in mid-1918, they were compelled to begin virtually from scratch.[24]

Indeed, the explosive reemergence of Jewish politics after February was itself, ironically, perhaps the heaviest brake on renewed cultural institution-building throughout 1917—and, in Ukraine, again in late 1918—because the imperative of political engagement weighed heavily on Jewish culturists across all lines of commitment. Most were aligned with one of the half-dozen parties that defined themselves in nationalist terms: the general Russian Zionist movement, its left-leaning Tseire Tsion (Youth of Zion) fraction, the breakaway Marxist-Zionist party Poale Tsion, the Menshevik-aligned Bund committed both to Marxism and Jewish national autonomy, the newly founded Ukraine-centered socialist-nationalist Fareynikte, or the nonsocialist diaspora autonomist Folks-Partey. Throughout 1917, each of these parties strove to publish "newspapers, party organs, brochures, election tickets" not only nationally but also regionally, in two or even three languages.[25] Each needed activists to travel around the region and debate, propagandizing a Jewish public hungry for political engagement. Each was desperately short not only of material resources, but also of what the Bundist Moyshe Rafes called "literary powers."[26]

These shortages meant that the parties themselves could make only limited contributions to cultural revival even when they wished to. Furthermore, sympathetic cultural producers felt pressure to mobilize themselves politically. Many Hebraists felt drawn to work on behalf of Zionism, which emerged from its long inter-revolutionary doldrums suddenly poised to win hegemony in the organized Russian Jewish community. Thus, in the March 17 issue of the Moscow Zionist newspaper *Ha-'Am,* one activist argued that the movement's recent focus on cultural and educational work now had to yield to expanded efforts to win political power.[27]

Even more dramatic were the effects of political mobilization on the revival of Yiddish cultural activity, in part because this upstart movement seems to have had a smaller core of dedicated culturists. Some complained that the demands of politics consumed virtually all the energies of the Yiddishist intelligentsia, and although this claim was partly tactical, it was not entirely wrong.[28] In the Jewish socialist camp(s), some who had taken part in Yiddish cultural activity in the inter-revolutionary years when direct political activism had become impossible now abandoned it altogether. One of these was Sh. Vaytsman (brother of Chaim Weizmann, the future first president of Israel), who had moved in Yiddishist circles since 1910 but by July was "entirely immersed in political matters" and in fact never looked back.[29] But more committed Yiddishists too threw themselves into politics in 1917. The Bundist pedagogical theorist Khayim Kazdan became vice-mayor of Kherson in 1917.[30] The leading Yiddish literary critic Shmuel Niger was elected to Petrograd's *kehillah* for the diasporist Folks-Partey, and his younger brother, Donyel Tsharni, an aspiring poet, administered the party's Moscow affairs.[31]

Thus the Jewish cultural sphere that reemerged in 1917 already divided down the middle had to start virtually from scratch, its bearers dispersed across Russia, impeded by material obstacles and the competing obligations of politics. That it reemerged at all despite the conditions of the time contrasted quite remarkably with the fate of Jewish culture during Russia's first revolution, the Revolution of 1905. In the previous Revolution, Jewish cultural and literary endeavor had declined precipitously, especially in Hebrew. Culturists had reacted with shock to this collapse. The Hebrew-Yiddish writer Zalman Ahronson (Anoykhi) had written perceptively of this "great and bitter blow to our literature" and drawn a pained comparison between the abandonment of Jewish culture and the enviable responsibility of Russian cultural creators:

> Even if these terrible upheavals should last for decades, when victory comes, the Russian people will be able to lift their eyes to their literature and find a great literature, great creations . . . Even during these upheavals, [the Russians] have people who concern themselves intensely with this task. The fighters fight, but the literary talents continue to perform their task, to write, make, create, and publish.[32]

It may be that some culturists had learned a hard lesson from this first revolution. More generally, the fact that in 1917, a dedicated if thin cohort of intellectuals insisted that cultural endeavor should not be neglected testifies to a deepening of commitment to culture as an end in the Jewish nationalist intelligentsia between 1907 and 1917.

Yet cultural endeavor in 1917 was not framed solely by a sort of grim commitment to staying at one's post. Rather, in many quarters, there was surprising optimism. Figures like Zlatopolsky and Persits were not alone in their sense that despite the devastation of the Jewish cultural sphere, the prospects for the Jewish cultural project had never been more favorable. Many of the roughly two hundred Hebrew writers, pedagogues, actors, artists, patrons, and activists who gathered in Moscow in mid-April 1917 in response to their letter evidently shared their views. Over four days, the delegates repeated the mantra that February had initiated a sea change in the conditions of cultural activity—that it was now possible not only to undo the wartime disruption of Hebraist cultural activity, but also to realize the Hebraist cultural revolution of which they had long dreamed. The new organization founded at the conference, Tarbut (Culture), issued this ringing declaration:

> Great days have arrived for our work. The political revolution has brought us too deliverance and relief. Chains generations old have been removed from us, the national energy which we squandered from day to day and from generation to generation in a difficult war for our very survival, for our basic human rights, has been freed. Now behold, deliverance has come and we are able to turn our spiritual energy to the work of national creation. Alongside all the liberated peoples of Russia we too can build for ourselves our internal national life as we see fit. Do not postpone the fulfillment of this great hour's commandment.[33]

Given the painful limitations on Jewish cultural revival in 1917, why were many of the Hebraists gathered at the meeting enthusiastic? Much of this optimism stemmed from a surprising local development: wartime developments in Moscow. Moscow was famed for its longstanding efforts to keep Jews to a minimum. But the war years had inundated it with waves of Jewish refugees ranging from wealthy businessmen from Kiev and Warsaw to tens of thousands of displaced persons seeking work in the city's relatively robust labor market. A prewar Jewish population of 15,000 had grown at least fivefold by mid-1917.[34]

Among the new arrivals was a strong cohort of Jewish political and cultural activists, mostly Zionists, who came to Moscow from Petrograd or the south in search of better administrative and economic conditions. The

Petrograd Zionist weekly *Razsvet* reopened in Moscow as *Evreiskaia zhizn'* (Jewish Life) in late 1916 and gave substantial space to cultural and literary matters. The most vibrant movements in Zionism, the party fraction Tseire Tsion and the youth movement He-Ḥaver, centered their most dedicated activists in Moscow; many of these were strongly committed to the importance of cultural renaissance. Both in the city and in the many refugee settlements around it, a growing number of Hebrew educators began to found schools on a Hebraist-Zionist basis. And in late 1916, such activists began to publish the only Hebrew newspaper allowed in Russia, the weekly *Ha-ʿAm* (The People) edited by a coalition of Hebraist cultural figures and Zionist leaders. The final element in Moscow's transformation was the resettlement there of some half-dozen of the most important prewar patrons of Hebraist causes, including Zlatopolsky and Persits.[35]

Months before February, then, Moscow had become a major center of Hebraist cultural activity. "The House of Zlatopolsky-Persits" transformed the local, legal branch of the Ḥoveve Sfat ʿEver (Lovers of the Hebrew Language) from a sleepy enthusiasts' club into a front for regionwide educational programming. This transformed HSE formed the basis for the Tarbut organization created in April 1917. In 1916, Persits managed to find that rarest of commodities in Moscow, Hebrew typeface, at the Institute for Oriental Languages (she discovered it while studying Arabic in preparation for eventual emigration to Palestine), and established her Omanut publishing house. These veteran patron-activists were joined by a number of newly minted patrons who had made their fortunes during the war itself. In late 1916, Avraham Yosef Stybel, the Polish Jewish hasid-turned-Hebraist (and clerk-turned-leather-magnate) took his first steps toward creating a publishing house devoted entirely to Hebrew literature and literary criticism; by 1917, his Moscow-based Stybel publishing house would blossom into the best-endowed and most culturally ambitious publishing venture in the history of modern Hebrew literature.

Such endeavors, initiated from above, could draw on the talents of young activists like Shmuel Ayzenshtat. Born in the western borderlands, Ayzenshtat was traditionally educated but held a law degree from Berne, was active in both Hebraist and Zionist endeavors, and before the war had cofounded both a young Hebrew writers' group and the Tseire Tsion political organization in Odessa. He typified the growing cadre of young Hebraist activists who administered Tarbut endeavors.[36] Other Hebraists of similar background included the Homel-born Hebrew pedagogue Yitzhak

Alterman (father of the Hebrew modernist poet Natan Alterman), who founded a pioneering Hebrew kindergarten; and Nahum Tsemah, a refugee veteran of the fledgling prewar Hebrew theater movement who cofounded the Hebrew dramatic society Ha-Bimah (The Stage) in 1916. Ha-Bimah was to serve Hebraist ends both by using theater as a means of cultural and linguistic Hebraization—founded under the auspices of the HSE, it envisioned the creation of Hebrew theater studios and theaters on a nationwide basis—and by creating a model Hebrew theater that would satisfy the aesthetic expectations of sophisticated audiences and perhaps even forge a new "Hebrew" aesthetic.[37]

This Hebraist milieu intersected with another unlooked-for development in Moscow: increasingly visible interest in the idea of Jewish culture among Russified Jews. By 1917, Moscow had supplanted Petrograd as the chief site of organized efforts by Russified but ethnically engaged Jewish circles to support Jewish creativity in the arts. The Moscow branch of the Evreiskoe Obshchestvo Pooshchreniia Khudozhestv sponsored Russia's second large-scale exhibition devoted to "Jewish art" in April 1917. Apparently, the real organizers were not the staid aesthetic conservatives who had founded the organization but the young avant-gardists Chagall, Natan Alt'man, and Lissitzky. By all accounts, these exhibitions generated great interest in a broader, highly Russified Jewish audience.[38]

Moscow's Hebraists eagerly sought to draw interested artists into Hebrew cultural life, reaching out to figures ranging from the academy painter and sculptor Leonid Pasternak to young Turks like Alt'man and Lissitzky.[39] Hebraists also sought to learn from the larger Russian milieu. The members of Ha-Bimah, determined to overcome their amateurism and intoxicated by the rich theater life of revolutionary Moscow (which boasted some thirty-two theaters in October 1917), turned to the doyen of Russian theater, Konstantin Stanislavsky, for aesthetic guidance. Stanislavsky, intrigued by their undertaking, appointed one of his chief students, Evgenii Vakhtangov, to train them.[40]

Word of the revival in Moscow began to spread even before the Revolution. It inspired growing excitement among Hebraists across the empire. The journalist and cultural critic A. Litai and the writer and editor of children's literature M. Ben-Eliezer gladly left their jobs working for Odessa's Zionist organization to join the Hebrew cultural sphere in Moscow.[41]

Yiddishists, by contrast, could not point to any site of cultural activity even remotely comparable in scope in 1917. At times, some voiced despair. In Petrograd, the literary critic Niger wondered whether the Jewish intelligentsia had any interest in Yiddish culture.[42]

But a sense of the era's new potential grew even among Yiddishists. Kiev in particular served as the site of Yiddishist resurgence in 1917. As socialist, liberal, and Ukrainian nationalist forces squared off for control of the region, this city with a socioeconomically differentiated Jewish population approaching 90,000 (some 20 percent of the whole) also naturally became a center of Jewish nationalist politics in both Zionist and socialist-autonomist forms. The Yiddishist milieu that emerged there in 1917 was dominated by prorevolutionary intellectuals and by literati affiliated primarily with the socialist-nationalist Fareynikte party. Its leading figures included Bergelson, the refined literary critic Yehezkel Dobrushin, and the violently combative Sorbonne-educated trilingual publicist, political leader, and cultural critic Moyshe Litvakov. These figures preached that while sociopolitical revolution was reforging East European Jewry into a proletarian nation, Yiddishist intellectuals had to cultivate the culture it would inherit: the modern, secular Yiddish high culture that had begun to emerge in the 1890s. This cultural renaissance-cum-reformation was deemed no less pressing than sociopolitical activism. A sense of their millenarian fervor can be gleaned from the acid comments of an observer who complained of "young men running around like poisoned mice" expounding their vision of a "Yiddish culture which stands in the very middle of 'storm problems'" and writers "who on a daily basis make colossal revolutions in the 'process of secularism.'"[43]

Whatever the cogency of their overarching vision, it propelled these radical Yiddishists toward ever more ambitious practical endeavors. While propounding their theories to "the workers" themselves through lectures at party clubs and through the socialist-Yiddishist daily *Di naye tsayt* (founded September 1917), these activists created the Kiever Farlag publishing house and launched a highly ambitious program of literary, critical, and children's publications. The goal was to generate an entirely secular, national-radical, and monolingual Yiddish literary culture that would—in keeping with their properly dialectical conception of cultural revolution— incorporate the best of European and the older Jewish culture (including Hebrew literature) through translation. At the end of the year, these activists went further; forging ties with Yiddishist elements in Kiev's other socialist parties as well as with nonsocialists, they reached out to pro-Yiddish elements across the empire with a call to coordinate all Yiddishist cultural activism through a League for Culture, a Kultur-Lige.[44]

These initiatives intersected—albeit imperfectly—with Kiev's rapid emergence as the most exciting center of Yiddish literary creativity in Eastern Europe. Dovid Bergelson's home became a literary center to a new generation of writers who would come to be called the Kiev-Grupe. Ranging from the uneducated but talented budding expressionist poet Leyb Kvitko, whom Bergelson arranged to have tutored, to Nokhem Oyslender, a Russified medical student turned Yiddish modernist, they were bound together not by a distinct aesthetic but by their shared desire for a mature Yiddish literature and the conviction that their diverse literary experiments had larger Yiddishist cultural import. Though this literary phenomenon was barely visible outside Kiev until 1918–1919, it lent further confidence to that city's Yiddishists that a Yiddish cultural breakthrough was imminent despite the practical difficulties.[45]

Not everyone shared their heated revolutionary certainty. But even more sober Yiddishists saw expanded possibilities for Jewish cultural renaissance under the new revolutionary conditions. Moreover, even those Yiddishists with a grimmer view of the situation felt the same cultural urgency that Bialik was expressing in the competing Hebraist camp. By late 1917, growing numbers of Russian Jewish nationalist intellectuals were becoming convinced that the cultivation of Yiddish culture was not a matter of secondary concern relative to political mobilization, but rather essential to whatever version of the Jewish national and social revolution they hoped to achieve. In Petrograd, a group of intellectuals linked to the democratic-populist Folkist movement, including most prominently the nationalist historian Semyon Dubnov; the Yiddish literary critic Niger; and the critic, scholar, and nationalist intellectual Nokhem Shtif, articulated a liberal nationalist version of this perspective in a journal that they founded in October 1917, the weekly *Yidishe folksblat:* "We must create the cultural atmosphere without which no society exists, without which all of our national-political victories remain suspended in mid-air."[46]

Between Possibility and Necessity

What factors fed culturist ambitions and convictions in 1917, even in the absence of visible infrastructures and resources? In the most general terms, of course, February meant complete institutional and expressive freedom in all spheres. After decades of government harassment, the Jewish intelligentsia suddenly found its cultural institution-building limited only by practical circumstance. Conversely, the wartime devastation of Jewish life in the Pale of Settlement had sealed the impression among many intelligentsia that the fabric of traditional Jewish religious culture was hopelessly and irrevocably torn.[47] The intelligentsia's imperative to create a new Jewish culture was thus reinforced, in their view, by history itself—and rendered all the more pressing. In that sense, February was pregnant with meaning for many culturists, but not in the sense we often associate with the rhetoric of revolution: it was not a rupture in time demanding a fundamentally new mode of behavior, but the capstone to the death of the traditional world that Jewish culturists had always aspired to succeed and subsume.

More concretely, several dynamics of political and sociocultural transformation brought both new confidence and new urgency to the culturist endeavor. For Jewish culturists, the astonishing political success of the Jewish nationalist movement in 1917 held a twofold promise. First, it signaled the possibility of fundamental change in the political and material status of Jewish cultural institutions. As Jewish nationalist forces collectively gained control of organized Jewish communal life, Jewish cultural activists could imagine real communal support for secular-national cultural institutions. Through much of 1917, they could even reasonably expect state support for Jewish autonomy, Jewish languages, and Jewish schools. Immediately after February, Russia's weak Provisional Government faced a chorus of demands by nationalists of all stripes that Russia's "prisonhouse of nations" be replaced by a republic of nationalities, each with broad political and cultural autonomy. And while Jewish nationalists waited for the Provisional Government to accede to this empirewide logic, a coalition of left-wing Ukrainian nationalists who were guiding the southern region toward independence in 1917 offered Jews robust national autonomy, including recognition of Yiddish as a national language and government funding of Jewish institutions under a Jewish ministry.[48]

Second, the swelling popularity of the Jewish nationalist movement seemed to many to herald a sea change in the *mentalité* of East European Jewry: the consolidation of a national identity in place of both assimilationism and traditional religiosity. This optimism proved wildly inflated. But Russian Jewish identity was in flux and discourses of national identity did find unprecedented purchase among disparate segments of East European Jewish society, as evidenced by the sudden upswing in Zionist and Jewish socialist party membership.

There was even some sign, particularly encouraging to Jewish nationalist intellectuals, of a nationalist shift among Russified bourgeois and intelligentsia elements. The transition was especially pronounced in Ukraine, where the growing influence of the Ukrainian national movement had brought pressures for de-Russification among Jews. While teaching Jewish history in a Yiddishist teacher-training seminar, Ben-Tsion Dinur was struck by the composition of the student body: Russified, well-educated Jewish women who would once have made their teaching careers in Russian. He was pleased to note that although their enrollment had little to do with preexisting attraction to Yiddish culture, some embraced the opportunity to engage seriously with it.[49]

This shift in self-identity came complete with numerous signs, for those who wished to see them, of greater openness to secular-national forms of Jewish culture in wide swaths of East European Jewish society. In mid-1917, the Zionist organization in the small southern Ukrainian town Pishtshanke informed the central organization in Kiev that more than a hundred adults had shown up for Hebrew evening courses, and begged for more Hebrew teachers. In another heavily Jewish town in the Ukraine, Hebrew classes were introduced into the curriculum of the local Russian-language secondary school; the younger son of the town's chief Hebraist and his friends donated Hebrew books and copies of *Ha-Shiloah* to the school library. In October 1917, a Hebraist group in the Russian-Ukrainian city of Poltava begged the noted Russian Yiddish writer and ethnographer Sh. An-ski to come lecture in service of the organization's efforts to "spread our literature among broader strata of the people": "the Jewish public is thirsty now, as you know, for a Jewish word, and it is a sacred duty incumbent upon all those who can to come to the aid of this public."[50]

In one respect, ironically, the war itself brought unanticipated benefits to the culturist endeavor. Initially invisible to the silenced and uprooted poets of Odessa and Moscow, these benefits were apparent to those culturists who served as educators and community activists. During the war, activists affiliated with the Petrograd-centered OPE founded hundreds of schools for Jewish refugee children. Both Yiddishists and Hebraists, who also founded a strong school network among the refugees, dominated many of these schools on a local level. Such schools and affiliated parents' groups could be used to project awareness of the new culture into local Jewish life. During the war years, moreover, the once-Russificatory OPE itself had decided that the language of instruction in its schools should be Yiddish, a testament to an ever-deepening national turn that the war had accelerated but that was actually rooted in the prewar decade.[51] As we shall see in Chapter 4, such developments inspired Jewish culturists to hope that they might now disseminate the new Jewish culture to East European Jewry as a whole.[52]

At same time, each of these developments was two-edged, suggesting to culturists that now was not only the best but also the last chance to realize such dreams. Some Jewish culturists understood that the collapse of traditional belief could just as easily lead to massively accelerated assimilation as to a Jewish cultural revolution—which is precisely what happened in Jewish life in the 1920s and 1930s everywhere except Palestine. And many culturists recognized that the reordering of life in Russia along ethnonational lines could bring new troubles to the cultural endeavor as well as benefits. They hoped for the creation of a federal Russian republic with a formal system of national autonomy for all, but also recognized the less savory possibility that the empire would break down into independent nation-states where Jews would be a prominent national minority. In addition to the dangerous political consequences of such a situation—which of course ultimately proved far worse than most culturists could imagine— it would also have the ironic cultural consequence of simply reinitiating the process of Jewish assimilation to the new state-backed cultures of a Ukraine, a Lithuania, and the like.[53]

Furthermore, the accelerating drive for substantial regional autonomy and eventually statehood in Ukraine and the Baltics, coupled with the larger Wilsonian shift in the international system, convinced Jewish nationalists that Jews as a group had to manifest to their neighbors a clear cultural profile. Having one's own "culture" was essential to claiming political recognition by other nationalist actors, by the Russian (or Ukrainian) state, and perhaps even by the international community. Moreover, in the borderlands, Jewish political leaders felt increasing pressure to counteract the common view among local nationalists that Jews were agents of Russification. As one Zionist activist put it in a discussion of Jewish secondary schools: "we in Ukraine must abandon Russian because it is hated by the local inhabitants, and if it is necessary to go over to a different language we must certainly go over to Hebrew, which is a language of culture."

Yiddishists echoed the same worried insights: "Our children will speak all seventy tongues and we will have to endure torments and scorn from our neighbor-peoples . . . Russians will bear a grudge against Polonized Jews: why are you seeking Polish schools, Polish culture here in Russia; Ukrainians—why are you trying to be Russians; and so on and so forth."[54]

The new political logic of culture deepened the various Jewish nationalist parties' commitment (in principle) to active support of Jewish cultural institutions. This was by no means a foregone conclusion. Significant lines of thought in both the Jewish socialist movement and Zionism posited strict limits on the sorts of Jewish cultural revival that should or even could be pursued. Although it is commonly assumed that the most powerful of the Jewish socialist-nationalist parties, the Social-Democratic Bund, was a bastion of Yiddishism, substantial parts of the party leadership actually rejected the constitutive Yiddishist commitment to the formation of a modern secular Jewish culture in Yiddish as an overarching goal. For many Bundists, called "neutralists," the question of whether a Yiddish-speaking proletariat would persist as a separate national organism with a distinct modern culture was a matter of indifference, and they held further that to view the creation of a separate Yiddish culture as an end was an unwarranted form of cultural nationalism. At the April 1917 conference of the newly legal Bund in Petrograd, the Odessa Bundist I. Nirenberg criticized the party's central committee for what he characterized as a negative attitude toward Yiddish since February. In response, the veteran Bundist leader Mark (Goldman-) Liber launched a pointed attack on the conflation of Bundism with Yiddishism. His warning against allowing "Jewish Social Democracy" to "blur into a Yiddishist bloc" was greeted by cries of "bravo."[55]

In 1917 certain lines of thought in Zionism were also brought to the fore that cast doubt not only on the relative but even the absolute value of Jewish cultural activism in the present. During that year, the Zionist activist Daniil Pasmanik published a pamphlet *Chto takoe evreiskaia natsional'naia kul'tura?* (What Is Jewish National Culture?). The title was misleading: the text was in fact a polemic against the idea that Jews could have a national culture in their present condition. A new Jewish culture, Pasmanik insisted, would only become possible within the framework of a separate "national economy, national politics, a national legal system, national language and . . . *national soil.*" Unlike the "neutralist" elements in the Bund, figures like Pasmanik accepted the paramount importance of "culture" as an ultimate end (even the ultimate end) of the national movement. More comfortable in Russian than in any other language, Pasmanik was nevertheless an uncompromising Hebraist, averring that Hebrew was "*the language of our national culture,* our spiritual distinctiveness, our national individuality." Yet ironically, the logic of his brand of Zionism deferred serious cultural activism indefinitely in time and placed it beyond the space of the diaspora altogether. Politics took precedence over culture in Jewish nationalist praxis not only for practical reasons, but also because cultural formation in a meaningful sense was impossible. Political consciousness alone constituted present-day Jewish nationhood: "We are a nation not because we *already* possess a national culture, but because *we strive toward an independent life.*"[56]

Yet within all of the Jewish nationalist and socialist-nationalist parties and movements, the voices that denied the claims of culture were overmatched by those that embraced them. Each movement boasted a more or less substantial cohort of genuine culturists, that is, people committed to the cultivation of the new culture as an end; indeed, by 1917, some of these had gained commanding positions within the party leaderships.[57] Pasmanik's skepticism about the very possibility of serious cultural formation in the diaspora found a hearing within the Zionist movement: in December 1917, the Zionist organization in Kiev ordered five hundred copies of the pamphlet.[58] Yet his skepticism found little echo in leading Russian Zionist organs. The main Russian-language Zionist newspaper of the period, the Moscow *Evreiskaia Zhizn',* continued the more mainstream Russian Zionist tendency, visible since the turn of the century, of embracing and encouraging "national creativity" in the present (and not only Hebrew-language creativity) without inquiring too deeply into the theoretical justifications for its existence.[59]

Many party activists were moved to support robust commitment to "culture" for political reasons. Not only was "culture" symbolically important for Jewish nationalist (and socialist) self-representation to non-Jewish political actors, it also seemed increasingly important as a symbolic stake within the intra-Jewish political sphere. As the struggle for popular support among the parties intensified and the reach of Jewish nationalist sentiment expanded, many activists deemed it not only ideologically proper but also strategically important that their parties proclaim broad agendas of national revival and self-determination.[60] As it had in the context of the 1905 Revolution, the Russian Zionist movement came under the dominance of activists who insisted that the movement could not confine itself to the pursuit of Jewish sovereignty in Palestine, but had to take the lead in the political, social, and cultural regeneration of diaspora communities. A sense of the twofold political stakes and the way in which they strengthened the significance of "culture" may be gleaned from a 1918 Yiddish-language handbill published by Ukraine's Zionist organization:

> (3) . . . The Zionist Organization will demand that the organs of national autonomy *satisfy all the needs of the Jewish population* according to its historic form of life. Its sphere of competence should include the founding, maintenance, and support of institutions which concern themselves with:
>   (a) cultural and educational matters; (b) the meeting of religious needs; (c) socioeconomic aid (cooperatives, professional training, etc.); (d) the colonization of the Land of Israel; (e) healthcare.[61]

The striking order of priorities speaks for itself.

Whatever the combination of reasons, in 1917 all of the Jewish nationalist parties formally declared their support for "Jewish culture" as an integral part of Jewish national revival (or national and social revolution). The Bund concluded its April conference by calling for a system of state-recognized, democratically elected institutions with authority over the development of "the entire cultural life of the nation: the school- and educational-system, the development of the literature, of art, and of scholarly and technical knowledge." Among Zionists, delegates to the May conference of the Tseire Tsion fraction in Petrograd exhibited a deep concern with matters of culture and committed the fraction to an extensive program of cultural activism alongside "pure Zionist work." This cultural activism, framed by an uncompromising Hebraism, was to extend beyond the support of schools and reading rooms to embrace the organization of "literary, musical, artistic, theatrical and other such societies." Finally, at the Seventh Congress of the Russian Zionist movement, held at the end of May, a full day was devoted to matters of cultural policy, and the Zionist organization committed itself to building Hebrew cultural institutions and securing state support and recognition for them.[62]

Stretched to the limit, the parties actually had little practical help to offer culturists and much to demand of them. Yet their principled agreement with culturist claims led them to accord Jewish culture unprecedented symbolic significance in Jewish public life. The organizers of the All-Russian Jewish Congress, the ill-fated joint effort by the competing nationalist and socialist-nationalist parties to formally constitute an all-Russian system of Jewish national autonomy, invited the writer An-ski to serve as a non-party deputy. A conference of Jewish local communal bodies in Kiev invited him to read from his already-storied drama "Between Two Worlds (The Dybbuk)." A similar invitation was extended to Haim Nahman Bialik in 1918 by the Ukrainian-Jewish successor to the Congress experiment, the Temporary National Assembly.[63]

These choices were perhaps inspired as much by the signal presence of cultural figures in the political councils of coterritorial national groups— in 1917–1918, for example, the Ukrainian writer Volodymyr Vynnynchenko served as the de facto president of the emerging Ukrainian nation-state—as by culturist ideals. In the Wilsonian political moment, poets were visible symbols of national distinctiveness. But to the delight of culturists, such idealization of Jewish literary figures also enjoyed popular resonance. In Odessa, the November 1917 funeral of the Hebrew-Yiddish literary pioneer Abramovitsh (Mendele) drew thousands of mourners. One of the participants in the procession, the budding Jewish historian Saul Borovoi, recalled that the crowd included many Jewish students and soldiers, and that the funeral took on the valence of a nationalist demonstration.[64]

As the symbolic value of "culture" rose in ever-widening circles of the Russian Jewish public, other developments suggested enhanced prospects for the creation of the new culture itself. Hebrew and even Yiddish writers were astonished by a sudden proliferation of enthusiastic, even importunate, patrons. Some of these patrons were not especially rich but simply were enamored of Hebrew or Yiddish literature. Released in 1917 from a prisoner-of-war camp outside Kiev, the Hungarian Hebrew poet Avigdor Ha-Meiri (Feuerstein) was bemused, and vaguely disgusted, by the largesse of a Hebrew-literature enthusiast who sought him out.[65]

More importantly, 1917 brought a doubly unexpected influx of new literary and artistic talents. First, Yiddishists and Hebraists were heartened by the appearance of a new generation of enthusiastic would-be writers— even as Jewish youth were becoming more steeped in Russian or Polish culture with every passing year. Even Yiddishists far from the emerging literary center in Kiev could take heart from these developments. In Petrograd, the literary critic Niger received a stream of letters from younger literary aspirants seeking a place to publish. In October, he was contacted by Dovid Hofshteyn, one of the Kiev-Grupe poets, who included a sheaf of unripe but promising poems like the following:

> Confusion of stone houses, belted with streets,
> But on all four sides it yields!
> Through the broad suburbs lines stretch out
> into the far field . . .
> From high windows, with stone sealed round,
> A twig gives oft a green smile,
> A bird in a cage
> At times throws down a tattered song . . .
> With quieted eyes, small faces
> through spotless panes regard the street,
> and mothers watch them, delicate and good
> and dove-quiet.
> Confusion of stone houses, belted with streets . . .
> But on all four sides it yields!
> Through the broad suburbs lines stretch out
> into the far field.[66]

Soon Niger would be contacted by a still younger poet wrestling with the same poetic problem of the transition between rural settings and the city, with all that entailed: the transition from lyric romanticism to modernism, *Gemeinschaft* to *Gesellschaft*, national and individual wholeness to modern fracture or perhaps a new maturity. Moyshe Kulbak, a product first of Lithuania's yeshivas and then of the secular Hebraist movement, began to write Yiddish poetry in the provincial city of Kovne under German occupation, spent some time in Minsk in 1918, and by 1919, having resettled in Vilna, began to evolve beyond Romantic lyricism and revolutionary effusions to a more innovative voice: "the city sounds in heavy streaming, / The stone-voice murmurs in the yoke of steel."[67]

Perhaps even more than Yiddishists, Hebraists had worried for the health of their endeavor ever since the turn of the century. A Hebraist literary revolution similar to that taking place in the Yiddish literature of Kiev would have to wait until the mid-1920s, in Palestine. But Hebraists too could point to hopeful signs in 1917. Even a backwater like the southern commercial city Ekaterinoslav offered signs of Hebraist success in the form of a hand-produced, mimeographed Hebrew anthology of poetry and essays, *Shevivim* (Sparks), composed in late 1916 by students at the P. Y. Cohen

Hebrew Gymnasium. One of the authors in this anthology even published a poem, at age eighteen, in Odessa's *Ha-Shiloaḥ*. The poem itself, "In the Silence of Despair," was an epigonic production that bespoke the outsized influence of Bialik's poetry in Hebrew letters as much as the actual despair of an adolescent subjected to the blows of revolution in Russia's disputed south: "There burst forth a wind, which blew from the north, / and severed the threads of my wonderful dreams. / The idols are lying shattered to pieces / in the isolate corner it ruined." But the poem showed a command of the language that spoke well of the modern Hebraist-Zionist schools in which the budding poet had spent the past six years. What became of *Shevivim*'s other participants is unclear, but the author of "In the Silence of Despair," Avraham Shlonsky, would go on to become the dominant Hebrew modernist of the 1920s.[68]

Both Yiddishists and Hebraists could also draw satisfaction from the first signs of a shift in the gender constitution of the Jewish cultural project, which had long been the preserve of men even more than most cultural spheres of the time.[69] Hebraists in Moscow thrilled to the remarkable case of Yeliziveta Zhirkova, a Russian poet who had grown interested in Jewish life before the war and now began to remake herself as the Hebrew poet Elisheva under the tutelage of Hebraist friends like the Ha-Bimah cofounder and Tarbut teacher Menahem Gnesin, her soon-to-be-husband Shimon Bikhovsky, and the poet David Shimoni (Shimonovits). Not only one of a new generation of women writing in Hebrew, but born non-Jewish and a Russian poet to boot, Elisheva came to represent the most radical possibilities for an evolving Hebraist culture.[70]

A second development that fed Jewish culturist hopes and ambitions was first visible in Moscow: a swelling interest in the idea of Jewish culture among cultural figures who were firmly part of the mainstream Russian cultural world. Many artists and composers of Jewish descent had begun to experiment with Jewish thematics before the war, and had even created organizations devoted to supporting Jewish artistic expression like the Jewish Society for the Encouragement of Art and the Obshchestvo Evreiskoi Narodnoi Muzyki (Society for Jewish Folk Music).[71] While these organizations remained agnostic about whether such Jewish artistic expression would come to comprise a separate Jewish national culture or flow into a multiethnic Russian one, between 1917 and 1919 it actually seemed as though some metropolitan artists might fully embrace the ideals of the Jewish cultural project—that is, to think of their own work as part of a collective effort to cultivate a distinct modern Jewish artistic sphere. In Petrograd, a circle of nationalist intellectuals who hoped to create a modern Yiddish theater were astonished when their endeavor drew the talented young avant-garde director Aleksandr Granovsky, who stemmed from a wholly assimilated background and in fact spoke little Yiddish.[72] Both the old lion Pasternak and the young star Marc Chagall, fresh from triumphs in the West, sketched portraits of leading Jewish culturists with whom they now grew close (see fig. 1). In April 1918, Lissitzky wrote to the Yiddishist Niger: "I want to express to you my happiness that we are approaching the time of the new Jewish book, a book created with love towards [the thing] itself and towards the coming culture whose bricklayers we wish to be."[73]

By 1919–1920, Lissitzky, his fellow experimental artist Alt'man, and many others would begin to renounce these aspirations and reorient their art toward the new horizons of the victorious Revolution and the international avant-garde. But their engagement with "Jewish" art lasted long enough to convince many Jewish culturists that a new Jewish culture embracing all the arts was in the making. Hebraists and Yiddishists greeted the apparent "return" of ethnically Jewish artists and musicians in February's wake with great excitement.[74] Both camps strove to draw these artists more deeply into their versions of the Jewish cultural project, especially as illustrators (see figs. 2–9), while expanding the place accorded to questions of art, music, and theater in their own publications and cultural organizations.[75]

Reviving the Cultural Project

To committed Jewish culturists, all these factors appeared no less real than the miseries of daily life or the promise of revolutionary social change. They acted accordingly. The first and most spectacular resurgence of Jewish culturist endeavor occurred in Moscow during the first months of 1917. Looking back, participants struggled to explain their sense that Moscow's Hebraism was something unprecedented in scope. One recalled: "Those days were holidays, the holiday of the February Revolution: people were still full of hope and a splendid future was visible on the Jewish street too. New faces filled the noisy streets of the capitol, new centers for culture and scholarship blossomed every morning. Jewish authors and scholars burst forth as though from out of the earth and the hands of the activists were filled with work: a time for doing!"[76]

Throughout 1917, a swelling stream of Hebraists arrived in Moscow, drawn, in the words of the young literary critic Grinblat (Goren), by what seemed like "grand plans, solid constructions, the redemption of our literature knocking on our windows."[77] One of the new arrivals was the aging Hebrew critic, editor, writer, and translator David Frishman. A finicky aesthete whom scholars have found easy to dismiss, Frishman was also an influential editor who for years devoted himself to the promotion of a properly European Hebrew belle-lettres—something he viewed as an end in itself and as the only true means to Jewish national regeneration, reader by reader.[78]

Precisely these ideas had most shaped the Hebraist ideology of the newly minted literary patron Stybel before the war, and it was he who invited Frishman to Moscow to guide the publishing house in early 1917. By mid-1917, Frishman and Stybel had initiated a program of Hebrew literary publishing on a scale never before seen in Jewish letters. Their emphasis was literature, above all translations from European and world literature, to be published both in book form and in a massive flagship quarterly, *Ha-Tekufah,* which devoted some seven hundred pages per issue almost exclusively to literature. The funds for all this were provided by Stybel himself in the form of an endowment of one million rubles—some 500,000 U.S. dollars in late 1916—out of his personal wealth. Within a year, Stybel Press had twenty translated literary works in print or production and over forty more commissioned. The press employed a number of young Hebrew writers full-time, and with Frishman's continual urging, virtually every Hebrew writer in Russia took part in the endeavor.[79]

At the same time, the institutions nurtured during the war by Zlatopolsky and Persits now blossomed into a robust Hebraist-Zionist network reaching beyond Moscow to southern Russia and ultimately into Ukraine. Persits and Zlatopolsky presided over the transformation of *Ha-'Am* into Russia's only Hebrew daily in mid-1917.[80] In July 1917, Omanut began to publish Hebrew materials for children, including an impressive journal for young adults, *Shetilim*. Under the editorship of the newly arrived Hebraist M. Ben-Eliezer, *Shetilim* exemplified the ideals of the publishing house. It included original literary work by leading Hebrew writers alongside translations from European literature by Wilde, Mickiewicz, and Daudet; folk literature of the world, including a collection of "Stories from Korea"; pieces on both Jewish and general history; and descriptions of the land of Israel in both contemporary and mythic terms alongside travel and descriptive literature on "other lands and states." It also made extensive room for visual arts: it offered readers an article by M. Antokolski on the nineteenth-century Jewish realist Max Lieberman and an article on August Rodin, and was filled with illustrations ranging from rather staid realist drawings to striking illustrations by figures like Lissitzky, sometimes on the same page (see fig. 4). In short, it was designed to serve as a vehicle for the creation of a Zionist, Hebraist youth that would be both fully Jewish and fully European. A second Tarbut-affiliated publishing house, Aḥinoar, was created in Ukraine to publish modern Hebrew literature and translations for young people; Alt'man produced its sigil (see fig. 2).[81]

It was in this context that Zlatopolsky, Persits, and the Hebraist activists and teachers of Moscow moved to create the Tarbut organization in order to coordinate the Hebraist endeavor on a pan-Russian scale. The April 1917 meeting at which the Moscow chapter of the Ḥoveve Sfat 'Ever was refounded as Tarbut brought together Hebraists of widely varying ideological commitments. They ranged from members of the democratic populist Tseire Tsion and Marxist-Zionist Poale Tsion to staunch antisocialists, from secularist educators who called for a mixed-gender Hebrew school system to religiously orthodox Hebraists who sought to "unite life and To-rah," from those who advocated compromise between Hebrew and Yiddish to those who decried Yiddish as "jargon." The conference proceedings were marked by intense, sometimes heated debates over the democratization of Hebraist cultural work, the nature of the education to be provided in the new Hebrew school and the place of religion in it, the language question, and the relationship of Hebraist cultural and educational work to the Russian Zionist movement.[82]

Given these divisions, what was truly striking about the program yielded by the conference was the depth of agreement on the Hebraist agenda. Despite their differences, participants shared a unitary Hebraism that sought both to cultivate a modern, high Hebrew culture as an exalted end in itself and to project this post-traditional Hebrew national culture to the broader Yiddish- and Russian-speaking Jewish society. The guiding figures of Tarbut aspired not only to support and institutionalize Jewish cultural creation in all of the arts, but also to provide intensive Hebraist education to children and adults—and to serve both of these very different goals through Hebrew theaters, art exhibitions, and clubs. The ultimate objective was a full-fledged Hebrew cultural revolution: the immediate transformation of Jewish society into a nation defined by a shared Hebrew culture. In the immediate wake of the April meeting, the new organization quickly assumed a central coordinating role in organized Hebrew cultural activity.

Tarbut brought existing Hebrew schools under its administrative umbrella and rapidly founded new ones, created several hundred local chapters across Russia, absorbed Omanut and its Hebrew publications, and moved to support other budding culturist endeavors in Moscow and across the country.

Taken together, the Hebraist endeavor in Moscow aimed at a threefold revolution: the reformation of Hebrew high culture itself, a dramatic expansion of the role of the Hebrew language and the new Hebrew culture in East European Jewish cultural life, and the transformation of East European Jewish society and consciousness through Hebraist cultural activity. Moscow's Hebraists shared a burning desire for a properly encompassing Hebrew high culture centering around literature yet embracing all forms of secular cultural creativity. Zlatopolsky eagerly supported the Ha-Bimah theater troupe, arranged for the acquisition of An-ski's *Dybbuk* for them, and was the first to appeal to Bialik to translate this Russian-Yiddish work into Hebrew (a translation then published in Stybel's *Ha-Tekufah*). The excitement generated throughout the Hebraist milieu by the April exhibition of Jewish art found parallels in Persits's (unrealized) desire to publish a journal devoted to the arts and in Tarbut's stated goals of helping to fund and organize Hebrew theaters, art exhibitions, orchestras, and "schools and leagues for art in all its forms."[83]

Another striking feature of Moscow Hebraism was its forceful recasting of Hebrew culture not as a private affair but as a public good. At the April conference, a number of delegates criticized the character of the organization to date for what they perceived to be its elitism, and warned more generally, in the words of one delegate from the radical center Minsk, that Hebraism that did not descend to the broad masses "would remain merely a sort of sport." The correspondent covering the conference for the Hebrew weekly *Ha-'Am* agreed that the moment had come to "build all the work on new, social foundations."[84] In fact, the conference revealed complete unanimity regarding the need to transform Hebraism into a genuine mass movement. The very patron-leaders targeted in these attacks acknowledged their legitimacy. Zlatopolsky averred that he himself knew "that work done outside the broader ranks has no fruit and cannot last." Persits complained in a report on the organization's budget that "this money is not a contribution of the people but came from individual patrons. And it is not proper to base the work of the people on the contributions of individuals."[85]

Radiating outward from Moscow, "this Hebrew renaissance . . . raised a storm across the entire expanse of Russia," inspiring would-be creators of Hebrew culture not only in long-established centers like Odessa, but also in the refugee-swollen cities of the Russian-Ukrainian south like Kharkov and Ekaterinoslav. Money and organizational infrastructure radiated outward too. Stybel and Frishman sent word across Russia and Palestine that work was available for any capable Hebrew writer or translator. Stybel even sent emissaries: young Hebraists in Kharkov's Tarbut chapter were thrilled when writers Kh. Sh. Ben-Avram and Valpovsky arrived bearing encouragement and generous advances.[86]

If Yiddishist efforts paled alongside this Hebraist renaissance throughout 1917, developments in Kiev in 1918 more than made up the difference. By late 1917, Yiddishist hopes for Kiev had spread beyond the ideologues of the Kiev-Grupe, in large measure because of the prospects for formal Jewish cultural autonomy in the hands of the Yiddishist left. Although the majority of those who voted in Jewish elections in Ukraine consistently supported nonsocialist parties, above all the Zionist movement, the left-wing Ukrainian nationalists who presided over the region's move toward independence were inclined to grant control to their fellow socialists regardless. As institutions of Jewish autonomy took shape in late 1917, Yiddishists in Kiev appealed to compatriots elsewhere to take part in this extraordinary development. In a letter to Niger and the nonsocialist Yiddishist scholar and teacher Zelig Kalmanovitsh, the formerly Zionist-socialist, now-Bundist educator Shimen Dobin urged his friends to listen to the "voice of history."[87]

In fact, this autonomy was short-lived; in April, power was seized by anti-socialists backed by the resource-hungry German army. More interested in order than in Ukrainian national revolution, the new regime (the Hetmanate) constricted the sphere of political activity, suppressed socialists, and rolled back the autonomy granted to national minorities. It did not, however, suppress Jewish cultural life to nearly the same degree as the newly established Bolshevik regime to the north; Kievan Ukraine still offered some formal autonomy, a high degree of organizational freedom, and livable political and economic conditions. Thus, even as Yiddishists lamented the rise of the Hetmanate, Yiddishist endeavors begun in 1917 blossomed throughout 1918.

The most striking Yiddishist development in Kiev was the creation of the Yiddishist answer to Tarbut, the Kultur-Lige. Initiated at the close of 1917 as a pan-Russian organization, it was founded concretely only in

April 1918 by a coalition of Yiddishist figures drawn from across the socialist spectrum and, in at least one case, beyond. Setting itself "the task of developing and disseminating to the people Yiddish secular culture in all spheres of human creativity, such as literature, art, music, theater and others as well as aiding in the construction of the modern Yiddish democratic school and other educational institutions," the Kultur-Lige moved quickly to consolidate and shape Yiddishist cultural efforts in Ukraine.[88]

In the scope of its efforts, the range of its ambitions, and its character as an organization, the Kultur-Lige was unprecedented in the history of the Jewish cultural movement. Its founders aspired to unify all forms of Yiddishist cultural activity, from educational and cultural work among the "Jewish folk-masses" to the cultivation of the most rarefied forms of Jewish high culture. Like its Hebraist rival Tarbut—which was itself shifting its operations to Ukraine in light of deepening Bolshevik control in Russia— the Kultur-Lige undertook pioneering initiatives in the creation, administration, and guidance of educational institutions and the fostering of cultural organizations outside the main urban centers and intelligentsia circles. One critical observer credited the Kultur-Lige in September 1918 with real success, noting that some of its local branches were running networks of kindergartens, schools, and clubs "with libraries, reading rooms, cinemas and the like."[89]

At the same time, the Kultur-Lige created active sections for literature, visual arts, and ultimately music and theater as part of its larger vision of a full-fledged Jewish high culture unified around Yiddish language and literature. Its art section brought together young avant-garde artists like Issachar Ber Ryback, Iosif Tchaikov, Alexander Tishler, and Lissitzky with theorists of the new secular Yiddish culture like Dobrushin to create a distinct Jewish art scene in Kiev. In studios and in artists' colonies organized in the summer and winter of 1918, these modernists worked closely with literary publishing houses in Kiev to produce what Lissitzky had called "the new Yiddish book" (see figs. 3, 5, 7, 8) while seeking to define a distinct Jewish visual aesthetics. Its theater section aspired to recreate Yiddish theater in accordance with both the standards of Russian theater and modernist sensibilities. This effort was part of a larger trend that included both the Hebraist Ha-Bimah and Yiddish theater ventures taking shape concurrently in Petrograd and Vilna.[90]

Most broadly, the Kultur-Lige hoped to carry out a structural revolution in the Jewish cultural sphere: the creation of a stable financial and institutional framework within which a new Jewish culture could develop and be disseminated. The organization took innovative steps to organize Yiddish publishing. It not only founded its own press, which specialized in text-book production and classic Yiddish and translated literature, but also established a central bookstore and an impressive system of book distribution across Ukraine. It parlayed this influence into exclusive distribution contracts with Yiddishist publishing houses across Ukraine, and used this leverage in turn to try to shape their productions.[91]

As the Kultur-Lige took shape, a host of other grassroots Yiddishist initiatives added to Yiddishist excitement. The Kultur-Lige's aspiration to shape a new Yiddish school system reflected not mere theoretical conviction but excitement over the spontaneous development of dozens of Yiddishist-secular elementary schools across Ukraine and beyond. Stated plans to guide the further development of Yiddish print culture drew conviction from a sudden shift in the fortunes of Yiddishist publishing in 1918. As of late 1917, Yiddish publishing in Kiev had consisted of the Kiever Farlag and a halting effort by Boris Kletskin, the prewar pioneer of Yiddishist publishing in Vilna, to set up a branch of his Vilner Farlag there while Vilna remained under German occupation. Yet despite Kiev's extremely limited Yiddish print resources—a legacy of tsarist-era legal restrictions on Jewish settlement in the city and the longtime publishing dominance of Warsaw and Vilna—a half-dozen Yiddishist publishing houses sprang up there in 1918, with another half-dozen in other nominally Ukrainian cities such as Odessa, Kharkov, and Ekaterinoslav.[92]

The grandest of these ventures was the Folks-Farlag, founded in October 1918. Its founders were diaspora autonomist intellectuals affiliated with the Folks-Partey: the publicist Zeev-Volf Latski-Bertoldi, the teacher and scholar Kalmanovitsh, the critic and literary historian Shtif, and a number of ideologically sympathetic patron-investors. Though it began initially with a focus on political publishing in close association with the Folks-Partey, the Folks-Farlag quickly metamorphosed into one of the most ambitious publishing ventures in the history of Yiddish culture.[93] A stock company, the Folks-Farlag was far better off materially than most Yiddish publishing efforts. Yet it subordinated the search for profit to Yiddishist and cultural nationalist principles. It apparently offered to pay important writers as much as they needed to make ends meet. More broadly, its administrators aspired to shape the newly emergent Yiddish cultural sphere as a whole; they hoped, as Shtif put it in retrospect, that the Folks-

Farlag "would be *the* cultural institution to build our literary cultural work and chart a path!" Their expansive publishing program included literature (original and in translation from Hebrew and European languages), children's literature, drama, scholarship on matters of Jewish concern ranging from history to contemporary economic analysis, and nationalist-democratic political theory. They focused particular attention on realms they deemed especially weak or critical for the new Yiddish culture: Jewish history, Yiddish translations of biblical and rabbinic literature, and translations for the Yiddish theater. The Folks-Farlag also sought an international reach: it established a Petrograd branch, recruited writers in Vilna, and tried to establish an international literary yearbook.[94]

In this ambition to be not merely a quality publisher but also an authoritative voice in shaping a new Yiddish culture, the Folks-Farlag was both compatriot and competitor to the Kiever Farlag, the Kultur-Lige, and the other institutions of Kiev's radical Yiddishist scene. Its guiding figures dissented from many of the tendencies that characterized Kiev's radical brand of Yiddishism: revolutionary politics (their attitudes ranged from careful sympathy on the part of Latski-Bertoldi to skepticism from Kalmanovitsh and Shtif), modernist aesthetics (although this did not stop the press from publishing the best of the young Yiddish modernists), or the faith that these two commitments, welded together, should constitute the organizing principles of the new secular national Jewish culture. Thus, the Folks-Farlag became part of the Kultur-Lige's distribution network, but remained at arms' length; Shtif and other leading figures themselves avoided extensive involvement in the Kultur-Lige and hoped at one point in 1918 to turn the local branch of the OPE into a competing umbrella cultural organization. The Folks-Farlag also tried to assume a different stance toward Hebrew culture, in keeping with the view, as Shtif put it, that the Hebrew book "was, is, and will be" even after the consolidation of a full-fledged Yiddish secular culture: it published an anthology of historical sources in Hebrew and planned to publish an anthology of modern Hebrew literature.[95]

All of this organized cultural activity was embedded in a vital literary, artistic, and intellectual life that only grew richer as the political situation in the Ukraine grew murkier. As the brief but spectacular success of the Kultur-Lige's art section testified, the rapprochement of Russian-Jewish artists to the Jewish cultural sphere first visible in Moscow in 1916–1917 was repeated in Kiev. In 1918, too, the landmark Yiddish literary anthology

Eygns (One's Own) was published. Under the guiding hand of Bergelson, the anthology brought together the full range of new departures in East European Yiddish writing: the masterful lyricism of Hofshteyn, the raw expressionism of Kvitko and the newcomer Peretz Markish ("What are you buying—corpses? Rags? / Or already-dead fathers? / Hey, losing a buyer— / Die and be reborn!"), Bergelson's subtle prose modernism, and the layered symbolist parables of Pinkhes Kaganovitsh, who wrote under the pen name Der Nister (The Hidden One).[96] Beneath the anthology's aesthetic eclecticism lay an emphasis on the individual rather than collective prerogatives of literary creativity, a shared insistence that Yiddish literature be judged by universal standards, and a common desire to take part in the pan-European literary revolution (tellingly, the editors chose the ethnically neutral title *Eygns* over *Yidish-Eygns*).[97]

The larger culture-building aspirations of Kiev's radical Yiddishists found expression in the Kiever Farlag's journal *Bikher-velt,* in which the principles of the new Yiddish culture were elaborated by Kiev's Yiddishist intelligentsia, with the political and cultural radicals in the vanguard. Appearing in January 1919 at the high point of Yiddish cultural life in Kiev, *Bikher-velt* surveyed Yiddish culture internationally in order to "classify the published work, assist the reader in orienting himself in all that which appears in Yiddish, and . . . awaken interest in the serious Yiddish book." The Jewish "book-world" that it presented was entirely secular, Yiddish, and high; contemporary Hebrew culture appeared only in vitriolic asides or as something to be translated and appropriated, while "lowbrow" Yiddish publications were simply anathematized.[98]

The early promise of autonomy; the impressive achievements of the Kultur-Lige; the formation of a substantial network of Yiddishist schools, publishing houses, and cultural institutions across Ukraine; and the fact that Ukraine was a major demographic center of East European Jewry inspired Yiddishist hopes and drew Jewish intellectuals to Kiev not only from the surrounding region, but also from Petrograd, Moscow, and Vilna. The young historian Dinur was struck by Kiev's rich "Jewish culture 'climate'" and especially the large, supportive audiences for the new Yiddish culture. This audience was derived, he observed, from the concentration of Jewish nationalist intelligentsia that had gathered in Kiev since the Revolution— teachers and trainees in Kiev's Jewish pedagogical institutions, party workers, newspapermen, and hundreds of Jewish students who "saw themselves as the future bearers of Jewish culture and its various manifestations."[99]

These "future bearers" included some Hebraists, like the teenager Yocheved Zhelezniak, whom Dinur taught in the Tarbut seminar; she would soon become the poet Yocheved bat-Miriam, first in the Soviet Union and then in Palestine, where she would write pioneering modernist verse until the death of her only son in Israel's 1948 War drove her to silence. Most seem to have been inclined toward Yiddishism, like the student Buzi Spivak, who knew all of Kiev's Yiddish writers and mixed intense activity in the Kultur-Lige youth section with equally intense activism in Bundist circles. For his Bundist activism, he would spend the last fifteen years of his life in Soviet hard-labor and concentration camps, where he sought both to expose his fellow prisoners to Yiddish literature and to organize resistance among them. His efforts ended when he was executed with a shot to the back of the neck.[100] But such grim endings lay in the future. For now, the signs were better than Yiddishists could have hoped. Contemporary observers noted with delight and surprise that Yiddish books sold beyond any previous expectations for the limited Ukrainian and Russian market. In just one year, Kiev had become the most vibrant Yiddish cultural center in the former empire.[101]

February as Unfettering

The year 1917 brought an outpouring of new cultural initiatives in Jewish culturist circles, but for the most part, these represented the enactment of long-standing plans. Zlatopolsky and Persits were not alone in viewing February as a return to a path on which they had embarked many years earlier. Even committed revolutionaries like Litvakov and his fellow radical Yiddishists in Kiev conceived their "Jewish cultural revolution" as the culmination of a process begun years earlier. It was no accident that the first programmatic publication of these circles in 1917 was a celebration of the recently deceased neo-Romantic and protomodernist writer Y. L. Peretz, who had long been a symbol for Jewish cultural nationalists of synthesis between old and new, folk and elite, tradition and modernism, indigeneity and cosmopolitanism, nationalism and socialism.[102]

These mutually antagonistic culturist circles had something else in common: they aspired to more than the mere renewal of Jewish cultural activity. They sought, rather, something far more ramified and collective: to organize cultural activity and pursue it systematically, to approach it as a collective project.

The poetic trajectory of the Yiddish modernist Moyshe Broderzon illustrates this sensibility. Driven from Lodz to Moscow by the war, Broderzon found his time there tremendously fruitful despite the material hardships. Under the influence of the city's Russian avant-garde, he threw himself into aesthetic experimentation: he composed a book of Yiddish *tankas* (a Japanese five-line poetic form) on themes of romantic love; produced, with Lissitzky, the era's most beautiful Jewish book-as-aesthetic-object, the illustrated poem *Sikhes-khulin* (see fig. 6); and pioneered Futurist verse in Yiddish. Apart from his choice of literary language, Broderzon might seem to have been a typical denizen of the Russian avant-garde, embarked on his own idiosyncratic aesthetic project and antagonistic toward the old, prewar world: "If I am young / I'll younger myself yet further: / . . . O, my fingers, stretched out long, / you beam out my every heartful thought / and pull down every clamp of laws / of every sort!"[103]

Yet even as Broderzon pursued his own avant-gardist literary projects and invoked Futurist rhetorics of rupture, he worked tirelessly toward a larger collective and entirely old-fashioned end: "the aesthetic renaissance of Jewry on the basis of Jewish creativity and by an organic rapprochement to general European art."[104] Seeking out Russian Jewish artists and composers at home in Moscow's cultural scene such as the noted critic and translator Abram Efros, the composer Aleksander Kreyn, and the artists Lissitzky and Tchaikov, he sought to knit them into a ramified collective project spanning all of the arts. He planned a publishing house that would "publish, in all three languages of the Russian Jews, various works of young poets, composers, graphic artists, etc.," a Yiddish journal devoted exclusively to art and culture, a Yiddish theater studio, and a club that would host exhibitions by Lissitzky and Tchaikov, "intimate literary and chamber music evenings," as well as "drama, opera, ballet."[105]

Broderzon operated with a kind of double vision. He pursued his own avant-garde poetic project while simultaneously cultivating—in a disciplined, even classicist fashion—a Jewish culture modeled on Europe's shared metropolitan template. An outlandish figure largely isolated in Moscow's largely Hebraist milieu, Broderzon was nevertheless absolutely typical in this respect. This double vision was one of the essential framing conditions of the Jewish cultural project.

Jewish cultural activity in the cities of Russia and Ukraine comprised numerous independent, diverse, even conflicting initiatives. Yet these initiatives and most of their participants shared not only a distinctive sociology relative to the larger Russian cultural sphere but also, more importantly, a distinct set of intentions. Like Broderzon, participants felt they were engaged in a collective project of cultural formation over and above (and thus, too, potentially in tension with) their own individual efforts.

Across the battle lines of politics, linguistic ideology, and aesthetic sensibility, Jewish culturists shared a great many assumptions about what sort of institutions, practices, and qualities a proper Jewish culture would entail. As Broderzon's own strange mix of rhetorical Futurism and de facto classicism suggests, moreover, despite the inroads of avant-garde and revolutionary rhetorics of rupture among Jewish cultural producers at the 1917–1919 juncture, the shared vision of culture that they pursued was rooted in nineteenth-century ideals and hopes.

— 2 —

The Constitution of Culture

In this time when it is possible for spiritual culture to develop freely, one begins to feel the need to unify our powers, to organize cultural work, to bring a coherent plan into all cultural undertakings, to bind together all initiatives.

—*DI GRUNT-OYFGABN FUN DER KULTUR-LIGE*, 1918

Any politics that seeks . . . to lay its hands on "culture" in order to enslave it to its needs rather than to serve it—such a politics is destined to become coercive, and a people which values its soul and its happiness will keep distant from it. The true happiness of the people depends . . . on the free development—absolutely free—of all the powers of its spirit.

—HAIM NAHMAN BIALIK, "TARBUT VE-'POLITIKAH,'" 1918

In an age when many writers and artists gave full rein to fantasies of political and psychic transformation, a few Jewish culturists, too, indulged in the dangerous pleasures of utopian writing. Viewing the revolutionary events of 1917 from Kharkov, to which he had been driven from Kovne (Kaunas) during the war, the Yiddish writer and publisher Kalman Zingman was moved to write *In der tsukunft-shtot "Edeniya"* (In the City of the Future Edeniya), which improbably reimagined the grubby southern industrial city as a high-tech utopia of ethnic harmony and national efflorescence. In Edeniya, Jews, Ukrainians, Russians, and Poles live harmonious but separate national-communal lives under autonomous administrations; in this respect, as Gennady Estraikh notes, *Edeniya* was part of a burst of programmatic literature on Jewish national autonomy produced during the first hopeful years after February.[1]

Yet *Edeniya* is not easily placed among the competing Jewish political ideologies of the day. Politics in the narrow sense is actually absent from the imagined life of Edeniya, although memories of political struggle are central to the city's multiethnic harmony ("together they fought, together they died"). Rather, it is *Kultur* that stands at the core of the collective and individual lives of Edeniya's imagined Jews.

The public life of Edeniya's Jewish population is organized around "mass spectacles" staged at a grand central theater and, even more so, around belles-lettres; theater may be the cultural-educational idiom of the city's civic life, but writers are its patron saints. At the center of Edeniya is a statue of the Ukrainian national bard Taras Shevchenko (suggesting that Zingman penned his utopia during the brief honeymoon of Jewish national autonomy in Ukraine in late 1917 and early 1918), but the city is also home to an imposing landscape of Jewish cultural symbols and institutions. Traversing streets named "Mendele" and "Sholem Aleichem," the novel's protagonist—a visitor from the future Palestine with the suspiciously self-referential name Zalman Kindishman—encounters a statue of Sholem Aleichem and posters advertising a Jewish ballet company, Jewish classical music, and a Yiddish opera about King Solomon. Arriving at the central theater-square shared by the city's nationalities, he witnesses a secularized, Yiddishized celebration of the Jewish holiday Lag Ba-Omer (a favorite of Jewish nationalists for its pronounced national and nature motifs). The book's climax comes when Kindishman attends a crowded public lecture devoted to the "Hasidic" stories of the canonical Yiddish writer Peretz—stories that, for Yiddishists, epitomized how East European Jewish religious tradition could be recast as aesthetically compelling Jewish literature.[2]

Edeniya is a fantasy of what it would actually mean to achieve a "modern Jewish culture," and several aspects are especially striking. First, Edeniya's Jewish culture is self-contained and encompassing. It is not a minority culture or merely ethnically marked expression in the shadows of the Russian metropole—in contrast to the Jewish culture of Zingman's day, it is a complete high culture with its own ballet, opera, and art museum.

At the same time, Zingman imagines that this encompassing Jewish culture can be sustained without sealing it off from the rest of the modern European cultural sphere: the highest reward that Edeniya's Jewish administration extends to Jewish artists is a sponsored tour of the world's "richest and most beautiful culture cities." Indeed, Edeniya's Jewish culture is strong enough to reclaim "its own" from the pull of the former metropole. In his inventory of the city's Jewish art museum, Zingman cleverly includes Lissitzky among the otherwise invented roster of future Jewish artists. In Zingman's utopia, Lissitzky is no longer a Russian modernist interested in Jewish themes but part of a "now"-independent Jewish artistic sphere.[3]

Edeniya left little discernible impression on contemporaries, no doubt because, as one arbiter of Yiddish literary taste suggested, it was aesthetically dreadful.[4] Yet Zingman's utopia embodied typical elements of the Jewish culturist imagination. Above all, Zingman's utopia captures in schematic form the nub of the Jewish cultural project: the aspiration to a metropolitan secular-national Jewish culture.

Many of the specifics of his vision would have met with vociferous rejection in various quarters of the Jewish culturist milieu. Hebraists would have found little in it to appreciate. In *Edeniya,* the new Jewish culture is exclusively in Yiddish and Hebraism is present only in a passing, negative reference to the "handful of oppressors" in the future Palestine, where the Jewish working class itself cultivates a Yiddishist option. In addition, the book's diasporism could hardly speak to Zionists. And finally, Zingman's conception of the content of the new Jewish culture, suffused as it is with secular adaptations of traditional Jewish texts and motifs, would have been deemed unduly parochial by many Hebraists and Yiddishists alike.

But in its aspiration to a Jewish culture that would be separate and encompassing of all the arts, *Edeniya* articulated shared core principles of Jewish culturist ideology. Divided along multiple lines of political and linguistic ideology, Jewish culturist circles nevertheless shared an essentially unitary vision of what a Jewish culture would entail. This underlying model of culture permeated their activity and oriented them toward one another as interlocutors, coworkers, or intimate enemies.

One of the truly remarkable features of Zingman's *Edeniya* is its absolutely unreflective conviction that art is the essential dimension of culture. Nationalist scholarship, which includes folklore collection and the writing of national histories, is given only the briefest of mentions, even though scholars of Eastern Europe tend to see this scholarship as utterly central to the regional intelligentsias' cultural nationalisms. By the same token, nobody in Edeniya philosophizes about Jewish identity, nor is there any sense that the city's Jewish life inscribes the sort of separate national ethos whose elaboration is also generally seen as a fundamental obsession of cultural nationalism. The closest the text comes to such matters is in its description of public rituals like the holiday festival, but even this is simply depicted as secular moderns enjoying a ritual in which content has been wholly displaced by aesthetic performance. The city's streets and statues represent belletrists, not national intellectuals (or representative national heroes), its museum is an art museum rather than a museum of national history, and its climactic lecture concerns the literature of Peretz rather than the historiosophical or philosophical speculations on Jewish nationhood or identity that could be found in the writings of some Jewish nationalist intellectuals.

In short, the defining practice of Jewish culture in Edeniya is the production and consumption of art, and what makes Jewish culture separate is not some essential Jewish-national sensibility but the materialities of separate institutions, a separate place, and a separate language. In this regard too, *Edeniya* typified the bid for a Jewish culture at the 1917–1919 juncture.

No less important and representative is the fundamentally old-fashioned—we might even say nineteenth-century—tenor of Zingman's conception of the place of aesthetic experience in culture and, concomitantly, the place of the cultural sphere in society. Zingman's utopia was of its time and place in many respects: communist in the literal sense (there is no money in Edeniya), cheerfully accepting of the need to use violence to bring about the revolution (it projects this violence safely into Edeniya's past but, of course, Edeniya's past was still the future as of 1917), and unabashed about the role that it assigns to the state in cultural life. Its conception of culture itself, however, is entirely at odds with the ideas we tend to associate with Europe's postwar political and cultural avant-gardes. Edeniya is not an avant-garde paradise in which life itself is remade as art and the distinctions of bourgeois society regarding culture, politics, and society collapse. *Edeniya* figures culture less as a realm of individual integration into the collective than as the essential medium for the free play of individuality. Despite his attention to the role of "spectacles"—a nod to the Revolution and to the monumentalist streams in Russia's avant-garde art—Zingman firmly privileges the interior domain of literary experience, as embodied in his main character's endless private meditations on the statues of various classic Yiddish writers. Zingman's society shows no trace, moreover, of the programs of total sociopsychological transformation that intrigued many Russian *intelligenty*. It is inhabited by individuals pursuing private satisfactions in art and eros, and even nuclear families with *echt*-bourgeois piano-playing daughters:

They sat for a time. There in the little "gazebo," there was always a little library of "garden-literature," as it was called: light stories, pieces for declamation. There was also a piano, where one could play the best musical numbers; Hannah began to play Einhorn's sonnets.[5]

Jewish cultural activists in this era shared Zingman's sensibilities. Even among Jewish culturist circles open to revolutionary rhetorics of rupture and to the avant-garde's simultaneous critique and hyperinflation of ideas of culture, the potential existence and value of a separate sphere called "culture" remained (as yet) unquestioned. It was against this conceptual ground that "Jewish culture" could reemerge as a project for so many.

Just as Zingman's *Edeniya* laid bare part of what we might call the unwritten constitution of the Jewish cultural project regarding the primacy of aesthetic experience and the system of the arts, his contemporaneous activity as a Yiddishist editor and publisher captured another essential feature of that cultural constitution: an insistent distinction between "culture" and "politics." As we saw in the previous chapter, organized Jewish cultural activity reemerged after February's deliverance in the shadow of a burgeoning and contentious Jewish politics, involving a bewildering array of parties occupying every location on a grid of divisions between diasporists and Zionists, class-sensitive and integral nationalisms, socialist and liberal ideology, and revolutionary versus reformist attitudes. Most Jewish culturists were themselves committed to one or the other of these political movements. In a larger sense, few questioned the importance of organized, ideologically coherent political action; Parnassian notions of a cultural elite standing above the world of political and social conflict found little resonance among Jewish culturists in Eastern Europe. Given this, along with the material difficulties attendant on culture's reemergence in 1917, it is also unsurprising that many of the cultural institutions that developed in 1917 were linked to one or another Jewish political movement.

In particular, it was altogether natural that Jewish nationalism's (and socialism's) political and cultural projects should have been closely linked from the first, and given the unprecedented successes of Jewish political movements in 1917, we might imagine that culturists would have eagerly sought to tighten this linkage for the material benefits and authority it might bring. Yet many culturists were deeply uncomfortable with the initially tight relationship between their project and the Jewish nationalist and socialist political endeavors in which they themselves took part. More broadly, many of them conceived the sociopolitical mobilization attendant on the

Revolution more broadly as a development that not only offered a promise of cultural advancement but also potentially threatened "culture" itself.

Zingman proved the Jewish cultural project's "representative man" in this last and most paradoxical respect as well. Zingman was by no means indifferent to the political fate of Russian Jewry or of Russia. He was deeply committed to ideals of Jewish autonomism and, despite the essentially socialist vision of his utopia, seems to have moved primarily in Folkist circles in 1917–1918, though in 1919 he moved precipitously into the pro-Communist camp.[6] Yet Zingman framed his Yiddishist activity in 1917 in terms at odds with any of these political commitments. Discussing plans for a Yiddish journal, he exploded: "It's about time, upon my soul [*kh'lebn*], that alongside the proclamations and announcements which the Revolution has given us, we should possess at least one substantial monthly for literature, art, and criticism. It's about time, upon my soul!" Even more significant, when queried about the journal's political stance, he responded that it would be "a purely literary-artistic [one] without politics" to which all Yiddish readers could relate regardless of political affiliation.[7]

As described earlier, Jewish culturists complained bitterly throughout 1917 about the nationalist movements' relative neglect of cultural matters. Yet ironically, by mid-1917, a growing chorus of culturists (often the same people) began to act on the conviction that the health of the new Jewish culture depended not on yoking it to the juggernaut of Jewish nationalist and socialist politics but on quite the opposite: insulating cultural activity and institutions from parties and even from "politics" as such. Zingman's effort in mid-1917 to create a suprapolitical Yiddishist publishing house and journal at a moment when the few significant Yiddishist publishing ventures (the Petrograd *Folksblat,* the Kiever Farlag) were linked to parties might seem no less utopian than his speculative fiction. In fact, in his own small way he proved a pioneer in a process that gained clarity and momentum by late 1917 and early 1918: a drive by Yiddishists and Hebraists alike to assert the autonomy of cultural institutions and cultural practice from the dictates of parties and the zero-sum sensibilities of a political age. Ridden by tensions and outright contradictions, this drive to assert the autonomy of culture nevertheless had real institutional effects. At the same time, it embodied—and thus reveals to us—further fundamental assumptions by the culturist intelligentsia: that culture consisted of a set of activities different by nature from those constituting political action and that this distinct cultural realm was no less vital to the national interests of the putative Jewish nation than was "politics."

Culture's Constitution

The disparate cultural initiatives outlined at the end of Chapter 1 inscribed in practice what Zingman had imagined in fantasy: they sought to shape an encompassing Jewish culture independent from the metropoles yet like them in sweep, and to do so in a way that consciously reenacted the prerevolutionary ideals that had shaped these metropolitan cultures in the nineteenth century. The Kiev Kultur-Lige's aspiration to a Jewish culture that would grow beyond Yiddish literature to encompass all the arts is sometimes cited as a distinctive feature of that organization. But although the Kultur-Lige was remarkable for its concrete achievements on this score, its aspiration was altogether typical. Well before the Kultur-Lige's founding, Moscow's Hebraist Tarbut aspired to the same end: "to found Hebrew theaters, schools for art, to exhibit Hebraic exhibitions, etc."[8] Although sociological limitations forced the organization to focus primarily on educational work, its founders continued to entertain these ideas. In June 1918, as Persits sought to refound the organization in Kiev, she nursed plans to "put out an entire series of propaganda pamphlets on questions of Hebrew culture, education, literature, and art."[9]

Moreover, this aspiration to a Jewish culture spanning the arts had been born long before 1917. It had seen its first halting and marginal articulations as early as the 1880s, in the writings of such figures as the Hebrew poet M. Z. Mane and the novelist-publisher Sh. Ben-Avigdor. It had become normative in the decade before 1917.[10]

This shared will to an encompassing Jewish high cultural sphere also found expression in the parallel drives of the Hebraist and Yiddishist camps to detach Jewish cultural life from the metropolitan Russian cultural sphere so as to erect a separate Jewish cultural milieu equal to Russian culture rather than a mere idiom within it. This may seem a surprising claim to some readers. In recent years, scholars have devoted special attention to the unprecedented interaction between the Jewish national cultural project and the metropolitan Russian cultural milieu at the 1917 juncture, especially in theater and the visual arts. And the idea of promoting "Jewish" expression was not intrinsically at odds with commitment to the Russian metropolitan culture. In 1917, for example, the composer Aleksandr Kreyn created musical settings both for a work by Bialik and for the symbolist Aleksandr Blok's "The Rose and the Cross."[11] There was also a seeming rapprochement in the literary realm between Yiddishists and Hebraists from the borderlands and Russian-Jewish writers at home in the metropolitan literature. The writers Andrei Sobol' and the young Il'ya Ehrenburg published in literary collections linked ideologically to the Hebraist or Yiddishist camps. Moscow's Safrut (Literature) publishing house, founded in mid-1917 by the Zionist activist and editor Leyb Jaffe, made a special effort to recruit Russified figures like the prominent literary critic M. O. Gershenzon. Jaffe even recruited Vladislav Khodasevich—a Russian poet, Polish Catholic, and the regretful descendant of Russian Jewry's most notorious apostate-informer Iakov Brafman—to collaborate on an anthology of contemporary Hebrew poetry in Russian translation.[12]

Yet it is wrong to characterize the Jewish cultural endeavor of the era as a rapprochement with Russia. Cooperative relations between Jewish cultural activists and mainstream Russian cultural actors were in fact framed by a commitment to carve out a separate "Jewish" culture spanning all art forms. This is true even of the most manifestly cooperative ventures like Ha-Bimah, whose founders' desire to learn from the great Russian theater tradition went hand-in-hand with a separatist Hebraist culturist agenda. Linked from the first to the Moscow Hebraist organization that eventually constituted the core of the Tarbut organization, Ha-Bimah's founding program called not only for the creation of a single professional theater company but also for Hebrew theater schools, classes, studios, public performances, and full-fledged theaters across the country. Its founders soon abandoned these grandiose organizational plans in order to train themselves in the theatrical arts, but this aesthetic commitment was itself separatist in its telos. Even as they sought Stanislavsky's help, the troupe's leading figures Tsemah and Gnesin conceived their relation to the Russian theater world in essentially dialectical rather than dialogic terms: their immersion in the Russian theater tradition was to facilitate the creation of a distinctive "Hebrew" theater aesthetic and lay the cornerstone for modern Hebrew theater in Palestine.[13]

In fact, almost all of the era's organized Jewish cultural ventures hoped to detach Jewish culture as much as possible from the metropolitan Russian cultural sphere. Seeking to establish a material and ideological framework for the consolidation of distinct, permanent, and self-perpetuating Jewish art establishments, Kiev's Kultur-Lige pursued a two-pronged strategy of competing directly with Russian studios and conservatories. It sought to make itself the primary framework in which Jewish artists, composers, and musicians would train and work, and at the same time tried to tie fledgling Jewish music and plastic arts to the Yiddish literary scene. In 1919, its art section made the revealing boast that it had "interested and drawn near the best young talents of Kiev, the most gifted Jewish painters and sculptors," including many students trained by the painter Alexandra Exter, whose studio had served as a hothouse for the emergent Russian visual avant-garde in prewar Kiev.[14] The Kultur-Lige's Kiev theater studio, established in 1919, competed directly for talented youth of Jewish extraction with Russian- (and perhaps Ukrainian-) language studios; its administrators crowed that "the more talented Jewish students from all other non-Jewish studios" in Kiev were "practically running" to join it.[15] Once it had gotten hold of these talented creators of "Jewish art," the organization invested great effort in deepening their connection to Yiddish literary culture. The art section worked to further the trend of Jewish artists illustrating Yiddish books, the music school included Yiddish literature in its curriculum, and the theater section not only sought to teach its heavily Russified actors proper Yiddish, but also immersed them in the Yiddish literary tradition.[16]

The depth of the culturist intelligentsia's drive to make room for a full-fledged Jewish culture is exemplified by the almost universal rejection of Russian as a language of Jewish culture by a generation of culturists more at home in the language than any of their forebears. By 1917, most Russian Jews used Russian to some degree, a substantial minority used it exclusively, and Russification as a process was proceeding ever faster. Younger Jewish culturists were generally fluent in Russian and steeped in Russian literature. Yet with very few exceptions, they denied Russian any legitimacy as a language of their new culture.

Committed Yiddishist and Hebraist organizations like the Kultur-Lige and Tarbut used Russian when they had to in their propaganda and, to a limited degree, their internal administration (though less so than we might imagine).[17] But both organizations defined Jewish culture in absolutely monolingual terms and held to this standard in all literary publications. Indeed, almost all of the major organizations committed to "Jewish culture" in Russia were resolutely Hebraist or Yiddishist. Almost none of the declaredly Jewish publishing houses of the era published anything in Russian. Hebraist and Yiddishist journals gave scant or no attention to Russian-language Jewish literature.

More to the point, by 1917 there was no longer a substantial constituency that insisted on a significant role for Russian in the new Jewish culture. Scholars have noted the flood of Russian-language Jewish newspapers and other media intended for Jewish readers in 1917. Yet by contrast, the production of Russian-language high culture for Jews was paltry: no theater troupes to compare with the Yiddish and Hebrew ones, the merest trickle of Russian-Jewish literary publishing. Moreover, even this literature came from publishers who held that Russian was merely a temporary expedient, not an intrinsically valuable medium of Jewish culture.

Thus, the most significant Russian-language Jewish publishing house in Odessa, Kinneret, published little on cultural issues, and what it did publish was meant to introduce contemporary Hebrew culture to Russian Jewish readers—such as the Hebrew literary figures Tchernikhovsky and Avraham Mapu. The same is true of the era's most important Russian-language Jewish cultural publishing project, the aforementioned Safrut. Funded by the "committed Hebraist Fayvl Shapira," Safrut was expressly committed to Hebraist ends. The editor Jaffe's introduction to the house's eponymous anthology defined the Russian-language Jewish book merely as something "intended for those circles of readers for whom the Jewish language is inaccessible." Although the anthology served as one of the few substantial sites for Jewish literary creativity in Russian, the press did not intend to support the development of a Russian-language Jewish culture. Rather, its self-appointed task was to acquaint Russified Jews with Jewish nationalist ideas, Zionist activity, and Hebrew culture (see fig. 10). Safrut's most notable publication was an ambitious anthology of contemporary Hebrew poetry in translation, *Evreiskaia antologiia*, and its publication list was heavily dominated by translations or treatments of Hebrew writers from the Hebraist ideologue Ahad Ha-'Am to the medieval poet Yehuda Ha-Levi.[18]

One of the few other substantial Russian-language Jewish literary anthologies, the 1918 *Evreiskii mir*, also seems to have begun as an initiative by a Jewish printer to offer Russian-language readers an anthology of recent Yiddish writing. Its editor conceived it as "an anthology of young Yiddish writers . . . in Russian" and turned to Yiddishists for help in selecting the best new work. Although it ultimately contained work by Russian-Jewish writers of note, among them the young Il'ya Ehrenburg, *Evreiskii mir*, like the products of Safrut and Kinneret, was not born of an ideal of Russian-language Jewish culture, but rather represented an effort to find a market among Russified Jews for a Yiddish-centered literary culture.[19]

Even organizations that had once actively embraced Russian as one language of Jewish culture now rejected the use of Russian. The collapse of the OPE in 1917 (tellingly, into competing Hebraist and Yiddishist camps, as we saw in Chapter 1) marked the end of the former empire's most important exponent of Jewish linguistic integration. In Petrograd and Moscow, remnants of the old OPE circles would persist into the early 1920s and publish journals that defined Jewish culture in nonlinguistic terms.[20] But the rump branches of the organization in borderland cultural centers like Kiev, Vilna, and Kovne (Kaunas) simply erased Russian from their brief. In Kiev, the local branch, revived by figures with Folkist leanings like the pedagogue Haim Fialkov, Shtif, and Latski-Bertoldi, signaled the end of an era when it announced its intent to sell useful books in "Yiddish, Hebrew, and, so far as possible, also in other languages."[21]

There were a few exceptions to this delegitimization of Russian. In Moscow, the circle of Jewish writers, artists, and critics around the Yiddish poet Broderzon established a publishing imprint called Shamir in order to publish works of Jewish culture "in all three languages of the Russian Jews."[22] Yet the delegitimization of Russian as a language of Jewish culture was so pervasive that it affected even those cultural actors who could not help but continue to think and create in Russian. Thus, in a note to the Yiddish literary critic Niger about his collaborative work with Broderzon, El Lissitzky actually apologized for asking Niger to "endure me in Russian."[23] The Russian-Jewish writer An-ski, too, who had once defended a central role for Russian in Jewish culture, continued to write and publish in Russian, yet drew close to Moscow's Hebraists, proclaimed Hebrew "the language of my soul," and devoted the last months of his life to working with Vilna's Yiddishists to build a Yiddish-language branch of the Jewish Historical-Ethnographic Society.[24]

Alongside this will to institutional separation, Jewish culturists of all stripes showed a second tendency that was particularly surprising for their time and place: a deep commitment to a fundamentally old-fashioned conception of culture. This held even among those Jewish culturists who counted themselves "revolutionaries" or "avant-garde." Both revolutionism in its Promethean East European version and avant-garde ideas about art and society were potentially deeply antithetical to the very concept of "culture"—certainly the nineteenth-century vision of a high cultural sphere, exalted but distinct within social life. The ideology of revolution lent itself to wholesale rejection of the whole institutional and psychic order of nineteenth-century "bourgeois society." Expressionism's embrace of inner fragmentation challenged the axial principle of a stable expressive self as the ground of culture. And the left avant-garde's desire to shatter the wall between "art and life" took aim at the idea that the artist could speak to social and moral questions only through careful attention to the rules of art.

Some of these disruptive potentialities did affect the Jewish cultural sphere. In 1918, in the midst of a serious engagement with questions of Jewish art and Yiddish culture, Marc Chagall left Moscow to become a Soviet cultural commissar in his native Vitebsk. There, he embraced (however briefly) new forms of monumental public cultural production in the name of the Revolution—forms that took him far beyond the bounds of a Jewish cultural project or of a recognizable ideal of culture as a separate sphere. At the same time, first Yiddish and then Hebrew poetry would reel under the impact of a new generation of writers, some returning from the searing experience of war, whose poetry would seem on the face of it unassimilable to any collective project, much less one founded on humanist ideals. The most prominent of these was the aforementioned Peretz Markish, whose first poems combined a belated but consuming Decadent pessimism with aggressive Futurist iconoclasm—both stances recalcitrant to a faith in culture: "I take apart, / I unravel every [word], / Just as though from exhumed corpses/I strip the shrouds."[25]

Yet although some scholarship makes much of this double rupture, what is remarkable about the Jewish cultural milieu of 1917–1919, especially by comparison with the Russian one, is how limited the effects of such tendencies toward rupture actually were. Until 1919 at the earliest, notions of a radically new "Red" Jewish culture remained inchoate even among those Jewish culturists who preached cultural "revolution." The disruptive potentials of modernism were confined largely to a purely aesthetic debate, and even the most rebellious modernists were embraced by leading Jewish culturists as examples of, rather than challenges to, the development of a modern Jewish culture. What is truly striking about Jewish cultural practice at the 1917–1919 juncture is how fully even the modernists and declared revolutionaries remained wedded to nineteenth-century blueprints of a whole, harmonious culture.[26]

Here we might return to the Kultur-Lige as the exemplary case. The Kultur-Lige was founded and dominated by the most politically and aesthetically radical activists in the Yiddish cultural milieu. Yet it was committed structurally and ideologically to a wholly traditional conception of high culture: the undisputed primacy of aesthetic creativity and experience in human consciousness, the central place of literature, the significance of the full panoply of the other arts (and to some degree nationalist scholarship) orbiting around it, and a commitment to disseminating this high culture to "the masses" in an undiluted form. As the 1921 epigraph to the introduction suggests, this same vision—of "a broad, comprehensive modern culture" for Jews—persisted unchanged throughout the revolutionary period. This stance stood in stark contrast with the tendencies that dominated the best-known equivalent to the Kultur-Lige in the Russian cultural sphere, the Proletkult, whose many leading figures preached an iconoclastic vision of a new culture stemming directly from the experimental strivings of workers. The distinctive conservatism of the Kultur-Lige's cultural program was quite apparent to contemporaries. Indeed, as discussed later, it became a focal point of the vicious criticism to which more radical circles subjected the organization in 1919–1920.[27]

This continued commitment to an old-fashioned conception of high culture was inscribed at the individual level too. Yiddish Expressionist poets like Kvitko and Markish shocked adult readers with their dark visions of decay, dissolution, and violent rebirth. But as good Yiddishists, both writers repeatedly suspended their own poetics to write lively, joyful poetry for the new Yiddishist schools and the Jewish children they hoped would be their inheritors. Thus, Kvitko offered children strange but cheerful fare like this playful portrait of birds taking flight at sunrise:

> And there on high—Old Bird-Uncle
> in a cap of magic-leaves
> in a coat of feathers—
> what a coat of feathers!
> Glimmer-glow rainbow!
> Fine gold drawn through!
> Birdie-birdlike cries:
> Old Bird-Uncle's flying!—
> His chariot is glowing, glowing![28]

This example of a cultural actor transcending his own ideological and aesthetic vision in service of a larger agenda of cultural formation helps explain another notable feature of the cultural sphere: the readiness of cultural actors with opposing aesthetic commitments to cooperate with each other. This readiness would eventually collapse under the weight of the Revolution's zero-sum logic, but until 1919 such cooperation was the rule rather than the exception. As in other cultural spheres, 1917–1918 marked the beginnings of sharp debates among Jewish culturists about the claims of modernist aesthetic departures: in February 1918, for instance, the Odessa Hebraist journal *Ha-Shiloah* carried a pseudonymous broadside against experimentation in the visual arts that denounced the new styles as a desecration of the human form.[29] Nevertheless, Hebraists eagerly solicited illustrations by modernists like Lissitzky and Alt'man (see figs. 2, 4, 10). In a similar push-pull fashion, leading figures at the nonsocialist Kiev Folks-Farlag like Shtif or Kalmanovitsh disliked the new modernist trends in Yiddish literature, but still helped recruit Dovid Bergelson as an editor and published Kvitko's first book of poetry, *Trit* (Steps), with its explosive expressionist rhetoric.

Also distinctive of the cultural programs of 1917 was a third feature of the culturist disposition that Zingman's utopia epitomized: a surprisingly sharp privileging of the arts over other forms of cultural creativity typically associated with cultural nationalism, like historical scholarship, ethnography, and excursions into "national thought." The idea that historical and folkloristic research marked the royal road to the authentic national self had been a central feature of East European nationalisms throughout the nineteenth century, and much recent work has demonstrated the prominence of this historicist-nationalist sensibility in East European Jewish cultural nationalism.[30] Similarly, the alternative notion of discovering or reconstructing a Jewish ethos or a distinct Jewish-national philosophical relation to the world is just as well documented in the history of Jewish cultural nationalism. The most influential Jewish cultural nationalist figure of the 1890s, the theoretician of cultural Zionism Ahad Ha-'Am, had argued that at the heart of classical Judaism could be found a distinct Jewish ethical relationship to life, one centered on a positive this-worldliness and an orientation toward virtuous individual life within the framework of community. This notion of a distinct Jewish ethos that could survive the death of religion had been embraced with equal fervor by non-Zionist cultural actors at the turn of the century such as the populist ethnographer An-ski and the Yiddish writer, folklorist, and culture-hero Peretz.

Similarly, for some culturists and especially Yiddishists, a search for the national self through a study of the "folk" remained the heart of cultural nationalism. By 1917, this view was epitomized by the peripatetic populist-ethnographer-writer An-ski. Deeming traditional folk culture a higher expression of "the human spirit" than mere "individual creativity," and convinced that East European Jewry had once maintained a distinct kind of moral imagination that Jewish moderns sorely needed, he worked tirelessly to collect Jewish folk culture and expose his fellow modern Jews to its vitalizing powers.[31]

Yet by 1917, a surprising number of Jewish culturists insisted vocally that aesthetic culture was both fundamentally different from other forms of cultural creation and of far greater significance. Thus, even many of the culturists who shared An-ski's interest in folk culture per se—and by no means was this interest universally shared—insisted both on a sharp distinction between folk culture and modern art and the self-evident superiority of the latter. In a programmatic 1918 essay on the uses of Jewish folk art for Jewish visual modernism, the Moscow art critic Efros credited An-ski's "truly historic collecting efforts" for "our long predestined encounter with folk art." But Efros, concerned exclusively with "the world of national beauty that has been revealed to us," offered no support for the idea that Jewish folk art was ideologically superior to modern artistic endeavors.[32]

Similar arguments came from within the core constituencies of the Jewish national-cultural camp. An-ski's acquaintance Niger asserted a sharp distinction between "ethnographic" and "aesthetic" interest in folklore. Whereas the ethnographic eye failed to appreciate folk culture as "a treasure, . . . a source of aesthetic pleasure,"

> for us, however, folk-creation is more than a "key" [to the psychology of the "folk"]. For us, it is a treasure, something which we wish to enjoy in itself. We seek in it not the soul of the people but an additional soul [traditionally held to inhabit Jews on the Sabbath]. We judge it according to the artistic pleasure, not the scientific use, which it brings us.[33]

Concomitantly, Niger dissented from the widespread approbation for An-ski's Russian-Yiddish-Hebrew drama *The Dybbuk* because he deemed it more a "folklore collection" than "literature."[34]

A similar hierarchy could be found in the writings of the young Yiddish modernist Moyshe Kulbak. Kulbak, like Niger, saw the folk culture of East European Jewry as an essential source for the new Jewish art; his writings in the 1920s might be regarded as the most successful marriages of modernist aesthetics and East European Jewish folk tradition in Yiddish. Nevertheless, in 1918 the young writer resolutely asserted the subordinate status of folk culture relative to the aesthetic capacities of the modern, self-conscious Jewish artist. The modern literary work surpassed the "primitive fineness of folk-creation": if it was in the "mouth of the folk" that Yiddish had first become a language capable of beauty, it was in the "souls of the Yiddish artists" that it had "performed its purifying ablutions . . . and won its aesthetic visage." Significantly, Kulbak located the mechanism of this aesthetic achievement precisely in the feature that most separated the modern artist from the hypostasized "folk": his or her "conscious" approach to aesthetic problems and to the manipulation of language. Whereas the creators of Yiddish folk song had shaped Yiddish "unconsciously," without "assessing the artistic value of the word," modern Yiddish writers had "consciously purified the language."[35]

Furthermore, while many culturists did recognize the uses of scholarship and the cultural value of ethnography, they showed virtually no interest in philosophical formulations of a new Jewish identity. Flaunting the contemporary presumption that the modern Jewish culture movement was in essence an effort to substitute a secular Jewish identity for a religious one, many culturist writings of the period, public and private, either ignored Jewishness as a philosophical problem or dismissed it as irrelevant. Significantly, this does not indicate the culturist intelligentsia's general disinterest in philosophical treatments of the modern condition. There is plenty of evidence, for instance, of culturist interest in works by Nietzsche, Bergson, and Russian counterparts such as Lev Shestov and Dmitri Merezhkovsky. Rather, the absence of any interest in the question of Jewish identity, which stood in stark contrast to their vast interest in the problems of a Jewish aesthetic culture, reflects a considered understanding by the intelligentsia of what "Jewish culture" could and could not be for secular moderns like themselves.

Thus, although An-ski's urgent commitment to ethnography did resonate with some contemporaries, notably the Jewish nationalist intelligentsia of postwar Vilna, very few Jewish intellectuals seem to have taken seriously his views about ethnography as a key to an occluded Jewish ethos. Tellingly, all of the other organized ethnographic efforts undertaken by Jewish culturists in 1917–1919 eschewed any rhetoric about recovering a national ethos, and focused solely on the desired aesthetic effects of exposure to the recovered works. The Kultur-Lige's art section, for instance, explained its decision to publish a collection of Jewish primitives as a means to orient Jewish "artistic thought to the beautiful folk-source."[36]

Hebraist institutions and journals showed a parallel indifference to the sort of nationalist thought about the "essence" of the Jewish ethos that had once been at the core of Russian Hebraism. This indifference infuriated Bialik, who lambasted his contemporaries for imagining, as he put it, that a few lyric poems marked a higher cultural achievement than Nachman Krochmal's *Moreh nevukhe ha-zeman,* the nineteenth-century Hebrew philosophical treatise that marked the high point (and, given its almost complete isolation, the nondevelopment) of systematic Jewish philosophy in Eastern Europe.[37]

A 1923 letter from the most ambitious Hebraist publisher of the 1917–1919 juncture, Stybel, suggests that many culturists did indeed believe that modern works were more significant, and begins to suggest why. Addressing the suggestion that the publishing house commission more translations of philosophical classics, Stybel wrote dismissively:

> Philosophy has been studied and written by us all these 2,000 years and nevertheless [Jews] turned and abandoned [the language]. Our chief aspiration now is to return and connect the young Hebrew reader to our Hebrew literature, and this can be done only if we provide him with Maupassant, Zola, Tolstoy, Dickens, Dostoevsky, Turgenev, and also Boccaccio and even Cassanova in Hebrew, and then it is possible to hope that he will also read Spinoza and Windelband in Hebrew.[38]

The culturist intelligentsia's unbounded faith in the significance of secular art and its equally deep doubts about other forms of cultural creativity had prerevolutionary roots; note that Bialik's angry and accurate diagnosis of this malady was written in 1915–1916. In his biography of Ahad Ha-'Am, Steven Zipperstein too has drawn attention to the precipitious decline in that figure's perceived significance sometime between 1905 and 1910. Not coincidentally, a great many of the culturists who sought to realize the Jewish cultural project in 1917–1919 had entertained Ahad Ha-'Am's ideas in their youth; it was they who had turned their backs on his notions of an ideational regeneration of Jewish culture in favor of an aesthetic framework.[39]

This shift had also occurred in the Yiddishist camp. In the last years of his life, the great Yiddish writer Peretz complained that the aestheticist culturism preached by his self-declared followers was dangerously unmoored from an authentically Jewish ethos. But although younger Yiddishists venerated Peretz, his late critique was basically ignored.

Beyond explicit declarations of aestheticism, what is remarkable about Jewish culturist activity in 1917–1919 is how fully aestheticist presumptions dominated cultural practice. While the revived Hebraist-Zionist flagship journal *Ha-Shiloaḥ* continued to cultivate its mix of Zionist writing, Jewish philosophy, arts, and secular-national Jewish scholarship in the grand Russian intelligentsia tradition of the "thick journal," almost all of the other culturist journals of the era devoted their pages exclusively or overwhelmingly to the arts. This was true of landmark publications like the Hebraist *Ha-Tefukah* and *Erets,* as well as Yiddishist productions of the Kiev Grupe such as *Eygns* and *Oyfgang;* it was also true of forgotten or unpublished works such as the Yiddishist *Kunst-ring* or Moyshe Broderzon's planned journal for the arts. The Kiev *Bikher-velt,* devoted to assessing all Yiddish publishing from a Yiddishist standpoint, made some room for discussions of scholarly projects, but almost all of its articles and rubrics took for granted that art was the centerpiece of the modern Yiddishist project.

The same story holds at an organizational level. The Folks-Farlag established a special section for scholarly publishing, but other leading culturist presses like Stybel, Omanut, and the Kiever Farlag slighted it. Although the Kultur-Lige initially declared its support of Yiddish-language scholarship, it made virtually no effort on its behalf, in stark contrast to its organizing endeavors in the arts and literature. Concern for scholarship was remarkably absent even in the most ambitious plans of Tarbut. Both organizations conceived the anatomy of their work in the same terms: Shoshana Persits defined Tarbut's brief as "culture, education, literature, and art" while the Kultur-Lige defined its three "pillars" as "Yiddish popular education, Yiddish literature, and Jewish art."[40] By the same token, all of these journals and publishing houses strongly privileged artistic expression over anything we might call "Jewish thought." One of the few exceptions, Moyshe Litvakov's book *In Umruh* (In Turmoil), privileged the aesthetic realm as the highest and in some sense only legitimate end of Jewish national-cultural endeavors within a multiethnic socialist society.

This valorization of the arts and aesthetic experience might be thought of as having a double genealogy. On the one hand, it was redolent of the fin-de-siècle sensibilities about art, selfhood, and experience in which the now-dominant generation of culturists had been immersed in their youth. Yet on the other, it was not wedded to the sorts of Parnassian indifference, bohemianism, incipient avant-gardism, or world-renouncing attitudes associated with "Decadence" in Eastern as well as Western Europe. On the contrary, as the quotation from Stybel's private letter suggests, Jewish culturists construed the larger social meaning of their aestheticism in es-

sentially Schillerian terms: culture, and above all art, was not a site of elite
retreat but a public good, the property of the nation that it was supposed
to organize and regenerate. Many culturists took for granted that culture
was a national concern to be organized on a public basis: immediately after
February, the young poet Menahem Ribalov urged the national movement
to take advantage of the Revolution's new freedoms to establish a large-
scale publishing house, revive the Hebrew press, and "found a literary institute, a sort of academy for art and literature, which will gather around it
all of our literary powers."[41]

Politics and Autonomy

Ribalov's insistence that "culture" had a distinct public significance and
thus a claim on the attentions of the Jewish public and its representatives
was altogether typical of Jewish culturists. Indeed, it was the same conviction that had structured Zingman's culturist utopia. Thus culturists could
not fail to be struck by the fact that by 1917 the most important representatives of the putative Russian Jewish public were the competing Jewish
political parties. Given their prominence, the question of the relationship
between Jewish culture and Jewish politics would have loomed large for
Jewish culturists in the revolutionary period even if this relationship had
not carried with it a history fraught with tensions, controversy, and mutual
recriminations.

In practical terms, as we have seen, the explosive development of the
Jewish parties and the larger Jewish political sphere affected the bid for
Jewish culture in contradictory ways. On the one hand, throughout 1917
especially, the practical demands of mass politics consumed the lion's share
of the Jewish nationalist intelligentsia's energies and resources. Many culturists were deeply unhappy over what they saw as the parties' neglect of
culture throughout 1917. Klausner, the editor of *Ha-Shiloah*, worried "lest
culture now be put aside for politics" and cast the journal's mid-1917 resumption as a means to combat this development. Across the battle lines
that divided Odessa's Zionists and Jewish socialists, the Poale Tsion activist,
humorist, and translator M. Kitai expressed the same worry: that political
mobilization of the Jewish "proletariat" and "broad folk-masses" was not
being matched by the revival of "the Jewish book" and "national culture."[42]

On the other hand, as we have also seen, the takeoff of Jewish nationalist
politics in 1917 (and the larger growth in nationalist discourse and mobili-

zation across Eastern Europe) also redounded to the benefit of Jewish culturists and the Jewish cultural project: the spread of nationalist sentiment generated new levels of public interest in the idea of a "Jewish culture" and the parties themselves embraced, at least in principle, the central significance of culture and cultural policy. Culturists were generally pleased when the parties and movements acknowledged the importance of Jewish culture as a matter of public policy.

Yet at the same time, from the first, culturists in the various camps also expressed a deep, and at first glance puzzling, suspicion toward the parties and a more general antagonism toward "politics" as such. At its April founding, Tarbut agreed to become part of the resurgent Russian Zionist organization only with regard to external policy matters, that is, relations with state bodies and other Jewish organizations. But its leadership insisted on complete independence from the larger Zionist organization regarding cultural and educational work—even though the vast majority of the organization's members were evidently Zionists. There seems to have been a real and well-grounded concern that the Zionist movement, a big-tent effort with many constituencies, would not commit itself to Tarbut's uncompromising Hebraist and anti-Yiddish agenda. But some participants in the debate framed this organizational autonomy as a matter of principle. The head of the organization, Zlatopolsky, grounded the move in an essential difference between politics and culture: "In general terms, we are not a political organization [*histadrut medinit*] but a cultural one, and we must and wish to work separately." The patron (and committed Zionist) Y. Nayditsh averred that Tarbut ought not to work "in an official fashion under the Zionist organization's banner" because "the Hebrew language is neutral and stands above all parties, and if we recognize that—we will strengthen our organization."[43]

The first substantial Yiddishist journal of the revolutionary period, Petrograd's *Yidishe folksblat,* went a good deal further. The *Folksblat* was not a journal of the arts, reflexively concerned to distance itself from the rough and tumble of politics, but a gathering point for Yiddishists deeply committed to political activism on behalf of nationalist-autonomist ideals. Its editors were convinced that cultural revival was essential to the political goals of the national movement, averring that the neglect of culture threatened to leave "all our national-political victories . . . suspended in mid-air."[44]

Yet for the journal's editors, it was not only the chaos of the revolutionary moment that threatened Jewish national revival, but also the hypertrophy of party politics itself:

> We have undertaken to publish our weekly under difficult conditions. The Jewish press has just now begun to revive after two years of suppression, but our noisy political life has brought forth purely party publications, which set themselves political party-goals. These publications are maintained from party funds and distributed by and among party comrades. The circle of Jewish readers which drew its cultural nourishment entirely or in part from Yiddish sources has divided itself into various camps. Cultural and literary goals are neglected . . . and literary talents who cannot press themselves into the frameworks of party publications stand outside the Yiddish press.
>
> A weekly that sets itself literary and cultural goals above all, that hopes to gather all of our best literary powers and formulate a Jewish democratic ideology, faces a very difficult situation. Such a weekly must first create anew its audience, its community of readers. It must accustom the audience once again [to the idea] that we have cultural and literary goals which stand beyond parties.[45]

What lay behind such direct attacks on organized Jewish politics by persons who were themselves politically active? In the case of the Tarbut organization, the claim to autonomy was driven by a concrete matter of cultural policy: a well-founded concern by Tarbut's intensely Hebraist members that the larger Zionist organization might take a more compromising line regarding the use and recognition of Yiddish in Jewish institutions. In part, that is, claims to autonomy could reflect actually differing agendas on the part of cultural and political actors within the same political camp.

But as the text of the *Folksblat*'s cri de coeur suggests, culturist suspicion toward the parties stemmed not only from policy differences, but also from factors rooted in conceptions of culture itself. Of course, we might read the *Folksblat*'s argument as merely party politics in another guise: according to this view, its invocation of civil society and the autonomy of culture might be read as a means of attack by Folkists against the socialist parties, above all the Bund, which dominated the Yiddishist camp. In a larger sense, certain traditions in the historiography of the Russian Revolution would mandate that we read critiques of the hypertrophy of "politics" as little more than an attack on revolutionary demands for the reorganization of society, polity, and culture, that is, as an antisocialist political effort disguised in the ostensibly neutral language of "culture."

Clearly, there is some truth to both readings. Claims to supraparty ideals did play an especially important role for nonsocialist diaspora autonomists like some of the editors at the *Folksblat* precisely because socialist elements in diasporist camp, like the Bund, were so much more successful as mass movements than they. Some defenses of culture's autonomous prerogatives in Jewish culturist circles were direct reactions to the emerging revolutionary culture and the steadily radicalizing claims of the revolutionary movement. At some point in 1918, the founders of Ha-Bimah decided to demand an oath of the troupe's members. After proclaiming their full acceptance of "the high national and cultural approaches and goals of the Ha-Bimah theater," the members were to promise "not to relate to my work as to a business, a profession, a craft, but as to a mission and an exalted calling. Because Ha-Bimah is not a business undertaking, I herewith promise not to relate to its managers as though to employers or bosses, but rather as to leaders and guides, and therefore I will not employ against them the means and tactics of class struggle."[46]

But there is good reason to reject such narrowly political readings of discourse like that which appeared in the *Folksblat*. In August 1918, Bialik published an essay entitled "Tarbut ve-'politikah'" (Culture and "Politics") in the unlikely venue of the Odessa Hebraists' recently founded journal for pedagogy, *Ha-Ginah*. It was a fierce protest against the idea that one could reshape the consciousness and culture of the nation through political discourse and action. It was here that Bialik voiced the worries cited in the epigraph: that "any politics which seeks . . . to lay its hands on 'culture' in order to subordinate it to its needs rather than to serve it—such a politics is destined to become coercive, and a people which values its soul and its happiness will keep distant from it."[47]

Given Bialik's longstanding opposition to the Russian revolutionary movement and its inroads among Russian Jewish youth, it would be easy to read these words as merely an attack on the revolutionary political culture emerging across the border in Bolshevik Russia (Odessa was at this time still nominally part of independent Ukraine). Yet the essay was explicitly directed not against revolutionary politics but against a danger that Bialik perceived in his own political camp, the mainstream, nonsocialist Zionist movement. "Culture and 'Politics'" was a riposte to an essay in a previous issue of the journal by the leading figure in Russian Zionist politics, Menahem

Ussishkin. Ussishkin's essay had concerned an ongoing discussion in the Zionist movement concerning the proper pronunciation system for the Hebrew language being revived in Palestine. Bialik's essay took as its starting point Ussishkin's conviction that such cultural questions were not merely to be decided by "linguists and writers," but "also, and perhaps first and foremost, by the helmsmen of our national politics."[48]

But it was not the topic of Ussishkin's essay that concerned Bialik, who laughingly (and prematurely) dismissed the notion that pronunciation could be decided by official dictates. Rather, what could not "be passed over in silence" was "the general tendency which bubbles up from every line of Ussishkin's essay and from the 'epigrams' interspersed among them. These epigrams teach us little about the matter under discussion, but they do teach us something about the general system of thought of our 'helmsmen' and about the relationship between their 'politics' to the values of our culture and those who create them."[49]

Bialik's critique was rife with contradictions. At certain junctures, the essay dismisses the notion that political dictates could affect consciousness. At others, it asserts a counterclaim to power and authority within Zionism by insisting on the writer's unique capacity to shape the nation—an old argument on Bialik's part and one to which I will return.[50] But lacking the religious resolve of a Luther, Bialik evidently could not sustain much faith in the resilient inviolability of spirit. Rather, the dominant theme of the essay is the danger posed to the work of culture and to the nation itself by a hypertrophic politics: "I and many others like me regard this system of thought [*shitah*] as harmful, and if it should triumph, it would bear grave danger for all our work of national revival . . . "[51]

In a broad sense, Bialik's essay was a reaction to the emerging sensibility of his postliberal age: the vague but potent desire to use the capacities of political discourse, political action, and state infrastructure to reshape any and all aspects of human culture and consciousness. This general concern was inscribed as well in his literary works. In a sketch entitled "Lememshelet ha-Marsh" (Toward the Dominion of the March), written during the war, a poet's creative process is violently disrupted by the blare of a military band outside his window. With great effort, he shuts out the noise and triumphantly completes his poem, only to find to his horror that in place of amphibrachs or dactyls, the poem obeys "the rhythm of the march."[52]

But significantly, the 1918 "Tarbut ve-'politikah'" does not frame its opposition to the rise of this same tendency in Zionism in terms of the moral-cum-aesthetic claims of the poet's interiority against the noisy realm of public life. Rather, "Culture and 'Politics'" mounts a nationalist defense of the project of Jewish cultural regeneration. That is, Bialik was not taking issue with Zionism or with Zionist political activism as such; the essay was not a political polemic in the guise of a cultural one. Instead, the guiding assumption behind all of this flailing essay's disparate and even mutually contradictory claims was that "culture" in fact denoted a distinct realm of human activity (individual and national) that operated in ways fundamentally different from the mode of reason and practice associated with politics. Further, the imposition of the political mindset on cultural practice was not simply ideologically objectionable but actually distorted the acts of cultural creators and ruined their work—and hence was mortally dangerous to the very Jewish cultural revival that Zionists desired.

Thus rhetoric about the danger of "politics" to "culture" was not found only in contexts of debate and struggle among the parties. It could also be found in the very bosom of the Zionist Hebraist movement, asserted by a figure virtually synonymous with Zionism in the broadest sense to an audience of Hebrew readers who certainly almost all shared both Hebraist and Zionist commitments.

Moreover, the antiparty principle of Jewish cultural circles was not born in 1917.[53] In fact, all of its variants had been formulated more or less word for word, often by the exact same actors, in the years of and after the 1905 Revolution, which significantly constituted another era of open Jewish party-political differentiation, mass politicization, and ideological delineation in general, and the ascendancy of revolutionary socialist ideas in the national movement in particular.[54] Thus in 1908, the first East European Yiddish journal formally devoted exclusively to literature and the arts, the Vilna *Literarishe monatsshriften,* defined the very concept of a purely cultural journal in direct opposition to party divisions in the Jewish national intelligentsia:

Peculiar, abnormal conditions have [created multiple] sociopolitical camps [*rikhtungen*] within the Jewish people, sharpened their corners and made them disproportionately antagonistic toward one another. The rising culture-renaissance demands that all the vital powers of the people be unified on its soil, on the soil of cultural creation. "Fortify our national bastions!"—That is the slogan which hangs in the air. Others should fortify them politically and economically, and their work will, unavoidably, have to split according to their various paths and contradictory means. We wish to aid in the building of our culture-fortress through the efforts of all creative forces.[55]

Famously (and infamously in the eyes of many Jewish socialists), the three founder-editors of the journal, Niger, A. Vayter, and Shmarye Gorelik, came out of opposing political parties (Niger was from the Socialist-Zionist party, an ancestor of the Fareynikte; Vayter came out of the Bund; and Gorelik had been a pro-Zionist publicist for the Zionist Yiddish daily *Der fraynd*).[56] And in fact, although their supraparty principle was attacked then and later as the heresy of renegades from political responsibility, such ideas began to emerge within the parties themselves during the Revolution. At the First District Conference of the Seymist party (the other socialist-autonomist ancestor of the Fareynikte) in Vilna in March 1907, vigorous debate over the question of literature and its place in party work led to the conclusion that literature had to command more attention from the party and its journal. The conference wrote into party dogma a surprisingly sharp distinction between art and politics: "We must strive [to ensure] that everything printed in our organ will have literary value and not merely narrow party content . . . Art-literature and art must take their proper place, and the time has come that art-literature should be supplied to the conscious proletarian in its pure and true form."[57]

Nor were these ideas confined to the prewar Yiddishist world, locked as it was in an intimate tension with the Jewish left and especially the Bund. As Dan Miron has noted, assertions of art's fundamental difference and of the author's necessary distance from "politics" (including the organized Zionist movement) characterized a whole generation of Hebrew writers who came of age between 1900 and 1910. And such notions were not only taken up by writers. They became common coinage among Zionist publicists as well. In 1902, upon his accession to the editorship of the preeminent Hebrew journal *Ha-Shiloaḥ*, the editor (and staunch Zionist) Klausner proclaimed that alongside its Zionist essays and Judaic scholarship, the journal would make a central place for good Hebrew literature without any ideological preconditions because "beauty, like thought and ethics, has great value in itself." By 1908, when the Zionist movement had refounded its flagship Hebrew periodical *Ha-'Olam,* the editor L. Jaffe advertised to writers his aspiration to make the journal not only a site for Zionist writing but also a central organ of "Hebrew art" and "art-literature" as such.[58]

Contemporaries emphasized the importance of insulating cultural expression from political determination even in contexts far removed from any discernible strategic concerns. Odessa's *Ha-Shiloah* was an assertively Zionist journal and its editor Klausner was as fiercely committed to active political Zionism as to Hebrew cultural revival. Yet in his capacity as a self-appointed cultivator of Hebrew culture, he regularly praised Hebrew writers for distancing their art from political concerns and repeatedly asserted the principle that good literature could only be created under such conditions. He praised the Hebrew writer G. Shofman, a figure altogether distant from his brand of Zionism, for creating a true "art literature" free of "political commentary and philosophizing and moralizing." He ascribed the achievements of the Hebrew Romantic poet Tchernikhovsky to his refusal to bow to "any party or to any movement" and a commitment to "art alone—to the perfection of the artistic idea, to perfection of the form."[59]

A variety of sources suggest as well that the distinction between culture and politics had deep affective dimensions, that is, it was neither merely polemical nor simply some sort of theoretical reflex. When Jewish political forces jointly extended special courtesies to cultural figures of national stature like An-ski or Bialik, they did so not only as a calculated act of political symbolism but also because such figures genuinely bore suprapolitical significance. In his memoirs of revolutionary Kiev, the left-liberal political activist M. Goldenveizer relates an event that occurred during a visit by An-ski to the Ukrainian parliament (Rada), in which the Jewish parties were also represented. When a local rabbi asked delegates to stand in honor of the ostensible affinities between the Revolution's freedoms and the ideals of the Jewish tradition as represented by the Torah, the anticlerical Bundist delegates attempted to shout him down. An-ski, Goldenveizer relates, quieted the delegates with a raised hand and insisted that the Torah was not merely a religious object but a symbol of Jewry's age-old culture, at which point everyone stood.[60]

In the year that followed this incident, relations between Zionist and Jewish socialist-autonomist camps became so antagonistic that such expressions of culture's supraparty authority in a public setting became unthinkable. When Ukraine's Temporary Jewish National Assembly invited Bialik to preside at its opening in November 1918, the invitation evidently came from the victorious Zionist bloc alone; Bialik himself had run in second place on the Zionist list.[61] Yet even in that poisonous atmosphere, the January 1919 issue of the Kultur-Lige's flagship Yiddishist cultural journal *Bikher-velt* ran a deeply respectful obituary for a leading figure in Ukrainian Zionism, M. N. Sirkin. The obituary, written by the literary critic Mayzl, lamented the death of this "talented Jewish journalist, activist, and lover of Yiddish literature." Speaking from personal experience, Mayzl credited the Zionist leader with playing a pivotal role in the *Yiddish* cultural revival to which *Bikher-velt* was pledged. Upon settling in Kiev in 1907, Sirkin had "led a very intensive effort for Yiddish and Yiddish literature. His lectures, which bore an inspired love for Yiddish literature, had a great effect on the student-youth." Mayzl acknowledged the transformation that had occurred between 1907 and 1919, yet in his view this only underscored Sirkin's merit: "In the last few years, when the differentiation of the sociopolitical camps in Jewish life grew so much stronger, M. N. Sirkin grew distant from the core of Yiddish creativity, but in his own circles, in Zionist-Hebraist circles, he did not cease to fight for Yiddish. Among the Zionists, M. N. Sirkin was one of the few who seriously loved and treasured Yiddish and Yiddish literature."[62]

Mayzl's essay was no exception to the anti-Zionism of Kiev's Yiddishist and socialist circles. But it did take for granted that a Zionist could love Yiddish literature and culture—an admission that cut against the grain of both socialist and Yiddishist propaganda. Mayzl wrote from personal experience, but he was still able to distinguish conceptually between cultural and political commitments as late as 1919. No less significant, the Yiddishists of *Bikher-velt,* who were themselves mostly socialist, saw fit to run the piece in their journal.

The most meaningful measure of what culturists really meant by their distinction between culture and politics must be sought in culturist practice. Throughout 1917 and into 1918, against the increasingly massive pressures of Manichean political conflict, many culturists genuinely sought to enact an ideal of culture's autonomy from party politics in their institution-building and their relationships with other cultural actors. To a limited degree, this tendency extended even across the more fundamental chasm dividing the Jewish intelligentsia into hostile Zionist and diaspora-autonomist camps. Finally, this tendency made itself felt even in the socialist-Yiddishist camp, where it had to overcome postulates of materialism and class struggle that would seem to render such notions inherently indefensible.

Petrograd's *Folksblat* matched its self-representation as "an organ for free Jewish thought" with genuine efforts to recruit "the most respected Yiddish literati regardless of party and ideological allegiance." Most of its writers were affiliated with the Folks-Partey. But participants also included the old socialist Yiddishist writer Avrom Reyzen, the Bundist writer N. Lurie, and Kiev writers affiliated with the Fareynikte like Bergelson, Nister, and Dobrushin, who served on that socialist party's culture committee.[63]

The *Folksblat*'s form of autonomy for cultural expression remained strictly within the ideological bounds of secular diaspora nationalism. But an organization created by the same actors in 1918, the Kiev Folks-Farlag publishing house, transgressed this line of political division too. In service to their ambitious program of Yiddish cultural formation, the founders of the publishing house chose editors regardless of party affiliation. Joint charge over its statistics and economics list and its textbooks list fell to the sociologist and Marxist Poale-Tsion activist Yankev Leshtshinsky and the Bundist Lurie, respectively. The press recruited the Hebraist Ben-Tsion Dinaburg to work alongside Zelig Kalmanovitsh in its Jewish studies section. And it placed its literary section under the radical Bergelson and the eminent Yiddish critic Eliashev (Baal Makhshoves), who was one of the few significant Yiddish cultural figures with expressly Zionist sympathies.[64]

As the readiness of these editors to participate suggests (though no doubt they were also driven by material needs), there was a genuine eagerness among culturists for such institutions. In October 1917, as the Yiddish poet Broderzon described his plans for a new journal devoted exclusively to culture, he lamented: "but where can one find a good Yiddish, non-political printing establishment?" Though he reflexively sympathized with the Revolution and would publish in journals affiliated with Poale Tsion, he nevertheless took for granted that a serious cultural journal had to be free of party affiliation.

The archives reveal a variety of similar if more fleeting efforts to find some realm of shared national cultural life beyond the divides of party and movement, and even across the fundamental Hebraist-Zionist versus Yiddishist-diasporist divide. The old Zionist activist Y. H. Ravnitsky and the diasporist Yiddishist Niger, for instance, endeavored to work together on a number of literary projects, though these did not come to fruition.[65] And in early 1918, Niger's brother reported plans by Yiddishists in Moscow for a literary anthology that was to include work not only by those prominent in the diaspora autonomist and Yiddishist movements, but also by

Eliezer Shteynman and Natan Grinblat, two writers affiliated with the opposing Hebraist and Zionist camp.[66]

In more public settings, some contemporaries attempted to avoid the Solomonic competition over the legacy of canonical writers and instead acknowledge their broader national cultural significance across party lines. In December 1917, the Moscow Jewish community council organized an evening in memory of Abramovitsh (Mendele) that explicitly set aside divisions of party, movement, and even linguistic ideology; the unlikely list of invited speakers ranged from Niger to the Zionist activist Jaffe and even the head of Tarbut, Zlatopolsky. Collectively dominated by the various nationalist parties, the council was also divided among them; the success of its initiative depended on the agreement of the various party representatives.[67] The evening thus represented accession to ideals of suprapolitical nationhood and national culture. It also suggested the potential of an elected national body to create a sort of neutral ground in which party divisions could be suspended, at least for a time.[68]

Finally, and most remarkably, efforts to institute a distinction between culture and politics extended beyond the Jewish liberal nationalist camp to the socialist milieu. The status of culture within the Jewish socialist-nationalist parties was itself a matter of debate, as I have noted. More to the point, many of those within the parties who did acknowledge the importance of culture nevertheless adjusted their cultural vision to their revolutionary ideals: the party's concern should be the cultivation of culture among and for "the workers" (or, at the most, "the masses"), the party could only support other instances of Jewish culture that accorded with its sociopolitical vision, and the notion that there existed a larger sphere of "Jewish culture" standing above political determinations was dubious or even counterrevolutionary.

In March 1918, at the first meetings of the Fareynikte's culture commission in Kiev, several participants were at pains to uphold such principles. When the committee decided to solicit information about cultural life in the provinces, some took for granted that the questionnaires should concern only cultural institutions organized by party branches. When it was suggested that the questionnaire solicit information on Jewish cultural life more generally, the activists Levitan and Rashkes (leading figures in the party, both of whom later became Communists) argued forcefully against the idea on principle: only workers' institutions and their needs merited party attention, not the general cultural situation.[69] A slightly less restric-

tive version of the same sensibility played out at a contemporaneous Poale
Tsion meeting. Calling on local branches to organize evening courses for
Jewish workers, the participants stipulated that the courses might be formally nonparty but that the initiative for holding them had to be taken by
"party-people," "our best cultural powers."[70]

Yet looser conceptions of cultural policy were also visible at these meetings. At the Fareynikte meetings, one activist, Y. Epshteyn, pushed the
party to "take the lead in cultural work on the Jewish street." In the dense
code of the revolutionary parties, this statement suggested a more cooperative relationship with independent Yiddish cultural initiatives. In the
face of opposition by the more orthodox Levitan and Rashkes, however,
Epshteyn scaled back his demands and merely insisted that the party
should solicit information on Jewish cultural life in general so that it could
"exert influence on those institutions in which the Jewish working class has
a vital interest."[71] At the Poale Tsion meeting, this more liberal sensibility
triumphed, at least temporarily. The party tasked itself with organizing
cultural institutions for "the broad masses" and conceived the goals of
these institutions in essentially culturist terms: it resolved to organize "dra-
matic-literary circles" and "literary evenings" not for the sake of revolutionary education and agitation, but in order to refine the "aesthetic feeling" of the "masses" and "more closely acquaint the Jewish *demokratye*
with Literature." Pledged to these ends, it also went beyond the Fareynikte
regarding its relations with the nonparty cultural intelligentsia: although it
was preferable for cultural initiatives to be under Poale Tsion control, "if
we have few [party-affiliated activists], cultural powers from outside our
party must be drawn in."[72]

The principled defense of culture's political autonomy received only
halting, defensive formulation within the socialist parties. But in more
neutral settings, socialists who also shared culturist commitments asserted
this claim more forcefully. In an article in the Kultur-Lige's *Bikher-velt* concerning plans for the first full-fledged Yiddish encyclopedia, the Poale
Tsion activist and scholar Leshtshinsky forthrightly declared that the project would transcend the limitations of party division in the cultural sphere.
Most significantly, Leshtshinsky viewed this development not as a temporary deviation from a properly party-centered cultural policy, but as the
beginning of a new and positive stage in the process of Yiddish cultural
formation: "The cultural work of the Jewish democratic world [*fun der
yidisher demokratye*] is becoming broader and more ramified. From iso-

lated efforts and from incidental cultural undertakings by parties or party activists, we are beginning to go over to collective creations, to greater and broader works, which demand an organized effort on the part of entire groups of people, of experts in various branches of culture."[73] Leshtshinsky enacted these principles in his own daily life, combining his political activism with work at the nonsocialist Folks-Farlag and in the Kultur-Lige.

It was Kiev's Kultur-Lige itself, the most significant Yiddishist experiment of the era, that constituted the most significant expression of the distinction between culture and politics in revolutionary Yiddishist circles. The Kultur-Lige represented an unstable combination of two visions of the culture-politics relationship. It was, like Tarbut, closely linked to part of the Jewish political spectrum, in this case the Jewish socialist-nationalist parties the Bund, the Fareynikte, and Poale Tsion. It was dominated by cultural figures affiliated with the various Jewish socialist-nationalist parties, oriented toward the same "folk-masses" whom the socialist parties hoped to mobilize, and openly antagonistic to Zionism and other forms of Jewish liberal-nationalist politics. In addition, several of its publications presented its cultural goals in explicitly revolutionary terms.[74]

Yet the organization also proclaimed an aspiration to stand above party politics and "rikhtungn." This supraparty or nonparty principle could mean two different things (and evidently meant different things to various actors in the organization). In a narrow sense, it could (merely) mean the suspension of differences among the socialist-nationalist parties alone in the name of a shared socialist Yiddish cultural project. Measured against the intense sectarianism and ideological dogmatism of the Jewish socialist parties, even this flexibility represented a substantial victory for principles of culture's autonomy in the socialist camp, but it was a far cry from the more robust autonomy advocated by many culturists.

The Kultur-Lige was later represented by several participants purely in these narrow terms as "a Yiddish-socialist organization."[75] But in fact, this socialist-culture model vied with a considerably more extensive vision of autonomy, which found expression both in the organization's formal brief and in its actual operations throughout much of 1918: the principle that the Kultur-Lige existed to unite all Yiddishists and even mere friends of Yiddish culture across all party lines. From its formal inception in April and May 1918, the Kultur-Lige's executive committee included not only members drawn from the three Jewish socialist parties, but also a member from the nonsocialist Folks-Partey and one figure declaredly unaffiliated with any party, the tireless and self-effacing Yiddishist activist Zelig Melamed. A different (Bundist) source puts the number of nonsocialist Folkists at three, alongside nine Fareynikte, seven Bundists, and two Poale Tsion activists.[76] This arrangement reflected socialist dominance. But it nevertheless represented a break with the dominant socialist view that nonsocialists with particular talents or indispensable skills could be tolerated as "specialists" (*spetsi,* in later Soviet parlance) but certainly not accorded any formal authority.

Contemporaries described the composition of the board as a triumph of a cultural principle over a political one. In a retrospective article, Moyshe Katz, a socialist activist and former editor of the Fareynikte's Kiev paper *Di naye tsayt,* emphasized the supraparty motivations of those who took part in the organization's founding: "No struggle for places took place among the parties. The only condition for election was that the candidates should be a capable person and a sincere adherent of a secular Yiddish culture." While some of the socialist figures on the initial executive board were full-time party activists, others (Bergelson, Dobrushin, Mayzl) were first and foremost cultural producers who commanded authority due to their creative work.[77]

Some of the leading figures within the organization had actually hoped for a still more politically neutral profile, as a document from the earliest stages of the Kultur-Lige's development attests. Although the organization was formally constituted in April and May 1918, the initiative that led to its creation had begun several months earlier. In January 1918, the activist Melamed contacted Niger in Petrograd on behalf of the "temporary executive committee" regarding the planned "Kultur-Lige." In the letter, the committee asked Niger to sign an enclosed announcement and to seek the signatures of other notable Jewish cultural figures in Petrograd, including the dean of Russian Jewish historiography and spokesman for nonsocialist diaspora autonomism Dubnov, the literary historian Israel Tsinberg, the Folkist activists and Yiddishist publicists Shtif and Yisroel Efroykin, the artists Chagall and Alt'man, and the Russian Jewish composer Lazar Saminsky. At the same time, he noted, a similar letter had been dispatched to Moscow, asking Fareynikte activist Dovid Hokhberg to attain the signatures of Efros and the composer Yulii Engel. Few of these figures were socialists by any standard. Several could not even be said to be Yiddishists, at least not in the Kultur-Lige's maximalist sense of the term. And at least one, Dubnov, was an outspoken and uncompromising critic of the very idea of applying class politics in Russian Jewish life. The common denominator of these figures was, simply, their sympathy to the project of Yiddish culture and their commitment more generally to Jewish cultural advancement.[78]

This fundamentally apolitical Yiddishism was expressed decisively in the organization's January 1918 statute of incorporation. The founders declared that the Kultur-Lige's goals consisted in "the development and spread among the Jewish people of secular culture in all areas of human creativity . . . and assistance in the formation of the new Jewish democratic school and other educational institutions." Reference to the "democratic school" was the only vaguely political formulation in the founding document, which went on to note that membership in the organization was open to anyone who accepted its platform and paid dues.[79]

It seems likely that this degree of political neutrality was simply too much for the socialist parties, and that the original initiators of the Kultur-Lige were forced to accede to a heightened revolutionary profile as the price for socialist party support. It also seems clear that the January initiative stemmed not from party circles but from specifically culturist circles in Kiev's Yiddish cultural sphere; the leading figure was Melamed, who not coincidentally developed a reputation as someone committed exclusively to a Yiddishism unalloyed by any discernible politics.[80] Yet other members of the initiative group (Bergelson, for instance) were indeed politically active socialists. The point is not that the Kultur-Lige was founded by apolitical people, but that it was founded by people who drew a distinction between their own political and cultural commitments, and that this distinction still possessed power at the organization's refounding.

Tension between narrower and more expansive principles of cultural autonomy also influenced membership and recruitment. On paper, membership remained open to all supporters of Yiddish cultural development. But evidently, many in the organization took for granted that the organization would in practice bring together "Jewish workers" and members of the three socialist-autonomist parties for a joint but socialist-minded Yiddishist effort. Katz, who was willing to attest to the essentially culturist principle that decided the composition of the executive board, described the organization's initial recruitment policy in terms of the narrower version of the culture-politics distinction: "After it was decided to found the Kultur-Lige, the founders issued a call to all Jewish workers to found branches in the provinces. In this regard, we did not turn to the party [*parteyishe*] organizations, which inevitably would have obstructed one another, but to the Jewish worker-masses and activists in general, merely making use of the party connections which we already had."[81]

Yet even at the level of membership, the more expansive ideal carried weight. As contemporaries noted with astonishment (either positive or negative), a substantial number of Zionists joined the organization.[82] Further data are maddeningly thin, because sources on the actual operations of the local organizations are few and scattered, but one archival trace is richly suggestive. At the founding meeting of the Kultur-Lige branch in the small town of Novgorod-Seversk in November 1918, greetings were extended not only by representatives of the Fareynikte, Poale Tsion, and Bund, but also by a representative of the Tseire Tsion (Youth of Zion). Throughout the 1917–1919 period, Tseire Tsion attracted populist but unabashedly Zionist youth. Although socialist ideas made inroads into its leadership and rank and file in 1917, the party remained a committed part of the umbrella Russian Zionist movement, unlike the genuinely Marxist left wing of Poale Tsion. Although we might hypothesize that this local Tseire Tsion branch was somehow deviant, the rhetoric of the local Kultur-Lige branch itself supports a different conclusion: a proposed telegram to the central organization represented the Kultur-Lige not as a servitor of the "Jewish workers," the "working masses," or even "the masses"—the range of normally acceptable formulations in the socialist-Yiddishist lexicon—but as an organization serving the *"folks-demokratye"* and "culture in our mother tongue."[83]

Nor was this development confined to the provinces or the rank-and-file. Two of Odessa's most prominent Hebraists, the activist-editor Ravnitsky and the poet Yaakov Fichman, joined the city's Kultur-Lige branch, and Fichman became vice-chairman. Both men distinguished themselves in Hebraist circles for their continuing sympathy toward Yiddish-language culture, but both wholly identified with the Zionist camp. Ravnitsky was one of the founding figures of Odessa Zionism. Fichman ran as a Zionist in the elections to the Temporary Jewish National Assembly in 1918; indeed, he was listed as vice-chairman of the Odessa Kultur-Lige on the Zionist electoral bill itself, alongside inveterate opponents of Yiddish culture.[84] This astonishing development not only testifies to these Zionist cultural figures' own differentiation between politics and culture, but also points to the readiness of the socialists who served on the committee to accept the Kultur-Lige's suprapolitical character. One of these was the Bundist

Nirenberg, who chaired the committee. Tellingly, it was Nirenberg who, at the Bund's 1917 conference, had criticized the party's central committee for its inadequate commitment to Yiddish and provoked the party leader Liber to assert a sharp distinction between socialism and Yiddishism (see Chapter 1). This fact, and a separate indication that nonsocialist Yiddishists respected Nirenberg, suggests that even in the Bund, the idea of keeping culture somewhat separate from socialist politics had made inroads by 1917–1918.[85]

Ultimately, the most concrete expression of this principle within the Kultur-Lige was the degree of independence enjoyed by its constituent sections. All evidence suggests that at least its literature, art, and music sections were led by the literati, artists, and cultural intellectuals active in them, and that neither the socialist parties nor the party-affiliated members of the executive committee exerted any substantial direct influence over them. Nonsocialist activists like Kalmanovitsh and Dinur were treated with respect by both colleagues and rank-and-file constituents.[86]

Skeptical or hostile critics on both sides of the political spectrum noticed the supraparty ethos of the Kultur-Lige. When the Folkist Kalmanovitsh arrived in Kiev in September 1918, his first impression, recorded in a personal letter to Niger, was that the Kultur-Lige was essentially a socialist organization that "only members of socialist parties" were joining. He observed that members of the Folks-Partey, those who shared his and Niger's sensibilities, were inclined to remain distant from the organization, and sourly noted that when the Hetman's regime arrested "a Bundist committee," the Kultur-Lige was automatically disrupted. But two months later, Kalmanovitsh's correspondence with Niger sounded a much more positive note: he reported that "even the Zionists are joining," praised the organization's ambitious publishing work, and noted that he himself had begun to teach in its teachers' seminar.[87]

Kalmanovitsh's sentiment was echoed, ironically, in mounting attacks from within the organization by socialists who could not abide such compromise. During the Kultur-Lige's second national conference in May 1919, there were sharp debates over membership policy, with many pushing to include a clear political test. Moyshe Litvakov, who was by then moving toward a pro-Communist position, expressed disgust at how far the principle of apolitical Yiddishism had gone. He claimed that allowing figures like An-ski and Niger into Vilna's branch of the Kultur-Lige threatened to turn the organization into a branch of the OPE—which to Yiddishists meant cultural work dominated by half-measures and lingering sympathy for Hebrew and/or Russian, an emphasis merely on education at the expense of high culture, and "bourgeois" leadership.[88]

The principled distinction between culture and politics could sometimes be employed as a political gesture. In a 1918 Fareynikte pamphlet that addressed the place of Hebraist organizations in the coming system of Jewish national autonomy, the author had a ready answer: "as regards party-political [*partiinykh*] societies and organizations (for example, Tarbut), their inclusion in the network [of state-supported organizations] will only be possible when they . . . consent to submit to the properly expressed will of the people." In other words, even though by any measure Tarbut had considerably more support from the Jewish public than did its Yiddishist competitors, Hebraism was an innately sectarian phenomenon while secular Yiddish culture belonged to the realm of the General Will.[89]

Similarly, the institutional successes of this principle must themselves be explained "politically": not as choices that flowed from the pure power of a concept but as outcomes of a specific play of forces and interests in specific settings. The readiness of the various socialist parties in Kiev to cede their authority over cultural affairs to the formally nonparty Kultur-Lige thus no doubt owed much to unique local conditions. At the time, Kiev's Yiddishist milieu revolved around a tight-knit, relatively well-off, highly educated circle that had a much more independent identity than most Yiddishist circles before or after. And the Jewish socialist scene in Kiev was peculiar in that the Fareynikte party, which exerted negligible influence elsewhere, enjoyed substantial support in the Jewish nationalist intelligentsia and commanded the sympathies of most of the significant cultural producers, while the Bund, generally the dominant force on the diasporist left, was relatively weak. Where such conditions did not obtain, the Bund (including some of the very same individual actors) would prove far less open to the principle of supraparty culture: when the founders of the Kultur-Lige later refounded it in independent Poland, they encountered strong opposition from the powerful Polish Bund.[90]

These qualifications, however, do not detract from this essential fact that by 1917, many of those who sought to create the new Jewish culture were committed to the principles that culture and politics were fundamentally different realms and that culture should be insulated from some or all of the political ideologies and conflicts that pervaded Jewish life. This commitment did not translate into a full-fledged depoliticization of the Jewish cultural sphere. But neither was it merely a defensive or justificatory discourse. It substantively shaped the practice of Jewish culture throughout the 1917–1919 period, albeit against ever-steeper opposition.

The drive to protect cultural endeavors from political influence stemmed from two fundamental, and somewhat contradictory, intuitions. There was an urgent sense that "culture" and especially the artistic process had to be shielded from the corruptions of party politics precisely so that they might serve a higher form of national politics: the representation and production of nationhood (or, alternatively, Revolution) itself. Thus, Bialik's 1918 defense of art's autonomy from political determinations ultimately pivoted, ironically, on an assertion of art's unique political capacities. Citing Renan's famous dictum that "Dante, Petrarch and the artists of the Renaissance laid the foundations of Italian unity, and Goethe, Schiller, Kant, and Herder created the German Fatherland," Bialik insisted that politics "in its broad sense" was in fact a matter of "culture"; "the spirit" was the "true leader, even if hidden, of the ship of politics"; and artists were the vessels of that spirit.[91]

Of course, Bialik's rhetoric might be read simply as an author's deploying a common nationalist trope in order to claim greater authority within the Zionist movement; certainly, he had made such moves at various junctures since the emergence of a politically mature Zionist movement in 1897. But "Tarbut ve-'politikah'" contains a particularly striking formulation that frustrates such an instrumentalist reading and points to genuine convictions about art and its potentials. Pointedly, Bialik drove home his claim that art as such had far more power to shape the nation than did political discourse and action by arguing that the contributions of the Hebrew writers "Mendele, Peretz and Frishman [to] the revival of the nation and the language have been immeasurably greater" than those of Zionist propaganda and practical politics. What would have struck Bialik's readers immediately was the common denominator shared by these three Hebrew writers: all were famous (and infamous) in Zionist circles for their non- or even anti-Zionist views. Unlike Bialik and most prominent Hebrew writers active since the 1880s, they had not merely kept their distance from organized political Zionism but explicitly rejected Zionism's diagnosis of the Jewish condition and prescription for its cure.

For Bialik, in other words, the national potentials of art, though a kind of politics in themselves, were wholly independent of political ideology: an anti-Zionist Hebrew writer of talent could do more for the revival of the nation by creating Hebrew art than could any number of political activists who shared Bialik's Zionist convictions. It followed that the political representatives of the national movement should specifically refrain from intervention in cultural matters and indeed encourage the development of a depoliticized national cultural sphere. Only in such a space could artists of genius emerge and truly serve the nation.

Such notions could be heard on the other side of the Jewish culture sphere as well, among Yiddishists sympathetic to socialist and revolutionary ideals. The Yiddish poet Moyshe Kulbak sympathized strongly with radical visions of revolution in the 1917–1921 period. But in a 1918 piece published in a Bundist newspaper in Minsk (a perennial center of Jewish radicalism), Kulbak gently suggested that Yiddishism would "win more through its blooms than through its propagandistic-paper swords."[92]

The idea that an artist or poet of genius might forge a nation through the aesthetic power of his art was, of course, a commonplace of nationalist rhetoric (and a highly self-aggrandizing argument in the hands of a leading poet), but there is no reason to doubt the sincerity of those who reiterated it. First articulated in English and German Romanticism, the notion of the poet as the true legislator found powerful purchase throughout Eastern Europe. Indeed, there it achieved a peculiar sort of self-fulfilling sociological truth in that growing numbers of readers, deprived of any political state (or, in the Russian intelligentsia's case, deprived of a state they would wish to call their own), actually do seem to have tied their sense of nationhood to their literary classics.

But figures like Bialik were not only contemptuous of "politics" but deeply fearful of it as well. In part, this had to do with a kind of inchoate conviction among Jewish culturists of all political stripes that politics' apodictic, authoritarian, and divisive dimensions inevitably trammeled or crippled the artistic process and undercut the alchemical process by which nation-forging artworks might emerge (see Chapter 5).

This was not the only source of culturists' fear of political hypertrophy, however. In the writings of figures like Leshtshinsky or the self-representation and structure of an organization like the Kultur-Lige, the autonomy of culture from party politics was conceived as the enabling condition not (merely) for a higher form of constitutive national politics-through-culture, but for the development of a realm of experience and self-cultivation fundamentally different from that demarcated by concepts of politics and national identity. Jewish culturists recognized that intense and violently sectarian politics was the natural, inevitable outcome of the predicament in which East European Jewry had found itself since the nineteenth century. They themselves were committed by and large to the necessity of political choice and thus the utility of political ideology. So why did they think that "culture" demanded insulation from such phenomena? Evidently, they conceived of culture as a realm with distinct modes of creativity and human relations fundamentally different than those that obtained within politics—yet no less significant in the life of a nation.

In their insistence on the importance of preserving an autonomous space for culture in relation to the pervasive politicization of Jewish and Russian life, culturists regularly invoked tropes of coordination: the Kultur-Lige would bring together producers in all realms of culture regardless of party affiliation, the Folks-Farlag would bring together the finest talents, projects like a Yiddish encyclopedia demanded a concentration of expertise across party lines, and so on. This rhetoric of coordination intersected with a pervasive language of development, potential, and also belatedness. Jewish culture stood on the cusp of a new stage or had just entered a new stage of development. But it could only develop further if the nation's collective powers (located both in collectives and in individuals) could be coordinated across the nation's divides. And, dangerously (or tragically), Jewish culture had come to this stage not only late in relation to other, older modern cultures but also at the worst possible time in history: a moment of hyperpoliticization that threatened to make such coordination impossible. The separation of culture from politics was constitutional in the true sense of the word: culture could not continue to develop or exist without this essential demarcation.

Shared Truths, Shared Questions

For a substantial cohort of writers, activists, intellectuals, and patrons who had long sought to create a modern Jewish culture, the developments attendant on the February Revolution of 1917 seemed to promise an environment in which they might realize their long-standing aspirations—or, in the view of more realistic culturists, seemed to demand that they renew their efforts lest they lose their last chance. As we have seen, the cultural initiatives with which they responded to this environment of opportunities and challenges were structured by deeply shared assumptions about culture's form, the nature of its core institutions, and the objective demands of its development.

Of course, those culturists who imagined that they could realize their old dreams proved colossally wrong. Throughout the period under discussion, cultural work and the activists who pursued it were subjected not only to violence and disease, but also to mundane but no less devastating disruptions in transportation, markets, and access to the basic necessities of life. The Yiddishist pedagogue Avrom Golomb recalls lecturing at Kiev University in the summer of 1918 clad in a "suit" made from old sacks; his embarrassment was partially assuaged when he saw that the Bundist cultural theorist A. Litvak wore a worse outfit made from salt bags.[93]

Moreover, transformative ideologies and forces were sweeping through the region and proved much stronger than stateless, powerless, and minoritarian Jewish culturism. Within six months of Tarbut's founding, the Bolsheviks took power and within a year, by mid-1918, the Moscow-centered Hebraist dream had begun to collapse even as its first fruits—the Ha-Bimah theater troupe, the *Ha-Tekufah* literary journal—made triumphant appearances. Alongside many other Jews fleeing Bolshevik rule or simply hunger, many Hebraists made their way south in mid-1918 to the freedoms and relative calm of what was then nominally independent Ukraine. They sought to reestablish their recently created institutions in Odessa and Kiev. But by 1919, most had despaired of igniting a Hebraist cultural revolution in Eastern Europe and had shifted all their hopes instead to the emerging Hebrew society in British Palestine. Yiddishism would have a much more complex encounter with Communism, but Yiddishists too had the same disorienting experience of seeing the real fruits of their 1917–1918 efforts ripen in 1919, just as the Bolsheviks took control of Ukraine and began to rewrite the rules of culture and Jewish nationhood.

Yet if culturist efforts at the 1917–1919 juncture ultimately failed, they also laid bare the logic of an underlying Jewish cultural project. Jewish cultural life during this period was divided down the middle into Hebraist and Yiddishist camps, which themselves mapped closely onto deep political chasms dividing the Jewish national intelligentsia between Zionists and (mostly socialist) diasporists. Yet as we saw in this chapter, this division meant not a halving but a doubling of a preexisting Jewish cultural project. Within each group, actors with the same goal of creating a modern, full-fledged Jewish culture built parallel institutions and launched parallel initiatives (hence the difficulty of any cooperation or amity between the two camps—both sought to occupy the same space of national culture). Yet their initiatives reflected shared understandings of culture itself: they had a common vision of how a proper, achieved culture should look and function; a shared notion, however inchoate, that in some ways culture was like a system or a machine that had to be built in a certain way if it were to achieve its goals; and a singular vision (especially with regard to the ineffable creation of art itself), of culture as being like a garden that had to cleared, planted, and cultivated so that individual and national creativity could flourish:

> Art and music require, however, very positive circumstances in order that they might freely develop. We have many Jewish artists, a great number of talented Jewish musicians, but we have merely the beginnings of Jewish art and Jewish music. The reason is understandable. The atmosphere was quite unsuited to their blossoming.
>
> The Kultur-Lige has created a section for art and music which has worked out a broad plan of action. It will unify our existing artistic powers, cultivate the young shoots which can grow and blossom, and undertake to create an appropriate atmosphere for them.[94]

If, in the Jewish culturist imagination, culture was a system to be built or an environment to be organized, it followed that a proper culture could not be achieved without certain distinct sorts of programmatic structuring, cultivation, and above all, insulation from heterogeneous factors that would distort its workings—in particular, the Jewish culturists' own political goals, whether nationalist or socialist.

It is against the backdrop of these shared assumptions that Jewish culturists within both the Hebraist and Yiddishist camp confronted three essential questions concerning the content and ends of the new Jewish culture. First, was a modern, secular Jewish high culture to be bounded by some essential "Jewishness" of content or form? Second, what was the proper relationship between the formation of a high culture and the cultural education of "the nation" or, for the socialists and radicals, the "Jewish masses"? And finally, and most fundamentally, was the Jewish cultural project a means to forge a new Jewish collectivity and stable Jewish identity for mass and intelligentsia both, or an end of irreducible significance in its own right?

Just as the intelligentsia's conceptions of culture were born long before the Revolution, so too had all of these questions accompanied the idea of Jewish culture from its beginnings. In 1917–1919, however, such issues confronted Jewish culturists with unprecedented concreteness and urgency as they tried to put old visions into practice.

— 3 —

Unfettering Hebrew and Yiddish Culture

We do not divide literature into a "literature of Jewishness" and a "literature of humanity" . . . A living people, which speaks and thinks in a living language, knows of no dividing lines in its poetry.

—MOYSHE LITVAKOV, "DI SISTEM FUN IBERZETSUNGEN II," 1919

The literature of the world——God Almighty! Is this not the thing longed for by all those Hebrews who aspire to wholeness of spirit, all those for whom it is hard [to bear] both intellectual abstinence and the intellectual assimilation which comes through perusal of books written in foreign tongues?

—A. BEN-MOSHE [LITAI], "SIFRUT HA-'OLAM," 1918

By the time Dovid Hofshteyn began his rapid ascent in Kiev's Yiddish literary sphere, he bore little resemblance to the dreamy rural wanderer who inhabited much of his lyric poetry. He had completed a Russian gymnasium education in Kiev ("with Greek," as he noted), served in the Russian army in Armenia, traveled through the Caucasus in Pushkin's footsteps, and studied briefly in Petersburg's Psychoneurological Institute. He had also married for love and become a father, and the material demands of this situation brought him back to Kiev to study at the local Commercial Institute. A born poet, however—at various junctures he also experimented in Hebrew, Russian, and Ukrainian—he could not refrain from attending philology lectures at Kiev University, and soon devoted himself entirely to Yiddish letters.[1]

Readers encountered Hofshteyn's work in *Di naye tsayt*, the Kiev organ of the socialist-territorialist Yiddishist Fareynikte party, then in more definitively culturist venues like the landmark avant-garde Yiddish literary anthology *Eygns* (1918), in readings to enthusiastic audiences at the

Kultur-Lige's literary evenings, and finally in his book *Bay Vegn* (On Roads) in 1919. Many were especially taken with Hofshteyn's many poems of the young (Jewish) man awakening to selfhood through communion with a reenchanted nature. Written in an unprecedentedly unrhetorical, lyrical Yiddish that many deemed Hofshteyn's greatest achievement in itself, these poems also constituted a sophisticated effort to create a belated Yiddish version of European Romanticism's lyric tradition. Famously, part of one of these poems, "In vinter farnakhtn" (At Winter Dusks), would later be sung by Soviet Jewish soldiers during World War II.

Yet for the sophisticated Yiddishist critic Dobrushin, Hofshteyn's most important achievement consisted in poems that emerged from a more mature perspective: a series of poems about fatherhood and Hofshteyn's love poetry to his wife. In Dobrushin's eyes, these poems possessed not only "great aesthetic worth," but also "true cultural significance" for a Yiddish culture on the cusp of a metamorphosis.[2] Dobrushin's excitement holds a key to comprehending the defining concerns that freighted the aesthetic endeavors of Jewish culturists at the 1917–1919 juncture.

One of the poems that captured Dobrushin's imagination was "Nemen" (Names), about which he declared: "Manifestly, one must, together with the poet, grow to such a modern Jewish-secular comprehension of cultural-aesthetic impressions."[3]

> My children play like young wolves
> like young wolves the both of them:
> the elder's name is Shammai—
> the name of my grandfather,
> a half-blind old man in the deaf little town,
> and the younger's name is Hillel . . .
>
> Another name waited
> on a close rung of the shadowed ladder
> but I, from the midst of the wide world,
> of the boiling swarm,
> saw there suddenly,
> how the height of my tender years soared
> there over the old homey mold *[nestn-shiml]*—
> and the elder's name is Shammai,
> and the younger's name is Hillel . . .

> My children play like young wolves
> like young wolves the both of them,
> and scratch at each other
> with fiery, wild angry looks.
> And I, I watch with quieted gaze
> from a blind heart,
> how old names roll around,
> like young wolves, like thread-spools of young joys.[4]

"Nemen" opens with a disjuncture that would have struck any reader even marginally familiar with Jewish tradition: the contrast between the utterly natural, animal character of the children and the Jewish cultural weight of their names. Shammai and Hillel, leading interpreters of Jewish law in antiquity, were resonant symbols of the rabbinic ethos for East European Jews even nominally educated in Jewish culture. But the poem frustrates the temptation to read this resonance ontologically; despite their names, these children belong to nature, not culture, and certainly not to the rabbinic moral universe with its anti-Hellenistic denial of physicality's value. The poet-persona's choice to name the elder son Shammai is traditional in a more local sense, because calling him after a deceased grandfather adhered to the naming practices of the East European Jewish folk tradition. But the reader is then subjected to another arresting reversal: the choice to name the latter son Hillel rather than by another name from family tradition marks a break with this very folk tradition and the "old homey mold" of shtetl culture—a break born of a moment of insight ("plutsem dort derzen") afforded by the poet's own immersion in the roiling chaos of modernity.

Hence the reader is brought to the central problem of the poem: why did the Hofshteyn-figure name his second child Hillel? Representing the return of this "old name" as a phenomenon with its own agency through a reflexive construction ("vi alte nemen kayklen zikh / vi kleyne velfelekh"), the poem suggests that in play here are the secularization and aestheticization of tradition. An accidental conjuncture of the two names at an earlier stage in the Jewish experience, in rabbinic narratives, endowed them with a lasting association for Jews, and this remains as a purely aesthetic residue even after the national "content" ceases to bear any meaning. Yet what also evidently impressed Dobrushin was the poem's depiction of this tradition's lasting claim on the Jewish poet-father regardless. Secularized and aestheticized, the Jewish tradition does not cease to be compelling; in fact, it may be even more meaningful because it operates not in the head but in the "blind heart" of the thoroughly modern Jewish individual. Dobrushin's sense of the poem's affective weight would have been deepened by his knowledge that Hofshteyn had, in fact, given these names to his own young sons (see fig. 11). Thus, "Nemen" parlayed the intimate scene of fatherhood into an artful reflection on whether a Jewish tradition born both in classical rabbinic texts and East European folk tradition might somehow retain a creative vitality for moderns, even after it has been stripped of its religious and national-collective meaning.

If "Nemen" connoted dialogue with tradition, Hofshteyn's contemporaneous love poetry seemed to Dobrushin to mark something very different and more significant: a radical renunciation of Jewish tradition in favor of wholly alien cultural resources. One of the love poems that Dobrushin found compelling was "Kh'hob derzen zi bam taykh" (I Saw Her at the River):

> I saw her at the river
> under branches,
> under the green, sky-patched roof.
> Several dozen steps away,
> upon the earthly silence
> there a stone was mute
> a stubborn limb
> from my old country's bones, scattered and turned to dust . . .
> I saw her in the naked joy of her flesh,
> in the disheveled crown of her fragrant hair,
> I heard from the depths of age-young years:
> —This is what one calls a wife![5]

What struck Dobrushin as so forcefully new about a love poem like this one was the poet's choice to avoid the erotic resources of the Jewish tradition, either in classic Hebrew texts dating back to the *Song of Songs,* or in the Yiddish folksong tradition that Jewish culturists had rediscovered over the previous two decades: "the associative paths of Hofshteyn's poetic moods do not connect to the national homey Jewish environment nor even to the overly familiar cultural history, as was the case with all of our previous significant poets."[6]

Moreover, Dobrushin offered a striking explanation for Hofshteyn's ability to transcend the narrow world of familiar Jewish reference in much of his poetry: an unprecedented "Europeanness" born of education in the deepest sense. Behind the refinement and subtlety of Hofshteyn's lyric verse and its thematic refusals, he perceived a "poetic conception of the world [that] stems from general cultural history and the best representatives of modern European poetry." Hofshteyn's innovation, and his importance for Jewish cultural development, stemmed not merely from his lyrical talent but also from the fact that his poetry epitomized what was "for us a new, truly European culture of feeling."[7]

Yet for Dobrushin, these "European" poems emancipated from a narrow lexicon of Jewish themes and images were not a departure from the project of building a Jewish national culture but precisely what that project demanded. He declared Hofshteyn "our first non-'national' poet in the usual narrow-bourgeois [*eyng-balebatish*] sense of the word"—meaning, as he made clear in the essay, that Hofshteyn was indeed a national poet in a broader sense. Hofshteyn's poem transcended any parochial national frame and participated in something more "general" and "European"—yet it was precisely from this fact that it derived its decisive national significance.[8] Hofshteyn's poems and Dobrushin's interpretations sketch the aesthetic-cum-intellectual question that most preoccupied Jewish culturists in 1917–1919 as they sought to give definitive shape to their modern, secular culture.

Even as Jewish culturists grappled with the common questions that now consumed intellectuals across Europe—questions of modernism, revolution, the cultural meaning of the war—they also returned with renewed fervor, across all spectra of linguistic, political, and aesthetic allegiance, to the basic definitional questions that had dominated the cultural project at its inception some thirty years earlier: what was the proper scope of a "modern Jewish culture" and on which sources and traditions should it be built? Hofshteyn, and most of the Jewish writers and artists of the day, approached this question as something to be explored rather than answered, as only one productive question among many, and through the lens of their own personal artistic projects. But many Jewish culturists, like Dobrushin, felt that the time had come for a more decisive answer. They were driven by a shared sense that Jewish culture had reached a decisive and even dangerous moment in its evolution—that unless these questions were answered correctly and soon, the new Jewish culture might actually collapse not because of external, political, and material factors, but due to aesthetic and intellectual exhaustion. In its sharpest formulation, the question was posed thus: would a healthy and compelling Jewish aesthetic culture be more successfully achieved by deepening its intentional orientation toward "the Jewish," however understood, or, conversely, by pursuing a countervailing imperative of willfully un-Jewish, unparochial "European" or "universal" expression?

The first of these principles, that of strengthening ties to the Jewish tradition, naturally found powerful expression in the Jewish cultural project.[9] By 1917, its most prominent living exponent was Bialik, who had long preached a strategy of recasting the indigenous traditions of Judaism as a secular-national patrimony. Bialik advocated the refounding of modern Jewish culture on the basis of a national canon drawn from the entire universe of Jewish texts of every age and genre, but especially from the various strata of premodern Hebrew texts. Under the rubric of *kinus* or "gathering," culturists were to cull the entire textual tradition to find those works that could offer creative revitalization and national-cultural guidance: "If we want to restore to our literature something of its vigor and its influence on the people, it is incumbent upon us . . . to turn and make a new 'ingathering,' national, of course, and not religious, of the best of Hebrew literature from all eras."[10] The alternative, he warned, was cultural disintegration. As he put it in 1913, addressing a Conference for Hebrew Language and Culture in Vienna, "the sons, if they wish to avoid being scattered in the world's wind, must turn and turn this earth, must plough and harrow it again and again . . . for if there is no earth there can be no growth, and if there is no tradition and chain of transmission in a literature—there can be no enlargement and development, and no renewal."[11] Insisting that "our poverty [lies] not only in what we *lack,* but in the fact that we do not properly use the possessions that we *do* have," he warned that only *kinus* could fill modern Hebrew literature with "new content," save it from "feeding on its own flesh," and redeem it from an essential absence at its heart which rendered it a "national literature which is not national."[12]

Not all culturists who sought a Judaic-European synthesis gave pride of place to the classical Hebrew canon. Some who sought to adumbrate a new Jewish culture connected to the wellsprings of "tradition" opted instead to privilege the Yiddish-language folkways of Eastern Europe—and in so doing created a situation of full-fledged internal duality rare in the annals of cultural nationalism. Thus, while Bialik developed his idea of *kinus,* the other leading figure of the prewar Jewish cultural project, the Warsaw Yiddish-Hebrew writer Peretz, produced an influential corpus of neo-Romantic stories on Hasidic and folkloric themes that demonstrated—at least to their many enthusiasts—that the most parochial expressions of East European Jewish tradition could provide a compelling symbolic grammar for modern Jewish culture.[13]

These sensibilities did not disappear in 1917. For some Jewish culturists, the devastation of the war and the transformations heralded by the Revolution reinforced the conviction that an adequate modern Jewish culture had to be founded on "authentic" traditional Jewish cultural expression. For the writer-ethnographer An-ski, the war reaffirmed his belief that only by absorbing the distinct national spiritual culture embodied in this "folk-creativity" could a properly Jewish "individual creativity" flourish.[14] The Hebraist educator Pinhas Schiffman (Ben-Sira) took for granted that effecting a synthesis between Jewish tradition and modern European culture remained "the fundamental essence of the cultural-national problem . . . on the agenda."[15]

We might ask how it could be otherwise. To many scholars, negotiation between the modern self and premodern Jewish expression seems like the essential concern of modern Jewish culture, with the recovery of classical Hebrew sources the defining Hebraist cultural posture and folklorism, that of Yiddishism. This in turn corresponds to a regnant assumption in most work on the relationship between nationalism and culture, namely, that cultural nationalism means the valorization of indigenous cultural traditions by native intellectuals in a fundamentally defensive reaction to more metropolitan cultures.[16]

What, in other words, could Jewish culturists have meant by "Jewish culture" if not the negotiated marriage of post-Renaissance European forms with indigenous Jewish content? Yet there was an opposing tendency among champions of a modern Hebrew or Yiddish culture. Perhaps the most tireless dissenter from the cult of the indigenously Jewish was the Hebrew literary critic, writer, and gadfly Frishman. In a lecture delivered at the same 1913 Hebraist conference at which Bialik presented his most forceful formulation of the indigenizing strategy, Frishman dismissed the idea that a renewed acquaintance with Jewish classical sources—even if "[changed] a bit with regard to their form and style, so that they will be accessible to everyone"—could compel a younger generation of East European Jews to engage with modern Hebrew culture. The sons of Hebraists like himself, he argued, were moderns for whom the foregone achievements of Jewish tradition had no bearing on the only essential cultural question: "whether we still have the power to give birth." These comments capped decades of insistence on Frishman's part that the Jewish tradition, far from being a repository of vitalizing forces, was itself to blame for the stifled creativity of the Jewish nation. What Hebrew literature needed was not more Jewish tradition but decidedly less: "It is not the book that we need in the first place, but literature, not the dead *library* but the *living creative work,* not the mummified soul which lies in a shelf on the wall in the form of books, but the force which lives and gives life, which draws the heart and not just the mind . . . not the *book* but the *writer.*" By 1913, moreover, Frishman's audience would have known well the positive alternative preached by this pioneering translator of Nietzsche, Byron, Pushkin, and Tagore: the salvation of modern Hebrew culture through a thoroughgoing, humble reorientation toward an altogether non-Jewish tradition—modern European literature.[17]

Frishman's dissent has enjoyed little resonance in the work of historians of Jewish culture, evidently on the assumption that these were merely the contrarian sensibilities of an idiosyncratic aesthete standing at the margins of the Jewish national and culturist milieus. Yet in the reemergent Russian Jewish cultural sphere of 1917, another alternative vision of Jewish cultural formation emerged that was far more in the spirit of Frishman than that of Bialik. In March 1917, the Moscow newspaper *Ha-ʿAm,* an official organ of Russian Zionism, carried an article insisting that the most important item on the Hebraist agenda was, *pace* Bialik's call for organized efforts at *kinus,* the creation of an organized, publicly funded program to translate "the famous works of the great figures of the nations of the world" into Hebrew. The author of this piece was not some Parnassian like Frishman, but Aharon Litai, a lifelong Zionist activist and mainstream figure in Russia's Zionist-Hebraist camp. Traditionally educated, he was equipped to understand Bialik's bid to reconnect modern Jewish culture to tradition. Yet by 1917, he had come to agree with Frishman that the perpetuation of the modern Hebrew cultural project—and even "our national language" itself—depended not on a negotiated return to tradition but on the embrace of "the literature of the world."[18]

Such ideas stretched across all the linguistic, political, and aesthetic lines that subdivided the cultural project. Writing in early 1919, the Kievan Marxist, diasporist, and avant-garde Yiddishist Litvakov issued a similar urgent call for systematic translation that opened with a ringing rebuke to ideas like Bialik's or An-ski's: "Our literature has by now almost entirely exhausted the spring of its traditional, folksy-Jewish [*yidishlekhe*] themes and motifs, thoughts and feelings . . . Yiddish literature has already completed the provincial-nationalist phase of its development, and it must become a metropolitan-universalist literature, with inclinations and orientations toward taking a place in world literature, not thereby losing but perhaps, on the contrary, deepening its unique national character."[19]

Both of these figures, and many others, sketched a very different cultural vision, one defined above all by a desire to break with any definitive Jewish canon or tradition. This tendency, having already gained ground well before 1914, exerted tremendous influence in culturist thought and practice during 1917–1919. And at root, this deparochializing drive reveals an alternative form of cultural nationalism. Those who sought to unfetter Hebrew or Yiddish culture from any Jewish essentialism did so in the name of the nation and its cultural regeneration no less than did those who sought to build a thickly "Jewish" modern culture. Their goal was the attainment of full expressive freedom for themselves and for their fellow Jews, and the essential medium of this paradoxical cultural nationalism was language.

Translation and the National Interest

In early 1918, a year after his alarmed insistence that only a program of massive literary translation into Hebrew could save the Hebraist cultural project, A. Litai took up the same theme in the essay quoted in the epigraph. But this time he wrote not as a voice crying in the wilderness, but as witness to practical efforts to actually realize this goal, and as one voice among many.[20] By 1918, a number of intellectuals, critics, writers, and activists had reached the same conclusion and separately articulated the proposition that what Jewish culture now needed most was not the indigenous but precisely the foreign: the systematic, massive, and immediate literary translation of a posited unitary canon of Western literature into Hebrew or Yiddish. Litai's fellow Hebraist, the editor and children's writer Ben-Eliezer, had in fact preceded him in advancing this idea. Writing in a 1916 anthology edited by Bialik himself, Ben-Eliezer had rebuked those who claim "that we do not need to bring into our literature the 'offspring of aliens,' and that just as the Hebrew people did not exert itself to bring in converts, so it is fit that our Hebrew literature keep distant these creations which did not issue from the womb of Israel." On the contrary, Ben-Eliezer insisted, there could be no further literary development except through translation: "But those who believe in the revival of Hebrew literature and its development, and see a great necessity in this, must follow after all the young literatures which maintain themselves from translations."[21]

Across Hebraist-Yiddishist battle lines, the leading figure of Kiev Yiddishism, Litvakov, made the same argument. In his 1919 essay "The System of Translations," carried in Kiev's *Bikher-velt,* Litvakov argued that Yiddish literature had reached a stage of stagnation beyond which it could move only by means of a massive, systematic program of translating the "world poetry of all generations, peoples, and languages," especially the "living waters" of contemporary European literature.[22] Such a project required planning, a focus on helping Yiddish literature become a self-sufficient and all-encompassing art form, as well as the leadership of the intellectual elite. Litvakov both emphasized the critical significance of this undertaking and invoked a model for it by reminding readers that early nineteenth-century German and Russian literary elites had undertaken ramified programs of translation "as a type of national-cultural function on behalf of the vital interests of the national literature."

Moreover, by the time Litai, Ben-Eliezer, and Litvakov wrote to preach the same ideal to the now mutually opposed Hebraist and Yiddishist camps, such notions were no longer confined to the realm of theory but were embodied in an unprecedentedly massive translation program: that of the magnificently endowed Stybel Hebrew publishing house in Moscow. As noted earlier, the publishing house's wealthy founder Stybel and his editor-adviser Frishman focused above all on commissioning and publishing literary translations. The range of works included a strong selection of Russian classic prose and poetry (Pushkin, Lermontov, Tolstoy, Dostoevsky, Chekhov); other giants of nineteenth-century prose (Dickens, Flaubert, Zola) and poetry (Mickiewicz, Heine); and a strong representation of fin-de-siècle and early modernist work (Wilde, Maeterlink, Ibsen, Hamsun, Przybysewski, France, Strindberg). At the same time, Frishman called for writers who "know their strength" to take on translations of Shakespeare, Goethe, Schiller, Byron, and the great playwrights and poets of ancient Greece and Rome.[23]

The story behind Stybel's and Frishman's unprecedented endeavor is so remarkable that it is often treated as an accident of fate, in which a wartime financial windfall gave an unusual opportunity to the Hebraist Stybel, who just happened to be an ardent follower of Frishman's ostensibly peculiar brand of "European" Hebraism. Before he made his fortune dealing American leather to the Russian army, Stybel had long been attuned particularly to Frishman's ideals; indeed, he credited a reading of Frishman's translation of *Daniel Deronda* in the 1880s as a signal moment in his Hebraist conversion. But although the Stybel-Frishman project was certainly extraordinary in scope and ambition, by 1917 it was not ideologically peculiar. In fact, culturists as ideologically disparate as the Zionist Hebraists Litai and Ben-Eliezer, and the Marxist Yiddishist Litvakov, entertained essentially the same ideal.

Adherents of the Jewish Enlightenment or Haskalah had devoted themselves to translation throughout the nineteenth century, and in a sense, one could argue that the very idea of "Jewish culture" connoted translation—the transposing of European genres into a Jewish key. But the figures who preached the importance of translation in 1917 meant something very different. In conscious repudiation of most previous Hebrew or Yiddish translation practice, these figures insisted that individual translations avoid adapting foreign works so they would be well received by Jews. Rather, the task of the translator was to expand the Hebrew or Yiddish literary language by finding the means to represent the most "un-Jewish" settings, characters, and tones. Litvakov made such avoidance of unwarranted Judaization in translation an explicit principle. *Ha-Shiloah*'s editor Klausner hailed a 1918 Hebrew translation of Wilde's *Picture of Dorian Gray,* published by Stybel, precisely because it was "the *first complete* Hebrew translation" of a "story which has no connection to Israel [Jewish matters]."[24]

The translation program preached by Frishman, Litvakov, and Litai was not merely a declaration of literary principles, but the sharp end of a full-fledged alternative vision of Jewish cultural formation. These ideologues wedded their conception of nonadaptive translation to the idea of regrounding Hebrew or Yiddish culture through the systematic, rapid importation of a compensatory European or world literary canon. The distinctiveness of this idea is evident in the surprising gap between Litvakov's own extremely radical aesthetic commitments on the one hand and his classicist translation program on the other. As a literary critic and theorist, Litvakov was an aggressive proponent of the most avant-garde literary streams and an impatient critic of anything old-fashioned. He was also, by mid-1919, a committed supporter of the Bolshevik Revolution; by the time the second half of this article was published in August 1919, he held a position in the Yiddish cultural institutions of the newly installed Bolshevik government in Kiev (the first half, published in January 1919, was written before the Bolshevik takeover). Yet neither of these commitments found much echo in Litvakov's translation program, which might as well have been Frishman's and Stybel's:

> These must be translated: works which have had the most significant influence on the formation and development of our literary feelings, thoughts, and ways of speaking, whose images, symbols, figures, and expressions have made their way into our everyday lives [tog-shteyger]. Works which have called forth particular literary-social streams and become a jumping-off point for a new development. Works in which the eternal beauty of the artistic word is crystallized. The major epic works of the various peoples and lands. Works of writers who characterize or embody a significant epoch or interesting stratum of society. Above all, works which represent boundary markers in the development of literary forms, genres, and tendencies.[25]

Not everyone made the same surprising double move of imagining a translation program divorced from one's own aesthetic and political commitments. One reviewer for the same journal welcomed a Yiddish translation of Byron's *Heaven and Earth* in part because of Byron's ostensibly unequaled readiness to "make from his art a direct means of struggle . . . with that world which the great Revolution has just outlived."[26] But the leading proponents of translation shared Litvakov's views. The Hebrew prose modernist Eliezer Shteynman was a man of strong aesthetic and political commitments who alienated many in the Hebraist circles for his outspoken embrace of the Revolution. Yet in the pages of the 1919 Hebrew anthology *Erets,* which itself yoked together Bolshevik sympathies, Zionism, and a call for "youth" revolution in Hebrew literature, Shteynman praised the Stybel publishing program for avoiding particular political or aesthetic commitments in order to bring "everything, everything to us: from the first fruits of realism, from the flowers of Romanticism, and from the grapes of modernism."[27] The journalist Litai opined that the Stybel press should translate fewer Decadent works and more Romantic ones in view of their salutary influence on Jewish consciousness, but also welcomed both the encompassing effort to bring "the literature of the world" into Hebrew all at once and the absence of a political line in Stybel's journal *Ha-Tekufah.*[28]

Furthermore, the primary purpose of the envisioned global translation was not the direct reshaping of the broad Jewish reading public; in this respect, this program of translation differed both from earlier Jewish nationalist precedents and from the most dramatic coterritorial translation program of the day, Maxim Gorky's massive Vsemirnaia Literatura (World Literature), which harnessed Russia's finest writers to create a "foundational library" that would instill an internationalist humanism in Russian readers.[29] Flying in the face of generations-old assumptions that translation into Yiddish in particular was above all a means of popular education, Litvakov rejected any notion that his translation program should limit itself according to the needs of present-day Yiddish readers: "there are phases in the history of a national literature when neither this or that individual translator-devotee nor the public but rather [the literature] itself requires translation for its growth and development."[30] Although these champions of translation certainly hoped that readers might benefit, the goal was to reorient Hebrew or Yiddish literatures as institutions toward an ever-more universal European literary culture by infusing them with a compensatory European literary tradition. Thus, Litvakov's surprisingly catholic translation program would transform Yiddish literature into "a metropolitan-universalist literature, with inclinations and orientations toward taking a place in world literature" not by emphasizing one particular aesthetic line but by infusing it with world literature's entire panoply of "fundamental motifs and moods, visions and images, symbols and figures, legends and myths."[31]

Litai, Litvakov's polar opposite in political and linguistic-ideological terms, shared precisely the same vision of what literature was, how it worked, and what Jewish literature should be. He imagined the relationship among "fully developed" literatures like those of England, Germany, and Russia as a constant process of "mutual influence" through which these literatures "renew themselves and enrich themselves from day to day." It was self-evident that "our literature," which by "a European measure is only at the beginning of its development," should aspire to join this company, and that only programmatic translation could provide the necessary "universal" fundament.[32]

Whereas each individual translation of merit might help transform Hebrew or Yiddish into more flexible literary languages, the overall effort would also reeducate the Jewish writer. Champions of translation shared the hopes of another long-standing advocate of such efforts, Frishman, who maintained that such a body of translations would serve not as a source for mechanical imitation—indeed, he believed that only by translating these works accurately and making them an "integral part of Hebrew culture" could imitation be avoided—but provide inspiration, benchmarks, and an aestheticizing and Europeanizing influence on Hebrew writers.[33] Litvakov articulated a similar view: "Should the future and even present Yiddish writer cleave spiritually and psychically to this wonder-world of great artworks, if he should reforge them in the flame of his intuition, our literature's 'Pale of Settlement' will perforce be abolished."[34]

Translation was, thus, neither merely a matter of national stature nor the mere provision of raw material. Rather, the translated works were meant to reshape the new Jewish literature in two ways: by expanding Hebrew or Yiddish as literary languages and by educating the authors who employed them. In practice, this demanded, first, that each individual translation had to be a genuine literary achievement. One means to this end was the harnessing of the most talented Jewish writers to take on the job. In the name of all Hebraists who wished for "the revival of our language," Litai hoped Bialik would undertake to translate "the classic foreign works."[35] Independently, Frishman and Stybel plied Bialik with requests that he translate *Evgenii Onegin* on the grounds that he was the "only one" who could do so; Stybel's first assistant, the newspaperman Ben-Tsion Katz, had made particular efforts to recruit the great poet and translator Tchernikhovsky (a practicing doctor) to work full-time for the press.[36]

In addition, foreign literatures could only have the requisite influence if they were imported as a complete set of canons and genres, so that the Jewish writer might internalize the whole embodied history of a putatively universal literary development.[37] Hence the disgust of the Kiev Yiddishist literary critic Ezra Korman with an anthology that purported to offer translations of the most important modern European poetry but merely proffered an unsystematic smattering arranged not by national literature but by translator.[38] Hence too the oft-repeated desire to see translation organized in some central fashion.

The Jewish discourse on translation at the 1917–1919 juncture smacked of a previous age. For although individual Hebrew and Yiddish writers recast external influences in ways no less sophisticated than their European modernist counterparts, the revolutionary-era Jewish advocates of translation were concerned not to "enrich" Jewish literature but to refound it.[39] Their vision was part of a self-consciously belated program of culture-building: culturists such as Litvakov and Frishman quite penetratingly invoked as models the Russian and German literary spheres of the previous century, with their multidecade quest to master the literary powers of their neighbors to the west.[40] Despite deep ideological differences, they shared a notion of a universal "Literature" with a single if evolving package of genres, styles, and sensibilities that Jewish literature in Hebrew or Yiddish had to encompass (in part so that they would be able to grow beyond it). Ben-Eliezer captured this sensibility in language tellingly drawn from the realm of capital and investment: world literature in translation was "spiritual capital [ha-hon ha-ruhani ha-zeh]" that "the young peoples take on credit from their older neighbors" and that served "as the foundation for the edifice of their national literature." This figuration of literary translation as a form of capital investment is revealing: literature may be qualitatively unique and irreducible, but it can also be transformed through translation into a form of liquid capital that can be employed universally and serially by any "investor" nation.[41]

These conceptions of literature stemmed neither from naïveté nor lack of sophistication, but on the contrary, a firmly historicized and even coldly analytical perspective regarding what made for a strong national literature. These champions of translation saw that the non-Jewish literatures they knew best (Russian and German) had become great "national literatures" precisely and paradoxically through translation.[42] Furthermore, the modernists among them, like Litvakov, knew that literary revolutions were only possible when framed as a response to a canonical framework. And they knew that they were embarking on this project late, at a modernist moment when the very notion of a single, stable Literature was under attack by much of Russia's avant-garde and Europe's "Generation of 1914." Hence the paradox that a figure like Litvakov could see this belated translation project as a necessity, even if it was at odds with his radical cultural and political ideals.

De-Judaization and Revival

Running through some of these arguments for programmatic translation was a broader vision of what we might call cultural de-Judaization. Some framed translation not as a timely supplement to strengthen the new Jewish culture but as the sharp wedge of a larger effort to deparochialize it altogether—to make Jewish literature as encompassing of human experience as any other. The young Hebrew writer Shteynman struck this stance when he declared that the massive importation of world literature would bring Hebrew literature "off its narrow path, its side-track."[43]

The same assumptions drove many critics of the period to approve of translations that assumed not some parochial "Jewish reader" but a mature, modern reader who could occupy any reader-position demanded by a work. Klausner hailed the aforementioned Hebrew translation of *Dorian Gray* for making no cuts or changes on the assumption that certain things would not be interesting to the Hebrew reader, "as even the 'Europeans' among our translators were wont to do up to the present day."[44] Shteynman, too, poured scorn on prewar Hebrew publishers who, unlike Stybel, had shaped their programs based on "their assumptions" that the needs of the Jewish reading public were "somehow special."[45] And in Kiev, Litvakov put these sentiments more programmatically: the confidence to reject any sharp division between "'Jewishness-literature' and 'humanity-literature'" was the mark of a "living people, which speaks and thinks in a living language."[46]

These and other radical advocates of deparochialization-through-translation indeed openly rejected the idea that premodern Jewish culture should serve as the essential basis of the new cultural enterprise. Litvakov's aggressive vision of translation's task went hand-in-hand with a denigration of the place of folk culture in the emerging Yiddish culture; in his view, a literature that remained wedded to folk culture would be merely one of "regurgitated old-Jewishy feelings, experiences, and images." Litvakov did not rule out the possibility that folk-cultural remnants might still be useful to a genuinely modern Jewish literature; he recognized the merits of the symbolist writer Der Nister, whose work was redolent with seeming reference to the Jewish mystical tradition and its tropes. But Litvakov preached a dynamic model of literary development in which folklore could not maintain a stable significance—much less implicit aesthetic-cum-ethical superiority. Tellingly, even the great Yiddishist culture-hero Peretz was not insulated from this uncompromising vision of literary development. Breaking with an emerging pietistic Yiddishism that hailed Peretz as the incarnation of a successful synthesis between modern Yiddish culture and the East European folk tradition (a unidimensional view that did disservice to Peretz's actual complexity), Litvakov charged that "even Peretz," despite his "universalist leanings," had become a point of departure for old, worn-out modes of "Jewishy" writing. Similarly, Litvakov dismissed the poetry of the Polish Jewish writer Alter Katsizne as mere scraps from Peretz's plate, a cruel but clever jibe that mocked Katsizne's folklorically inflected poetry by invoking the Hasidic mystical practice of eating the scraps of the rebbe's meal.[47]

Parallel attacks could be found in Hebraist circles. Klausner, a radical Hebraist and integral Zionist who could not have been more distant from Litvakov ideologically, demonstrated a strikingly similar conception of literary exhaustion and development, not least in his brutal critique of the "parochialism" he saw in the work of the Hebraist culture hero Bialik. In Klausner's view, the greatest talents of all other peoples like Shakespeare, Goethe, Byron, or Pushkin were "world-embracing spirits" who drew on all materials of world civilization—"every true poet is also a pantheist"— to address "truly great and deep general-human problem[s]." By contrast, Bialik remained parochial in his themes and sources. Significantly, Klausner's argument suggested that this failure not only rendered Bialik's work less universally significant, but also lessened his worth as a national poet. Unlike the great Biblical prophets who were simultaneously national and universal in their teachings, Bialik could neither offer answers to the great problems of humanity nor serve as a guide to a better Jewish future: "and even in our small world, in the Hebrew [Jewish] world, he showed us only the brightness of the recent past and spread light on the dark places of the present, but did not make windows for us to the glittering future and did not cleave open for us the sunrise of revival that a poet-seer ought to herald while darkness still covers the land and the fogs of exile the people Israel."[48]

Klausner offered an alternative for Hebrew cultural development in Bialik's perennial "other" in Hebrew poetry, Tchernikhovsky. Devoting the August 1918 issue of *Ha-Shiloah* to Tchernikhovsky on the twenty-fifth anniversary of his poetic debut, Klausner trumpeted him as the living resolution of all the poetic "problems" that afflicted Hebrew literature. In a Jewish diaspora culture that was unfree, "to which every [all-]human thing is foreign," Tchernikhovsky was a "miracle" and "riddle": "a Jew-man whole in body and spirit" who did not overintellectualize, mourn, or show undue reverence for the Jewish community. Nor was Tchernikhovsky merely superior to his predecessors; Klausner also systematically contrasted him to all of the shortcomings that contemporary Hebrew writers detected in their peers and themselves. He was free of "fissures in the heart," the defining condition of the Jewish national intelligentsia first diagnosed in the turn-of-the-century writings of the Hebrew-Yiddish-German writer and

Jewish Nietzschean Berdichevsky.[49] He was not "a preacher or a rebuker or a philosophizer [*mitpalsef*]" but rather a poet full of joy and creative vitality. He differed even from those who might seem his ideological followers: rather than constantly talking about "*the necessity* of strength and courage, *the necessity* of beauty, *the necessity* of transvaluation of values," Tchernikhovsky actually manifested these in his work and his person. He was committed to the Zionist idea, yet refused to compromise poetry itself: refusing to bow to "any party or to any movement" he was instead a "poet entirely given over to art alone—to the perfection of the artistic idea, to perfection of the form." And "the main thing": Tchernikhovsky was a European poet who attained to "a level on which stand the more perfect poets of Europe."[50]

A still more encompassing Hebraist attack on the continuing authority of the classical Hebrew tradition, parallel to Litvakov's critique of the continued power of the folkloric tradition, could be found in the Hebrew literary anthology *Erets*. There, the pseudonymous writer Aleph (probably the aforementioned Shteynman) furiously dissented from Bialik's cultural strategy of *kinus* and its assumptions. First, he rejected the indigenizers' insistence that the texts of the classical rabbinic tradition could and should remain the ground of Jewish cultural creativity. Where Bialik claimed to see untapped literary potential even in dry rabbinic legal discussions, Aleph saw only crippling diminution of the creative imagination: "We created the 'Talmud,' which we dubbed 'a sea'—and we were lost among its waves . . . Because we were merely interpreters. And this is our punishment."[51]

Directly confronting the terms of Bialik's *kinus* idea, Aleph's essay also rejected the indigenizers' more general principle that only a vitalizing relationship to some aspect of Jewish tradition could generate a significant Jewish culture. In his decisive 1913 essay "The Hebrew Book," Bialik had argued that successive generations of Jews were able to remain culturally creative only because Jewish cultural elites had, at critical junctures in Jewish history, selected, delimited, and proclaimed certain texts to be canonical—*hatimah*—whereas other works were denied an active presence in the cultural consciousness—*genizah*. *Genizah* had saved Jews from being crushed under the proverbial weight of their heritage, whereas *hatimah* had rendered half-forgotten texts active sources of new cultural creation. Taken together, these operations constituted *kinus,* which might yet save Jewish culture again if—and only if—it was undertaken collectively and systematically by a Hebraist elite properly committed to its own Judaic-Hebraic heritage.[52]

Aleph's essay "Genizah ve-ḥatimah" offered a radically different histori-cal narrative. In this view, the history of Jewish creativity since the exile had been an unending chain of struggles between a conservative religious-cultural elite committed to suppressing and extruding all forms of creativ-ity that deviated from a particular conception of Judaism and, on the other side, a succession of defiant cultural rebels ranging from the storied hereti-cal rabbi of Roman Palestine Elisha Ben-Abuyah, to Jesus, to the heretical thinkers of the Western Sephardic diaspora Spinoza and Uriel Acosta, to Heine. In Aleph's historiosophy, drawn from Berdichevsky, all of these fig-ures were isolated creative spirits who naturally rebelled against the rabbis' traducement of human (and Jewish) creativity. The triumph of the censo-rious conservative side had choked off Jewish national creativity. Far from clearing a space for further Jewish creativity, *ḥatimah* and *genizah* had sup-pressed anything genuinely new and self-confident; stifled "in advance" the genuinely new "book" that would have arisen from the nation's "*havayah*," the organic, lived life of the nation; and reduced future generations of the nation to "inheritors, grandchildren, interpreters, and imitators."[53]

Aleph drove home the presentist concerns of the essay by insisting that the conflict had continued into the current era, pitting conservative think-ers, above all Ahad Ha-'Am and his many "disciples" (evidently meaning Bialik) against rebels like Berdichevsky and a new generation—his own, of course. At a personal level, Aleph was evidently driven in part by a sense that his generation had been overlooked or insulted in contemporary He-brew literature. Thus, he raged against Ahad Ha-'Am, imagining him as a nobleman who spends "his days strolling about the cultural estates [*nikhsei-ruaḥ*] of Judaism with the ease of an wealthy man, and tours with prideful pleasure the wide expanses of the estates, and tastes with pleasure from the citrons of the ancestors, [and] mocks, like a true man of property, at any fresh sprout." In this sense, his essay might be explained away as the grumblings of a new generation with little cultural capital compared to ex-isting cultural elites, right down to the telltale rhetoric of class resentment. But his dissent was novel in its approach. Rather than asserting some kind of aesthetic superiority of his own literary generation over the previous one, as the Russian Futurists or Yiddish avant-garde poets were doing, he wove together an old-fashioned Romantic concept of the creative individ-ual throughout history with a more modernist concept of the flux and plenitude of "life" (*havayah, ḥayim*) to assert the rights of every individual and generation to react creatively to its own experience, with no special voice given to past authority or tradition. In so doing, he sketched a distinctive alternative vision of a new Jewish culture, one defined as no more and no less than the sum of individual acts of creation issuing from personal experience and expressed in Hebrew.

Competing Visions in Practice

Questions regarding the scope and content of the new Jewish sphere were not confined to debate alone. Rather, they resonated in all realms of cultural practice: in the arts, in the choices and strategies of cultural organizations, and in the preferences and desires of audiences, readers, and museum-goers. And in all of these realms, essentialist conceptions of a Jewish culture rooted in indigenous traditions confronted a diffuse but increasingly pervasive urge to create a different kind of Hebrew or Yiddish realm.

At an organizational level, many still spoke of mobilizing indigenous sources to advance Jewish cultural creativity. Even as publications by the Kultur-Lige carried the anti-folkloric critiques of Litvakov, for example, its art section published a collection of Jewish folk art in order to orient Jewish "artistic thought to the beautiful folk-source."[54]

Yet in the most significant realm of organized Jewish cultural production—Hebrew and Yiddish publishing—the emphasis was shifting in the opposite direction. As mentioned earlier, the most notable feature of culturist publishing programs across the ideological spectrum during 1917–1919 was the unprecedented investment of resources, effort, and planning in literary translation. Alongside Stybel's press, the two other leading Hebraist publishers of the day also made a substantial place for translation. Moriah sought translations of Homer and Shakespeare from Tchernikhovsky and of Grimm's fairy tales by Frishman.[55] Moscow's Omanut press, which focused most of its efforts on literary publishing for children, laid particular emphasis on translations from European children's literature, producing an impressive array of "storybooks and tales for children from the best of world literature."[56] This emphasis was also evident in the press's 1917 Hebrew journal for young adults, *Shetilim,* which placed Hebrew writers like Bialik, Tchernikhovsky, Fichman, and Shteynman alongside Wilde, Mickiewicz, Daudet, and even Korean folk tales.[57] Omanut's effort was paralleled by the program of another Hebrew publishing house, Aḥinoar, which was founded in 1917 in honor of Bialik by Hebraist patron-admirers. This children's book publisher planned to publish some 150 children's books, drawn mostly from world literature.[58]

Litvakov's call for a grand translation program into Yiddish came against the backdrop of a similar explosion of translation in the reemerging Yiddish publishing sphere. The Yiddishist-radical Kiever Farlag, with which Litvakov was linked, made translation a central part of its efforts to re-shape Yiddish literature as a whole, publishing Andersen, Tolstoy, Pushkin, Ivan Franko, Wilde, Longfellow, and Daudet. Other smaller Yiddishist houses in Kiev published Andersen (Onhoyb) and Byron (Dorem-Farlag). The publishing houses Literatur in Odessa and Universal in Warsaw both initi-ated a "universal-library" series modeled on similar endeavors in other Eu-ropean languages.[59] Kharkov's Farlag "Idish" planned a "folks-bibliotek" that would include Byron, Jack London, and Knut Hamsun.[60] The small Moscow publishing house Khaver produced an anthology of European po-etry, *Fremds,* as well as translations of Tolstoy, Kuprin, and Maupassant.[61] And the most ambitious and well-funded private Yiddishist publishing ventures of the day, Kiev's Folks-Farlag and the Kultur-Lige publishing house, both made translation a central aspect of their self-declared (and competing) missions to guide the reemergent Yiddish cultural sphere as a whole. By mid-1919, the Kultur-Lige Farlag had declared its intent to fo-cus on the publication of "classic works, original and translated." Like Omanut, the Folks-Farlag's division for children's literature emphasized translation of "the classic works of world-literature which usually com-prise the reading material for youth." Its literature division aimed to trans-late "the classic works of the European novel-literature" and "modern lyric poetry." In its brief existence (founded in late 1918, it dissolved in the dras-tically altered circumstances of Bolshevik Kiev by 1921), its translation di-vision "prepared translations of the writings of Tolstoy, Chekhov, Byron, Flaubert, Maupassant, and many, many more. And it announced that it planned to translate a selection of the works of Shakespeare, Ibsen, Goethe and Schiller."[62]

Undoubtedly, many motives lay behind the plans of these collectives, not least a desire to find buyers for the publishers' wares.[63] Yet many clearly shared the desire of champions of translation to refound Jewish culture on a broader, more European basis. Most of the publishers themselves did not entertain radical deparochializing views. The Europeanizers Persits and even Stybel contributed funds to an album of Jewish folk art planned by An-ski.[64] And leading figures at the Yiddishist Folks-Farlag like Kalmanovitsh and Shtif saw great cultural value in the Yiddish-language folk tradition and even in the classical rabbinic tradition. Yet by 1917–

1919, even figures such as these had, in their capacity as publishers and culture-builders, come to share the translation camp's perception that an infusion of non-Jewish culture had become a pressing need. And even self-proclaimed folkists like Shtif now spoke in terms of deparochialization: "Once again, we are over-full with Jewishness, albeit in a new, 'national' incarnation . . . [National phraseology] is poisoning us, stuffing us once again with self-love, makes an idol out of every little thing we've created, every [decorative] pole and chapbook."[65]

As publishers sought to decide these questions at the level of material production, Jewish artists and their audiences also wrestled with them. In Hebrew letters, one figure above all others incarnated this question: the towering Romantic poet Tchernikhovsky. Since his fiery arrival on the Hebrew scene in the 1890s with poems that celebrated vitalism and eroticism, Tchernikhovsky had been read by many as Hebrew poetry's first "pagan." What his poetry meant for the new Jewish culture was a matter of dispute, however. Whereas some, like Klausner, celebrated him as a "European" or a "Hellene," others feted him as symbolizing a return to a repressed and occluded "Israelite" or even "Canaanite" culture. Both stances were equally at odds with the sort of piety toward Jewish tradition that marked indigenizers like Bialik or An-ski at times. But one interpretation connoted an unabashed celebration of the foreign, while the other heralded a deeper, nativist form of essentialism.

As Tchernikhovsky moved from Petersburg to Moscow to Odessa to escape the Bolsheviks, he wrote a series of poems that have since been read in both ways and might seem to constitute an internally contradictory confirmation of each. His 1919 sonnet "'Ashtarti li, halo tasihi li" (My Ashtoret, Won't You Tell Me—which has been taught to generations of American students as typifying Tchernikhovsky's poetic project) speaks in the voice of an ancient Israelite woman. In the poem, she beseeches an *ashtoret*—a personal idol of the pan–Near Eastern love goddess whose cult the Biblical prophets repeatedly sought to stamp out—to bring her a handsome lover. The speaker in the poem exemplifies a "Canaanite" transvaluation of values that some Jewish culturists, especially in Palestine, hoped to achieve: a woman unselfconscious in her love for the material beauty of the idol itself, completely pagan in her religion, and unashamed about her desire, she is a systematic inversion of what contemporaries took to be orthodox Judaism, exemplified by the figure of the male spiritual adept (prophet or rabbi), uncompromising monotheistic principles, and the denigration of the aesthetic and the erotic. A different but equally unvarnished Israelitism seems evident in a second sonnet, "'Od yesh bi-sdeh Moav ve-Yehudah" (There Still Stands in the Fields of Moab and Judah), in which an ancient Israelite stone dreams of a new "mighty generation" that would return to the land, declare victory "over the fathers," and displace the markers of a dead and petrified past with renewed celebration and dance.

Conversely, Tchernikhovsky's continued intensive engagement in literary translation during this period hewed to the ideas of the Europeanizing camp. In his introduction to a translation of the Greek Anacreon poems done for Stybel, Tchernikhovsky wrote: "There is no cultured nation which does not have in its literature something from those poems which are called Anacreonic . . . These poems, poems of the pleasures of life . . . are entirely absent only from our literature." Tchernikhovsky thus asserted an unvarnished cultural anti-essentialism worthy of Stybel or Frishman themselves: the point of the translation was not to supplement a unique "Hebraic" culture with a dose of the "Hellenic," but to bring Hebrew literature closer to an ostensible universal stratum of literary tradition and cultural sensibility shared by all "cultured nation[s]."[66]

The same stance seems inscribed in Tchernikhovsky's grand project of the period, his *Iliad* translation. Tchernikhovsky strove mightily to retain the *Iliad*'s dactylic hexameter: "Kokhoh hifkidu ha-Troyim shomrehem; akh bene ho-Akhaim / retet aḥozom vo-faḥad, ha-aḥim li-eymoh u-mnusoh."[67] As Aminadav Dykman notes, this choice of form was not at all a given in earlier Hebrew *Iliad* translations or in the Russian and German translations that Tchernikhovsky would have known.[68] His attempt to capture the formal feel of the Homeric poetry reflects his choosing to put form before "meaning" (or rather, to reject any distinction between the two in the name of a sovereign logic of poetry). Equally consonant with the programmatic concern for Europeanization was his effort to avoid invoking any Jewish textual traditions. In Tchernikhovsky's case, this involved trying to avoid the biblicization that had characterized all previous Hebrew translations of Homer. As Dykman notes, to turn Greek epic into Biblical epic was the culturally obvious choice for Hebrew translators (Erich Auerbach's famous emphasis on their difference notwithstanding) if one regarded translation as cultural mediation. Tchernikhovsky's decision to avoid it— and his efforts more generally to escape the gravity of any of the literary languages of the many-layered Hebrew textual tradition—bespeak a will not to mediate but to preserve the aesthetic object's strangeness.[69]

These opposing sides of Tchernikhovsky's creative practice might be attributed simply to the distinction between his roles as poet and translator. Certainly, internal contradiction was not hard to find in a literary sphere in which the distance between one's cultural-ideological commitments and the autonomous creative process could be substantial. No less a radical deparochializer than Tchernikhovsky's fellow Hebraist Frishman devoted much of his own literary effort in this period to a series of stories, *Bamidbar,* set in the context of the Israelites' wanderings in the desert and the Sinaitic theophany.

Tchernikhovsky, however, was not only aware of the tensions exemplified by his own practice, but addressed them directly in his poetry. His major poem of the period, the corona "La-shemesh" (To the Sun), dated 1919, must certainly be read in part in this light—although it can hardly be reduced to a metapoetic commentary. Formally complex even for Tchernikhovsky (a corona consists of fifteen sonnets in which the last line of each serves as the first line of the next, and the fifteenth is composed of the first lines of the preceding fourteen), "La-shemesh" is no less ambitious in its range of philosophical, historiosophical, and humanistic concerns. At one level a vitalist hymn to the sun, "La-shemesh" is also a poem of "innocence and experience," as Boaz Arpali puts it, that projects this dyad well beyond the biographical frame to dramatize questions of nature and culture, rural life and urban society, the world of premodern shamanistic consciousness and the disenchanted world heralded by science. The poem's most famous passages concerning Tchernikhovsky's experiences as a Russian army doctor in World War I meditate on the morally bewildering doubleness of light and heat as sources of both life and death, through stunning images of the flash of artillery and the light in a dying soldier's eye.[70]

Yet as critics have recognized since the poem's publication in 1921, it is nonetheless clear that "La-shemesh" makes the literary-cultural tensions of the indigenous and the European a central theme. Several constituent sonnets address this tension directly but without apparent resolution. At one point, the poem seems to signal an unalloyed cultural pantheism. Declaring "I fathomed an age's sorrow, each nation's song bewitched me," sonnet 5 asserts the essential unity underpinning such disparate cultural utterances as a Druidic inscription, a Chinese talisman, and significantly, inscriptions to the Near Eastern deity An: cloaked in differences of languages, place, and belief, Western, Eastern, and Canaanite cultures share with each other—and, the poem suggests elsewhere, with modern science itself—an essential posture of awe before the mystery of life's birth out of light and heat. Other sonnets, however, qualify the implied author's universality. Although he derisively rejects normative Judaism ("the God of the vulgar people") and looks forward to the future overthrow of life-denying monotheism (represented by both the Biblical El and the "crescent moon" of Islam in sonnet 10), he elsewhere affirms his own links to an Israelite origin: "in my heart the dew yet lodges that descends on Edom's steppe."[71]

This contradiction is inscribed more deeply still in the vital question of the poet's source of inspiration. Whereas the opening lines of the poem locate this source firmly in the universal order of nature—"grow, sproutling, and burst forth / With your song, festive song, in the jagged thorn"—sonnet 13 suggests that despite the implied author's love for both Hellenic and Northern European culture (Tchernikhovsky famously shared the Russian Symbolists' interest in Finnish myth and had translated the *Kalevala*), the "spark that says within me Repeat, . . . this flash is from the East, from Canaan I preserve it." Amplifying this indigenist trope ("in Ur of the Chaldees did I worship"), sonnet 13 ends with the naked question of whether the poet should orient his "worship" to the Israelite-Canaanite ur-culture from which his own poetic "spark" derives or to the Hellenic culture that has "seized me, and I have no escape!"

> Where's the way I must choose, and where is the path?
> Shall I anoint my oil for Yah [the Israelite God], or Zeus shall I choose,
> Or the last age's icon in the kingdom of the idol?[72]

Sharpening the thrust of the question still further is the poet's inversion of what would seem to be the poem's general tendency to valorize nativity over civilization: one of the striking features of Greek culture, the poem avers, is that it can indeed reshape and "convert" all who encounter it regardless of their origins: "all who touch it know beauty, / Loveliness became its wisdom, its wisdom became loveliness, / and it scattered its beauty over Hades and Ocean."[73]

A reading of "La-shemesh" committed to reconciliation of these tensions might posit that the poem rejects the regnant division between "European/Greek/foreign" and "Israelite/Canaanite" in favor of an idiosyncratic valorization of all cultures sharing some essential vitalism; this view would find support in Tchernikhovsky's preference as a translator for texts redolent of mythic consciousness and "pagan" violent or erotic intensity. Another of Tchernikhovsky's metapoetic poems of the period, however, the 1920 "El ha-sonetah ha-'ivrit" (To the Hebrew Sonnet) responded to the indigenous/European dyad with a more surprising move:

> How dear you are to me, how dear, oh sonnet, "song of gold"!
> From the days of the Renaissance have you been preserved for us.
> The "Immanuel"—he loved the echo of your song
> And singular men in their generation preserved you in Italy,
>   and you did not die.[74]

On the one hand, invoking the Renaissance Hebrew poet Immanuel of Rome, Tchernikhovsky proudly claims a lineage for the sonnet within the Hebrew poetic tradition in the name of a collective "us." His own turn to the sonnet is, then, not humble borrowing from a more advanced European culture but a return to an occluded Jewish poetic tradition. But on the other hand, the poem roots that very tradition in the Renaissance (using the pan-European French term), the birth of European high culture. The indigeneity of the Hebrew sonnet, ironically, lies precisely in the Europeanness of the Renaissance Hebrew poets. Fittingly, elsewhere in his writings, Tchernikhovsky used the Hebrew sonnet not only for "Israelite" expression but also for poems of personal voice without any clear Judaic reference.[75]

Like Hofshteyn, then, Tchernikhovsky approached the question of the Jewish and the European with subtlety and no small measure of ambivalence. But much as Dobrushin did with regard to Hofshteyn, many of Tchernikhovsky's contemporaries read him much more programmatically at the 1917–1919 juncture, in a manner that testifies to the deepening tension between indigenizing and deparochializing imperatives. Tchernikhovsky's incorporation of ancient Israelite themes in some of his poems moved some to hail him as the symbol of a return to a supposed ancient Israelite culture; the Zionist pioneer, agronomist, and writer Shlomo Tsemah hailed Tchernikhovsky as "the first Israelite poet since the Bible" who transcended European poetry for a new Israelite ideal ("The statue of Apollo is overthrown, the altar to Ashterot and Baal is raised").[76]

But others (no less politically Zionist than Tsemah) hailed the "European" Tchernikhovsky with equal fervor as the new fundament of Hebrew literary and cultural consciousness. The formulations of Klausner, cited earlier, were echoed by many contemporaries.[77] Strikingly, such praise of

Tchernikhovsky was regularly paired with increasingly sharp attacks on the figure to whom he had always served as an "other," the "Jewish national poet" Bialik himself. The Hebrew poet Elihu Meitus declared that whereas Bialik had "torn open windows to the sun for us," Tchernikhovsky "brought us outside and gave us the sun and the moon and the stars . . . and taught us to love—to love everything . . . to love man, and to love life, the world and all it contains, without any accounting."[78] Although Hebraist, Russian-language Zionist, and even at times Yiddishist publications continued to issue pro forma declarations of Bialik's preeminent status, these jostled with a genuine outpouring of doubt about Bialik's continued primacy or even relevance as a literary model, expressed both in critical reflections on his work and highly defensive efforts to salvage his status. Importantly, both the critiques and the defenses shared the same standard: both asked whether Bialik could transcend an ostensible Jewish parochialism in favor of a "European" or "universal" poetics.

Among the most naked declarations of Bialik's parochial limitations came from an outsider to the world of Hebraism, the noted Russian (ethnically Jewish) literary critic Gershenzon. Brought to his interest in Hebrew poetry (which he could only read in Russian translation) in part by an encounter with Bialik, Gershenzon recognized the poet's greatness. Yet in his introductory comments to the Safrut publishing house's 1918 anthology of modern Hebrew poetry in Russian translation, Gershenzon declared that Bialik's younger contemporaries had already surpassed him because Bialik was "still almost entirely absorbed in Jewish matters—to him, it has still not been granted to go forth into the expanse of human freedom."[79]

It is perhaps unsurprising that an outsider to Jewish national cultural concerns like Gershenzon should take this stance. But similar criticisms were evident in works of unvarnished cultural nationalists. As we have seen, the most vociferous articulation of this stance within Hebraist circles issued from the pen of Yosef Klausner, who had personal scores to settle with Bialik. But younger Hebraists who shared neither Klausner's well-defined cultural-ideological agenda nor his personal animosities read Bialik through precisely the same lens. Bialik, Meitus lamented, "still stands with one foot on the doorstep of the *beit-ha-midrash* [the traditional house of study]."[80]

Perhaps more telling still, even those who defended Bialik's continued literary preeminence invoked the same set of antiparochial standards as did his detractors. In *Ha-Tekufah,* the sensitive critic Grinblat (Goren) at-tacked those who claimed that Bialik was "more Hebrew that European" and maintained that "a book of Bialik's poems is not a *sefer ḥitzoni* [a book standing outside the Jewish canon]." On the contrary, Grinblat insisted that Bialik's poetry was in its "very essence . . . none other than that art which is entirely *'ḥitzonit* [foreign to the Jewish tradition]." Bialik's great-ness, in other words, inhered precisely in his transcendence of the Jewish tradition in favor of "European" modes of art.[81]

The audacity with which Hebraists flattened out the work of two great poets in the name of deparochialization found a close parallel in the Yiddishist camp, in the hyperbolic outpouring of excitement that greeted the cohort of young Yiddish poets retrospectively dubbed the Kiev-Grupe: Hofshteyn, Kvitko, and Markish. Leading Kiev Yiddishists like Litvakov, his fellow critic Dobrushin, and the translator-critic Korman hailed these three still very young poets as collectively inaugurating a new epoch in Yiddish literature. Significantly, as the previous discussion of Hofshteyn indicates, these and other critics located the core of these poets' innova-tions and their larger cultural significance in their minimization of obtru-sive Jewish themes and intertexts. In the journal *Baginen*—published in mid-1919 under the auspices of Kiev's new Bolshevik occupiers—one P. Reyland praised all three poets as "the new today, the new tomorrow" and grouped them all under the rubric of a full-fledged break with "the spe-cifically Jewish past." Their poetry represented the maturation of a new Yiddish literature insofar as it manifested a new Jewish personality type untroubled by the past; intoxicated by the present; "wanton" in its relation to nature and beauty; and most importantly, brimming over with an ag-gressive, confident individualism that Reyland saw more generally in "our youth"—their sense that one was "lord over the entire world and stands at its center."[82]

For some of these critics, this deparochialization could not go far or fast enough. Figures like Litvakov and Reyland saw Hofshteyn's complex negotiation of the problem of tradition in his poetry—which readers like Dobrushin and Bergelson welcomed—not as a virtue but as a limitation. Far more satisfying was the unalloyed anti-traditionalism of Hofshteyn's younger contemporary Markish, who gained fame with poems like this 1917 lyric:

> Don't know if I'm at home
> or if I'm afar [*tsi in der fremd*]—

I'm running! . . .
my shirt's unbuttoned,
there are no reins on me,
I'm nobody's, I'm unclaimed [*hefker,* also: wild, licentious],
without a beginning, without an end . . .
My body is foam,
and it reeks of wind;
my name is: "Now" . . .
If I throw out my hands,
they'd give the world a smack from one end to the other,
my eyes if I let roam about,
they'd guzzle down the world from bottom up!
With eyes open, with an unbuttoned shirt,
with hands stretched out,—
I don't know if I have a home
or have a-far,
if I'm a beginning, or an end . . .[83]

Such poems moved radical deparochializers like Litvakov to declare that Yiddish literature was on the cusp of achieving the all-embracing voice that was the supposed seal of modern "universal" literature.[84]

Such a programmatic choosing of sides was also evident in the competing visions of the avant-garde Jewish art-theater groups that were then emerging in and beyond Russian space. In keeping with the indigenizing ideal, the Hebraist Ha-Bimah aspired to elaborate a distinctively "Jewish" aesthetic while simultaneously attaining metropolitan standards of artistic seriousness. Thus Ha-Bimah's Menahem Gnesin justified the choice of Dovid Pinski's *The Eternal Jew,* a Yiddish play, for the theater group's first full-length production with the telling remark that "although it wasn't originally written in Hebrew, it was nevertheless entirely Hebrew in content and it was deemed very proper to perform it at Ha-Bimah."[85] By contrast, the fledgling theater troupe that would eventually become the famous Soviet Yiddish theater group GOSET initially aspired to a "European" Yiddish theater free of any "specific repertoire": "We say: Yiddish theater is first of all a theater in general, a temple of shining art and joyous creation—a temple where the prayer is chanted in the Yiddish language. We say: The tasks of world theater serve us as the tasks of our theater, and only language distinguishes us from others." Nor was this simply the stance of the troupe's director Granovsky, a newcomer to Jewish cultural concerns whose views had been formed by his prewar involvements with German avant-garde theater. M. Rivesman, the literary director of the Petersburg Jewish Theater Society that had sponsored the troupe, proclaimed a widely attested desire among Yiddishist activists to "refresh the dirty, moldy Yiddish repertoire and illuminate it with masterful translations" alongside "truly literary, original dramatic works."[86]

The desire for a capacious Jewish culture was so powerful that it even found expression in the visual arts. At one level, the very idea of a "Jewish art" (and mutatis mutandis, Jewish music) seems to presuppose some notion of a fixed Jewish content or aesthetic tradition, though Jewish artists or composers could and did fight over whether this tradition was to be found in a posited "eastern" fundament or in the folk art of East European Jewry. Certainly, even some of the most sophisticated expositors of "Jewish art" at the 1917–1919 moment were committed to an indigenizing ideal. The best-known essay on Jewish art from this period, "Aladdin's Lamp" by the critic Efros, which appeared in the 1918 Moscow Jewish anthology *Evreiskii mir* (Jewish World), took for granted that a new Jewish art meant a creative synthesis between universal avant-garde principles and "the true folk material" cleansed of "alien accretions and borrowed embellishment."[87]

But even as they embraced this ideal, a number of painters who identified with the Jewish cultural project at this juncture struggled with the limits it imposed. As the art critic Rachel Wischnitzer-Bernstein put it, "Today's generation, analyzing itself, announces with an understandable pride that it doesn't feel obliged to the previous generation, that there is no need for ethnography and the anecdotal. Their mission is not to depict the Sabbath in a Jewish home but to express their own spiritual quest."[88] When, in 1919, the artists Boris Aronson and Rybak published a prescriptive essay on "The Paths of Jewish Painting" in the Kiev Yiddishist anthology *Oyfgang,* they subtly demoted Jewish folk culture from an identifiable tradition to a vaguely posited repertoire of distinctive shapes and colors.[89] Other self-declared Jewish artists sought to go further still, gropingly moving beyond any notion of authentic tradition toward the view that Jewish art meant simply the artistic expression of self-consciously Jewish selves. The young painter Solomon Nykritin wrote in a diary entry: "Here I am walking along the street. My silhouette, form, and color are inside of me, and I do not wish to delve into any psychological depths,—I am a painter . . . and I am proud of it. And isn't my art national?"[90] It is difficult to know how such feelings could have been translated into artistic practice. But arguably, one can discern among the era's self-declared Jewish artists a movement away from Jewish folk imagery. For instance, in his cover illustration for an anthology devoted to Peretz, the Odessa artist Yankev Apter avoided any sort of Jewish figures in favor of pure abstraction (see fig. 12).

The urge to deparochialization was no doubt limited to a certain educated stratum. Certainly, many continued to identify "Jewish culture" with Judaic themes tout court. Indeed, the artwork that generated the most immediate and widespread excitement among general audiences open to secular culture was An-ski's play *Dybbuk,* which embodied the ideal of indigenization. In European Russia and then in Vilna and Warsaw, many reacted with unprecedented enthusiasm to the play in its various stages of presentation. An-ski's 1917 reading of a Yiddish or Russian version of *The Dybbuk* to a Hebraist-Zionist circle at the Moscow home of Tarbut's patron-founder Zlatopolsky provoked such excitement that Zlatopolsky apparently purchased the rights to the manuscript on the spot for the evolving Ha-Bimah theater troupe. He then delegated the Hebraist journalist Sh. Tshernovits to solicit a translation from Bialik himself. The rumor that Bialik would translate the play thrilled many Hebraists (though by no means all: Litai lamented that Hebrew's greatest writer should squander time on this "completely mediocre" play about "dybbuks" rather than furthering "the redemption of our language" through translations from world literature like the *Quixote* he had previously begun).[91]

But the countervailing desire for a Jewish culture that would not be confined to works like *The Dybbuk* was not limited solely to a few cultural critics. Many of those who dilated on the importance of deparochialization suggested that it was not merely desirable in itself but also necessary to retain the allegiance of a younger "generation" for Hebrew or Yiddish culture. Litai's 1917–1918 essays on translation framed his program not only as an absolute good for Hebrew culture, but also as the only way out of an intolerable choice between "mental abstinence or assimilation" that threatened to drive a generation of Hebrew-literate youth and even authors away from Hebrew. Concretely, Litai contended that the modern Jewish person, however strong his nationalist and Hebraist commitments, could not be expected to confine himself solely to the existing corpus of works in Jewish languages. Yet the obvious recourse to coterritorial non-Jewish languages—particularly Russian—for access to world literature and thought virtually guaranteed linguistic and cultural assimilation. Litai invoked a previous generation's experience as proof and warning: "The *maskilim,* that is, those who apart from their knowledge and learning in Hebrew attained for themselves general education to a certain degree and mastered one of the culture-languages—these abandoned Hebrew literature because she could not satisfy their mental and spiritual needs."[92] The only solution was to bring "the literature of the world" into Hebrew, as Litai put it in his 1918 followup essay, a piece that amplified his sociologically framed urgency with the revealing language of individual psychic need cited in one of the epigraphs to this chapter. This argument for translation transposed the issue from cultural ideology to sociology (and from the needs of literature itself back to the reader, albeit in this case, a member of the intelligentsia). It was driven by the conviction that this intelligentsia simply would not stand for a self-limiting culture, no matter how much it respected figures like Bialik.

This conviction had been the basis of Frishman's critique of Bialik's "Hebrew Book" back in 1913. There, Frishman had explained his insistence on the irrelevance of Hebrew's past glories and the overriding importance of producing new Hebrew works in explicitly generational terms. What had brought him to the Vienna conference, he averred, was concern that his own son, and by extension the sons of his whole Hebraist generation, should not abandon the Hebrew culture that Frishman loved so ardently. But such abandonment, he insisted, would be entirely natural and unstoppable unless Hebrew culture itself changed "to attract the hearts of our sons." Whereas once Hebrew readers had been educated in traditional Jewish texts before discovering secular literature, the new generation of potential readers was "European":

> Our new reader is also a different type, utterly different from the sort we had previously. He too no longer comes from the traditional school, for the most part, and certainly not from the study house or yeshiva; rather, he is someone who had read other literatures before he began to read in Hebrew, or who reads them simultaneously. For the most part, he is the son of a Zionist—and of that sort of Zionist who, in educating his son, even though he wished with the best will in the world to make him a complete Hebrew, could not but give him a real modern education, an education that includes high school, university, and all the other modern necessities. And this sort of reader, because his taste has been purified and improved by a great literature . . . , demands a modern literature from his own authors, an art-literature with all of the requisite orna-

ments—and because he does not find such a literature among [the Hebrew authors], he turns up his nose and leaves, never to return.[93]

More educated by European standards and more cosmopolitan than their fathers, such young people would simply move beyond Hebrew culture if it refused to speak to them beyond its narrow ambit of "Jewish" themes. Frishman's conclusion was clear and urgent: a proper Hebrew literature in the universal European mold was "the only means by which we will be able to attract our sons, the youth audience, that they might not betray us and our ideals but rather remain true to them."[94]

We might dismiss Frishman's or Litai's invocation of sociological necessity as a convenient rhetorical means to win support for their particular cultural vision. But many other sources suggest a real sociological basis for their claims. One memoir of Yiddishist cultural life in Kiev records: "The youth would gather in the writers' club of the Kultur-Lige and react with excitement to the appearances by Peretz Markish, black-haired, burning and stormy; Leyb Kvitko, tall and thin and with his pipe always in his mouth; the dreamy and silent Dovid Hofshteyn; and others. Sometimes they broke into a stormy dance and the song: 'instead of a beard without a Jew, better a Jew without a beard.'"[95] The arresting mantra chanted by the Yiddishist youth at the Kultur-Lige's literary club had many parallels. By all accounts, the 1917 announcement that Tchernikhovsky had undertaken to translate the *Iliad*—long deemed the very antithesis of classical Jewish literary expression—generated tremendous excitement in the Hebraist literary community.[96] The transplanted Hungarian Hebrew poet Ha-Meiri recalls a bizarre conversation in Kiev with a would-be patron, a fluent Hebrew speaker from Ekaterinoslav, who promised not only to pay him by the poem, but to pay double for love poems and even cover any expenses the poet might incur in courtship because "[w]e have no true love poems in Hebrew literature" and Ha-Meiri was "a European" who had it in his power to rectify this omission. And in his memoirs, the Yiddishist Tsharni boasted of his encounter with a Jewish soldier who had sung Tsharni's prewar Yiddish translations of the Russian Byronic poet Lermontov with fellow Jewish servicemen during the war.[97]

What all of this suggests is a growing community of people for whom Hebrew or Yiddish culture was a passion, but who were also firmly oriented toward Russian and other metropolitan cultures. Significantly, by 1917, Bialik himself acknowledged that this was the case, however unfortunate he may have deemed it. Laying out his vision for the future of Hebrew culture at the founding conference of Tarbut, Bialik grouped "translations of the works of the world geniuses—Shakespeare, Goethe, Heine" among the essential tasks that Hebraists would have to carry out if they had any hope of transforming East European Jewry. Bialik had long acknowledged the importance of translation, despite his criticism of excessive "European-ism" in Jewish cultural life. He had taken a leading role in the prewar Turgeman publishing imprint for children's-book translations and made a place for the world classics in his agenda-setting 1913 "Hebrew Book." Yet he had never left any doubt that the translation of "alien" works was to occupy a strictly subordinate place relative to the recovery of the Hebraic tradition for moderns. It is against this backdrop that his little-known speech at the 1917 Tarbut conference is so remarkable, for Bialik declared such translations a necessity on precisely the objective sociological grounds that Frishman had once invoked against him: only such an expansion of Hebrew culture's bounds could keep the allegiance even of "our national-ist youth" because this youth, despite its solid nationalist commitment, "do[es] not belong to us in their heart and soul, but to other worlds . . . to Tolstoy and to Turgenev and not to Isaiah and [Yehudah] Ha-Levi."[98]

This concern with a generation slipping away thus cut across the com-peting visions for Jewish culture. It plausibly explains the motives of those writers, critics, and publishers from Bialik to the Folks-Farlag's Shtif who did not share the deparochializers' antagonism to indigenous sources but nevertheless laid heavy emphasis on translation at the 1917 moment. The Revolution, with its universalist promises and seductions for so many young Russian Jews, no doubt intensified this concern among culturists, but the 1913 debates testify that both the concern and the hunger for widened ho-rizons that spurred it long preceded the Revolution.

A Different Cultural Nationalism

In actuality, only a few Hebraist and Yiddishist actors were aggressive pro-ponents of deparochialization. Most contemporaries favored shifting Jew-ish culture's center of gravity rather than expelling tradition altogether. Even the broadsides of Litvakov, Klausner, or Aleph against the cultural authority of tradition betrayed in various places a countervailing admis-sion that at some level, this was a strategic righting of a cultural balance, and that, rhetoric aside, no Jewish culture would want to obliterate all traces of its own tradition. Thus, Klausner's commitment to a "Hebrew humanism" freed of a hypertrophic Jewishness did not prevent him from recognizing that it was deep engagement with this tradition that had produced much of the best modern Hebrew literature. Litvakov, for his part, was far more interested in the cultural uses of traditional forms and images than many left-wing Yiddishist cultural theorists, and his genuinely dialectical Marxism gave a place of honor to the cultural achievements of the old world so that these might be bequeathed to the coming Jewish "proletarian nation."[99]

Moreover, even the radical "universalizers" were by no means opposed to the development of specifically Jewish idioms in modern Hebrew or Yiddish literature. Indeed, these figures cherished the hope that their engineered deparochialization might lead, dialectically, to new literary works that were distinctly Jewish. Klausner, Shteynman, and many of their contemporaries repeatedly invoked the hope that "the most universal poet" would also give birth to "the most national" poetry. None other than Litvakov held out the hope that through Europeanization, Jewish literature would "not los[e] but perhaps, on the contrary, [deepen] its uniquely national character."[100]

Finally, at the level of emotion and sensibility, even the most disciplined "cultural engineers" did not maintain wholly coherent stances. It is not simply that some of the most radical champions of deparochialization in 1917 would later veer in the other direction (Eliezer Shteynman would spend his late years producing compendia of Hasidic stories for Israeli readers). Even in 1917–1919, essentialist and anti-essentialist conceptions of Jewish culture jostled in the same essays, even the same paragraphs, because almost without exception, even those Jewish culturists who wished to move beyond the felt limitations of any defined Jewishness found at least some indigenous Jewish sources deeply compelling.[101]

Yet despite their mixed feelings, by 1917 substantial numbers of Jewish culturists felt compelled to choose one "side" or another in these debates. At this historic juncture, subtle negotiations between the claims of indigenization and deparochialization carried out in the poetry of figures like Tchernikhovsky and Hofshteyn wrestled with increasingly strong perceptions of a zero-sum conflict between these two cultural imperatives. It was no accident that many articulations of the translationist and deparochializing positions invoked the figure of a journey through space (Shteynman's "side-path" and "royal road," Klausner's rhetoric of exile), or an evolution through time in which Jewish literatures had arrived at a point of danger, paralysis, and fateful choice (Litai, Litvakov, Ben-Eliezer). What all of these discourses and programs shared was a powerful conviction that Jewish aesthetic culture had arrived at a crisis that could only be resolved by liberating it from Judaic essentialism.

Although the Revolution's rhetorics of futurity and cosmopolitanism no doubt played a role in these concerns, it was at most a catalyst in this as in all other aspects of the cultural project. There was no necessary connection between revolutionary ideology and the deparochializing stance. Among the most vocal champions of cultural deparochialization, Litvakov was a part of the Russian revolutionary intelligentsia and the Hebrew writer Shteynman came to embrace the Revolution, but Klausner was a committed anti-revolutionary. Latski-Bertoldi, though formerly a socialist, had moved so far from support for revolution by 1917 that he helped revive the nonsocialist Folks-Partey. Conversely, revolutionary sympathies coexisted with indigenizing visions quite nicely well beyond the revolutionary period. Many Yiddishist socialists considered the folk roots of modern Yiddish culture from a social-revolutionary vantage point. Among Hebraists, one of the most outspoken supporters of the Revolution was Tsemah, who dreamed of a Hebrew culture that would return to its ancient Israelite roots.[102]

More to the point, a broader historical perspective reminds us that the deparochializing impulse was a part of Jewish culturist discourse and practice almost from the beginning. In a debate famous in the annals of Hebrew literary history, the major Hebraist cultural authority of the 1890s, Ahad Ha-'Am, squared off against an array of younger Hebrew writers over whether Hebrew literature's scope should be defined by national concerns or by the full panoply of modern, individual questions and longings. In parallel debates, other culturists of the 1890s spoke of the need to balance "Jerusalem" with "Athens"—to bring foreign beauty into a literature still ostensibly dominated by an overriding ethical imperative and a tradition of anti-aestheticism. Klausner, then a rising young critic, made his critical reputation by defending the legitimacy and even national significance of Hebrew poetry that explored personal, romantic, and erotic themes deemed too "alien" by many cultural nationalists. In 1894, he praised now-forgotten Hebrew love poetry by Peretz as a step toward the necessary Europeanization of Hebrew literature. A few years later, he was among the most vociferous defenders of the young Tchernikhovsky, who was anathematized as an "alien shoot" by many in the turn-of-the-century Hebrew press for his willingness to celebrate beauty, vitality, nature, and erotic love; his explicit Nietzschean orientations; and his open commitment to remaking Hebrew poetry in dialogue with Greek, Latin, Russian, German, and other European poetic works.[103]

These ideas began to find institutional purchase well before 1917 too, in Klausner's own *Ha-Shiloah* or in the Tushiyah publishing house of the Hebrew writer Ben-Avigdor. Ben-Avigdor anticipated Stybel's insistence that translation was a matter of utmost cultural and literary importance. In the decade before the Revolution, such ideas also began to make themselves felt in Yiddishist circles, particularly through the mediation of the socialist-nationalist thinker Khayim Zhitlovsky.[104]

For the most part, this pre-1917 legacy constituted less an alternative program than a countertradition of disconnected reactions. Thinkers who argued for the importance of deparochialization and Europeanization sometimes retreated from this stance. The most famous case might be Peretz, a proponent of Europeanization in the 1890s who from the turn of the century became the very symbol of Jewish cultural regeneration through the vitalizing power of Yiddish folk culture.

But already by 1914, deparochializing sensibilities were leading to more aggressive and coherent formulations. In that year, the leading Yiddish journal *Di yudishe velt* carried an unvarnished dissent from pieties about the secular *Ueberdichtung* of tradition and its national value:

Modern Yiddish literature . . . how many hopes have the nationalists placed on it in a worldly, secular sense . . . and how Yiddish literature has fooled them . . . a Hasidic aesthetic, religious Romanticism has become its fundamental tone, the poetic core of all new literary creations . . .

[W]hat really remains of our freethinking, while the crown of our Diaspora Jewishness, the central star of our nationalism, remains the rabbinic Sabbath-and-holiday-ideology, which has become a sacrosanct plank in the most radical programs? Like the cloud at Mount Sinai, this ideology has surrounded us, and we cuddle at the rabbinic breast and breathe in the poetry of Jewish national peace. This entire Sabbath-poetry of do-nothingness and weakness, which comes from not feeling any responsibility for the maintenance of the world and of our own people, this Hasidic-feminine beauty and Hasidic-feminine desire to negate our will only in order to achieve a feeling of inner happiness, this whole pessimistic Jewish aesthetic has intoxicated our souls and allows us to go around in an unreal world, allows us to trade a national life for national symbols.[105]

Thus, well before 1917, the question of "Jewishness" and "Europeanness," or their cognates, had become an explicit problem for the would-be creators of a new Jewish culture.

What makes their dissatisfaction significant for our understanding of the Jewish cultural project is how this evolving alternative vision of Jewish aesthetic cultural formation intersected with Jewish nationalism. No less than the indigenizing program, the deparochializing urge was a nationalist one. Klausner, Litvakov, and their cohort were not dissatisfied simply as individual cultural consumers, but as nationalists committed to the ideal of a great modern Hebrew or Yiddish cultural sphere. They wanted to see these cultures flourish despite their backwardness relative to more developed cultures—perhaps the most basic core of cultural nationalism. And they declared their nationalist intent clearly: the goal of unfettering Hebrew and Yiddish literature was to make possible a modern Jewish national culture. Klausner, for example, saw Tchernikhovsky's very freedom from an oppressive Jewishness as a sign that the poet himself was "himself entirely Revival [*meshorer, she-hu' kulo tehiyah*]"—he represented in his person what the national culture as a whole had to become.[106]

Klausner's notion of freeing the nation from Judaic limits on its cultural creativity and Litvakov's invocation of the developmental needs of the national culture itself were not mere figures of speech, but expressions of an alternate Jewish cultural nationalism. This same nationalist logic was already implied in Aleph's essay. Jewish expression freed of any prescriptions and limitations would yield as-yet-unknowable cultural assemblages that would in their own way be unique, and distinctly Jewish.

Other Hebraist and Yiddishist voices outside the translation debate also married the ideas of cultural anti-essentialism and cultural nationalism. In a 1917 essay entitled "Bor'ba za natsionnal'nu'iu individual'nost'" (The Struggle for National Individuality), the young Tarbut activist and Zionist thinker Haim Grinberg (who later became one of American Jewry's leading Zionist intellectuals) depicted national culture as a constantly evolving national "I" that at any given time was the "sum of the historical life of the nation" or, like a chemical compound, a unique but changeable mix or "system of elements" that were themselves universally available and present in different constellations in other human cultures. From these mutually contingent developments arose each nation's "unlimited and indefinable potential."[107]

Explicitly rejecting ideas of an essential Jewish national ethos which he associated with the Zionist thinker Ahad Ha-'Am, Grinberg defined "Zionism" as no more and no less than "a struggle for Jewish individuality—a struggle not for the preservation and fruitless conservation of this or that fixed trait of this individuality, but for the establishment of a free background for its unceasing re-formation, for its free and (to use the terminology of Bergson) 'cinematic' development." In other words, the cultural end of Zionist state- and society-building was not the preservation of some existing Jewishness nor the recovery of some new Israelitism, but the unfettering of an unforeseeable and always changing national culture that is linked to what comes before only serially, much as one image in a film is linked not in essence but only in proximity to the previous one.[108]

Grinberg's essay appeared in *Safrut,* the Moscow Zionist journal intended for assimilated and cosmopolitan Russian Jews. Yet a similar anti-essentialist vision of open-ended Jewish cultural development was presented to the much more traditionally rooted Hebrew-reading constituency of Tarbut in Ukraine a year later. In a 1918 essay published in the Hebrew organ of the organization's Ukrainian branch, the young Hebrew writer and Zionist-Hebraist activist Natan Bistritsky (Agmon) insisted that the ultimate cultural benefit of the Zionist creation of a territorially and linguistically normal nation would be not the formation of a new Jewish or Israelite ethos and philosophy, but quite the contrary: the liberation of Hebrew cultural creation from all forms of intellectual and aesthetic limitation hitherto imposed in the name of "Jewishness." Grimly assessing the cultural effects of diaspora, Bistritsky argued, much as Berdichevsky had in the 1890s, that Jewishness, deprived of the organic horizons of land and language, had become a religio-ideological system that sustained itself and the nation by forever reimposing fixed "philosophical principles" on Jewish life. The resulting "ghetto for emotion and thought" had constricted Jewish culture itself because "the Hebrew individual could not conquer for himself all the paths of universal creativity." Most striking was Bistritsky's anti-essentialist but overtly nationalist vision of what a properly liberated Hebrew culture would be: a "new national culture" that "will not be afraid to renew and change its content and forms: this culture will become a rich and splendid, kaleidoscopic world culture."[109]

Parallel notes were sounded by the Yiddishist activist Latski-Bertoldi in an admiring review of Litvakov's writings. Much less politically radical but no less culturally radical than Litvakov, Latski-Bertoldi shared Litvakov's vision of a dialectical secular-cultural revolution from within Judaism. Writing in 1919, he enjoined Jewish political radicals of Litvakov's ilk to carry out their revolution, as Litvakov himself demanded, within Jewish national culture rather than outside or against it. Were they to do so, "your rebellion will be a blessing for you and for the Jewish people" alike.[110]

All of these conceptions of a Jewish national culture completely freed of essentialist assumptions could only be realized at some future moment. Compounding this vagueness was the propensity of some to invoke Romantic ideas of a Jewish individuality or genius inhering in the individual author. This tendency could even veer in racialist directions: the Hebrew poet and later far-right nationalist Ha-Meiri praised the Hungarian modernist Ady Endre for a synthesis of Decadent poetics and nationalist content that pivoted on the simultaneous freeing of "the national artist from the crude chains of politics" and the reorientation of his poetry toward "his racial and instinctual qualities."[111]

But the anti-essentialist visions were not entirely abstract. It was no accident that the most radical advocates of deparochialization like Klausner, Litvakov, Frishman, and Shteynman also numbered among the most fervent monolingualist Hebraists and Yiddishists of their day: even as they rejected notions of a definitive content for Jewish culture, they pressed just as hard to make language central to the ongoing development of a self-sustaining Jewish culture. Their vision of language followed the logic of their larger commitment to deparochialization: Hebrew or Yiddish had to be transformed into languages "sufficient to all the needs of feeling and thought and description of the modern person," as Klausner put it.[112] But use of Hebrew or Yiddish guaranteed that all expression by the modern Jew, regardless of its content, would remain part of an open-ended national culture.

The anti-essentialist view of the role of national language was different than the more familiar form of linguistic nationalism in that it had more to do with form than content. The more familiar mode, identified with Herder and generally imputed to all linguistic nationalism east of the Elbe, involved, as Charles Taylor puts it, an "expressivist notion of the special character of each people": that is, each language was thought to bear within its traditions and perhaps very structures a particular national character, which it thus both preserved and communicated "naturally" to all acts of individual expression.[113]

By contrast, the anti-essentialist stance conceived of language as a container rather than an essence. Infinitely expandable and semi-permeable (via translation), it was also at once a storehouse in that it ensured that the self-expression of any one speaker would be available to all other speakers of the national language in perpetuity, and an echo chamber in that the creations of individual speakers would orient themselves most naturally and most often to other creations within its bounds. Rooted in the omnipresence of Hebrew or Yiddish in everyday life, education, and culture (hence the monolingualist fervor), this orientation would not be threatened by attention to works in other languages, and would only be enriched by translation. It would produce indigenous literary traditions not by fiat but by simple, unforeseeable cumulation. Jews would come to be "like every people which lives its natural life and spins the thread of its creation *unintentionally and without particular purposes*," as Bistritsky put it. With a universal fundament gained through translation and sustained by constant cultural interchange, a new Jewish culture might be as wide as humanity but also self-contained and self-sustaining.

— 4 —

To Make Our Masses Intellectual

To make our masses intellectual, our intelligentsia Jewish—that is
the goal of the Kultur-Lige.

—*KULTUR-LIGE*, 1919

The year 1918 marked the twenty-fifth anniversary of Yosef Klausner's debut in Hebrew letters and the fifteenth anniversary of his accession to
the editorship of *Ha-Shiloah,* Russia's leading journal of Hebrew literature
and Hebraist and Zionist thought. Among his letters of congratulations
was one from the executive committee of the Tarbut branch in the small
Ukrainian town of Zvinihorodke. The committee expressed the hope that
Klausner's journal—"which was and is the school of the Hebrew intelligentsia"—and its editor would soon have "the merit to ascend to the Land
of Israel . . . and from there to spread its Torah to the reaches of the exile."
The letter was written in the sort of florid, old-fashioned Hebrew that *Ha-
Shiloah* had actually sought to stamp out in favor of lean, modern clarity.
Its trope of a small cultural elite in Palestine disseminating a new national
"Torah" to the Jewish diaspora invoked the ideals of the journal's first editor Ahad Ha-'Am, and was quite out of keeping both with the postwar Zi-
onist movement's heightened commitment to mass mobilization and colo-
nization and with Tarbut's more militant and encompassing vision of total
Hebraization in the diaspora.

Yet the authors of the letter also seemed open to the very different Hebraist vision that Klausner preached. The committee thanked the "author-
teacher" Klausner in particular for his ideas about "the synthesis between
Judaism and humanism"—a topic on which, they informed him, their
branch was concurrently organizing a lecture. As we have seen, by 1917–
1918, the forty-four-year-old Klausner had become a leading advocate for
an ideal of "Hebrew humanism" that combined uncompromising devotion
to Hebrew—a university-educated man completely at home in Russian

and German, Klausner insisted on using Hebrew as much as possible—
with deep contempt for any "parochialism" in Jewish life and culture.
Klausner's Zionism involved not only a right-wing, vitalist, integral nationalism for which he would later become (in)famous in interwar Palestine, but also a vision of transforming blinkered diaspora Jews into cosmopolitan, European Hebrews. When Klausner had first begun to preach this
ideal in the 1890s, it had been seen as the upstart "Hellenism" of a few mad
poets and university students. But by 1918, this Europeanizing Hebraism
was being taught to small-town Ukrainian Jews.[1]

A few months later, Klausner received a note from the young Hebraist
activist and aspiring writer Natan Bistritsky concerning a different facet
of his role as a national "author-teacher." Newly arrived in Kiev on behalf
of Tarbut, Bistritsky hoped to bring the gospel of the new Hebrew culture
not only to those who could already understand the language—migrants
to the city from the "Zvinihorodkes" of the region, as it were—but also
to Kiev's deeply Russified Jewish youth. In particular, he wanted to famil-
iarize them with the poetry of Tchernikhovsky, the vitalist, nationalist
Romantic whom many contemporaries touted as the most "European"
and unparochial of Hebrew poets. Klausner had long championed
Tchernikhovsky in precisely these terms. He had, indeed, anticipated the
young activist's conviction that it was only through exposure to such unparochial poetry that Russified Jews might open up to the fledgling
Hebrew literary culture. He had written a booklet in Russian on
Tchernikhovsky as the "poet of the revival" *(Saul Tshernikhovski—Poet
Vozrozhdeniia)* for that very purpose. Now Klausner's booklet became a
tool for Bistritsky, who deemed it well suited for "the community of young
readers who most need this sort of booklet."[2]

How Klausner reacted to both letters we cannot know, but both most
likely pleased even this cantankerous man, because each seemed guardedly
optimistic about a question that had long troubled him and many fellow
Hebraists: what was to be the relationship between the properly modern,
"European" Hebrew high culture that they sought to create and the larger
"nation" to which it was either conceptually or linguistically foreign? This
question had not really tormented a previous generation of Hebraists, the
men of the 1880s, who assumed that any Hebrew cultural revival would at
first pertain only to members of the secularized traditional elite like themselves and would exert positive effects on most East European Jews only in-
directly, by being a beacon of national revival.[3] Klausner's generation, how-

ever, which had been forged in the age of mass politics and the 1905 Revolution, aspired to a full-fledged Hebraization of East European Jewry, as epitomized by the goals of Tarbut. Moreover, to a far greater degree than their predecessors, they confronted the ever-accelerating Russification of Russian Jewry's more urban, wealthier, and younger elements.

Ultimately, the effort was hampered most by the simple sociological fact that most Russian Jews, traditional or Russified, simply didn't know much Hebrew. It might seem, then, that Yiddishists were in a better position to implant their new culture in Russian Jewry as a whole. Yet Yiddishists faced problems of their own. Hebrew at least commanded unquestioned status among Jews. Yiddish was not only already in decline as a language of everyday life, but was also viewed with indifference by many (arguably most) of its speakers and outright contempt by many more Russified or Polonized Jews. Moreover, although certain aspects of the new Yiddish literature had become visible to a mass audience, especially through mass-circulation dailies, in the years before the war, Yiddishism was in many respects far less institutionally developed than its Hebraist competitor: only within the last decade had proponents of the language acquired proper publishing houses and founded the first secular Yiddish schools.

Against this backdrop, Yiddishists, like Hebraists, considered dissemination to be not a given, but an urgent challenge. One of the most hypertrophic elements of Kalman Zingman's Yiddishist utopia *Edeniya,* first discussed in Chapter 2, was its lovingly detailed fantasy of a single, unitary, secular, Yiddish-language culture shared by the city's entire Jewish population. Zingman imagined a world in which both religious tradition and assimilation had been utterly defeated by the secular intelligentsia's cultural project. In Edeniya, there is no trace of traditional religious practice or of Eastern Europe's Orthodox Jewish population. Although the central character possesses a traditional knowledge of Jewish texts, Judaism persists only as aesthetic experience, as shown in the holiday celebration or the lecture on Peretz's Hasidic stories.

By the same token, in Edeniya, Russification and assimilation have been completely reversed in all domains of East European Jewish life. Zingman's choice to set his Yiddishist utopia not in Vilna or even Warsaw or Kiev but in Kharkov, an industrial city whose prewar Jewish population had been famously and precociously Russified, was itself part of the utopia.[4] *Edeniya* matched this symbolism of place with a fantasy centering on the relationship among generation, gender, and language. In the utopia's penultimate scene at the lecture on Peretz, the novelist's artistic gaze lingers on a pair of "darkly beautiful" female university students conversing enthusiastically about "contemporary" Yiddish literature. At the end of the lecture, as "the thousand-headed youthful audience" erupts in applause, the women students in the audience let fly the flowers they are wont to throw to "their favorite professors." An embarrassing piece of wish fulfillment on Zingman's part, this last detail was also a clever way to capture, in miniature, culturist dreams of overcoming Russification. By 1917, it was a grim article of faith among both Hebraists and Yiddishists that their projects had barely reached Jewish women, especially educated Jewish women. These women—who not incidentally included sisters, relations, and love interests of the young men who dominated culturist ranks—were deemed particularly vulnerable to the attractions of Russian, Polish, and other metropolitan cultures.[5] Zingman's beautiful *studentki* throwing flowers to a lecturer on Peretz, however absurd, thus offered a perfect metonymic shorthand for the triumph of Yiddishism over the juggernaut of Russian metropolitan culture in the hearts and minds of the empire's Jews.[6]

Finally, and most fundamentally, Zingman's utopia elides any distinction of cultural habitus among the city's Jews. All of the novel's characters are indistinguishable in any way except generationally, and all of them—Kindishman's guide, the guide's charming daughters, Kindishman's lover and muse Naomi, and of course the enthusiastic crowd at the lecture—are equally enthusiastic about the new Jewish culture. In Edeniya, everyone belongs to the intelligentsia.

Zingman's fantasy vision depicted a central urge of the cultural project at the 1917–1919 juncture. During 1917, Jewish culturists launched efforts of unprecedented scope and ambition to disseminate their culture-in-the-making to the entire East European Jewish population. The most dramatic element of these efforts, and the one most familiar to scholars, was the intensive and rapid development of full-fledged school systems by both Hebraists and Yiddishists. During the 1917–1919 period, both the Hebraist and Yiddishist movements devoted tremendous effort and probably the bulk of their resources to elementary education. For Hebraists, this focus was a demographic necessity; the founding conference of Tarbut recognized that education in the broadest sense was necessarily "the center of our work." Yiddishists did not have to stake their transformational endeavor on formal education to the same degree, given that Yiddish was the vernacular of the large majority of East European Jews. But they too saw children, as yet uncorrupted, as the most likely bearers of their dispensation.

Yet schooling deferred the question of culture's extension to the next generation. How did Jewish culturists attempt to bridge the gap between themselves and other Jewish adults? And what do their efforts tell us about their conception of culture?

The era's most ambitious Jewish cultural organizations, Tarbut and the Kultur-Lige, both viewed the mass dissemination of the new Hebrew or Yiddish secular-national culture as a central task. They dreamed that the new culture might simultaneously replace traditional religiosity, cultural assimilation, and the new Yiddish popular culture of boulevard theater and pulp novels. The notion that the chaotic revolutionary moment offered unprecedented possibilities for such a transformation was not distinctive to the Jewish nationalist intelligentsia. Parallel enthusiasms motivated Ukrainian nationalists in the borderlands and broad swaths of the metropolitan Russian intelligentsia, from writers like Maxim Gorky to the statist liberals of the Provisional Government to significant parts of the revolutionary left.[7] Certain sociological peculiarities of the Jewish case seemed, indeed, especially promising. By contrast with the Russian and Ukrainian cases, Jewish culturists did not have to face (or repress) the reality of an effectively illiterate rural mass. Those whom culturists dubbed the Jewish "folk" or "masses" were actually largely literate, urban, and indeed more thoroughly modernized than culturists themselves recognized. Intoxicated by the unexpected rise in the fortunes of Jewish nationalism in 1917, Jewish culturists were also free of the Russian intelligentsia's dread that their own national "masses" in fact hated them and everything they represented, a fear fed throughout 1917 by peasant jacqueries and the widespread hostility of lower-class Russians toward everything "bourgeois."[8]

Of course, the actual dissemination efforts born of these goals were incessantly and often violently disrupted. For much of 1917–1919, centers like Moscow, Odessa, and Kiev were largely isolated. Yiddishist efforts did not really get under way until 1918; and although the Hebraist project began earlier, its leaders were forced to start from scratch again when they left Bolshevik Russia for Ukraine. The intensification of the Civil War in later 1918 further isolated cultural centers from each other and from the Jewish population in the provincial towns of the borderlands (especially in Ukraine), where a bewildering array of armies warred on each other and on the Jews.

No less a hindrance was the fact that the East European Jewish population targeted for national-cultural transformation was itself radically various and fractured. Disproportionately concentrated in the region's urban centers, the population was also still heavily represented in small towns. Decades of economic transformation had widened the gaps between haves and have-nots within the Jewish population and laid the groundwork for intensifying social conflict within it.

Culturally, a substantial portion of this putative nation was already deeply acculturated to Russian or Polish metropolitan culture, a trend that would only be intensified by the new possibilities and pressures of the revolutionary era.[9] At the same time, another substantial part of the Jewish population remained committed to traditional East European Judaism in its various forms, though with varying degrees of self-conscious opposition to modern movements and temptations. Although this way of life now became still more porous and embattled, it remained significant not only in smaller Jewish communities but even in most of the cities where the new Jewish nationalist and culturist intelligentsia had its home. For many traditionalist Jews, culturist ideology with its humanist valuing of art and self-expression above or against piety and law, with its frank preference for the cultural forms of non-Jewish Europe over those of the rabbinic tradition, could only be anathema: as one Hasidic leader put it in the 1920s, the "sickness" caused by the "deadly poison" of "free literature" (sifrut hofshit) had "torn away from us our sons and daughters with a breach that will never heal."[10]

By 1917, most Jews in the rump empire were probably neither fully Russified nor fully committed to orthodox Judaism; certainly, orthodox circles deemed their version of Judaism to be in terrible crisis.[11] In that sense, by 1917 substantial parts of the region's Jews had become far more receptive to the general terms of the Jewish nationalist cultural project than had been the case thirty or even fifteen years earlier. Yet the decline of traditional Judaism did not mean an embrace of secularism or a full-fledged European culture: this amorphous and as yet understudied population lived a hybrid cultural life very different from the forms of cultural practice and ideals advocated by the intelligentsia.

The concern of this chapter, however, lies not in cultural outcomes but in culturist intentions, and what they reveal about the Jewish cultural project itself. How did culturists seek to bring their culture to this broad and variegated mass of non-intelligentsia? How, by 1917, had they come to conceive the proper relationship between their desire to forge a Jewish high culture on a par with Europe's metropoles and the desire to carry out the mass cultural reformation of East European Jewry? As of 1917, Jewish culturists freed of state interference might have chosen to create, alongside their own high culture, a second nationalist "popular" culture tailored to the imagined needs of these masses and imperatives of identity formation—to give East European Jewry, in Matthew Arnold's words, "an intellectual food prepared and adapted in the way they think proper for the actual condition of the masses." Such behavior would have been in keeping with regnant assumptions about the innate authoritarian-populist tendencies of East European nationalisms. Yet it seems that during this period both Hebraism and Yiddishism embraced a very different vision: the belief that the whole of the nation could share in the intelligentsia's elite culture without compromising that culture itself. In fact, although culturist dissemination efforts were laden with contradictory impulses, one of the most powerful of these was what might be called an elevationist ethos. The Kultur-Lige wished to "make our masses *inteligent.*" Tarbut aspired "to make the works of Hebrew culture the possession of the entire people." "Elitist" in its fierce desire to stamp out "low" culture, this sensibility was thus democratic in its urge to abolish the gap between intelligentsia and folk by making everyone *"inteligent,"* capable of enjoying and even creating high culture.[12]

Zingman's utopian fantasy thus captured an aspiration to cultural revolution in Jewish society that was shared by culturists across all their linguistic-ideological, political, and aesthetic divides. At the same time, *Edeniya* sketched a second kind of relationship between culture and the public: in his fantasy-city, the new Yiddish culture is not merely the object of public enthusiasm, but also a public good instantiated in the state and entirely supported by state funding. The state itself, we are told, controls paper, assigns the hours that a printer works, publishes cultural texts in an "all-nationality printing house," and supports artists of merit. Though works of art are produced freely by individual artists, the members of a *bildungs-rat* (Commissariat of Enlightenment) within the regional "kultur-lige" decide what should be published. They do so on purely aesthetic or scholarly grounds, Zingman assures the reader, presumably because in this ideal future, all political divisions have been resolved. The astonishing statism and deeply censorial sensibility embedded in this vision deserves further examination in another context. Here what is significant is the other implication of all this state support: all cultural products in Edeniya are free.

Zingman's effacement of any nexus between capital and culture reflects in part the lineage of the deep, almost reflexive anticapitalism common to Eastern Europe's intelligentsias, as evidenced by an arresting spatial metaphor: asked why no shops are to be seen, Kindishman's guide explains that the city has been reorganized into separate "production-quarters, consumption-quarters, and culture-quarters."[13] Culture is sacred, and cannot be profaned by mere production or consumption. *Edeniya* here also offers a fantasy resolution to one of the deepest predicaments of the Jewish cultural project: its economic weakness (which held true for both Hebrew and Yiddish culture, albeit for different reasons). Exacerbated by the disruptions and hyperinflation of the era, this economic weakness was nevertheless more deeply rooted in precisely the situation that culturists hoped to overcome in their dissemination efforts: the relatively low levels of public support for, and hence consumption of, the new culture. Going beyond even the command-economy pricing mechanisms later used by the Soviet Union, Zingman's vision freed Yiddish culture utterly from the market— meaning, at the level of fantasy, from the cruel collective logic of the actual Jewish population's revealed preferences. It also imagined that even stateless Jewish culture could benefit from support by the substitute on which all metropolitan modern cultural spheres depended to some degree: the ostensible representative of the public's better self, the state.

In this respect too, Zingman's utopia points to an essential feature of the culturist endeavor at the 1917 conjuncture. Even as they dreamed of national communion and equality in culture, Jewish culturists sought ways to sustain and institutionalize their new culture that would be independent of mass support. In particular, they sought to decouple culture from the market.

Creating an Audience

Dissemination efforts launched after February were entirely dominated by proponents of mutually exclusive, radically monolingual Hebraist and Yiddishist cultural ideologies. In the years before the Revolution, the primary candidate for the coordination of any large-scale project of cultural dissemination would have been the Russificatory OPE. But the collapse of the Russificatory impulse among Jewish nationally minded intelligentsia did not even have to await the OPE's implosion in 1917. Already during the war years, ascendant Yiddishist elements within the organization were working to erase its Russophilic tendencies. In 1915, Zelig Melamed (the

Yiddishist activist who would later play a central role in the organization of Kiev's Kultur-Lige) had argued as a member of the organization's library committee that OPE-supported Jewish libraries should not purchase Russian-language translations of Jewish authors or any Russian-language literature for children. In 1916, such Yiddishist sensibilities had become the rule rather than the exception when the OPE decided that all of its refugee schools had to operate primarily in Yiddish.[14]

Hebraist and Yiddishist visions of dissemination conceived their audiences differently. Most Hebraists claimed to speak to the whole of the "nation" regardless of class or religiosity; this was the official policy of Tarbut. By contrast, organized Yiddishism of the Kultur-Lige's variety was increasingly dominated by political and cultural radicalism, which posited only the "masses" and the "intelligentsia" as the legitimate bearers of Jewish culture (and inheritors of the Jewish future).

In practice, however, both Hebraist and Yiddishist efforts addressed the same two constituencies. On the one hand, both had to address themselves to relatively educated (and increasingly Russified) audiences, usually conceived under the overlapping categories of "the youth" and the "Jewish intelligentsia." Socialist Yiddishists loudly excluded "the bourgeoisie" from their purview in a way that Hebraist efforts did not, but arguably, most of the actual population delineated by terms like "the intelligentsia" and "the youth" actually consisted of members of the professional classes as well as the children of Russia's Jewish middle- and lower-middle classes. On the other hand, both sides vied for the "masses" or "folk." Though these terms themselves were of course ideologically overdetermined, they nevertheless captured the sociological reality of an array of potential publics for whom modern high culture as such, Russian or Jewish, had hitherto been at least partly inaccessible: the Jewish lower classes living in Ukraine's cities and in refugee communities in Russia, and the Jewish population outside urban centers. Hebraists and Yiddishists alike imagined these "masses" as literate but uncultivated, rooted in tradition and hence backward—or worse, debased by exposure to Yiddish boulevard culture.

Hebraists and Yiddishists evidently hoped to reach their more educated target audience primarily through the products of high culture itself, especially the arts. In Kiev, the Kultur-Lige organized a rich menu of cultural events in all the arts (although some of these initiatives, particularly in the nonliterary arts, only bore fruit later under the very different conditions inaugurated by active Soviet involvement in Jewish cultural life). Recollections of outside observers suggest that much of this activity presupposed a sophisticated audience.[15] Thus, in Moscow, the founders of Ha-Bimah and their supporters in Tarbut conceived one of the Hebrew theater company's chief tasks as creating productions that would appeal to an audience already immersed in the aesthetic standards of Russian theater.[16]

The degree to which these organizations actively sought to draw in fully Russified Jews is difficult to establish. Although the Kultur-Lige declared one of its goals the "yiddishization" of the Jewish intelligentsia, I have found little trace of Yiddishist cultural propaganda in Russian. The Kultur-Lige did not produce anything like the 1918 anthology *Evreiskii mir* (Moscow), which brought together local Yiddishists like Niger with Russified Jews interested in the question of Jewish culture and sought to acquaint Russified Jewish readers with Yiddish literature in translation (see ch. 2). This may be because the contempt of the organization's leaders for the "bourgeoisie" and deep populist commitments inclined them to focus on creating a "folks-intelligentsia" from below. But more likely, they simply assumed that most Russified Jewish youth could be reached in Yiddish too.

By contrast, Hebraists could make no such assumption about linguistic accessibility. Nor, with the exception of the movement's Marxist left, were they formally hostile to any class. Consequently, Hebraists made substantial efforts to make their cultural attainments and goals visible in Russian. As I noted in Chapter 1, Hebraists in Moscow and Odessa founded two Russian-language publishing houses, Safrut and Kinneret, that sought not to cultivate a separate Jewish culture in Russian but rather to propound Hebraist ideals among Russian-language readers.

For both Yiddishists and Hebraists, the most promising way to reach the educated and urbane elements of Russian Jewry was through formal adult education. In centers like Kiev and Moscow, the Kultur-Lige and Tarbut could offer students access to leading intellectuals and artists. In Kiev, students at the Kultur-Lige's *folks-universitet* studied Yiddish literature with the formidable theoretician Litvakov and the European classics with A. Koralnik, who would later become one of Yiddish literature's most interesting literary critics; in Moscow, adult students of Hebrew studied with Ha-Bimah's Menahem Gnesin.[17]

Hebraists and Yiddishists also launched efforts of unprecedented scope to bring their new Jewish cultures to a much broader public. At one level, this involved essentially propagandistic efforts to foster ideological—and emotional—commitment by the masses. Free to organize on a national level, both Tarbut and the Kultur-Lige moved to link fundraising to consciousness-raising. Tarbut planned the creation of "a great cultural fund to meet our essential needs."[18] The Kultur-Lige created a similar fund, the "Yiddish Culture-Fund in Memory of Mendele, Peretz, and Sholem Aleichem." Though intended in part to raise money, these fundraising efforts were primarily designed to engage the mass public. The *Kultur-Fond* solicited support in such miniscule sums as five, ten, and fifty kopeks while Tarbut, amply supported by its wealthy patrons, set the initial membership fee at a single ruble so that "all ranks of the folk" might participate as equals in "the work of the people."[19]

Tarbut and the Kultur-Lige also sought to project the new culture into Jewish public life. As part of the Ukrainian Zionist movement's "Week for the Land of Israel" in autumn 1918, Tarbut called on local branches to organize public performances of Hebrew poetry or drama by children and gatherings for adults with Hebrew "lectures, plays, declamation, music, and so forth." The letter emphasized the importance of working with the local Zionist branches in charge of the events to ensure that Hebrew culture would have a clear presence.[20] At roughly the same time, the Kultur-Lige held a "Week of Culture" during which local branches in some seventy locations offered "concerts, lectures, spectacles." Organizers deemed the event "the first great demonstration for the new Yiddish culture."[21]

For Hebraists and Yiddishists, however, it was not enough to create broad interest in the new culture through spectacle. They sought to generate more sustained popular engagement as well. One well-established strategy was the creation of "model institutions" and guidance to ideologically compatible local initiatives. In Kiev, the Kultur-Lige gradually forged ties with a range of workers' clubs, cooperatives, and professional unions that already had adult education programs, theatrical circles, and libraries—and that, by late 1918, showed an interest in "joint cultural work" with organized Yiddishist forces. By April 1919, it had ties to similar bodies in Kharkov, Odessa, Berdichev, Ekaterinoslav, Zhitomir, Uman, Beletserkove, Rovne, and Homel.[22]

But Tarbut and the Kultur-Lige also aspired to have a much more direct influence over nonelite cultural consumers. Both organizations placed great hopes on local branches that might coordinate local events, raise funds, and support the backbone institutions of secular cultural life: elementary schools, adult courses, libraries, and drama clubs. This branch strategy was especially central to Tarbut and Kultur-Lige efforts to project their versions of Jewish culture into the provincial towns, where roughly half the East European Jewish population still lived. Cultural activists in Russia and Ukraine had initially hoped to bring the fruits of the new Jewish culture to the "provinces" through traveling lectures, readings, theater productions, exhibitions, and museum exhibits, but Revolutionary-era conditions disrupted these plans. By contrast, branches proliferated, even in small towns. By November 1917, Tarbut had seventy-nine branches, mostly in European Russia; by early 1919, the Kultur-Lige had more than one hundred in Ukraine, and Tarbut some two hundred.[23]

These branches were meant to encourage local cultural initiative and enthusiasm, but they were also supposed to follow the cultural blueprints of the overarching organizations. Thus, Tarbut was not merely content to seek symbolic support from the provinces, but sought to ensure that local branches would adhere to its goal of using Hebrew as much as possible, in as many settings as feasible. Although its platform offered membership to any man or woman who espoused its goals, it also stipulated that the leadership elected by any branch had to be able to actually conduct the meetings in Hebrew.[24]

In a different vein, Hebraists and especially Yiddishists explored new ways of bringing secular Hebrew or Yiddish culture to a larger audience. Jewish culturists remained as convinced after the Revolution as before it that the printed book would be the cornerstone of the new Jewish culture and consciousness. As Kiev's Yiddishist Folks-Farlag put it: "the Yiddish book must become our cult, our form of worship."[25] One goal was to cultivate a coming generation of readers. The flagship publication of Moscow's Tarbut-affiliated Omanut publishing house was the children's journal *Shetilim,* which devoted extensive effort to orienting young readers toward both modern Hebrew literature and European history and culture. It sought to create a new generation of cultural consumers who would simultaneously seek sophisticated forms of culture yet also naturally progress "into the world of our Hebrew literature."[26]

Most ambitiously, some cultural activists sought to develop means of direct, immersive high-cultural education whereby adult audiences might rapidly acquire the capacity and desire to participate in elite culture. Some Hebraists cherished such hopes, as evidenced by Ha-Bimah's initial conception of its task as not only aesthetic but educative: "to promote the study and spread of Hebrew dramatic art among Jews" through Hebrew theater classes as well as public lectures and performances.[27] Yiddishists pursued such dreams empowered by their twin assumptions, however illusory, that their linguistic commitments gave them unmediated contact with the "Yiddish masses" and that their high culture was somehow directly linked to the folk. The Kultur-Lige's approach to art education reflected this sensibility in two ways. First, the organization envisioned an ongoing program of mass education in the history of Jewish artistic expression, centering on a "universal Jewish museum" that would gather "all the artistic creations of the Jewish people in every sphere of human culture." By this means and through traveling exhibitions, the masses would be educated in "their own" folk-art tradition. But their tastes would also be cultivated, so that they might become intelligentsia-like consumers and indeed creators of a new, evolving Jewish art: once the Jewish public was "acquainted with the treasures that exist" it would be "easier to cooperate toward the creation of new ones."[28]

At the same time, some in the organization cherished still more ambitious goals, imagining that the mass audience might be educated to appreciate avant-garde Jewish art. This sensibility was evident in the organization's decision to recruit avant-garde artists for its stamps, as well as in the Kultur-Lige's art exhibition organized in Kiev in April 1920. Smaller than previous Jewish art exhibitions of 1917–1918 in Petrograd and Moscow, it had an ambitious outreach agenda: the art section brought in groups from local educational institutions (most of them presumably Yiddishist institutions affiliated with the Kultur-Lige), employed the artists themselves as exhibition guides, and organized discussions with the artists and Yiddish literati.[29]

The Elevationist Ethos

What these last elements of culturist dissemination programs indicate is a deep desire to bridge the cultural gap between the intelligentsia and the masses without compromising culture as the intelligentsia understood and valued it. In seeking to wrest cultural dissemination from the corruptions of the market, choke off popular culture at its source, and replace the patchwork culture of East European Jewry with unified secular, monolinguistic Hebrew or Yiddish cultures, the culturist intelligentsia was clearly seeking cultural authority. But the entire project was also infused with an intense democratizing telos.

The signal feature of both Yiddishist and Hebraist cultural practice in this period was a deep optimism that high culture could be attractive and accessible to all. This is why both the Kultur-Lige and Tarbut set leading intellectuals and artists to work in adult education programs, and why the Yiddishist Visnshaft publishing house in Ekaterinoslav assured readers that "we know that more than anything, the reader needs classic literature. And we intend to meet this burning need first and foremost."[30] Some extended this optimism to include even the most abstruse forms of modernism—consider those Hebraist and Yiddishist publishers who solicited the most sophisticated Russian-Jewish plastic artists to illustrate their books or the Hebraist and Yiddishist drama troupes that presented challenging modes of modernist stagecraft to mass audiences.

As further evidence of their democratic intent, the Jewish intelligentsia of 1917–1919 eschewed any program calling for the creation of a separate, second-tier "national-popular" culture for the masses. Like some Russian and other regional intelligentsias, the Jewish nationalist intelligentsia had at various junctures cultivated precisely this idea: during the Ḥibat-Tsion movement of the 1880s and 1890s, for example, some leading adherents juggled a commitment to the goal of a modern Hebrew culture with the production of poetry and novels in Yiddish designed for the "folk." The second-tier approach was also evident in the Jewish socialist Bund during the first years of the twentieth century (and beyond). As the then-Bundist activist Moyshe Olgin noted critically in 1909, his fellow Bundist intellectuals had essentially produced a narrow Yiddish popular-radical culture for the movement's followers while living their own inner lives with Russian literary and intellectual traditions.[31]

By contrast, Tarbut's program of disseminating the new Hebrew culture on a mass level, coupled with its uncompromising hostility to Yiddish, represented a rejection of the whole classic mode of bifurcated Hebraist activity. Certainly, most East European Jews' relative ignorance of Hebrew meant that Tarbut especially was compelled to develop outreach programs that could only be symbolic and ritualistic (it also meant that as a matter of practice, the organization devoted most of its money and energy to the education of children). But given this vast sociological challenge, Tarbut's organizers were willing to countenance remarkably little compromise of their Hebraist ideals.

Yiddishists were perhaps even more furiously puritanical, in part because the reviled Jewish popular culture stood in uncomfortable linguistic proximity to theirs. The founders of a Yiddishist theater group in Kharkov aimed to create "a true artistic theater in place of the surrogate for the masses which has hitherto obtained."[32] Spokesmen for the Kultur-Lige defined the organization's Yiddishism in part by organization's effort, as they saw it, to provide "in all realms of its work . . . not cheap peddler's merchandise [*bilige pak-skhoyre*], but rather products of fundamental cultural worth. The activists of the Kultur-Lige have kept in mind that popular does not mean vulgar, that bringing culture to the masses does not mean giving them something which would not be acceptable to oneself."[33]

The elevationist ethos found its ultimate expression in the culturist desire—bordering on obsession—to transform cultural consumers into cultural producers. As mentioned earlier, the Yiddishists of the Kultur-Lige, for whom the social gap between intelligentsia and folk could only be experienced as a scandal, imagined that general adult educational programs like the Kultur-Lige's Kiev *folks-universitet* might allow the "Jewish folkmasses" to "create their own intelligentsia."[34] In early 1919, the Yiddishist intelligentsia of Kiev was gripped with excitement over the appearance of a twenty-two-year-old playwright named Beynish Shteyman. Some of this excitement had to do with Shteyman's flawed but arresting experiments in expressionist drama. But much of it had to do with Shteyman's inspirational life story.

Born to poor parents and educated solely in the *ḥeder,* the traditional Jewish elementary school, he had left for the big city and studied to become a pharmacist. In the cultural imagination of the Yiddishist intelligentsia, this rather typical path led to one of two dismal ends: either upward mobility and assimilation or a sad diminution back in the shtetl as a petit-bourgeois pharmacist. Indeed, the most important Yiddish novel of the period, Dovid Bergelson's *Opgang,* revolved around a character with this very trajectory (Bergelson condemned the poor idealist-turned-pharmacist to suicide). But after serving in the army, Shteyman returned to his small town Kreslavke not to open a pharmacy but to found a Yiddish school and dramatic circle. He transformed himself, moreover, not only into a Yiddishist but into a creator of Yiddish culture—into a Yiddish playwright as well as a would-be modernist who set himself the task of translating Oscar Wilde's *Picture of Dorian Gray* and "Salome" and then turned to expressionist drama. Shteyman died in August 1919, while serving in the ranks of the Red forces mobilized to hold Kiev against the advancing Whites. But for Yiddishists hungry to believe in the possibility of true cultural dissemination, he remained a symbol. His obituary in the Yiddishist anthology *Oyfgang* presented him as a sign of a larger cultural apotheosis: "the proudest sign" that the "churned-up earth" of Jewish life was now fertile, that such fertile earth "already exists, and shoots are growing."[35]

In short, by 1917, the goal of virtually all organized Jewish cultural activity was precisely the elimination of the gap between intelligentsia and "folk"—not the creation of a new secular cultural hierarchy in place of the old, but the formation of a single "culture-nation."[36] The elevationist ideal at work in 1917–1919 was the outcome of a longstanding inner struggle by Jewish culturists to reconcile the intrinsic tensions between the cultivation of a high culture and their felt obligations to the wider Jewish public. The decade before 1917 had brought these tensions to an unbearable pitch. As Yiddishists had grown more unabashed in conceiving a Yiddish high culture as a legitimate end in itself—that is, as they had become Yiddishists— they had found themselves at odds with the lingering imperatives of the populist mission that had first moved them to cultivate culture in Yiddish.

Thus, in 1908, the pioneering Vilna Yiddish literary journal *Literarishe monatsshriften* had scandalized the pro-Yiddish socialist and populist intelligentsia not only by its brazen demands for a separation between Yiddish culture and Jewish politics but also by its eagerness to embrace complex forms of literature manifestly inaccessible to a mass readership. From the journal's opening pages, the editors proclaimed the right of Yiddish literature to develop in accordance with the interests of the intelligentsia rather than the needs of the masses. Yet for all their bravado, the intellectuals and writers of *Literarishe monatsshriften* had never been willing to abandon their responsibilities (as they saw it) to the "underdeveloped reader." Before and during Russia's 1905 Revolution, the three editors of the journal and many of their fellow Yiddishists had sought to reshape "the nation" or "the folk" directly, as activists in Russia's Jewish nationalist and socialist-nationalist movements. Ironically, this same nationalism, alloyed with a growing idealization of *Kultur,* had then compelled them to distance themselves from that "folk" so that they might have the freedom to cultivate a proper modern Jewish culture. But this same nationalism had also made it impossible for them to go as far as the Russian and French avant-gardes in their proclaimed indifference to audience. Declaring their independence from unmediated, direct service to the mass reader, the editors of the *Literarishe monatsshriften* nevertheless hoped to reach and elevate them to the level of the intelligentsia itself: "The goal of *Literarishe monatsshriften* is to be an assembly point for that which should be able to make our spiritual world richer, enlarge our cultural possession, improve the taste of the old reader and win new ones; step by step he approaches, the new reader. *Literarishe monatsshriften* wants to speed his coming and increase his number."[37]

Coming from a nearly opposite sociolinguistic and sociocultural starting point, Hebraists had converged on the same dilemma. As I have noted, the de facto (and often rather frank) elitism of late-nineteenth-century Hebraism had given way since the turn of the century to a growing desire to find a Hebraism that would somehow bridge the gap between literati and the nation. The mass dissemination dreams of Tarbut were anticipated by the programs of organizations like 'Ivriah (founded in 1906) and Tarbut's own direct ancestor, the Ḥoveve Sfat 'Ever (founded in 1908), which had established some sixty branches and founded a substantial number of local educational programs and libraries in Russia despite harassment by tsarist authorities.[38] Facing the rise of Yiddishism and a material crisis of Hebrew publishing after 1900, growing numbers of Hebraists had come to believe that the formation of a high culture inaccessible to most Jews for the foreseeable future was both irresponsible and potentially fatal. Yet while some Jewish culturists who had once entertained Hebraist ideals now abandoned Hebraism for Yiddishism, a core group remained for whom abandonment of Hebrew culture itself was unthinkable.

February and the events that flowed from it seemed initially to offer culturists on both sides of this divide an unprecedented opportunity to cut their respective Gordian knots. They might have sought to do so via a two-tiered approach or via elevation. Their choice of the far less realistic approach of elevation represented culturist sensibilities ascendant well before 1917. Back in 1908, *Literarishe monatsshriften* had presaged the Kultur-Lige's curt dismissal of the two-tiered option virtually word for word. Contrasting itself with the Russophile OPE, the journal had contemptuously declared that it would make no place for "*filantropishe kultur-tregeray,* for popular, counterfeit literature 'for the people.' The literature which is specially designed for a low degree of development is no artistic literature, just as the aspiration to 'lower oneself to the people' is absolutely not a democratic aspiration." By 1917, this once minority-held stance had not only become a point of wide agreement but also achieved institutional stability in durable formal organizations that fully rejected the idea of diluted culture.[39]

The Social Limits of Elevation

If the freedom and promise of 1917–1919 spurred Jewish culturists to formulate grand plans and articulate fundamental principles of cultural dissemination, the actual chaotic conditions of the era afforded them precious little opportunity to enact them.[40] Culturist efforts did find a much larger and hungrier audience than pessimists had feared. Arriving in Kiev in 1918, Ben-Tsion Dinur discovered "hundreds of young people with Jewish and general educations who saw themselves as the future bearers of Jewish culture and its various manifestations." The same picture emerges from recollections of Kiev's Yiddish cultural milieu by the Hebraist educator and Zionist activist Zeev Livneh:

> The Yiddishists in Kiev also developed a very extensive operation . . . The literary critics Dobrushin, Litvak, Litvakov, the brothers Yashe and Lipe Reznik and others would appear at meetings of the literary circles and a large audience would listen to them. Many of the youth participated in the arguments about literature. It all bubbled with vitality and enthusiasm.[41]

The participation of a large, enthusiastic audience of young people at the cutting edge of Yiddishist cultural debate was precisely the sort of achievement of which Jewish culturists dreamed. Yet sources like Livneh also suggest that those who came were drawn from a cohort already oriented toward the Jewish cultural project ideologically, or who were at least sociologically primed to embrace it. Dinur recalls that the large audiences for the new forms of Yiddish and Hebrew culture in Kiev consisted mainly of teachers and trainees in Kiev's Jewish pedagogical institutions, party workers, newspapermen, and hundreds of Jewish students. Another source amplifies this insight. The Kultur-Lige's Jewish Folk-University, founded in 1918, offered tracks in the sciences, the social sciences, and the study of Jewish culture. Although about seventy-eight of the approximately one hundred eighty students who attended in 1918 enrolled in the program on Jewish literature, history, and language, only nineteen of these could be categorized as the "workers or salaried people" whom Yiddishists had hoped to reach. The rest were "student youth"—evidently, people of the same cultural and professional background as their Yiddishist teachers.[42]

Some of these people may have come from the more Russified circles that Zingman and other culturists dreamed of reclaiming. That culturist efforts to reach more fully Russified figures did enjoy some success is suggested by the as yet only partially reconstructed history of those cultural producers who turned from Russian to Hebrew culture in this period, even before they emigrated to Palestine. These included many of the actors in Ha-Bimah and the extraordinary case of Zhirkova (Elisheva).[43] Yet for the most part, what the sources suggest is that despite their dual obsession with recapturing assimilated youth and reaching the benighted folk, the Jewish culturists mostly tapped into a new cohort of the same sort of people with whom the cultural project had always been linked: secularized youth from thickly Jewish cultural backgrounds with substantial exposure to metropolitan culture and a preexisting interest in the forms and values of *Kultur*.

It is worth noting that the close sociological proximity between the tutelary intelligentsia and its audiences sits uncomfortably with the common scholarly image of cultural intelligentsias as authoritarian *Kulturtraeger* imposing their views on voiceless subalterns. At the same time, this actual proximity testifies to the shortfall between intelligentsia dreams of a common culture and the difficulties of getting beyond the magic circle that had always circumscribed the cultural project. In a larger sense, too, culturist dreams of a common culture faced some very large obstacles.

Some of these obstacles were of culturists' own making. Yiddishist social radicalism virtually foreclosed substantial recruitment among the region's Jewish bourgeoisie, yet a great many of those whom leftists considered "workers" were in fact drawn either to traditionalism or to Zionist and Hebraist principles.[44] In addition, the vitriolic antireligious dimensions of much Yiddishist discourse and practice apparently alienated many who were otherwise sympathetic to Yiddishist principles. Striking evidence of this was the marked gender imbalance in Yiddishist schools: Jewish parents in Ukraine and later in independent Eastern Europe were far more willing to send daughters to these secularist schools than their sons, whom they considered the bearers of the core traditions that many still valued.[45]

Other obstacles sprang up where sociological realities met the ideological aspirations of the culturists. By contrast with the Kultur-Lige, the Hebraism represented by Tarbut targeted the entire Jewish community. Indeed, its declared openness to religious people led it to overrule secularist pedagogues who dominated its educational wing to allow single-gender schools, conceding that where local conditions—to wit, religious parents—demanded it, separate schools might be established. Hebraists and Zionists, unlike Yiddishists, had some access to religious society and could even recruit in synagogues.[46] Yet Hebraists could only take limited pleasure in Yiddishist self-limitation. Their own successes among those whom Yiddishists, as well as some radical Hebraists, called "the masses" only underscored the gap between the ideological appeal of their principles and the actual possibilities of transmitting Hebrew culture to a population that was largely Hebrew-illiterate.

Two examples from the Ukraine, one of the centers of Hebraist and Zionist success, illustrate the problem that Hebraists faced. In the small, largely Jewish town of Shpikov, local Hebraist and Zionist activists enjoyed broad public support and drew enthusiastic crowds to their lectures. But a memoirist's description of one of these lectures, declaimed by his older brother who was like him the product of a Hebraist household, is telling: "He would open the speech in Hebrew, continue in Yiddish, and end in Hebrew with a poem by Bialik or Tchernikhovsky." The "thunderous applause" that followed his speeches may have been a tribute to the symbolic evocation of Hebrew culture that bookended the speech—but the middle bit evidently needed to be in Yiddish in order for the audience to understand the actual arguments.[47]

Even in larger centers, the limits of Hebrew culture could be stark. During 1917 and 1918, Zionist organizations in the city of Uman sponsored a series of theatrical performances by what seems to have been a single group of amateur actors. These performances were evidently framed by the Hebraist principles formally adopted by Russia's Zionist organizations in 1917. Organizers printed up some of their playbills in Hebrew even though there could not possibly be any audience that needed them, and the actors themselves assumed typological Hebrew stage names like Yehudi (Jew), Bat Shalom (Daughter of Peace), and Ish Ḥofshi (A Free Man). But the troupe's performances themselves were almost entirely in Yiddish. Other than the Zionist national anthem "Ha-Tikvah" and some Hebrew songs about Jewish life in Palestine, the only glimmer of Hebrew high culture evident across a half-dozen handbills was one declamation of Bialik's poem "Levadi." And in one case, even the obligatory poem by the Hebrew national poet was his one major Yiddish poem "Dos letste vort." Most outrageous of all from a Hebraist standpoint, the staple of the troupe's performances were Yiddish plays by the recently deceased Sholem Aleichem, who, though a Zionist, was manifestly a Yiddish writer.[48]

There were examples of Hebraist success, to be sure. Even in provincial settings, there was serious engagement in the practices of the new Hebrew high culture. At a Hebraist high school in the heavily Jewish town of Vinitse in southern Ukraine, the young teacher-in-training Baruch Tshemerinsky mounted several Hebrew-language productions with his students in 1917–1918. He also headed a local drama society. Within two years, he was accepted into Ha-Bimah.[49]

But the gap between broad public support for the ideals of Hebraism and the hard sociolinguistic fact of a Yiddish- and Russian-speaking population was wide, and even radical Hebraists had to compromise on some points. Hebraist activists in Kiev demanded that *kehillah*-sponsored adult education programs teach "Hebrew, Hebrew literature, Jewish history, and knowledge of the Land of Israel" in Hebrew. But a draft of their proposal allowed, hesitantly, that while "in principle the language of instruction in evening classes for adults must be Hebrew," in practice "the language of instruction in the evening courses for adults might also be the spoken language [Yiddish], in accordance with the desire of the students."[50]

Moreover, Tarbut's compromising stance with regard to matters of religion, though no doubt effective in winning over some of the many Jews who combined Zionist-Hebraist and traditional sympathies, was not enough to make its essentially secular humanist Hebraism palatable to many traditionalists. The year 1917 marked not only a watershed in secular Jewish political and cultural endeavor, but also, as historians have recently begun to acknowledge, a new stage in the consolidation of a theologically uncompromising Orthodox counterculture. Not only Yiddishists faced the activism of *Akhdesnikes* (adherents of *Aḥdut,* an ultra-Orthodox political movement in Ukraine and Lithuania).[51] In Ukraine, a heartland of Hasidism, Tarbut also encountered substantial resistance from Orthodox circles.[52]

Finally, over the course of 1917–1919, both Hebraists and Yiddishists came to realize that neither their opponents in the opposite camp nor the Orthodox presented the greatest challenge to their cultural endeavor. The obdurate reality of continued acculturation by many East European Jews was this primary challenge. In 1918, an article in the pedagogical journal of the Kultur-Lige mocked a group of privately founded high schools where children of "the middle class" could continue to study in Russian and receive *praves* (official credentials). The journal scornfully accused these "middle class" parents of sabotaging pedagogical and cultural progress in favor of harsh discipline, uniforms with gold buttons, and "*klasne nastavnikes*" (using a crudely Yiddishized version of the Russian term *klassnyi nastavnik,* a sort of class preceptor and disciplinarian of the pre-revolutionary state school system, to parody both the conservative sensibilities and the continued Russificatory tendencies that they saw in these schools).[53] Yet beneath its hazy mix of Marxist and moralistic rhetoric, this critique reflected a recognition that for many Russian and Ukrainian Jews, culture still meant Russian culture.

Outwitting the Market

Partly in response to these realities, Jewish culturists sought ways to establish their new culture without mass support, if need be. First, many of them dreamed of harnessing the financial and institutional power of the state. In post-February Russia and Ukraine both, culturists sought and sometimes gained financial support from local, state-sponsored authorities such as the Jewish *kehillot* and even some municipal administrations *(zemstva).*[54] The most dramatic support occurred in Ukraine from December 1917 through April 1918, when real national autonomy led to state funding on a meaningful scale for secular Jewish education. Culturists entertained hopes of going beyond this support for schools to gain direct state support for the production of Jewish high culture. Such hopes flourished briefly when, in December 1918, the fall of Ukraine's German-backed Hetmanate at the hands of the Ukrainian nationalist-radical Directory led to the restoration of a Jewish ministry in Ukraine.[55]

These efforts to secure state support were both practical-minded and indicative of more encompassing notions of using the state to help institutionalize, legitimize, and even impose the new culture. Some Jewish nationalists looked forward to the day when there would be a distinct Jewish state; others did not. But as we have seen, the entire Jewish nationalist movement across the spectrum supported the institution of formal Jewish national autonomy in the states where Jews were found, and agreed that, at the very least, this national autonomy should include state recognition of and support for Jewish cultural and especially educational institutions. This support might be administered by a central body or channeled through local Jewish autonomous bodies, but it was the state's responsibility. The Kultur-Lige, which began its work in the shadow of the dissolution of the Jewish Ministry and necessarily took up many of its functions, never ceased to maintain its demand that much of the work that had fallen into its hands be taken up by "democratic state institutions" in a restored system of Jewish autonomy.

More broadly, like their Russian compatriots, many Jewish nationalists (particularly the socialists among them) saw a positive role for the state—in the sense of a public authority standing above private interest—in planning and shaping cultural life.[56] States could support the kinds of large-scale public institutions so hard to sustain through private initiative: museums, schools for art and music, orchestras, and performance and exhibition spaces. This, too, was not merely an issue of funding. In an age of art's internationalization at the level of content, it was arguably the state more than anything else that sustained separate "national" arts by situating artistic creativity by its citizens in national spaces, by tying material support to national affiliation, and by "consecrating" the resultant creativity as national.[57]

Jewish cultural nationalists in Ukraine received a foretaste of how the institutionalization of Jewish culture in a state might work in the last days of federal-level Jewish autonomy before the April 1918 coup. On April 22, the Kiev branch of the Jewish Society for the Encouragement of Art wrote to the Department of National Education at the Ministry for Jewish Affairs requesting a subsidy for Kiev's Jewish artists. The society's letterhead was in Russian, but the request itself was written in an old-fashioned, unwieldy Yiddish by someone clearly unused to official correspondence in the language. In a state where Jewish cultural nationalists had institutional power, there was reason for Jewish artists to declare themselves as such and accede to nationalist linguistic and cultural demands.[58]

There was another face to the Jewish culturist interest in the state: a readiness of some culturists to use the state to impose their vision of culture on the Jewish population. Zingman's utopia *Edeniya* took for granted a tutelary Yiddishist administration. The Yiddishists who dominated the short-lived Jewish Ministry erected in Ukraine in early 1918 made state recognition of Jewish schools contingent on the requirement that the language of instruction be Yiddish.[59] In this, they anticipated the policies of Hebraists invested with similar autonomy in British Palestine a few years later—and pinpointed one of the deepest tensions within the cultural project between the ideal of culture as a realm of freedom and the ideal (and practical requirements) of collective cultural revival and development.

But in practice, Jewish culturists had little opportunity to experiment with state power in 1917–1918: state support for Jewish culture remained largely an intriguing prospect rather than a reality until the Jewish cultural project was folded into the Bolshevik order (with fateful consequences for this dimension of the project as for many others; see Chapters 6 and 7). From the first moments of the cultural project's revival in 1917, then, culturists sought to find other means to sidestep the limitations of the market in their promotion of a new Jewish culture. The key site for this sort of experimentation was Hebrew and Yiddish publishing.

As we saw in Chapter 1, the proliferation of Jewish culturist publishing ventures since late 1916 had occurred against the backdrop of unprecedented material disruptions in the economy of the Jewish book. Despite this fact, the strange conditions of the time also made for some local successes: by 1918, the culturist publishers of Kiev and Odessa were enjoying substantial and unexpected profits.[60] Yet these publishers and the activists around them were well aware that their dreams of Hebrew or Yiddish cultural revolution through books faced challenges born not merely of immediate conditions, but also of endemic problems of cost and consumer base. The simple fact was that, for both Hebraist and Yiddishist publishing, there would be no adequate market for much of the literary culture they hoped to create.

Since the turn of the century, post-traditional Hebrew print culture had suffered from periodic market failure. A brief upswing of publishing activity and optimism after the disruptions of the 1905 Revolution had given way in the prewar years to a precipitous decline in the print runs and sales of Hebrew literature.[61] This decline may have been due in part to a growing divergence between the proto-modernist approaches that increasingly dominated Hebrew literature and the more traditional tastes of the established Hebrew reading public; more accessible genres like popular history and historical romance continued to be popular. More fundamentally, however, the decline revealed a crisis of demography and cultural reproduction: a shrinking readership base for Hebrew literature. Modern Hebrew literature had for the most part been produced by and for an already small minority of Jewish men steeped in traditional learning, and Hebrew literature seemed largely unable to secure a next generation of readers beyond this small pool. The growing proportion of the Russian Jewish intelligentsia educated in modern schools did not or could not naturally look to Hebrew as a literary medium, and even the growing strength of Zionism and Hebraism and the expansion of Hebraist educational efforts could do little more than ensure that the market for Hebrew textbooks would continue to flourish.[62]

New developments in the Hebraist cultural program itself also dictated a nonmarket strategy. The generation of Hebraists who had come of age by 1913 advocated new kinds of cultural production that could not possibly find a major market in the near future. Consider, for instance, the massive, organized program of literary translation from world literature into Hebrew (see Chapter 3). As one articulate supporter recognized, "such a thing at this moment, until such time as the number of those who know Hebrew and read it increases," could not possibly turn a profit.[63]

Although Jewish culture in Yiddish could rely on much larger demand, high-culture Yiddishists who aspired to create a Yiddish print culture that spanned the full range of genres and could appeal to sophisticated readers also faced critical market problems. Most of the Yiddish-speaking population could not be counted on to appreciate or consume the sorts of cultural wares that the Yiddishist intelligentsia began to produce in earnest during the first years of the twentieth century: experimental literary works, scholarly works, and journals devoted to the arts and to serious analysis of contemporary issues. The demographic that might have been expected to support these, the Russian Jewish intelligentsia, could satisfy its intellectual needs through Russian-language culture, and winning it over to active interest in Yiddish culture was a slow and uncertain process—in part due to long-held skepticism about the cultural capacities of Yiddish. In the years before the war, highbrow cultural production in Yiddish did manage to win a growing readership: the preeminent prewar Yiddishist journal *Di yudishe velt* claimed 3,308 subscribers and buyers in 1913, and this number may have risen to 6,000.[64] Yet the increasingly ambitious Yiddish literary community continued to depend on nonmarket sponsorship by ideologically sympathetic editors and patrons, and innovative Yiddish writers, even the most established of them like Peretz himself, struggled to find publishers willing to spend money on more daring or abstruse works.[65]

While several of the Hebraist and Yiddishist publishing houses founded or revived after 1916 soldiered on in the difficult task of seeking markets for their highbrow Hebrew and Yiddish books, others proved more innovative in the face of these challenges. The most striking nonstate effort to decouple cultural production from dependence on the market was undertaken by a new breed of Hebraist patron-activists willing to devote substantial parts of their own fortunes toward Hebraist culture regardless of existing demand. We have already encountered the most notable among these figures—Zlatopolsky, Persits, and Stybel—and examined their publishing endeavors and cultural undertakings in terms of their ideological substance. Now we turn to their innovative model for producing and disseminating their published works.

On the face of it, the most striking feature of the publishing work of Omanut and the Stybel press was that it seems to have been undertaken without regard for profit—indeed, with the expectation of loss. Omanut, which was founded in Moscow but moved to Odessa in 1918, produced works for children, youth, and Hebrew schools at a moment when the market was in shambles; Stybel focused on the publication of dozens of translations from world literature readily available in Russian, and published the massive literary "thick journal" *Ha-Tekufah* at a moment when the cost of paper was staggering. At least some of what both houses produced was, moreover, physically deluxe not only in light of the extremely difficult material conditions of printing in revolutionary Russia but by any standard. Nor were these deluxe volumes produced in limited editions for collectors, such as S. An-ski's album of Jewish folk art or some of the lovely editions of Hebrew and Yiddish books produced subsequently in Berlin. Stybel produced his *Ha-Tekufah* in print runs far greater than he could hope to sell well into 1918.[66]

Furthermore, the losses inevitably incurred by such ventures were evidently borne by the patron-publishers themselves. The exact financial structure of Omanut is not clear. It seems likely that Zlatopolsky and Persits simply put up their own money and absorbed losses; that the press was ultimately brought under the formal auspices of the Tarbut organization may have altered its funding structure, but it seems to have remained very much the personal concern of the Zlatopolsky-Persits family.[67] Stybel went further: in early 1917 he established out of his personal fortune an endowment of one million rubles to underpin the work of his press. At the time, this sum was worth some half million American dollars—between seven and fifteen million U.S. dollars in current terms.[68]

The motives behind these publishing policies, it seems, were twofold. First, by all accounts these patron-publishers wanted to support Russia's Hebrew writers and revive the Hebrew literary sphere: their presses provided support to dozens of Hebrew writers by commissioning translations, purchasing manuscripts, and employing them at their publishing houses as editors and even typesetters. Second, the publishers seemed to believe that it was necessary to decouple Hebrew literature from its dependence on the market given the tensions between their ideological commitments and the realities of the Hebrew book market. Stybel's focus on translation stemmed from his belief that Hebrew literature could only become modern and win a new generation of readers and writers among Jews steeped in modern European culture if it quickly offered the entire canon of literature and children's literature common to European cultures. In this respect, his indifference to the market was not a luxury but a necessity: no natural market demand could fuel a program of systematic translation on a scale sufficient to make up for centuries of literary "underdevelopment," especially because increasingly acculturated Jews could look to the robust corpus of translations in Russian, Polish, or German.

Other Hebraists of means were moved in this period to commit themselves to support Hebrew literature on a smaller scale but with the same distinctive ideological fervor. In Odessa, the patron Mordechai Sobol, approached by Bialik with a request for 30,000 rubles to support the families of several impoverished refugee authors, suggested a far more substantial undertaking: in 1918, with Bialik and Ravnitsky, he founded Devir, a stock company and Hebrew writers' cooperative (and a major Hebrew publishing house to this day). Devir drew tremendous support from patrons like Sobol, Pinhas Minkovski, and their friends in Odessa's wealthy Jewish business community, which helped raise an initial capital of 800,000 rubles at five thousand rubles per share; one source relates that "all the important figures of the city and almost all of the Hebrew intelligentsia in Odessa—doctors, lawyers, engineers—took part." Two other patrons, Moyshe Granovski and Tsvi Kleynman, contributed one million and 700,000 rubles respectively. Devir had ambitious plans to market and distribute its books—it was, in other words, not indifferent to readership and the market—but those who invested such massive sums in it could hardly have seen it as a serious business venture. According to the same source, Sobol's proposal stemmed from his enthusiasm over the Balfour Declaration—the British statement of support for a Jewish homeland in Palestine, issued in November 1917—and his belief that the time had come to place Hebrew literature and its authors on a new footing.[69]

In his recollections of revolutionary Moscow, publicist A. Ben-Yishai draws a contrast between prewar Hebrew publishing ventures that received help from patrons but depended ultimately on market success, and Hebrew publishing in revolutionary Moscow based, as he puts it, on "patronage-national" motives.[70] The patronage practiced by Stybel, Zlatopolsky,

Persits, and others with its "grand plans, solid constructions, and [commitment to] the redemption of the literature," was, in a sense, almost a movement unto itself, and arguably the first time that modern Hebrew literary culture had drawn the unreserved support of the wealthy to the same degree that both Russian culture and traditional rabbinic culture could rely on such support. Bolshevik suppression squelched these efforts, but the trend would continue elsewhere.[71]

Yiddishists who sought to circumvent the perennial and intensified market dilemmas of Yiddishist high cultural publishing could not hope for patronage of this kind: the status of Yiddish was just too weak. In addition, the wealth of the most committed Yiddishist patron, the Bundist-turned-publisher Boris Kletskin, did not compare to that of Hebraists like Zlatopolsky, Persits, and Stybel. Although he supported a number of Yiddish writers during the war in Bobruisk and returned immediately to publishing efforts in 1917, he could not single-handedly provide a new basis of support for Yiddish literature.[72] The Kultur-Lige, the most expansive and economically successful Yiddishist organization of the day, took patronage where it could find it but received little from what it called the "Jewish plutocracy," whose negative attitude toward Yiddish was no doubt compounded by the Kultur-Lige's aggressively socialist bent.[73]

So the Kultur-Lige tried a different tack. During 1918, more or less by accident, the Kultur-Lige secured a virtual monopoly over the distribution of Yiddish books in Ukraine. Its unique Ukraine-wide reach, coupled with the disruption of established book-distribution networks by the war, made its central bookstore the most effective distributor of Yiddish books in Ukraine. Consequently, all of the leading private Yiddishist publishing houses in Ukraine became affiliated with the Kultur-Lige bookstore, giving it exclusive distribution rights and paying it five to ten kopeks per book.[74] By the end of 1918, the Kultur-Lige bookstore and the publishers affiliated with it were doing a thriving business in Kiev; through sales to the organization's dozens of provincial branches; and to Yiddishist libraries, clubs, and schools. The bookstore itself reported that during the last three to four months of 1918, it sold some 92,000 books worth 160,000 rubles; the sympathetic but skeptical observer Kalmanovitsh wrote in November 1918 that Kultur-Lige's sales amounted to 5,000–6,000 rubles per day. By January 1919, the bookstore's own capital amounted to some 500,000 rubles: this at a time when the publishers affiliated with it were selling children's books for less than a ruble apiece, literary works for one to six rubles, and journals like *Eygns* and *Shul un Lebn* for eight rubles or less.[75]

The Kultur-Lige used this monopoly not for profit but in the service of Yiddishist dissemination. In an effort to reach poorer consumers, the Kultur-Lige sold its books at prices very close to cost and older books at their nominal cost, rather than adjusting the prices to inflation. At the same time, the organization looked to local Yiddishist institutions to serve as the chief medium of cultural education. It sought to ensure that books in limited supply (those from Warsaw or Vilna) would reach local Yiddishist libraries and clubs and offered a set of "the better books" to such institutions at half price before making them available to private buyers.[76] And naturally, it excluded from its unequalled distribution network "improper" sorts of Jewish books: Hebrew books, religious books, and popular entertainment literature, or *shund*. Though Yiddishists could not suppress such work directly (a situation that would change dramatically under Soviet power), Kultur-Lige activists took great satisfaction in the failure of two *shund* publishing houses in Odessa and Kharkov that, lacking the Kultur-Lige's extensive distribution network, presumably could not earn enough to stay ahead of the rampant inflation.[77]

No less important to the Kultur-Lige's goals than the mass distribution of the good Yiddish book was the material support of high-culture Yiddish publishing. The relationship between the organization and its publishers was symbiotic, framed by a common Yiddishism that saw the creation of the new Yiddish culture as the highest end.

Indeed, the Kultur-Lige was run by socialists who cherished a deep hatred of the market itself. By contrast, neither the Yiddishist Folks-Farlag nor the Hebraist publishing ventures of Moscow and Odessa disliked the market as such; indeed, the Folks-Farlag hoped that its production would ultimately yield profits. Yet all of these ventures saw the market as a problem to be overcome because none of them viewed the actual desires and interests of the "folk" or "nation" as a legitimate factor in determining the shape of the new Jewish culture. Indeed, not even the perceived and ideologically imputed "needs" of the nation were to determine cultural production. Even Yiddishists were willing to assert this, as *Literarishe monatsshriften* had a decade earlier:

> Literature cannot survive, cannot develop freely and expansively, if it depends on an underdeveloped reader, if it satisfies the spiritual-aesthetic wants only of those who have no access to the culture of other peoples. Yiddish literature has until recently depended on such strata of readers.

Its main user has hitherto stood on a low cultural level, and the literature itself has been primitive and coarse.[78]

At the time, the riposte of true Yiddishist populists, thoroughly anti-nationalist socialists, and Russifiers alike to this sort of argument had been the same: if so, why should there be a freely and expansively developed Yiddish literature? What was Yiddish if not, at best, a means to reach precisely such underdeveloped readers? Why develop a high Yiddish literature if no one needed it? The same question, mutatis mutandis, could be directed with equal force at Hebrew literature (as many Yiddishists themselves did): granted there was a storied age-old Hebrew textual culture, but if all Russian Jews could read Russian or Yiddish, why did there have to be a proper modern Hebrew one?

The answer was that by 1908, and certainly by 1917, such literatures were indeed felt to be burning needs—not for "the nation" but for the intelligentsia itself. For the Hebraists and Yiddishists who founded these publishing houses and organizations, the goal of creating a full-fledged Jewish high culture was evidently no less pressing than the goal of bringing the new dispensation to the nation or masses; hence the willingness of Yiddishist presses like the Folks-Farlag and the Kiever Farlag to publish challenging modernist works, and the Hebraist drive to produce translations of European literature. These Hebraists and Yiddishists were not part of that pan-European avant-garde for whom the small run and market indifference were paradoxical marks of pride and aesthetic success. Good nationalists, they hoped that the future would bring reconciliation between their high culture and a sophisticated national audience. But they also took for granted that the creation of the Jewish culture of their dreams could brook no delay.

Why a Shared Culture?

Taken together, the intelligentsia's programs of dissemination and the logic of its experiments with alternatives to dissemination may seem paradoxical. Jewish culturists were at pains to insulate actual cultural production from the very nation they aspired to serve. Yet they were obsessed with bringing this culture to the nation undiluted. They may have been elitists, but their elitism expressed itself not in an effort to set themselves apart as a separate and higher stratum of intellectuals, but rather in their desire to endow everyone with their capacities. It bears asking once again why they insisted on maintaining and enacting the idea that a single, undiluted culture should be shared by the whole of the nation, when instead (and probably more effectively) they could have taken up the older and regionally common practice of producing specially tailored forms of mass culture.

Culturist attitudes toward the popular or "low" culture they sought to displace offer an important clue. We know that culturists were obsessed with stamping out the culture of potboilers, boulevard theater, and light entertainment that many East European Jews enjoyed. But why should the Kultur-Lige have bothered to discourage workers' cooperatives from putting on fund-raising "spectacles" of unsatisfactory aesthetic and moral caliber? Why did its activists take such delight not only in the flourishing of their book program but also in the failure of pulp publishers whose wares probably didn't compete directly with those the Kultur-Lige published?[79]

The essentially religious language with which culturists motivated these arguments offers the answer. The Kultur-Lige worried that performing lowbrow theater would have a "debasing effect" on the drama circles that performed them. Bialik spoke for his entire cohort of Hebraists and Yiddishists alike when he described attendance at popular theater this way: "every night, people by the thousands . . . bathe their flesh and spirit in cauldrons of boiling filth and render eternally impure their mind and heart, their eyes and ears, the spirit of their mouth and the breath of their nostrils."[80]

What this language of debasement suggests is that culturists were convinced that aesthetic experience could have tremendous transformative (even crippling) effects on the individual psyche. It also explains why they were so reluctant to cultivate a second-tier, controlled "popular" culture even though such a culture might have better served their nationalist purposes in the cruder sense. Culture had a purpose or ultimate function, according to this view, which it could only fulfill if a worthwhile artistic experience were offered. This same logic, not incidentally, was invoked in culturist arguments for the insulation of "culture" from the dictates of party politics and political ideologies and for its liberation from demands that its content be "Jewish."

Figure 1. Marc Chagall, *Baal Makhshoves* (The Thinker), 1918. Baal Makhshoves was the dean of Yiddish literary critics and one of the few significant Yiddishists in revolutionary Petrograd. (© 2009 Artists' Rights Society [ARS], New York/ADAGP, Paris. Photo © The Israel Museum, Jerusalem, by Peter Lanyi.)

Figure 2. Natan Alt'man, logo for Aḥinoar publishing house, ca. 1918, reproduced in *Jüdische Graphik* (Berlin, 1923). Aḥinoar was a Hebraist publisher of youth literature. The style reflects Alt'man's prewar engagement with traditional East European Jewish art. Alt'man created works for Jewish culturist publications in Russian and Yiddish as well. (© Estate of Natan Isaevich Altman/ RAO, Moscow/VAGA, New York. Image courtesy University of Texas Libraries.)

Figure 3. Issachar Ber Ryback, cover illustration for *Oyfgang* (Kiev, 1919). Ryback was active in the Yiddishist circles that published this cultural journal and, with fellow artist Boris Aronson, cowrote a theoretical article in it entitled "The Paths of Jewish Painting." (Image courtesy Jewish National and University Library, Jerusalem.)

Figure 4. Page from H. N. Bialik, "Shlomo ha-melekh," *Shetilim* (Moscow) 6–7 (October 1917). Emblem by El Lissitzky, 1917. Like Alt'man's, Lissitzky's art was sought by both Yiddishists and Hebraists, suggesting that Hebraism and Yiddishism should not be seen as connoting clearly distinct aesthetic sensibilities, but rather as largely parallel versions of a single Jewish cultural project, both open to many aesthetic tendencies. Note how this page mixes Lissitzky's in-text illustrations with an utterly dissimilar illustration (artist unknown). (© 2009 Artists' Rights Society [ARS], New York/VG Bild-Kunst, Bonn. Image courtesy Jewish National and University Library, Jerusalem.)

Figure 5. Alexander Tishler, illustration for Book of Ruth, 1918. Tishler apparently completed this work under the auspices of the Kultur-Lige's art section; it was published by Kiev's Folks-Farlag. (© Estate of Alexander Tyshler/ RAO, Moscow/VAGA, New York. Photo © The Israel Museum, Jerusalem, by Avshalom Avital.)

Figure 6. Page from Moyshe Broderzon, *Sikhes-khulin* (Moscow, 1917), illustrations by El Lissitzky. (© 2009 Artists' Rights Society [ARS], New York/VG Bild-Kunst, Bonn. Image courtesy Jewish National and University Library, Jerusalem.)

Figure 7. Iosif Tchaikov, cover illustration for Dovid Hofshteyn, *Bay vegn* (Kiev, 1919). (Photo © The Israel Museum, Jerusalem, by Avshalom Avital.)

Figure 8. El Lissitzky, cover illustration for *Andersens mayselekh,* trans. Der Nister (Kiev, 1919). (© 2009 Artists' Rights Society [ARS], New York/VG Bild-Kunst, Bonn. Image courtesy Jewish National and University Library, Jerusalem.)

Figure 9. Iosif Tchaikov, cover illustration, *Baginen* (Kiev, 1919). Tchaikov had committed himself to the goal of a distinct Jewish art well before the Revolution, though his formal vision shifted dramatically in the revolutionary period. As a number of scholars have noted, the figure in this illustration thematizes the left-Yiddishist variant of the cultural project: half traditional Jew (with an earlock, blind) and half modern (shorn, open-eyed), blowing a *shofar* and looking to the right (the old world?), but with the naked body facing leftward and upward into the new. (Image courtesy Klau Library, Hebrew Union College–Jewish Institute of Religion, Cincinnati.)

Figure 10. El Lissitzky, Safrut emblem on back of *Evreiskaia antologiia,* ed. V. F. Khodasevich and L. B. Jaffe (Moscow, 1918). Note that although "Safrut" is written in Russian at the bottom of the border, it appears in Hebrew at the heart of the image—a testament to the firmly Hebraist goals of this Russian-language publishing house. (© 2009 Artists' Rights Society [ARS], New York/VG Bild-Kunst, Bonn. Image courtesy Jewish National and University Library, Jerusalem.)

Figure 11. Photograph of *(left to right)* Hillel, Fanya, and Shammai Hofshteyn, ca. 1923. (Gnazim, Fanya Hofstein Collection, 339. By permission, Gnazim, Tel Aviv.)

Figure 12. Yankev Apter, cover for *Tsum ondenk fun Y. L. Peretz* (Odessa, 1920). Note Apter's readiness to create a completely abstract image for a Jewish culturist publication, rather than one with recognizably Jewish content other than the letters. Apter also did extensive illustrations for Hebrew publications of the time. (Image courtesy Jewish National and University Library, Jerusalem.)

Figure 13. Cover illustration, *Tsu der erefenung fun der teater-studye Kultur-Lige* (Kiev, 1921). Anonymous. Note the stylized "eastern" or "Assyrian" imagery chosen for this Yiddishist (and Soviet) publication. Although it is sometimes assumed that such a style was naturally linked to Hebraism while Yiddishists naturally looked to East European Jewish folk art for their repertoire of forms, this image demonstrates the uneven fit between ideology and aesthetics in the Jewish cultural project. (Image courtesy Jewish National and University Library, Jerusalem.)

— 5 —

The Liberation of the Jewish Individual

Modern Yiddish literature . . . already walks the path taken by all literatures of modern, cultured nations——The writer writes for himself, not for anyone else; in himself alone he seeks the highest law of his creation. The writer and the reader are isolated, like the artist from the viewing public. For both, literature is already a separate category which possesses its purpose and justification itself, and one no longer seeks in it any external aims.

—NOKHEM SHTIF, *HUMANIZM IN DER ELTERER YIDISHER LITERATUR*, 1919

The question of our national culture in its full breadth and depth is the question of the liberation of the Jewish individual.

—NATAN BISTRITSKY, "SHIḤRUR HA-PRAT," 1918

In 1916, as tsarist repressions imposed an almost total silence on Hebrew and Yiddish culture, audiences in Odessa and Moscow flocked to hear a public lecture by the living symbol of Jewish letters, Haim Nahman Bialik. The lecture, which Bialik was compelled to deliver in Russian translation before publishing the original Hebrew text in spring 1917, bore the innocuous title "Halakhah and Aggadah." These were familiar categories of rabbinic hermeneutics designating respectively the realm of law and a diverse body of creative narratives and "lore" interwoven with legal discussions in classical rabbinic texts. Listeners familiar with Bialik's prewar views no doubt expected to hear a further elaboration of his arguments about the essential relationship between the new Jewish culture and the traditional canon.[1]

What they heard, however, went far beyond such questions of canon and content. Contemporary interpretations of this complex essay were dramatically divergent. But all recognized in "Halakhah and Aggadah" a savage indictment of the Jewish national intelligentsia as a whole, and Bialik's own fellow Hebrew cultural creators especially, for a terrible moral, political, and cultural failure. Interpreted in its proper context, moreover, "Halakhah and Aggadah" was not only a polemic, but an agonized expression of doubt about the most fundamental ideals of the cultural project: that a cultural praxis defined by the primacy of art and claims of secular individuality could generate a worthwhile new Jewish culture.

"Halakhah and Aggadah" embedded its urgent critique in a meditation on these two terms, which the essay construed not merely in a historical-philological register but as richly polyvalent metaphors for law and freedom, authority and creativity, form and flux, and ethics and aesthetics, with each pair operating simultaneously in both "life and literature." Bialik began by asserting that *halakhah* and *aggadah* should be understood not as fundamentally opposed phenomena—justice as opposed to mercy, clarity as opposed to ambiguity, duty against volition, prose against poetry—but rather as dialectically related moments in an ongoing process. Much of what followed was framed as a corrective to the unwarranted denigration of *halakhah* that, Bialik implied, afflicted his generation.

On one level, the essay seeks to demonstrate to its modern, secular readers that the corpus of ancient and medieval rabbinic law was relevant to the modern Jewish mind too: not as law, but as national culture. Rabbinic law, Bialik argues, had been a decisive cultural force within Jewish national history. The textual expressions of rabbinic law, properly read, were potent sources of national self-understanding and even self-revelation. Halakhic sources, like aggadic ones, were potentially the stuff of renewed Jewish literary creativity and even a new Jewish "national epic"—if only modern Hebrew culture had "true artists and divinely blessed creators" instead of a generation given to using "borrowed vessels and appropriating forms created by others . . ."[2]

The venom of this last formulation points to the deeper critical and moral agenda behind Bialik's essay. This second layer of the argument, which becomes fully clear only with the essay's agonized conclusion, begins with a second set of claims about *halakhah* itself: that *halakhah*, properly understood, is not the antithesis of art, nor merely a resource for modern Jewish art, but itself a special form of art—perhaps even "the greatest in the world." Significantly, its superiority to other arts ("sculpture, painting, architecture, music, poetry") derives from a difference of *purpose:*

Its craft is the greatest in the world: the crafting of life and its conduct. Its material—the living person with all his desires; its means—individual, social, and national education; its fruits—a continuous chain of a good life and good deeds, a straightening of life's road between the twisting ways and crooked paths of individual and collective . . . Halakhah is the trainer-art, the teacher-art of a whole nation.[3]

The section of the essay that makes this argument is primarily framed in historical terms. It is on one level a defense of the rabbis, who, it turns out, were not the close-minded, dry jurist-autocrats that rebellious Jewish culturists had imagined them to be, but great nationalist artist-leaders. Bialik even goes so far as to compare the premodern system of law elaborated by a thousand years of rabbinic effort to Europe's greatest works of religious art, the cathedrals of Cologne, of Milan, and Notre Dame of Paris.

Yet the purpose of his argument is not merely to redeem rabbinic civilization as a great national achievement in the eyes of contemporary Jews. Rather, Bialik is concerned above all to expose the absence of any such "art of life" in his own circles. The culmination of "Halakhah and Aggadah" shifts from the Jewish past to the present of Jewish modernity to announce a fateful and disastrous transformation: the disappearance of *halakhah* and the hypertrophic victory of an *aggadah* now wholly decoupled from it:

Now we have attained a generation which is entirely *aggadah*. *Aggadah* in literature and *aggadah* in life. The whole world is nothing but *aggadah* upon *aggadah*. Of *halakhah* in all its meanings there is no sign or trace.[4]

By this point in the essay, both of the key terms are purely metaphorical; as Bialik is at pains to emphasize, he is no longer speaking about the actual rabbinic law and its narrative counterpart but about two transhistorical modes of human consciousness and intention ("to each generation its own *aggadah;* to each *aggadah* its own *halakhah*"). Much of the essay's concluding section is devoted to elaborating what Bialik means by damning modernity as an age that is "entirely *aggadah*." In particular, his concern lies in the disastrous implications of this condition for the effort to reforge Jewish culture and collectivity. Although the essay's critique seems directed at moderns in general, Bialik directs the full force of his attack on his fellow Jewish intellectuals and cultural producers—and not merely Russian Jewish intelligentsia in general, but those who shared his nationalist political and cultural commitments in particular.

With furious strokes, Bialik's concluding section depicts the modern Jewish cultural sphere as corrupted and crippled in both "literature" and "life," overwhelmed by corrupting *aggadah* and on the verge of epochal failure:

> Our modern literature has for the most part sought for itself, like a true beggar, a fixed abode on the lowest level of cultural thought and feeling. All fifty gates of understanding are locked before it, and there remains only the narrow wicket of a dubious "beauty"—the *aggadah* of our time ... A few stories and a few poems—that is the whole of the poor man's portion in its haversack. The rest of the higher springs of the spirit have no influence.[5]

This failure of cultural creativity in "literature" is intimately linked to a parallel overgrowth of *aggadah* in "life":

> Thus a generation arises in an atmosphere composed entirely of slogans and refrains . . . A sort of Judaism of permission is taking shape. We preach nationalism, revival, literature, creation, Hebrew education, Hebrew thought, Hebrew work—and all of these hang by the hair of some sort of love: love of land, love of language, love of literature . . .
>
> Love [*ḥibah*]? But where is *duty* [*ḥovah*]? And from whence will it come?[6]

Contemporaries differed dramatically in their interpretations of what Bialik meant by this terrible excess of "aggadah in life." Haim Grinberg saw the essay as a veiled attack on the revolutionary enthusiasms widespread among Russian Jewish youth; others saw in it a demand that Zionists actually emigrate to Palestine; and in Palestine itself, the labor Zionist intellectual Berl Katznelson appropriated the essay to legitimate the new social order that he and his fellow socialist Zionists hoped to institute.[7] Clearly, however, Bialik meant to identify, among other things, a failure of what I have been calling the cultural project—of those who believed that the realm of culture ("revival, literature, creation, Hebrew education, Hebrew thought") had a central role to play in Jewish national revival and reformation.

It was in the gap between "love" and "duty" that Bialik located his contemporaries' failure. In literature and in life, Bialik's secular-national contemporaries, unlike the rabbis they reviled, had not found a way to transmute volition, will, and love of nation into national commandment—that is, into not merely positive injunction but a "law of the heart" that would lead perforce to right action.[8] The task of the Jewish national intelligentsia was, ultimately, the guidance of Jews toward this right action, which meant both cultural self-reconstruction as Jews in the face of modernity's challenges and nationalist political choices, which in Bialik's fondest imaginings would follow from the inner reconstruction.[9] The ultimate goal of Bialik's effort to recover the moral, national, and aesthetic greatness of *halakhah* was to confront the modern, secular national intelligentsia—and especially his own fellow culturists—with the scandal of their own failure to create a culture that could "shape life" and provide a new "Law" to the nation.

But why did they fail? At times, Bialik suggested in heated rhetoric that his fellow culturists were guilty of such personal sins as ignorance of Jewish tradition, laziness and irresponsibility, even immorality. But ultimately, "Halakhah and Aggadah" suggested that this failure stemmed from the Jewish intelligentsia's conception and practice of culture itself. In answer to his own rhetorical question as to whether he truly needed to spell out the applicability of his historical-phenomenological discussion of *halakhah* and *aggadah* to present-day Jewish culture, Bialik averred that, indeed, many of his contemporaries would fail to understand him because "among the 'aggadists' of our day there is a tendency to accord 'autonomy' [Heb.: *avtonomiah*] to literature—that is, [to preach] 'art for its own sake'—and there are those who place [literature] 'above life,' that is, *outside* it."[10]

The most famous response to Bialik's "Halakhah ve-aggadah" came not in Russia but in Palestine, where Y. H. Brenner, Hebrew literature's most unsparing critic of both the Jewish present and the Jewish past, read the essay as an ill-conceived attack on secularization in general. But Bialik's contemporaries in Russia's Hebrew cultural sphere, who were closer to the poet, interpreted Bialik's essay as I have reconstructed it earlier: as a focused attack on culturist ideals (which, ironically, they felt themselves to have learned not least from Bialik's poetry itself). Two fellow Odessans, the young literary critic Menahem Ribalov and Bialik's close friend Yaacov Fichman, saw in it an attack on their culturist faith in the sovereign rights and powers of art. In *Ha-Shiloaḥ*, Ribalov angrily defended the view that a Jewish literary renascence was essential to "our complete inner liberation from our deep slavery, which is rooted in the depths of our inner essence." Throwing Bialik's historiosophy back in the poet's face, he insisted that what contemporary Hebrew literature needed was precisely more "beauty," and for that matter greater liberation from "the bonds of the past." In the Odessa pedagogical journal *Ha-Ginah,* Fichman located the crux of

"Halakhah and Aggadah" in its equating of *aggadah* with modern literature and its contention that the practitioner of literature was perforce irresponsible insofar as his praxis yielded only dreams rather than realities.
In later memoirs of discussions with Bialik during the war years, he located the seed of the essay in Bialik's growing dissatisfaction with the modern distinction between beauty and truth, art and idea. Fichman recalled
Bialik's angry insistence that Judaism had "never distinguished between
poetry and thought . . . indeed, it always preferred matters of thought to
matters of poetry, and rightly so."[11]

A third reader, the young medical doctor, army veteran, and literary
critic David Aryeh Fridman, perceived a different target in Bialik's attack
on culturist ideals: the modern ideal of individuality. "What is [Bialik's]
ideology? It is short and simple: the one must serve the many . . . In a case
of the individual as against the collective *[klal],* the collective takes precedence." Fridman framed his reading of the essay in terms of a structural
tension between "shirat ha-rabim" and "shirat ha-yahid," poetry for the
many and poetry for the individual—as we can see from his audacious
comment that Bialik's own poetic development stood in tension with the
moral claims of "Halakhah and Aggadah":

> Thus Bialik once thought during that long period when he himself wrote
> poetry for the many. He believed then that that was his personal duty,
> and thus he believes now too, after he has already created a wondrous
> poetry of the individual and of the inner life of the individual [*shel ha-
> yahid ve-shel haye ha-nefesh shel ha-prat*]. He still believes that in princi-
> ple, the collective is what is important. In practice—he himself is also an
> individual poet.[12]

The responses of Fichman on the one hand and Fridman on the other
are significant for two different reasons. Fichman was one of Bialik's closest friends, disciples, and confidants. He was privy to the essay's gestation
over several years. Thus, his construal of "Halakhah and Aggadah" as above
all an attack on aestheticism, on his own and his generation's faith in the
sovereign status and unique powers of literature, has authority. And there
is certainly a great deal in "Halakhah and Aggadah," as well as later essays
by Bialik, to support his reading. For Bialik, the true scandal of the failure
of the new Jewish literature to move beyond "a few stories and a few poems" was that it had been partly intentional, a product of beliefs that Bialik
attributed broadly to the cultural intelligentsia. Jewish writers showed no
desire to raise themselves out of their "desolate pit" because they truly be-

lieved that "there is no 'literature' and no 'creation' [*yetsirah*] other than belle-lettres, and everything beyond it is unfit for use." Their failure in "literature" stemmed, according to this reading, from precisely that pervasive valorization of the aesthetic within Jewish culturism that I pinpointed in Chapter 2. Worse, Jewish culturists actually sought to "root this view in the hearts of the masses"—a striking anticipation in 1916 of the intelligentsia's refusal, examined earlier, to compromise the rules and contents of the new culture in order to disseminate it more readily.[13]

Conversely, what is striking about Fridman's reading by contrast with Fichman's or Ribalov's is how dramatically it reads its own concerns into "Halakhah and Aggadah." Fridman wrote as though Bialik had explicitly attacked the intelligentsia for cultural individualism, expressed in a propensity to create "poetry for the self" when it should have been creating "poetry for the collective." But although the essay contains a bit of rhetoric on which to hang this reading, "Halakhah and Aggadah" certainly does not elaborate any sustained discussion of individualism. Yet the question of individualism in culture seemed to Fridman to be the essay's self-evident core. As we shall see, moreover, he—and many others—found the same question inscribed everywhere he looked. Fridman's reading-in of this question suggests a link between Bialik's critique of culturist aestheticism and a parallel set of tensions clustering around the specter of a modern individuality taking root within the cultural intelligentsia—an individuality with anarchic implications for the demand that the new Jewish culture serve the nation as a whole.

Both Fichman and Fridman assumed a respectful tone in their discussions of Bialik's attack. But both insisted that the failure with which Bialik charged their cohort was not due to a lack of integrity. Both insisted that their generation's embrace of "aggadah" (Fichman) or "the poetry of the individual" (Fridman) was not a lapse in judgment but a choice made in full consciousness. And both went further still by agreeing with Bialik on a crucial point. Bialik's critique suggested that not only were the creations of Jewish culturists rendered barren by misplaced ideals of aestheticism, untrammeled expressive freedom, and individual desire, but that Jewish culturists had compounded their error by believing that a new Jewish national culture and consciousness could in fact be forged within the framework of such flawed ideals. Fichman and Fridman did not seek to blunt this attack: on the contrary, their responses suggested the view that aestheticism and individualism were not only compatible with the intelligentsia's national-cultural mission but essential to it. Between them, the antagonists registered the seismic effects of a twofold development within the Jewish cultural sphere among both Hebraists and Yiddishists: a growing tendency to conceive art as an autonomous realm with rules that could not be broken, and an inchoate but powerful longing for that most prized possession of Western modernity, a modern, capacious, creative individuality unfettered by any preconceived limits of "identity."

The Demands of Art

"Halakhah and Aggadah" attacked the Jewish culturist intelligentsia not merely for failing to create a law-giving art that would influence "the many," but also for rejecting such demands as violations of art's special prerogatives. Bialik placed that claim at the center of his critique still more baldly three years later, in a speech before an Odessa audience to celebrate the founding of a Hebrew opera company that aspired to refound itself in Palestine. The address was entitled "Ha-omanut ha-tehorah" (Pure Art), and its argument turned on a critique and redemptive transvaluation of this titulary idea. With biting irony, Bialik argued that under the banner of "pure art," Jewish theater artists had either "grazed amongst the lilies . . . in the vineyards of others"—that is, Russian culture—or, worse, created the Yiddish popular theater, which not only benefited no one but, indeed, corrupted the nation "by the thousands, the old, the young, widows, children." Against this twofold irresponsibility, Bialik imagined for his listeners "a truly pure art, pure in all of the good meanings of this holy word, art which will nourish not only the senses but also the spirit, which will exalt and refine the human rather than render him bestial." He gave this Schillerian invocation of an educative theater the nationalist twist we might expect: "our art will not only *entertain* the people, but also *educate* it." Yet strikingly, he framed this typical trope of theater as the site of national education in defensive terms: "our national and folk theater *at all of its levels* must be—I am neither frightened nor ashamed to say it—a theater-school for the people." Bialik imagined a chorus of critics rebuking him in defense of the ideal of "pure art":

> Heaven forfend that art should be confined in any way! You would rob it of its soul! You seek to inject into it a "tendency" for its sake? Art must perforce be "clean"! And clean art must perforce be free![14]

In other words, as he had in "Halakhah ve-aggadah," Bialik posited that to impute a nation-building task to art—something usually seen as intrin-

sic to cultural nationalism—was to hold a contrarian and unpopular position among his listeners, the Hebraist culturist intelligentsia. This defensive view was shared by other critics in both the Hebraist and Yiddishist
camps. From the very first moments of the reemergence of Jewish cultural
discourse in 1917, those who like Bialik continued to believe in the artist's
nation-forging duties wrote not as the champions of self-evident nationalist dogma, but as Jeremiahs witnessing an epochal moral-political failure
of their respective national literatures.

In a 1918 essay on the death of the Hebrew-Yiddish literary pioneer Sh.
Abramovitsh, the Zionist publicist Moshe Kleinman berated contemporary Hebrew writers for abandoning Abramovitsh's principle that the "true
artist" served both art and society and sought a synthesis "between artistic
truth and the truth of life." Like their Russian contemporaries "Turgenev,
Dostoevsky, Tolstoy, and Gleb Uspensky," an older generation of Jewish
writers like Abramovitsh had striven to be "not only creators of literary-artistic forms, but also seers and prophets to their people," and to influence
not merely other writers but also "enlightened people and activists, men of
state and creators of public culture."[15]

By contrast, in the contemporary Hebrew cultural sphere, the idea that
"the book must be in the service of life and the author must be a guide and
leader to his generation" was rejected as inimical to art itself:

> It is now customarily asserted that [any] tendency in a creative work less-
> ens its artistic value . . . The proclamation has gone forth: the artist does
> not need any guiding idea or public orientation in his literary works; one
> is not to ask the artist what he has come to tell us because the artist is free
> like a bird of the heavens to fly on the wings of his imagination and to
> sing the song of his soul.[16]

Across the Hebraist-Yiddishist divide, the Yiddishist Shtif perceived an
identical phenomenon in contemporary Yiddish literature. As we saw in
Chapter 3, Shtif shared what he identified as his generation's impatience
with an excessive reverence for things Jewish and its desire for a mature
humanist Yiddish culture that encompasses "the universal and the human
in art and in life." But in his occasional writings and especially in *Der
humanizm in der elterer yidisher literatur,* a 1919 study of Jewish Enlightenment literature, he registered deep concern with the implications of the
aestheticist principles that he, much like Kleinman, felt his generation took
as entirely self-evident. Shtif's *Der humanizm* was at one level a scholarly
work that sought to redeem the Yiddish satirical literature of the nine-

teenth century from the disdain of his sophisticated contemporaries, who thought it was "Jewish-parochial *[yidishlekh]* through and through," a relic of an "antique-pious, small-town cobweb-world" from which Jewish youth was still trying to escape "with all of our powers." Shtif framed his scholarly concerns, however, with a more pressing and presentist agenda.[17]

Contemporary writers and readers, he argued in his introduction, rejected the idea of a "goal-literature" in favor of a literature understood "as an *end in itself*, which seeks in itself its beginning and end, the goal and the way." Yet the literature of the Haskalah demanded respect not because of its aesthetic achievements, which he deemed limited, but precisely because of its passionate commitment to educating the nation in a humanist vein. Careful not to suggest that such a literature could be emulated in the present—a vital point to which we will return—Shtif nevertheless reproached his contemporaries' ostensibly unreflective aestheticism with another vision of what "national literature" should be:

> Among us, one measures literature now solely with an aesthetic measure, and from that perspective we often recoil when the older Yiddish literature is mentioned. We forget that aestheticism is only one of the methods by which one can approach literature, and not the only one. The literature of an entire people also has a *content*, a pathos; it does not separate itself by any means from the nation's way of life, from its dreams and its reality. On the contrary, it deepens it, it sees and aims further than writings on public affairs, than politics, and raises from the stream of everyday life that which endures and has weight.[18]

The attitudes to which Bialik, Kleinman, and Shtif alluded darkly or gloomily were very real and pervasive in Hebrew and Yiddish cultural life at the 1917–1919 juncture. In 1918, the Hebrew literary critic Grinblat asserted as a matter of course that poems written "in honor of the land of Israel" could not be considered by any serious "lover of poetry and person of good taste . . . as poems at all." He dismissed the self-consciously "Zionist" poems of Bialik and other Hebrew poets as the worst in their oeuvre.[19] Writing in the Folkist *Yidishe folksblat*, Niger, the leading Yiddish literary critic of the 1905 generation, defended the cultural value of Decadent trends in the previous decade's Yiddish poetry with the insistence that "*literature is an end in itself* . . . [I]f literature is a means and only a means for other ends, it may be anything you like but not literature (in the sense of art)."[20]

These critical arguments intersected with an increasingly unabashed insistence by writers themselves that the nature of artistic creation forbade the imposition of *any* programmatic "duties" or expectations on the artist. In 1918, the Zionist-Hebraist activist and budding author Bistritsky averred that any ideological imposition on authorial "inspiration" threatened to "constrict the original feeling of the individual, clip the wings of his imagination, and dry up the wells of his thought."[21] In ways reminiscent of English and German Romantic criticism produced a century earlier, by 1917 Jewish culturists of all stripes were operating with a vitalist conception of authorship, which held that themes had to emerge organically from the author's "soul" rather than from external didactic and ideological expectations.[22]

Yet it is important to recognize that the defenders of art's autonomy were not asserting an *"art pour le art"* ideology; contrary to Bialik's charges in "Halakhah and Aggadah," they too were speaking as nationalists. Nor can the differences between the critics and the defenders of this ideology be explained adequately by differences of role or institutional location (political activists versus literary critics and artists, for instance), although in a broad sense these factors no doubt help explain how such attitudes gained institutional traction. Figures like the Hebraists Grinblat and Bistritsky or the Yiddishist Niger (to whom we might add many of the figures encountered in Chapter 2, such as the utopia-writer Kalman Zingman and the Yiddish poet Moyshe Kulbak) were politically active, engaged nationalists with the same range of political affiliations as Kleinman and Shtif, respectively. All five were also well to the left in their social politics, which we might expect to have further strengthened an inclination to conceiving art as bearing a definite social responsibility. Grinblat was an active member of the socialist-Zionist Poale Tsion party who had even spent time in tsarist jails for his revolutionary activity, remained active in Jewish civic life, and would soon leave Russia for the Yishuv. Niger too defended the sovereignty of art while working actively for the Folks-Partey, and Kulbak was close to the Bund.

In addition, these figures framed their claims not as moral arguments for the autonomy of art but in objective, real-world terms, as stances that any reasonable person would take given the objective features of artistic creation and consumption. Significantly, one of the critics of intelligentsia aestheticism, Shtif, regretfully shared this perception:

Modern Yiddish literature . . . already walks the path taken by all literatures of modern, cultured nations. Here, literature is already a thing for itself, a partition between writer and reader. The writer writes for himself, not for anyone else; in himself alone he seeks the highest law of his creation. The writer and the reader are isolated, like the artist from the viewing public. For both, literature is already a separate category which possesses its purpose and justification itself, and one no longer seeks in it any external aims.[23]

Shtif's reluctant recognition that the growing disconnect between nationalist ideology and the arts was not merely the result of clashing beliefs but a matter of changing sensibilities points us to the complex sociology of attitudes and dispositions that lay behind these aesthetic debates. What both Shtif and the targets of his ire sought to articulate was that their aesthetic experience of art objects and their aesthetic perceptions as would-be creators of art were not really under their own ideological control. In a slow, recursive process of aesthetic experience and reflection on that experience, these culturists had come to apprehend art as a separate category with its own "rules" separate from nationalist ideology and hopes. In turn, their nationalist ideology had come to exert ever less influence over their experiential relationship to individual works of art as readers, viewers, participants, or creators—that is, over whether individual works of art or types of artistic creativity compelled them or left them unmoved. We can find evidence of this gap between cultural ideology and aesthetic-cultural commitments throughout the Jewish cultural sphere of 1917–1919.

One of the most striking examples of the autonomous power of art at an affective and experiential level is the strange relationship between Bialik, the living symbol of Hebrew art and Zionist cultural revival, and the avant-garde Yiddishists who were at the center of Kiev's burgeoning Yiddish cultural sphere after 1917. Figures like Litvakov, Bergelson, Dobrushin, Hofshteyn, and Mayzl shared the view that all aspects of Jewish culture and consciousness ought to be lived in a fully modernized, ramified Yiddish-language cultural sphere. By definition, this stance dictated that Hebrew culture would have to be relegated to the "museum," in Litvakov's terms, or at best incorporated into Yiddish via translation. In a move that was both cultural patricide and fratricide, Litvakov's fellow critic Dobrushin went so far as to proclaim that modern Yiddish literature "is truly a Torah," that is, a new foundational text of modern Jewish culture that could take the place both of tradition and of modern Hebrew culture.[24]

Yet even the scattered sources left to us by this chaotic period reveal that in the midst of their Yiddishist cultural revolution, these Yiddishists maintained a remarkable connection to modern Hebrew culture: they sustained an intimate relationship with Bialik's Hebrew poetry and with the poet himself. In January 1918, the Kiever Farlag editors Mayzl, Dobrushin, Bergelson, and Der Nister appealed to the "deeply respected H. N. Bialik" to write something for them in Yiddish. Their letter invoked the pivotal distinction between "culture" and "politics," noting that the Kiever Farlag had already sent Bialik some other publications that demonstrated "that our press is a truly literary press and that thus your participation is not only possible but desired." But they also couched their appeal in more strikingly personal terms: "we have always felt toward you a special closeness and we, from our side, have also felt the same feelings toward us."[25]

In part, this was a straightforward claim about individual friendships with the older poet. Dovid Hofshteyn enjoyed an intimate though increasingly fraught personal and poetic relationship with Bialik well into the revolutionary period, as did young Yiddish poet Osher Shvartsman, to whom Bialik was related.[26] Bialik was even a guest of honor at Bergelson's April 1917 wedding.

But these Yiddishists' critical writings about Bialik bespeak a far more complicated connection to the poet's art—one that reveals how aesthetic experience could outweigh the dictates even of fiercely held cultural programs. One of the most paradoxical productions of Jewish literary life in the revolutionary era was a long Yiddish essay on Bialik by the young critic Mayzl.[27] Occasioned in all likelihood by Bialik's 1916 anniversary, it was published as a monograph by the radical Yiddishist Kiever Farlag in 1917 (and sold out its first run by 1918).[28] Given the struggle between Hebraism and Yiddishism during the wartime era, parts of the book seem altogether heretical. For Mayzl, Bialik's poems in Hebrew were among "the most illuminated and magnificent pages in the new Jewish poetry." Flying in the face of the common Yiddishist insistence that Hebrew was a dead language weighing down the vitality of the folk, Mayzl's essay extolled the tremendous linguistic accomplishment of Bialik's Hebrew poetry: his ability to synthesize a vibrant secular poetry out of a largely unspoken language circumscribed over long centuries by the legal, pietistic, and mystical needs of the rabbinic tradition.[29] He avoided any effort to find in Bialik's small Yiddish-language output any basis for a Yiddishist countergenealogy, frankly acknowledging the aesthetic superiority of the Hebrew corpus. And in an act of astonishing inversion, Mayzl hailed Bialik's almost exclusively Hebrew prose of the same period as far more full of life than that of the canonical Yiddish writers: Bialik's Hebrew short stories of a contemporary, local Jewish life with "healthy strong roots, [which] grows and becomes strong by its own powers" were more vital in a national sense than Abramovitsh's vision of a Jewish life "about to die," Sholem Aleichem's creation of a Jewish life that "lives through miracles," and the social-critical stories of the early Peretz, "full of groans and sighs."[30]

These deviations from the Yiddishist "party line" based on the personal experience of Bialik's Hebrew poetry were not unique to Mayzl. The same assessment, delivered in cooler but no less certain terms, is evident in the writings of Mayzl's fellow critic Dobrushin, who grouped Bialik with Byron, Pushkin, and Verlaine as one who had already reached the "national-classical heights" to which Yiddish poetry should now strive. This was at once an act of distancing—Hebrew poetry was no more (though also no less) relevant to Yiddish poetry than English, Russian, or French—and an extraordinarily undisguised admission that the achievements of modern Hebrew poetry were as yet unmatched in Yiddish.[31]

These analyses did ultimately conform, in part, to Yiddishism's ideological dictates. Mayzl suggested that by failing to outgrow his love for "the culture which was already sentenced to become history" and instead draw vitality from the real-life of "the folk," Bialik had failed to create "the new style, *the* style which must stem from life into art."[32] Yet even in this comment, Mayzl demonstrated a second reason for his continued devotion to Bialik despite the ideological chasm between them: he also understood—or experienced—Bialik in Romantic terms as a poetic genius whose great talent existed independent even of language itself. Again, Mayzl was not alone in this understanding. This same assumption—that Bialik's genius might be transposed from Hebrew to Yiddish—underpinned the Kiever Farlag editors' effort to recruit him.

For these Yiddishists, the compelling power of Bialik's poetry was simultaneously national and personal—simultaneously a piece of the Jewish national cultural heritage that could not be ignored, and something that evidently continued to speak to them across the widening political and cultural divides. For Mayzl, Bialik's significance as "national poet" was independent of his "faulty" linguistic choice. In his finest poetry, Bialik laid the groundwork for future Jewish poetic development by elevating into art the fruitful tension between the "two powers" that struggle in "every great personality, especially among oppressed peoples . . . the purely personal (the subjective, the intimate)—and the national."[33]

Both the friendships and the critical writings of the 1917–1919 juncture were rooted in formative encounters with Bialik's poetry and the poet himself that dated back to the first decade of the century. Before the war, both Mayzl and Bergelson had sought out Bialik and considered him a literary and cultural guide despite the rapidly widening divide between the Hebraist and Yiddishist camps. Even as Mayzl cofounded one of the first Yiddishist schools in Kiev in 1912, he sought (in Hebrew) Bialik's insights regarding his literary criticism. A friend of Bergelson's reported to Bialik himself that the great poet had "influenced Bergelson during his stay here in Odessa, and influenced him for the good, and this influence has not faded since. Bergelson feels connected to you in general and misses you greatly."[34]

Scions of the old Jewish elite and students of traditional Hebrew texts before their break with tradition, these Yiddishists had been shaped by Bialik's poetry no less than were the younger Hebraists against whom they were now arrayed. We hear this profound connection in a passionate letter to Bialik written by Dovid Hofshteyn in 1923: "Reaching over the small minds and narrow hearts of the various mischief-makers who stand between us, I press your hand and thank you for all the joy you have given me . . . I feel the threads which lead from you to all that of ours which is mighty and delicate, bitter and beautiful."[35]

Even Litvakov, a man who would soon prove utterly at home in the Revolution's culture of absolute hatred toward anything deemed counter-revolutionary, could not wholly escape youthful commitments. Although in his critical broadsides Litvakov consigned Bialik to a "bookshelf" of culturally exhausted "medieval" works, astonishing recollections by the Hebraist A. Z. Ben-Yishai suggest another side of this relationship.[36] In November 1918, at the height of the political conflict between Zionists and the socialist-Yiddishist left in Ukraine, Bialik arrived in Kiev to take part in Ukraine's Jewish National Assembly. Litvakov, a Fareynikte representative to the *natsyonal-farzamlung,* was very clearly on one side of this divide, and Bialik was clearly on the other (as was the memoirist Ben-Yishai himself). Yet to Ben-Yishai's astonishment, in the midst of this confrontation, Litvakov showed up at Bialik's Kiev hotel room in order to introduce Bialik to the young poet Peretz Markish.[37]

After the meeting, according to Ben-Yishai, Bialik, lamenting Litvakov's betrayal of Hebraism and Zionism, nevertheless commented to Ben-Yishai that "something would come" of Markish—even though the young futurist's jarringly modernist poetry was in a very different voice than the folksy or neo-Romantic Yiddish literature that Bialik preferred. As for Litvakov, his visit bespeaks conflicting sensibilities. He clearly wished to confront the poet of the past with the poetry and language of the future, yet his very choice to bring his young prospect before the older poet testified to an undiminished sense of Bialik's poetic and cultural significance in Jewish letters.

During 1919, these encounters and contacts were to end due to mounting mutual ideological antagonism, both political and cultural. Yet the persistence of these kinds of supra-ideological connections for so long indicates a distinct world of values and assumptions within Jewish literary life that stood in an uneasy relationship not only with the Jewish nationalist political sphere but with the Jewish national cultural project itself. This was the sociological reality that Shtif was trying to articulate. And although Shtif would hardly have been bothered by this particular case of radical Yiddishists acknowledging the greatness of modern Hebrew poetry—he himself shared these views—he was, as we have seen, discomfited by the implications of a divide between ideology and a sphere in which art itself dictated the rules.

The Crisis of the Self

As Shtif mused on the problem of "art and nation," a younger contemporary published a series of anguished essays over the course of 1917–1918 that pivoted on a second conflict within the new Jewish culture, that between the nation and the individual: "The question of our national culture in its full breadth and depth is the question of the liberation of the Hebrew individual." The author of these essays was the aspiring Hebrew writer Bistritsky, whom we encountered earlier as a fervent advocate of a culture that would be both unparochial and unfettered by any external determinants; he also worked as a full-time professional activist for Hebraist and Zionist causes. In both content and tone, his essays point us back to a second wellspring of tension within Jewish cultural nationalism that we have already encountered in the debate over deparochialization: demands within the intelligentsia for modes of self-expression and self-development that conflicted with its national tasks.[38]

In the debate over the proper relationship between artistic prerogatives and national responsibilities, Bistritsky's essays articulated a deeply conflicted position. In one sense, his aesthetic dispositions placed him squarely in the "camp" of Niger and Grinblat: he denounced "wretched nationalist poetry" and deemed the "liberation" of "Hebrew creativity" from "the four ells of nationalism" a necessary precondition for a Hebrew literature worthy of the name. As Niger and Grinblat did, he framed this particular claim within a general assertion that any "external tendency" imposed on the aesthetic object—even "the ideal of preserving the existence of the nation"—constituted a crippling form of "inner exile."[39]

Yet Bistritsky's essays also show that, like Bialik, Kleinman, and Shtif, he worried that making aesthetic autonomy an inviolable principle might lead the Jewish cultural intelligentsia to abandon its national-cultural responsibilities. Like Kleinman and Bialik, he disliked the Decadent strains that had dominated recent Hebrew literature: "all the poets of the recent period were swept up in the stream of aestheticism. There was in that typical tendency much of the naïveté and excess of the yeshiva boy who has fallen into licentiousness."[40] Bistritsky's literary dissent from this "decadence" was paralleled by his public engagement. Unlike many of the still-young Hebrew writers of the previous generation, whose collective self-definition had involved demonstrative distance from any institutional involvements, Bistritsky was active both in the organized Hebraism of Tarbut and in the Tseire Tsion political movement.[41]

Bistritsky's sense of sharp conflict between his own literary and cultural-ideological commitments is evident in all of his writings of the period. In particular, three literary-critical essays, devoted respectively to the legacy of the recently deceased Peretz, the problem of the "silence of Bialik," and the significance of the younger Bialikian poet David Shimoni, strained to find in each writer signs of a "third way": a harmonious synthesis between the prerogatives of art and the responsibilities of national culture formation. A fourth essay, "The Liberation of the Individual," confronted readers with the bracing claim that this conflict could *not* be mastered by individual creativity but only by a fundamental transformation of Jewish life: the abolition of the Diaspora itself.

The title of this last essay brings into focus the distinctive feature of Bistritsky's thought: his central concern with "the individual." Each of Bistritsky's essays explained the conflict between the demands of art and nation as the expression of a more fundamental conflict among the extrinsic needs of national culture, the psychological makeup of the individuals who made up the nationalist intelligentsia, and the nature of art itself, which Bistritsky conceived in Romantic terms as the individual's revelatory self-expression. The "excess intimacy" that Bistritsky perceived in his poetic predecessors was not a result of moral irresponsibility or crass mimicry of European literary fashion, as critics like Bialik or Peretz had charged before the war, but a psychologically understandable response by selves-in-the-making "to an era which knew only the poetry of the collective." Bistritsky located the origins of this conflict between the collective and the individual precisely in the generation of the 1880s and 1890s, which had presided over the birth of both Jewish nationalism and the cultural project. From the beginning, the Jewish cultural project had been shaped by three contradictory "creative powers": "the rationalism of the Haskalah era that had not yet passed from the world; the romantic emotionalism of the era of nationalism: the going to the people en masse and the powerful aspiration to 'populism'; and a radical individualism" marked by a powerful drive toward "the individual's self-isolation."[42]

Bistritsky's argument ultimately collapsed these three concerns into two "'principle protagonists' of modern Hebrew history: *the public and the individual.*" On one side, he situated both the demand that culture serve socially regenerative ends (associated with the Haskalah and the revolutionary left) and the nationalist demand that culture preserve national tradition or protect the nation. On the other side he placed a drive to individuality that would bridle against any limitation of its expressive prerogatives. At times, Bistritsky embraced the effects of this conflict as positive for the nation:

> Hebrew creativity, which had contracted within the four ells of nationalism, had to be set free into the air of the wide and glorious world *at the hands of the individual,* his searchings and sorrow. The individual had to reveal new horizons in the narrowed Hebrew culture, . . . to find the thread of the worldly, the human, the universal in Hebrew creativity. And by means of this liberation was the individual to win for himself spiritual redemption, eternal redemption . . . Liberated Hebrew creativity was to have and could have freed the individual from the bonds of tendentiousness and exaggerated nationalism which pressed upon the national genius and its creations, and robbed them of their universal value. In this new creativity the individual found for himself the true and proper form of his new world that now rose to revival from amongst the tombs of the collective and the ruins of history. The redemption of the Hebrew individual and Hebrew creativity depended one upon the other.[43]

These notions resonated with the emerging alternative vision of Jewish cultural formation that I have been calling antiparochial nationalism. Indeed, Bistritsky's historiosophical vision of a traditional Jewish culture crippled by self-imposed limits and in need of aesthetic liberation—a vision he had inherited from Berdichevsky and shared with other deparochializers from Litvakov to Klausner—pivoted on the pathos of the individual creator fettered by the demands of the nation (or, more subtly, his or her own sense of responsibility to the nation). Bistritsky hoped that the new Hebrew culture would ultimately emerge not only from audacious programs of translation and aesthetic deparochialization alone, but more fundamentally from "the liberation of the individual" from Jewishness as an externally imposed ideal: "And perforce, when it is possible for the individual to express his individuality, when complete authority and freedom are given to him to seek and find new ways and paths of self-expression, to bring forth from the hidden treasures of his soul—perforce, the individual creates a new national culture."[44]

Unlike Litvakov or Frishman, however, Bistritsky deemed this mutual "redemption" of national culture and the modern Jewish self not only incomplete, but also intrinsically conflicted and even, perhaps, impossible without a radical change in the Jewish condition. The needs of national culture and prerogatives of individual expression were locked in tragic conflict. "Liberated Hebrew creativity was to have freed the individual from the bonds of tendentiousness and exaggerated nationalism," yet what had resulted instead was a "war" between individual and nation within the evolving national culture. This war had produced a painful "duality of the soul" and distorted the art even of great figures like Brenner, Berdichevsky, and Bialik. Now the same problem confronted Bistritsky's own generation undiminished.[45]

Bistritsky was hardly a systematic thinker. His essays are full of internal divergences and even contradictions regarding the exact nature of this tragedy of self and nation, under what conditions it could be solved, and indeed what the proper solution would be. His literary-critical essays on Peretz, Bialik, and Shimoni suggested that this conflict was a matter of psychic tension that could be resolved within individuals through the right mix of will and creativity. The Hebrew intellectual-artist, freed of unmediated national demands, would nevertheless consecrate himself to serve the "demands of the nation" out of "desire and complete inner freedom."[46]

But Bistritsky's larger, synthetic statement "The Liberation of the Individual" struck a very different stance. Whereas his essay on Shimoni deemed "the poetry of the individual" valuable insofar as it "serves as a transition to a new harmony, the synthesis of the poetry of the one and the poetry of the many," "Liberation of the Individual" envisioned no such moment of freely chosen self-subordination. On the contrary, Bistritsky went so far as to elevate freedom of expression to a transhistorical principle and precondition of all human advancement: "no renaissance in human history comes except in the name of a humanist idea—in the name of the liberation of the individual and the creation of more comfortable conditions for the development of the human being." The "end of history" was a situation in which national culture would simply reemerge as the sum of the cultural expression of individuals entirely freed of any explicit "demands of the nation." Subject to eternal metamorphosis, it would be "great" because it was produced by individual genius and "national" because individuals embedded organically in their social and linguistic framework would naturally, without any form of chosen self-abnegation, speak to the needs of the nation that shared this framework.[47]

Far from resolving the problem of self and nation even in the realm of fantasy, however, "Liberation of the Individual" sharpened the point of the dilemma by suggesting, contra Bistritsky's other essays, that a resolution of the conflict was in fact impossible so long as Jews were in the Diaspora. Deprived of stabilizing frameworks of land and language, the diasporic nation could persist only by demanding various forms of spiritual obedience and self-abnegation from its members, and this remained the case even— perhaps especially—after religious authority gave way to secular nationhood. Bistritsky's essay wavered between the argument that it was impossible for the Diaspora Jewish artist to attain full expressive freedom because the demands of the nation weighed too heavily, and the perhaps more disturbing notion that such freedom could be attained only by betraying the Jewish nation and the Hebrew language. Even as it held out the hope of a resolution to the problem of self and nation that would preserve the integrity of both, this last essay left its readers with a choice between the aesthetic tragedy of the Jewish inability to give birth to a great culture in the diasporic present and the moral tragedy of the *inteligent* who now had to choose between full expressive individuality and allegiance to the Jewish national cause.

Bistritsky's diagnosis of a crisis of the self and the resultant "tragedy of the Hebrew *inteligent*" was not idiosyncratic. The Hebrew poetry written by his contemporaries during the upheaval of the 1917–1919 period is permeated and even dominated by this concern with the divided self. Much of the poetry published in the first issue of *Ha-Tekufah,* for instance, consists of explicit treatments of this issue. The twenty-five-year-old Menahem Valpovsky was a war veteran who would soon emigrate to Palestine and spend three more years in a more voluntary sort of "army," the socialist-Zionist Labor Brigade. He found time between these collectivist involvements, however, to publish a confessional poem "Bat Lita" (Daughter of Lithuania) that hardly sounds like the work of the proverbial hardened veteran or the proud Zionist-socialist pioneer. "Bat Lita" turns on the conflict between the poet-narrator's love for a Jewish woman rooted in their shared Lithuanian home region and his aspirations to leave for Palestine. The poem's connections between woman and place are entirely transparent, and the reader might expect the poem to unfold as a hackneyed story of love against duty. Thus, the speaker instructs the woman from whom he is parting to "greet the blessed forests of Lithuania for him" and avers that the streets of his youth will always accompany him "wherever I go and whatever I suffer." Yet the poet undercuts this reading by representing his turn to the East not as a bold break with exile in favor of a return to true Jewish nativity, but as an effort to regenerate a depleted, stunted self: "For my days have already expired in the darkling gloom. / I have grown old, and what is my comfort? / To the East, to renew my youth and to blossom / my soul yearns and longs." This is not a story about personal longing against collective obligation, but an admission of inner Decadence: "for the heart is tired of storms without purpose."[48]

The same issue of *Ha-Tekufah* carried a long *poema* by David Shimoni (Shimonovits), a figure central to the arguments of Bistritsky concerning the problem of selfhood and nation. By 1918, the thirty-two-year-old Shimoni was best known for a series of Romantic idylls on the Land of Israel, based on a year's stay in Palestine in 1909. Yet his 1918 poem "Nedudim" (Wanderings, or Insomnia) told a different story suffused with dark Byronic tropes of the divided self (not coincidentally, Shimoni was simultaneously translating poetry by Byron's Russian heir, Lermontov).[49]

Narrating a series of restless dreams and visions, "Wanderings" sketches an insomniac, alienated, and decaying self, and through images of travel dramatizes the question of whether this self can be reconstructed. The persona dreams of departing on a ship, recognizes himself in a lone seagull unable to rest and enjoy the coming spring, and, in the most arresting part of the poem, imagines himself in a seaside tavern among sailors from all corners of the world confronting the question of homeland and selfhood. Singing their native songs, the "Cushite" and the "Briton" are paradoxically drawn together by their shared longing for their distant homelands: "The Nubian lion, the white bear are here combined / and on the border of the icy North—stands the Sahara." The silent persona-wanderer is alone not because he is foreign but because he is homeless: "Only I am without a native song." The poem is thus primed for the deployment of the essential Zionist trope. Yet it defies these expectations. Asked by the sailors to disclose his home, he proudly asserts:

> The mist of secrets and the distance of the riddle
> there is my land, there is my joy and sorrow . . .
> And my national brothers are the winds and the seasons
> and the seas and the mysterious wastes . . .
> and the creator of desert and creator of ocean
> him I will worship with freeborn songs.[50]

Spoken within the poem, this may be read as bravado. But the poem goes on to more fully subvert both Zionist tropes and the Decadent-Orientalist alternatives exemplified by Valpovsky. Beginning with the poetry of the Russian-Jewish Love of Zion movement in the 1880s, the psychic geography of Zionist writing was clear: from cold to warm, north to south, west to east, Russia to Palestine, loneliness to collectivity, exile to homeland. Yet here, it is not to the sunny East that the persona ultimately looks for "purification," but to the snowy north of Europe:

> Snow falls light and pure.
> I will not tarry! I go
> to the fields, spotless, cold,
> my brother Winter rules there . . .
> I go to the forests!
> Do not look on me that I have grown pale!
> My forest will return my power to me once again;
> Do not look on me that I have darkened:
> there in the expanse my woe will melt away.
> My forest will return my power to me once more![51]

Thus, a poem of the self in national exile, sounding familiar Zionist concerns, gives way to a concerted inversion of the logic we might expect from this avowedly nationalist poet. The poem's persona seeks his regeneration not in the Israelite-Jewish East but in "my" north, not in collective frameworks but in the utter isolation of the snows and forests. The paradoxical natural imagery of the poem caps this inversion: it is not the heat of the sun that will warm his frozen blood, but the snow.

At a formal level, both of these poems were hardly original works. Both poets were utterly indebted to Bialik for their language and imagery. Moreover, their themes were altogether familiar. The theme of an exhausted or incomplete generational self (which returns to close Shimoni's poem, undercutting, it seems, any hope for redemption) was a perennial one in Hebrew letters. It was most powerfully associated with the poetry of Bialik, especially his 1910 masterpiece "Before the Bookshelf," which undercut Bialik's own ideal of *kinus* by staging an encounter between a poet whose inspiration has run dry and the traditional books that once spoke to him but are now meaningless.

But whereas Bialik's poetry famously resonates with an unstable but compelling metaphoric synthesis between its lyric personae and the travails of the nation's psychic exile, these poems pointedly avoided such metaphoric possibilities. Valpovsky's poem avoided the rich, Bialikian imagery redolent of Jewish classical tradition. Shimoni did use this Bialikian imagery: he drew freely on Bialik's extraordinary descriptions of Russian winters, and even directly quoted his famous invocation "come, oh night." But what is striking, from our standpoint, is that he did so in a way calculated to frustrate any reading of the poem as a collective psychobiography of the Jewish nation.

The tensions in these poems and in Bistritsky's essays—all works by figures committed at once to political Zionism, cultural Hebraism, and an ideology of art—suggest the growing complexity of conceptions of the individual in Jewish cultural nationalism in general, and Zionist thought in particular. Taken together, they also point to a milieu haunted by a sense that the stunted individuality of the politically and spiritually unfree Diaspora Jew demanded not only immersion in a new Israelite collectivity but also, paradoxically, an insistent, Nietzschean striving toward self-formation that would sit uncomfortably with it.

The Demands of Individuality

Bistritsky's essays reveal startling assumptions about the nature of individuality itself. First, Bistritsky's essays insistently assume that the necessary precondition of great art—and a worthwhile national culture—is the free, concrete individual: "Only if the individual is given an environment of spiritual freedom, and no spiritual or ideational yoke whatsoever presses on his soul, only then can he walk the 'royal road' of full and perfect creation." Unlike critics of Western ideologies of individuality from the Slavophiles to Bialik, Bistritsky unreservedly embraced the "idea of the creative imagination," as Charles Taylor puts it in his *Sources of the Self:* the idea that art is (both essentially yet also only potentially) the highest expression of an "inexhaustible inner domain," a unique selfhood.[52] Significantly, Bistritsky's essays present this conception of art not as an ideal, but as a fact—an accurate account of what art is in essence; hence the necessarily crippling effect on artistic creativity of "any goal whatsoever . . . *born of any sort of prior and special deliberation.*"[53] That Bistritsky took this notion seriously is borne out by his essay "Bialik's Silence," which insisted that to overcome his silence, Bialik had to renounce "publicness" for a "poetry of the individual personality [*shirat-ha-ishiut*]."[54]

Second, Bistritsky's essays conceive the striving for individual selfhood and its prerogatives as a fact of the social-psychological makeup of the Jewish national intelligentsia, rather than a mere ideological construct peculiar, say, to the literary sphere. Consequently, in Bistritsky's analysis, Hebrew culture faced a twofold contradiction. On one level, the contradiction was a social one pitting the nation's artists against the nation's needs. In striving for the modern individuality that alone could create a great national culture, successive generations of artists had in fact fallen into forms of decadence and irresponsibility; the cure of the modern self was as dangerous as the disease of tradition or coarse nationalist ideology. Yet on another level, Bistritsky conceives the problem of individuality as one of a psychic division within each of the nation's would-be culture-makers. To describe this division, he used phrases like "fissure in the soul," made famous by his forebear Berdichevsky, but also sought terms for "the self"— "*ishiut,*" "*yahid,*" and "*prat*"—that he mixed promiscuously to triangulate concepts as disparate as personality in the psychological sense, the private as opposed to public self, and the sovereign individual as opposed to ideological or sociological collectives. Far from simply translating shards of Romantic discourse into Hebrew, Bistritsky was groping to express a structure of experience. Bistritsky's essays sought to make sense of an ideal of individuality which he and his contemporaries had internalized, complete with a drive to untrammeled expression, a desire for self-development, and deeply anarchic implications.[55]

Bistritsky was a polemicist, and his essays appeared at a moment when many in the Jewish national intelligentsia, even Zionists and Hebraists, were increasingly drawn to the Revolution's appropriation of humanist and universalist rhetorics. Yet to read these essays as essentially strategic interventions in public debates seems simplistic given that these essays were all published in solidly Zionist, Hebrew-language venues intended for consumption by the like-minded—and in light of Bistritsky's subsequent obsession with the same problem of individuality and national collectivity outside revolutionary Russia. Shortly after leaving Russia for Palestine, he was to take part in one of the most intense communalist experiments in the history of Zionism and later chronicle this far-reaching experience of self-making and self-abnegation in his one half-remembered literary work, the novel *Yamim ve-leilot.*[56]

And indeed, when we look beyond Bistritsky, these same concerns and conceits regarding the individual's place in the cultural project prove to be ubiquitous among Hebraists and Yiddishists of all types. The pseudonymous Aleph's 1919 attack on Bialik's idea of *kinus,* first described in Chapter 3, deployed terms absolutely parallel to Bistritsky's, imagining the history of Jewish culture as an unending conflict between the collective and the individual. Both of them, in turn, might have been echoing the Yiddishist Latski-Bertoldi's 1913 essay "Yudishkayt un yuden" (also detailed in Chapter 3). Latski-Bertoldi had conceived the history of diaspora Judaism in exactly the same counter-historical terms as Bistritsky: faced with the dangers of exile, the rabbis of the Roman era had "turned a people into a sect with one intellectual system, a sectarian Judaism-organization [*a sektantishe yandes-organizatsye*]." Latski-Bertoldi too had insisted that the central task of modern Jewish culture—indeed, modern Jewish nationalism—was to free the individual from intellectual subjection to "the thought of the collective."[57]

Bistritsky's convictions about the decisive connection between individuality and modern cultural creation were shared by many Jewish culturists—not least among his Yiddishist opponents. The "emancipatory national-secular content" that the Yiddishist-Marxist Litvakov found in some contemporary Yiddish literature, for example, was held to emerge precisely through its evolution beyond folk-culture toward the self-consciously literary expression of the modern individual consciousness. It was not the folk but "individual creators and poets" who were the "fathers of the new tradition that has come to itself."[58]

One of the new "individual creators and poets" to whom Litvakov was referring was Hofshteyn, and with due respect for the difference between theory and poetry, we may read Hofshteyn's poetry of the period as also articulating this ideology of individuality. Of course, it is almost tautologically true that lyric poetry articulates a self. Speaking in a formalist vein, we might say that simply by dint of embracing lyric poetry as a practice, successive generations of Jewish writers "activated" the thematic structures of the lyric "I" embedded in the genre. But Hofshteyn's poetry of the early revolutionary era manifestly transformed this generic property into an explicit and central theme, revisited it obsessively almost to the exclusion of all others, and spoke directly to the larger debate over the place of the self in relation to Jewish culture and Jewish nationhood.

Although Hofshteyn's art was resolutely focused on the short lyric, his 1919 book of lyrics *Bay vegn* may be read as coherent poem-by-poem investigation and articulation of a unitary self. This is signaled, first, by the organization of the book's poetry as a poet-persona's life history, one that matched Hofshteyn's own. The first three sections of the book "First Enchantment," "On Roads," and "Fields" invoke a rural youth in the bosom of Ukrainian nature. "Caucases" contains poems by an older Jewish soldier-traveler stationed in the region and making pilgrimages to places walked by Pushkin, much as Hofshteyn had done in 1912.[59] "Before Dawn" and "Streets" describe the persona in "the city" both as a husband and father in the privacy of his home and as a wanderer of its streets.

The focus on selfhood is also signaled by the dramatic repetitions within the poems, which—in phrasings characterized both by lyric mastery and striking economy of imagery—repeatedly revisit the same few scenes: the isolate poet-wanderer on the road or in the field; the poet and his wife in intimate moments; the poet as father; and the poet on the street either alone or in a passing encounter with a stranger.

Hofshteyn's poetry may be read as articulating a double move of self-formation. First, as we saw in Chapter 3, much of Hofshteyn's poetry in this period consisted of efforts to find a mode of first-person lyric poetry free of all parochially Jewish marks. As Dobrushin recognized, Hofshteyn's search for a neutral language of poetic representation specifically of the self was in itself a breakthrough to a new kind of "universal" lyric poetry. But it was also a means of articulating a historically new kind of Jewish self. Only a few of the poems in *Bay vegn* frame the poetic self in relation to a recognizably Jewish context of any sort.[60] Such poems are far outweighed by poems concerned to represent a selfhood at once wholly individual and wholly universal. The most exemplary of these is "A gantsn tog":

> A whole day
> To be possessed by roads [*in rshus fun vegn zayn*],
> a whole day
> with naught but wind before me,
> and between road and rough—just a narrow ditch,
> only young lashes between eye and sunlight—
> what in this world
> could be more beautiful?[61]

Here, the poet-speaker is no longer defined in any way by social order, origin or family. Resonating between an image of the authority exerted by the road itself and twin images of virtual boundlessness, the poem sketches a self poised between complete immersion in open space and complete freedom to move as it wishes. Significantly, Tchaikov's cover for *Bay vegn* depicted this wanderer, dressed in unmarked European fashion in cloak and walking stick (see fig. 7). Just as significantly, Hofshteyn took this poem as a kind of credo; it was this poem that he chose to translate into Hebrew when in 1924 he briefly attempted to make a life in the new Jewish society in Palestine.[62]

Hofshteyn's subsequent poems return this now-universal self to recognizable social settings. But "he" is now no longer the young Jewish man wrestling with his parents and Judaic collectivity, but an individual dividing his life between nights in the private, intimate sphere of his own home and days on the streets of a metropolitan Kiev. Consider one of Hofshteyn's several love poems, "Evening":

> Beloved!
> the world has now forgotten us,
> as we forgot her earlier . . .
> without asking us
> they've made it night there
> on the cheerful ringing street . . .
> the darkened door
> is pale and quiet,
> locked up deaf and mute . . .
> on the bright red fabric

> of our old sofa,
> night-ink has spilled out.
> My love! Lay your hand on my head
> thus . . .[63]

Here the Jewish love poem is reborn entirely free of collective resonance. Its theme is the relationship of two private persons bound in an erotic relationship tied to a concrete setting, and hence resistant to the allegorization that was the lot of traditional Jewish love poetry. The beloved of the poem is not the nation, and the nation is not the object of the speaker's address; the world itself is excluded from this intimate home of private selves.

Against this backdrop, the poet-speaker relates with no less unvarnished individuality to the other denizens of his city:

> I stride through my young day from street to street.
> From shadowed corners it smells of dawn,
> but already the sucking worries well up
> and the little coils of hot hatred roll about . . .
> The sun glows, heaven is soft and overhead,
> and I stride free and still from street to street . . .
> The sun together with the taut wires
> marks a path for me on the asphalt with thick shadows . . .
> I follow it, this path, I'm true to it as to all paths—
> but if another human brother [*bruder-mentsh*] comes hurrying in the
>   opposite direction
> how can I not spare him a bit of road?
> I step quietly off my shadow rails—
> my sunlit path I'll not betray,
> my sunlit path I'll yet find.[64]

The surprising political turn of this poem, "On the Street," completes Hofshteyn's representation of individuality's prerogatives. Even in the midst of gathering social and political upheaval, the speaker maintains both a sphere of private selfhood resolutely seeking its own path and a liberal politics of inviolable selves in which each person has a claim on the public road. The moral act is to recognize in one's "human brother," regardless of his or one's own intermediate affiliations (Ukrainian, Jew), the same claim to one's own path and inner need, however opaque these are.

The Nation and the Child

The culturist intelligentsia's struggle to adjudicate the relationship between nation-formation and the claims of art and individuality did not end at the margins of the printed page. In fact, during the 1917–1919 juncture the claims of art and self were elaborated even in a realm often depicted as ground zero of nationalist instrumentalism: the education of children.[65]

For both the Hebraist and Yiddishist movements, 1917 marked a chance for extraordinarily rapid development on the education front. By mid-1919, Tarbut and the Kultur-Lige were administering some two hundred elementary schools, another one hundred kindergartens, and several high schools across the expanse of Russia and Ukraine, with the balance in the Hebraists' favor. Both organizations rushed to establish teacher-training programs and produce curricula, textbooks, and educational journals.[66]

On one level, the educational programs that Hebraists and Yiddishists developed in this brief period reflected a nationalist belief that children were a means to reform the nation. Both Hebraist and Yiddishist pedagogy aimed at nothing short of cultural revolution in—and through—the lives of Jewish children. As each movement was quick to point out about the other, the breadth of their respective cultural-revolutionary ambitions meant that in many ways, each movement sought quite radically to uproot the child from his or her environment. Hebraists sought to supplant the Russian and Yiddish language world of the young with an institutionally created Hebrew culture. Yiddishists liked to claim that their pedagogical program, by contrast, was linked to the child's home environment by the medium of shared language; but they too were fighting substantial Russification by 1917. Moreover, organized Yiddishism's thoroughgoing radicalism and secularism meant that its pedagogical program was in many ways less connected to the home life of most Jewish children than were East European Hebraist schools.

Concomitantly, both movements engaged in reeducating both children and teachers. Hebraist pedagogues could not share other ethnonationalists' romance with the imagined healthy, *volkisch* home environment where infants absorbed the national language from their mothers' lullabies, because that Yiddish-speaking home environment and its Hebrew-illiterate mothers were serious obstacles to the Hebraization of Jewish society. One obvious means to combat this problem was an ever-greater emphasis on preschool education to Hebraize (and de-Yiddishize) the child. In the years before the war, a Hebrew nursery-school movement took shape under the guiding hand of Hebraist pedagogical theorist-activists like Y. Alterman and Yehiel Heilprin. As these schools flourished after February, Hebraists moved to bring further order into this work with curricular guidance through Tarbut and through a new journal, *Ha-Ginah* (The Nursery), founded by Heilprin and the poet Fichman in Odessa. *Ha-Ginah* recruited Hebrew poets to create Hebrew lullabies and children's songs—in effect engineering this most "natural" dimension of folk culture and childhood experience. *Ha-Ginah* also sought to provide guidance to the Hebrew nursery school teacher, particularly to the female teacher. Whether due to a sociological fait accompli or powerful conceptions of the role of women in children's formative years, Hebraist pedagogues construed women as the primary providers of preschool education. This in turn raised another thorny problem: due to the gender divisions of traditional Judaism, there were few women fluent in Hebrew. Journals like *Ha-Ginah* worked to shape these caretakers into appropriately Hebraized educators.[67]

Yiddishists directed similar efforts at reeducating and mobilizing their mostly women teachers.[68] As Kiev's Yiddishists noted in their pedagogical journal *Shul un lebn,* many of the women teaching in Yiddish schools had received only Russian-language pedagogical training. Yiddishist pedagogical activists deemed them linguistically unprepared and "entirely cut off from the masses"—that is, weak links in the effort to create a secular Yiddish-only education.[69] The theorist and critic Dobrushin prescribed immersion both in Yiddish and the "new Holy Law" of Yiddish literature for "our young teacher corps, and especially the woman teacher, the *Froebelistin,* [who] comes to us mostly from outside"; only in this way would the teachers be able to fill "the child's soul with new Yiddish-secular values."[70]

Yet even as these pedagogies concretized a tendency toward conceiving the child as a vessel for national identity, leading pedagogical theorist-activists in both movements aggressively combated the notion. The nursery-school educator Heilprin opened his programmatic article on "The Foundations of the Hebrew Nursery" by opposing his journal's viewpoint to two crudely substantive nationalist pedagogical tendencies: the idea that the nursery's primary task was to teach the Hebrew language, espoused by "the radical 'Hebraists' among us," and the idea that it ought to teach some sort of nationalist-historicist credo centering around the Land of Israel, espoused by "many of the 'avowed Zionists,' the party activists who seek the most primitive means to strengthen the national feeling in the heart of the child."

> The Hebrew nursery is not, in our opinion, a factory to teach the Hebrew language nor a workshop to produce little "Zionist" souls; the nursery is not a *means but an end* in itself . . .
>
> [It] derives its end only from within itself, from its essence, from the idea that gives it the right to exist, surely the principle goal toward which we strive in all modern education—to awaken in children *the power of creation.*[71]

Obviously, we might dismiss this argument as mere rhetoric—moreover, as rhetoric that in its defensiveness betrays something essential about an education undertaken in a context of nation-seeking. But why would someone like Heilprin feel compelled to make these claims—and not, crucially, in a debate with Yiddishists or with the Russifying liberals who had once dominated nontraditional Jewish education efforts, but in a Hebrew-language pedagogical journal intended for Hebraist teachers?

Furthermore, the same assumptions about the child as a creative subject to be cultivated rather than a vessel to be filled permeated pedagogical articles in both Hebraist and Yiddishist journals. Educators' writings were heavily laden not only with the already standard activity-based learning ideas of Friedrich Froebel, the early nineteenth-century creator of the kindergarten, but also the more recent and far-reaching arguments of Italian educator Maria Montessori regarding the distinctive character of children's minds and their rights to developmental autonomy. The fundament of such pedagogical orientations, as Hebraists and Yiddishist educators construed them by 1917, was a twinned concern with forming an individual capable of "independent thought" and with fostering an "original person" in the aesthetic sense. In their view, "to educate the child means to awaken the 'creator' in him, and with that, to strengthen his desire and ability so that he will wish to and be able to order his life in the future as he wishes and in a manner appropriate to his nature and his creative ability."[72]

Hebraist and Yiddishist pedagogues preached not only the doctrine of the child's individuality, but also the importance of aesthetic education. Typical was one Yiddishist educator who insisted that "aesthetic studies" were not a luxury but a necessity. Such study "develops the senses and the feelings, it allows the growth of the ability to create and the possibility of joyfully drawing from and satiating oneself with beauty—and the life-joy of encompassing everything and creating is, after all, the ultimate end of ends."[73]

Importantly, these pedagogical, psychological, and moral inclinations were held not only by the Russian-trained educators who had flowed into Jewish education from "outside," but also by some of the most ideologically committed nationalist activists of each movement. Though we lack an adequate sociology of Jewish nationalist teachers, sources from 1917–1919 suggest the real internalization of these sensibilities; certainly, they yield a very different profile than that of the teacher as proverbial instiller of national patriotism. The historian Dinur, who taught in Tarbut's Kiev teacher-training institution, describes the worshipful attitude of one young teacher toward Y. H. Brenner, Hebrew literature's most uncompromising critic of all Jewish nationalist pieties. This teacher's rejection of nationalist pieties typified his cohort; Dinur proudly records that the young man ultimately thanked him for having shown his cohort the value of "the Bible and Jewish history" (a value, in other words, that was in no way a given for this generation of Nietzschean Jewish nationalists).[74] Another Hebrew educator framed the importance of aesthetic education in the Hebrew school not primarily in terms of overcoming Jewish artlessness—a staple European criticism of Jews that had deep roots in modern Jewish circles—but rather in terms resonant with Schiller's *Über die ästhetische Erziehung des Menschen.* Aesthetic education was a necessary precondition, incumbent on all regardless of nation, for the transcendence of the "vicious animal within man" unleashed by the war, and for the creation of the "human being liberated from its yoke" who would build a new world.[75]

It seems that these principles were not merely preached and felt, but also practiced. Speaking to Hebrew educators, Heilprin prescribed the use of open-ended reading material that provoked questions rather than offered answers. He recommended the "new literary anthologies which are being written by the best among the teachers of all nations," thereby implicitly rejecting the more traditional nationalist anthologies produced for secular Hebrew teachers since the 1890s.[76] And in the Yiddishist *Shul un lebn,* a provincial teacher described his efforts to teach primary-school children not only to appreciate "poetic form" but also to write their own literature.[77]

Hebraist and Yiddishist cultural production for children beyond the school reflected the impress of these principles even more dramatically. In literary publishing for children, where the object was manifestly the direct shaping of the reader, the leading writers, critics, and publishers of both camps inclined decisively away from direct strategies of national subject formation. Substantively, the Hebrew and Yiddish children's literature of the period was dominated by the same deparochializing tendencies concurrently operating in the more rarified realm of high literature. Hailing a Hebrew translation of the Grimm fairy tales, Fichman rejoiced at the availability of this universally beloved book to Hebrew-reading children. Significantly, he drew no value distinction between this work and an original "Jewish" work, even though a previous generation of nationalist critics would certainly have done so. By the same token, the Kultur-Lige published a new translation of Hans Christian Andersen by the Kiev Yiddish writer Der Nister which, unlike previous translations into Hebrew and Yiddish, retained the Christian realia and references of several of the stories (see fig. 8).[78]

The original Yiddish and Hebrew children's literature of this period displayed and provoked similar responses. While some of the literature produced for children used Jewish traditional or folk motifs, some authors sought to avoid them. Writing in the flagship Yiddishist educational journal, one critic welcomed one such book, a collection of children's poems by Der Nister, because its center of gravity was not traditional Jewish folk life but rather "the world of elemental [*stikhishe*] spirits, the human being."[79]

As in the adult literary sphere, these deparochializing strategies signified not merely a broadened conception of "Jewish culture," but also ideas regarding the goals of culture and the proper character of the individuals who would consume, sustain, and eventually create it. By 1917, Jewish children's writers and nationalist publishers agreed with their counterparts in education that the child was not an empty vessel to be filled with national identity but a budding individuality deserving access to the full range of human experience. Even those editors and publishers who did not share the crusading sensibility of radical cultural de-Judaizers now took it for granted that the proper fare for children was not the nationalistically reconceived Jewish history and culture fed them by some of their predecessors, but a mixed corpus unfreighted by excess concern about Jewishness.

Children's journals like the Hebraist *Shetilim*, founded in 1917 in Moscow, and Kiev's Yiddishist *Shretelekh*, launched in 1919, mixed Jewish-themed texts with works ranging from contemporary European children's literature to Korean folk tales. Leading nationalist publishing houses of the era like the Hebraist Omanut or the Yiddishist Kiever Farlag focused especially on translating the international canon of youth literature "from which all the peoples of Europe drew sustenance."[80] Though these nationalists were anxious to win over Jewish children to Hebrew or Yiddish national culture—to "implant the Hebrew world in the heart of the young reader," as *Shetilim* put it—they clearly regarded access to a rich, unparochial Hebrew or Yiddish culture as a necessary enticement for children of the former Russian empire. But they also regarded such a harmonious blend of Jewish and world culture as the child's right and their own duty: one of *Shetilim*'s declared tasks was to bring the child "out of his narrow world."[81]

It is perhaps apposite that the two leading figures of revolutionary Russia's Hebrew nursery-school movement by 1917–1919, Heilprin and Alterman, raised sons—Yonatan Ratosh and Natan Alterman—who became two of modern Hebrew poetry's most formally innovative poets. They were raised by nationalists to be, among other things, "national Jews"; but their growth into creators rather than passive recipients of the nation's ostensible genius and eternity suggests that their parents succeeded in fostering creative individuals rather than obedient subjects. There is a vast body of critical educational theory that seeks to expose the incoherencies or even bad faith of such essentially liberal conceptions of education and individuality, and even scholars who differ with these theories cannot assess these phenomena on the actors' terms. But it is clear that these Hebraist and Yiddishist ideas about what was best for Jewish children made for a substantially different sort of pedagogy than that presumed in much writing on nationalism.

The Dialectic of Cultural Nationalism

Culturists concerned with the tension between national-cultural duty and the distinct imperatives of art and individuality agreed that these conflicts were rooted in experiences and ideologies that predated the Revolution. None of them, not even outspoken revolutionaries like Litvakov, saw aspirations to untrammeled creative expression and the cultivation of the self as products of 1917.[82] To the contrary, they conceived these preexisting aspirations as themselves decisive forces behind the cultural project's 1917 resurgence.[83]

An analysis of the longer history that birthed these aspirations would require a thoroughgoing reconstruction of the "sources of the self" (to use

Charles Taylor's felicitous term) for East European Jewish moderns. Here it suffices to note a few hallmarks of the processes that Shtif, Bistritsky, Bialik, and others sought to understand. As Bistritsky recognized, tensions among nation, art, and individuality had been present in the Jewish cultural project from its earliest stages in the 1880s and 1890s. Scholars familiar with the archetypal narratives of modern Jewish literary culture will think immediately, as Bistritsky did, of the famous polemical confrontation of the mid-1890s between the editor and ideologist Ahad Ha-'Am and the budding Nietzschean Hebraist Berdichevsky, described in Chapter 3. Ahad Ha-'Am's 1896 mission statement for *Ha-Shiloah*, too, had famously invited only those literary submissions that would contribute to "the awakening of thought and the spreading of the national idea among us" and rejected in advance "the creative work which has nothing in it but beauty, which awakens the flow of feeling for the sake of pleasure alone." Berdichevsky had dissented in favor of an encompassing, anti-essentialist vision of a Hebrew literature that would draw no predetermined lines between the concerns of nation and those of the modern individual. In part, he sought to defend a more expansive vision of Jewish culture. But in turn, he motivated this cultural agenda in terms of an underlying concern with the fate of the modern Jewish self: "We wish to be 'Hebrew humans' at one and the same time, in one spirit, nourished from one source. We feel a great and fundamental need to heal the great and terrible fissure in our heart."[84]

Berdichevsky's stance, though no doubt heartfelt, was also intensely polemical and performative. But the culturists of the 1890s iterated the same notion repeatedly in numerous other, less polemical frameworks. None other than Bialik, by 1917 the most powerful internal critic of the intelligentsia's "irresponsible" tendencies toward aestheticism and individualism, spent his formative decade as a poet locked in a guilt-ridden struggle to overcome forms of private, erotic, and intellectual subjectivity in his own work. In 1892, having already embarked on his meteoric rise to the status of Jewish national poet, he admitted privately to his older admirer Ravnitsky that in his own eyes, much of his own poetry was not properly "national."[85]

Similar developments made themselves felt in the fledgling Yiddish literary sphere of the 1880s–1890s. Although the pioneering Yiddish writer Y. L. Peretz later grew into the role of Yiddishism's symbolic progenitor, in the 1880s he was by no means sure that Yiddish literature possessed more than merely tutelary value en route to Jewish integration into a modern

"European" (in this case, secular Polish) culture. In a series of letters from 1888 concerning the tasks of Yiddish writing (addressed to another ambivalent founder of modern Yiddish literature, Sholem Aleichem), Peretz expostulated on the need to create a literature in Yiddish for "the folk" that would reforge the Jewish community as a modern, strong national collective able to better face its adversities, while simultaneously educating it. This trope was a typical one among East European ideologies. Yet in the same letters, Peretz sounded a very different note: "I write for myself, for my own enjoyment, and if sometimes I remember the reader, he is a person from a higher stratum of society, a person who has read and studied in a living language." In a further striking contrast, Peretz asserted the difference between his form of authorial subjectivity and that which he took to be Sholem Aleichem's: "I, as someone who writes for his own enjoyment according to the situation of his spirit at the hour that I grasp the pen, I have taken from all worlds at once."[86] Importantly, this stance was reflected (if also partially repressed) in Peretz's early Yiddish writings, which intrigued and infuriated contemporaries precisely because they obeyed the modern literary imperative of multivocality.

Bialik's and Peretz's early writings reflexively cast literary complexity as the product of an individual consciousness not unwilling but unable to subject itself to the ideological goals that, in principle, both authors embraced as the very reason for their literary work. Equally significant, both men articulated these felt contradictions privately and prior to any clear public articulation of such tensions in the Hebrew and incipient Yiddish literary fields. Their utterances must be read, then, not as a parroting of notions already in place in metropolitan literary fields, but as a description of an expressive self taking shape within them and their contemporaries.

In the first decade of the twentieth century, these sensibilities became the norm among Jewish culturists and began to transform cultural life. Speaking intimately about his own generation, in 1922 the Yiddishist Mayzl described his and his friends' cultural aspirations in the decade before World War I:

The pitying and condescending attitude toward Jewish art is uprooted. Yiddish literary creativity ceases to be a product of the intellectual for the "poor" folk. It penetrates into the intimate life of the intellectual, begins to satisfy and excite him himself . . .

Literature and art were confronted with great demands: they must be woven into the web of Jewish spiritual life and must express the entire sweep of experiences, problems, and woes of the modern Jew, who lives in the wide world, who bears universal problems and universal concepts, and is deeply and organically both Jew and Man.[87]

Mayzl here captures precisely the same process decried in Bialik's 1916 "Halakhah and Aggadah": a fateful sea change in the ideals and sensibilities of the Jewish national intelligentsia revolving around vaguely understood but strongly felt new structures of aesthetic consciousness and individualism. Bialik, Kleinman, and Shtif considered these developments a national disaster; Litvakov, Mayzl, and the Hebrew and Yiddish pedagogues construed them (at least in public) as an unalloyed advance. Hofshteyn and Shimoni approached these issues as productive cultural problems. Bistritsky conceived the structure of tensions surrounding these commitments as a tragedy in the true sense: the clash of two rights. But what almost all of these essays took as a given was that they were dealing with a deep process rather than a superficial one, that is, one that was at once ideological and cognitive, rhetorical yet also sociocultural, and hence not easily undone.

As Mayzl's text suggests, the once-marginal and controversial views of figures like Berdichevsky concerning the prerogatives of art and self had been internalized by many Jewish culturists between the 1890s and 1914. Indeed, a number of scholars have pointed to the ways in which tensions around "art and nation" and parallel tensions around "collective and self" moved to the center of the secular Jewish cultural sphere in the years before the war.[88] The quiet conflict between private desire and public duty among Jewish cultural producers in the 1890s became a publicly visible, discursively ramified problem that Jewish nationalism in general and Hebraist and Yiddishist culturism in particular had to confront. The events of 1917 did not fundamentally transform this problem, but rather intensified it tremendously. Zionists were presented with the tantalizing possibility of finally achieving some sort of Jewish statehood in Palestine, diaspora socialists were tempted with the promise of the Revolution, and autonomists were cheered by the apparent breakthrough regarding formal national autonomy. All of these possibilities demanded that the nationalist intelligentsia redouble their efforts to instill the appropriate consciousness and conscience in the prospective Jewish nation, masses, or *folk*. Yet at the same moment, the cultural sphere that reemerged was marked by refusals of unprecedented boldness: many culturists declined to wed culture to political organizations and their programs, to make aesthetic culture a carrier of ideology, to intensify the "Jewishness" of the culture being produced, and to use culture as a means of mass national pedagogy.

Given the high stakes, it is not surprising that many Jewish culturists proved open to the attacks mounted on them from within by critics like Bialik and Shtif. Bistritsky's sense that he was caught up in a tragic battle of conflicting duties to nation, art, and self was typical. By the 1917–1919 juncture, many Jewish culturists had evidently come to share the worries of Bialik that somehow the new Jewish culture and its makers were failing to create a culture that could "shape life." In a 1919 essay that became infamous in the annals of Hebrew literary criticism, the Zionist and political radical Shlomo Tsemah savagely attacked the work of the recently deceased Hebrew-Yiddish literary pioneer Sh. Y. Abramovitsh (Mendele Moykher-Sforim) for having failed to "influence life with the power of [the author's] creation " and thus failing to offer Jewish readers any guidance as to "what we must do to escape our abject situation."[89]

Even cultural figures who adhered deeply to the very ideals under indictment, ideals of aesthetic autonomy and the prerogatives of individuality, felt the power of Bialik's critique. This was true of both Fichman and Fridman. Fichman insisted, rather vaguely, that the artist who was truly a "master of aggadah" could in fact shape the nation through the represented power of his dreams. Fridman acknowledged that Bialik's demands on the intelligentsia were no doubt legitimate at the present moment of possibility and necessity.[90]

Yet however much Bialik's critique resonated with its targets, the pervasive claims of art and individuality proved stronger still. Indeed, these ideals of art and self help explain the peculiar culturist ideals examined in preceding chapters: the drive to insulate culture from direct political affiliation and direct service to the political programs that most culturists themselves actually promoted; the urge to sever cultural expression from any narrow concern with "Jewish identity" or any particular Jewish cultural corpus; and the concern to ensure that the demands of national education did not compromise the content and character of high culture. Thus, to take the case of deparochialization, it bears reiterating that even many of the more reluctant advocates of such a strategy saw it as the only possible means of rendering the new Hebrew or Yiddish culture appealing to their own cohort of young, nationally minded but cosmopolitan intellectuals. Thus, the Hebraist Litai's insistence that a massive program of translating literary works into Hebrew was a national priority derived from his view that the will to individual self-development through culture was stronger among the Hebrew-using intelligentsia than even the most conscientiously held nationalist beliefs. Litai's modern "Hebrew" bridled at the narrowness of Hebrew literature's Judaic concerns because he or she wished to develop a self with no predetermined boundaries. In the absence of translation, to do so meant to turn to literary works in other languages, like Russian; this in turn led to assimilation. Yet to simply demand that the modern Hebrew refrain from pursuing all paths of cultural experience (as Bialik's "Halakhah and Aggadah" essentially did) was to demand the psychologically impossible—to require, as Litai put it, "spiritual abstinence" *(perishut sikhlit)*. The unmistakable sexual overtones of his rhetoric (a *parush* was a figure associated with abstinence for the sake of religious devotion), which indeed tapped into the familiar motif of sexual frustration common to the young men who had shaped modern Hebrew culture, underscored the psychic, affective, pre-ideological dimensions of the intelligentsia's will to individual self-formation. Like sexuality itself, the desire for cultured selfhood could not be checked.[91]

By the same token, the culturist critique of political demands on culture owed much of its urgency to underlying ideas about art and self. Moyshe Kulbak's 1918 assertion in a Bundist journal in Minsk that Yiddishism would win more through its "blooms" than through ideological argument radically contravened Bundist principles. But it made perfect sense against the ground of Kulbak's own essentially Romantic relationship to art and aesthetic experience and his working assumption—also grounded, we must assume, experientially—that many Jewish youth in the borderlands shared this relationship. By the same token, it seems likely that the culturist intelligentsia's aversion to the tutelary "*Zweck*-culture," which a previous generation of Jewish nationalists had unhesitatingly created to influence the masses, reflected not mere white-gloved elitism, but an experientially based sense that such cultural products would simply have no appeal to provincial youth hungry for the real thing.

In short, by 1917, the Jewish cultural sphere was populated by people who were wholly committed to the creation of a modern "Jewish culture" yet had internalized ideals of aesthetic experience and self-cultivation that were independent of that project. Jewish culturists may have wished to enact dictates of the sort Bialik issued, but they could not help but relate to art as an exalted realm with its own rules and requirements, and they were driven by a deep desire to attain a modern, integrated, cultivated secular selfhood. The tensions of role and responsibility that emerged from this conflict were structural, and hence unavoidable.

Yet although the conflict between nationalist objectives and the primacy of art and self was growing in intensity, a second process was also under way: the inscription of prerogatives of art and self in the very project of Jewish cultural nationalism. By 1917, some culturists had begun to suggest that the creation of an aesthetically compelling Jewish art and the cultivation of mature secular individualities among Jews were fundamental objectives of Jewish nationalism that could brook no compromise. They were perhaps even essential preconditions to the realization of Jewish nationalism's other goals.

Earlier in the chapter, I cited the Hebrew literary critic Grinblat's blunt dismissal of all poetry written for explicitly Zionist ends. Implicit in his argument were the by now familiar assumptions concerning the inviolability (and fragility) of the artistic process and the individual's aesthetic experiences. But Grinblat's argument went beyond a defense of the prerogatives of art and self. He insisted that the simple act of writing good poetry in Hebrew—good by pan-European standards—was itself true cultural nationalism: "literary revival in its true meaning means the renewal and elevation of creativity, and each one who has enriched the literature . . . each who has plowed the earth, renewed form and content . . . behold, it is he who has revived the literature, the spirit of the people, and prepared hearts for redemption."[92]

In the same 1918 essay that took up the challenge of Bialik's "Halakhah and Aggadah," Grinblat's fellow critic Fridman made a different but parallel claim. Fridman approvingly surveyed recent poetry by Fichman (another participant in the debate) on the poet's prewar experience of Palestine. What struck Fridman about Fichman's poetry was the uncompromisingly personal orientation that he found in it:

> It is [customarily deemed] impossible to speak about the Land of Israel without accentuating its value for the collective, its grace and splendor which depend on the relationship between the land and the Hebrew people. And in truth, who could resist that temptation and think about the Land of Israel solely in the terms of an individual who wanders in it rather than as the son of a nation which longs for its homeland? But

Fichman knows only the poetry of the individual and the joy and woe of the individual [*ha-individ*]. Therefore, his relationship to the Land of Israel is also utterly different from the traditional relationship. He finds in it not our land, but *his* land.[93]

Fridman saw this stance not merely as a formal achievement but as a cultural—even political—one:

He is lacking in patriotism [*patriotiut*], some will say. He is not national, others will say. Indeed, that is true, and that is his glory. He is not a national poet and not a Zionist poet. He is a *true poet*. Would that all the individuals who comprise the Jewish nation could each find in the land of Israel his "own land"—then the land would perforce be "ours."[94]

It was likely no coincidence that both of these essays appeared in *Ha-Tekufah,* the journal published by Stybel and edited by Frishman. Frishman had long preached against ideas of collective identity and, already before the war, had articulated the essential move made by both Grinblat and Fridman: the reversal of the classically nationalist assumption that re-forming the nation's collective identity and reimplanting it in the individual were prerequisites to individual regeneration. As Frishman had put it in 1913 with deceptive simplicity: "Let us make makers, creators, oracles of a new word, and thus will we make readers, and thus will we make Hebrews."[95]

Frishman was the most significant anti-Zionist figure in Hebrew letters by the early twentieth century. Yet it would entirely miss the point to imagine that the individualist logic at work in the writings of Frishman, Fridman, and Grinblat necessarily dictated a rejection of Zionism (or some other form of organized Jewish nationalist politics). While Frishman drew that connection, the much younger Grinblat and Fridman combined equally strong individualist ideologies with deep Zionist commitments.[96] Both shared Frishman's aversion to cultural objects created in accordance with nationalist ideology or rhetoric, but their critiques of what we might call "nationalist culture" in no way renounced cultural nationalism. To the contrary, both essays framed their critiques of such cultural bastardization in terms of nationalism in general and Russian Zionism in particular. Nor was this some sort of subversive appropriation. In speaking of "revival" *(tehiyah)* and "homeland" *(moledet),* Grinblat and Fridman meant precisely what other Zionists meant: reviving the oppressed and debased East

European Jewish community by encouraging individuals to reconstitute a free nation in Jewry's historic territorial center. But because of their conceptions of art, individuality, and the interplay between the two in the consciousness of modern persons like themselves, they believed that these ends could only be served by art that was in no way burdened by any dictates made in the name of the nation.

Similar valorizations of the role of the individual appeared in explicitly Zionist venues. The pseudonymous Aleph's vociferous rejection of demands that modern Hebrew cultural creativity tie itself to the Jewish tradition employed the classic Berdichevskian rhetoric of the primacy of individual self-expression over and above any sort of group dictates. But Aleph went further: he cast this defense of the individual and his creative prerogatives as the truest form of Jewish cultural nationalism, properly understood: "To declare unfit in advance all the growth, all the souls in [the divine] treasury which are yet to descend to earth with the passing of generations, to strip from them the honor of a man and lower them to the status of inheritors, grandchildren, interpreters, and imitators—is that not truly the murder of souls and the spilling of the honor-blood of the nation [*shfikhat dam ha-kavod shel ha-umah*]?"[97]

In this tangle of fanciful imagery and purple prose lurked the same critical conceptual reversal proposed by Grinblat and Fridman. To trammel the expressive freedom of future generations of individual Jewish "souls" in the name of some fixed conception of Jewish national culture was actually a sin not only against Jewish individuals, but also against the Jewish nation. The reader was left to figure out exactly what about national culture and cultural nationalism motivated this claim (and indeed, Aleph's heartfelt but vague rhetoric may be an expression not of a well-developed ideological position but of precisely the sort of unmediated sensibilities about nation, art, and self described earlier). But Aleph's working assumptions were plain enough. Proper culture as such could only be created by the free and creative individual. Any national culture could therefore either be an open-ended collocation of the creations of free individuals or a scandalously crippled culture undermined by its own misplaced forms of essentialism and censorship. Hence, creating a proper Jewish cultural nationalism would mean not just accepting but embracing untrammeled individualism among Jews (or rather, Hebrews).[98]

Similar ideas were also to be found in Yiddishist circles by 1917. The political moderate but cultural radical Latski-Bertoldi proffered a vision of cultural rebellion and the autonomous individual as a national end:

> Living in your Jewish home, keep the world in view; do not fear to throw off the yoke, rebel against the old; don't let it matter that those around you hold "that the thinker becomes a heretic and the political activist and artist an impudent rebel"; you should imagine that you are on your own, discover your "I," the *human* in yourself and thus will you find the path to *humanity*—only, descend from the surface to the depths, be honest and whole everywhere, on the street and in *your home*. And then you may be certain that even in losing yourself you will find yourself, that your rebellion will be a blessing for you and for the Jewish people.[99]

Latski-Bertoldi's comments came as the conclusion to a commentary on Litvakov's ideas of "Jewish revolution." Like Litvakov, Latski-Bertoldi believed that rebellion against Judaism (in the largest sense) in the name of the individual and the universal could take dishonest or inauthentic forms—meaning denial of one's own Jewish cultural roots and conscious assimilationism. But Latski-Bertoldi was also convinced that as long as that pitfall was avoided, individualistic rebellion would serve rather than betray the cause of Jewish national regeneration.

Taken together, these essays (and those of Bistritsky, examined earlier) articulated in embryonic fashion several powerful claims about individuality, culture, and the nation. First, they suggested that respect for the special prerogatives of culture and of individuality would shape healthy Jewish national subjects more effectively than would more instrumental efforts to build national identity. Translated into Bialik's terms, this meant a profound skepticism toward any notion of a new "law" or law-giving culture, coupled with (and predicated on) a profound, almost Schillerian optimism that when East European Jews discovered culture in a humanist sense and reconstructed themselves as autonomous individuals, they would not abandon Jewish culture or the Jewish nation but commit themselves of their own free will to the regeneration of both. At the same time, these essays reflected a high water mark of Jewish culturism as a distinct ideological system, in that they took for granted that the formation of a culture in Hebrew or Yiddish that allowed for the full range of human expression and individual development was in fact the true end of Jewish cultural nationalism.

These essayists' unstable synthesis of liberal individualism and national-ism could easily slip back into familiar forms of coercive cultural national-ism. For example, the unspoken given of all these essays was a shared Jew-ish language (a prerequisite for the automatic "conservation," so to speak, of the individual's self-expression as a national possession); and what this meant in the multilingual context of Russian and East European Jewish life in 1917–1919 was an intensification of radical monolingualism and war against forms of Jewish expression in the "wrong" language. But, even leav-ing aside the question of whether any language could truly be freely chosen in 1918 Eastern Europe, what is significant for our investigation of cul-tural nationalism is that significant numbers of Jewish culturists not only came to accept regulative ideals of aesthetic autonomy and individual self-cultivation, but even attempted to inscribe these anarchic ideals into their nationalist doctrines and policies.

— 6 —

The Imperatives of Revolution

What is attractive in Bolshevism? Intellectually: its necessity, its
simplifying character. Ethically: its revolt against empty words.
Aesthetically: its elemental power, its totality . . . its plasticity. Politically: its activism, its will to power. In general cultural terms: its
laying bare the roots of culture—its forcing us to begin everything
anew; its wake-and-push-power, its giving to us a taste of the birth
pangs of the messianic age . . . psychologically (subjectively): the
fact that it possesses what I do not.

—SHMUEL NIGER, 1918

The Yiddish literary critic Shmuel Niger was a political and cultural moderate. Though he had played a leading role in a Jewish socialist-nationalist
party during the 1905 Revolution, by 1917 he had joined the nonsocialist
Folkist camp. A champion of new literary trends, Niger nevertheless had
no patience for notions of total cultural rupture. He was a firm secularist
who nevertheless remained convinced of the lasting importance of Jewish
tradition for the new Jewish culture-in-the-making. An early champion of
Yiddishism, Niger never ceased to acknowledge Hebrew's cultural importance; he even wrote in Hebrew on occasion and maintained friendly relations with Hebrew cultural figures as diverse as Ravnitsky, Stybel, and
Tchernikhovsky well into 1918.[1]

Most importantly, Niger was one of the most stalwart defenders of
culturist principles within Yiddishist circles. Since 1908, when he founded
the first Yiddish journal devoted exclusively to cultural matters, Niger had
sounded the same mantras. Cultural activity must respect different rules
than party politics. True artistic creativity required freedom from ideological demands. A secular high culture was essential to Jewish national formation but could only fulfill its task if created freely by individuals awakened
and committed to the specific rules of culture itself. He had elaborated
these increasingly normative culturist views in the first great Yiddishist

journal, the 1913–1914 *Yudishe Velt,* and reiterated them throughout 1917 wherever he published.

Niger left Red Petrograd for slightly less repressive Moscow in early 1918 still imbued with these views, and he never renounced them. Yet in mid-1918, his attitude toward the October Revolution began to change. An April diary entry records growing disillusionment, even contempt, for the Russian liberal and Jewish liberal nationalist circles in which he moved. In July, he wrote that "everyone who has any moral sensibility must *sympathize* with the Revolution. But the Revolution can be *made* by others and perhaps *only* by others." By November, he had appreciative words for the Bolsheviks' "drunkenness" and "maximalism."[2] Niger's evolution paralleled that of growing swaths of the Russian creative intelligentsia. As early as January 1918, the Symbolist poet Aleksandr Blok's apocalyptic *poema* "The Twelve" had given form to the sensibilities that now possessed Niger: a deepening conviction of the October Revolution's historical necessity, growing contempt for the "ineffectuality" of political moderates, and a mixture of repulsion from and attraction to Bolshevism's total vision.[3]

In mid-1918 Niger had altered his relationship to "October" in practice by taking a position at the Culture and Education Department of the central Jewish Commissariat (EvKom) in Moscow. The EvKom had been created shortly after the Bolshevik seizure of power by Stalin's Commissariat for Nationality Affairs (Narkomnats) as one of several commissariats concerned with the affairs of ethnoreligious or ethnonational groups; others included Muslim, Polish, Latvian, and Armenian commissariats. These government departments reflected in part a genuine commitment in the new regime to a sort of compensatory self-determination for nationalities repressed under the tsars. But their primary task was to project revolutionary ideology into the lives of the former empire's ethnic groups.[4]

Neither a party member nor a trusted revolutionary, Niger worked for the EvKom as a cultural "specialist." Along with his younger brother and fellow Folkist and Yiddishist Donyel Tsharni, he served as de facto editor of the first Soviet Yiddish cultural journal, *Kultur un bildung,* founded August 1918. There Niger began the process with which this chapter is concerned: a struggle to understand and help define the implications for the Jewish cultural project of his partial embrace of the October Revolution.

Niger never gave much ground to the vague but insistent rhetoric of cultural revolution that circulated elsewhere in the journal and in the larger revolutionary discourse by mid-1918. In fielding the question of the

proper relationship between high literature and the Revolution, Niger declared in the second issue of the journal that "all writings which are fabri-
cated in the name of some tendency . . . bear no relation to true art."[5]
A coworker at the EvKom, the loyal Communist Shmuel Agursky, later
wrote with disgust: "already from the first issue of *Kultur un Bildung* . . .
one could see very clearly that with such 'loyal' culture-people as Niger,
it would not be possible to create any new, revolutionary, proletarian culture."[6]

But Niger's change in attitude toward October did force him to grapple
ever more seriously with the question of the Revolution's meaning for
the Jewish cultural project. Niger left—or was forced out—of *Kultur un
Bildung* by October 1918. But when Bolshevik forces gained control of
parts of Lithuania and Byelorussia after the German withdrawal in November, Niger experimented once again with Yiddishist-Communist rapprochement. Resettled in his old adopted hometown Vilna, he became editor of *Di naye velt*, a second Soviet-sponsored Yiddish journal. There, in an
article entitled "The Revolution and the Poet" (concerning, in fact, Blok's
"Twelve" in Moyshe Broderzon's Yiddish translation), he continued to insist that literature could not be mobilized for directly political ends without losing its character as art. But he now accepted the claim that artists
could not ignore the Revolution in their art, and enacted this sensibility
by devoting extensive space in the journal to revolutionary lyrics by others
making the same rapprochement as he, like Broderzon and Moyshe
Kulbak. In essence, he now acknowledged the necessity of a "revolutionary" literature just as he acknowledged the necessity of the Revolution and
revolutionary violence.[7]

Niger was the first Jewish cultural figure of any significance to work
openly for a Soviet institution. Although it is sometimes still assumed that
the Russian Jewish intelligentsia as a whole had a special inclination to
Bolshevism, this was certainly not true of the culturist intelligentsia. As
Niger's brother put it, Moscow's Jewish intelligentsia assumed a "sabotage"
stance toward the Bolshevik cultural initiatives well into late 1918. The
Communist Agursky, who loathed both Tsharni and Niger as counter-rev-
olutionaries and certainly had no interest in defending their reputations,
recalled that Niger's decision caused "Jewish literary circles" to regard him
and his brother as "terrible heretics and . . . 'komisariattshikes'."[8]

If Niger was among the first culturists to be drawn by the raw power and
simplifying Manichean vision of the October Revolution, he was also

among the first to break off the romance. By mid-1919, Niger began to step back from his cautious embrace. By 1920, resettled in the United States, he became one of the Soviet Union's more vigorous critics on the Yiddishist left.[9]

But even as Niger ceased to be enthralled, many other Jewish culturists were beginning to trace his earlier steps, and many of these would go considerably further. At the end of 1918 and the beginning of 1919—some six months to a year after Niger's turn—a new openness to the claims of the October Revolution began to emerge among Jewish culturists, especially Yiddishists. By then, hopes were fading among much of Russia's liberal and radical intelligentsia that the Bolshevik regime would soon topple. The regime's internal opponents were suppressed or in disarray. By the winter of 1918–1919, the regime was in fact on the offensive in the context of the armistice that ended the world war and spurred a German withdrawal from the borderlands. In December and early January, working with local pro-Bolshevik forces, the Bolsheviks gained precarious control of parts of Byelorussia, Latvia, and historic Lithuania, including Vilna. At the same time in Ukraine, the Russian Communist party and its closely allied Ukrainian counterpart decided to seize power as the conservative Hetmanate government in Ukraine crumbled and a peasant revolt put a new left-wing Ukrainian nationalist government, the Directory, in power. On February 5, three weeks after Directory forces took Kiev, they were driven out by the Bolsheviks. To the north, the Bolsheviks soon lost control of Vilna to the armies of the new Polish state, but would hold Ukraine through the year and, except for a brief period in 1920, for the next seventy.[10]

These victories, and the revolutionary outbreaks and unrest that now convulsed postwar Europe, lent weight to Bolshevik claims that they were the vanguard of a coming world revolution. At the same time, for many in the region but for Jews especially, the range of passable alternatives to the Bolshevik regime was rapidly narrowing. The loosely organized Russian anti-Bolshevik movements that sought to overthrow the regime—the "Whites"—drifted toward ever more radical rightist and anti-Semitic principles. In the Ukraine, hopes for an autonomous Jewish national life had been briefly revived by the victory of the Directory, which restored extensive formal autonomy. But this optimism soon gave way to horror as a wave of monstrous pogroms swept across Ukraine in early 1919.[11]

These attacks had a profound effect on Jews across the ideological spectrum. Sending many into shock and despair, they also pushed many into the arms of the Bolsheviks, who in principle and for the most part in practice opposed anti-Semitic violence.[12] Nonsocialists and anti-Bolsheviks, like mainstream members of the Zionist movement, were left with few options. Where possible, they sought to make deals with tolerable local ethnonationalist forces: support in exchange for communal autonomy and protection. This took place at Zionist initiative in the newly established Lithuanian state in 1918, for instance.[13] For its part, the Jewish socialist camp within the national movement had always been pro-Revolution even when it was generally anti-Bolshevik. Hence, many within it were primed to interpret the events of 1919 as a confirmation that the October Revolution was the will of history—or at least that the only choice was between the Bolsheviks and the pogromists.

The actual Bolshevik conquest of Ukraine in February 1919 solidified these shifts. The Zionist and liberal diasporist intelligentsia could now only accede or emigrate. In the Jewish socialist-nationalist camp, the Bolshevik conquest catalyzed a full-fledged split: between February and May 1919, the Jewish socialist-nationalist parties in Ukraine split into Communist and anti-Communist camps. Meanwhile, a growing number of individual Jewish socialist-nationalists simply flowed directly into the Bolshevik party.[14]

It was in this context that growing numbers of Jewish culturists began to view the October Revolution as a reality that could not be ignored. The Hebrew prose writer Eliezer Shteynman was sympathetic to socialism but staunchly anti-Bolshevik well into 1918. In the April 1918 *Ha-Tekufah*, he called the Revolution an act of political violence that would do nothing to increase human freedom. But the winter of 1918–1919 changed his mind. An article published in March 1919 in an Odessa organ of the Marxist-Zionist Poale Tsion party registers his political despair and fury in the face of the pogroms. By mid-1919, he had undergone a dramatic transformation. In a pamphlet entitled *Ha-komunist ha-'ivri* (The Hebrew Communist), which made him notorious in Odessa's intensely anti-Bolshevik Hebraist milieu, he embraced the October Revolution, complete with its Manichean demands for merciless class warfare and apocalyptic violence.[15]

Concomitantly, Shteynman began to wrestle with the meaning of the Revolution for the cultural project. Sweeping declarations about a "Red Hebrew culture" in his pamphlet vied with a more conservationist sensibility that he confided to his diary:

If the change in regime brings a cure to the wounds of society, we too will say a blessing over the change and bring into the new life our language in all its forms and all the good that is stored up in our culture . . . And with the changing of the times, when life returns to its course and equilibrium is restored—behold, we will have guarded our national and human vessels: we will have preserved the treasure, and we will transmit it to our children as well in the spirit of the coming days.[16]

The depth of Shteynman's transformation was extreme, but the timing, trajectory, political and existential causes, and cultural-ideological consequences were typical. The pogrom wave of 1919 made a deep impression on culturists of all stripes. Most famously, Kiev's leading young Yiddish poets increasingly turned their attention away from their self-proclaimed task of creating "the new Yiddish poetry" toward the all-too-traditional task of collective mourning. One of their spokesmen later lamented the unlooked-for reorientation: "The poets who had just recently grown drunk on joy and carried away by the holiday-liberatory declarations and slogans put away their instruments of song and shaped true traditional laments."[17]

More generally, the Manichean logic of the Civil War loomed no less large for culturists than for Jewish political activists. Many left-wing Yiddishists in Ukraine greeted the new socialist-nationalist Directory with renewed hopes in November and December 1918; the cultural activists and educators in the Kultur-Lige saw it as an opportunity to recover real cultural autonomy after its dismantling by the Hetmanate.[18] But within this camp, too, growing numbers began to despair of the Ukrainian option even before Ukraine fell to the Bolsheviks. Already by late 1918, the young expressionist Leyb Kvitko had begun to compose the poetry that would win him the reputation of Yiddish poetry's first significant Communist poet.[19]

More to the point, by early 1919, no culturist could ignore the simple fact of Bolshevik rule. With the conquest of Ukraine, the main demographic concentrations of East European Jewry outside Poland and Galicia were under Bolshevik control. This included the main centers of the 1917 cultural revival: Kiev, Odessa, Vilna (briefly), and the secondary cultural centers of Minsk and Kharkov now joined Moscow, Petrograd, and Vitebsk.

The question of the Revolution's meaning for the Jewish cultural project was, finally, inflected by the specific features of an emerging Bolshevik policy regarding Jewish culture itself. Until mid-1918, the regime made no significant efforts to shape a policy toward Jewish culture. But between mid-1918 and mid-1919, first in Russia and then in Ukraine, the new regime emerged as a real actor within the Jewish cultural sphere. On the one hand, various representatives of the regime extended the promise of substantial, perhaps even unprecedented, cultural autonomy and material support for Jewish national culture. On the other hand, the regime's own newly created agencies for Jewish affairs signaled their readiness to suppress all those forms of Jewish culture and consciousness deemed anti-revolutionary. It quickly became clear that key forces in the new regime were intent on destroying Hebrew-language culture and that only Yiddish culture stood a good chance of winning regime recognition as an official ethnic culture. Thus, it was among Yiddishists especially that the meaning of the Revolution for the Jewish cultural project became a matter of intense debate and rethinking in 1919.

Jewish Culture under Bolshevik Power

In December 1917, after the shooting in the streets of Petrograd had died down, the great Jewish historian Dubnow wrote to Bialik and Ravnitsky that the Bolshevik Revolution meant not only the end of Russian Jewry's "holiday of freedom," but also the collapse of its cultural hopes, because the Revolution naturally sought "to do harm to everything which possesses a tinge of culture [Heb.: *kulturah*]."[20] Despite such despairing predictions, the first seven or eight months after the October Revolution were marked by relatively little Bolshevik interference in Jewish civil, political, or cultural life. The shaky new regime initially refrained from full repression of civil institutions and outright assault on Russia's literate urban public.[21] This included almost all Jewish secular-national organizations—perhaps because even the Bolshevik imagination could impute no threat to a population so politically isolated, without territory or allies, and victimized across Eastern Europe by Whites, Ukrainian nationalists, Polish nationalists, peasant mobs, demobilized soldiers, and anyone else who wished to harm them.

Jewish cultural activity in particular went almost entirely unmolested, in keeping with the overall fairly liberal cultural policy of those early days.[22] Indeed, the first six months of Bolshevik rule coincided with the blossoming of the Jewish culturist and especially Hebraist efforts that had begun in late 1916, especially in Moscow. During a March 1918 visit to Moscow, An-ski commented that "Jewish publishing is strongly developed here. Several dozen books are being published in Hebrew. A Yiddish press and a Rus-sian-Jewish press are in the process of organizing." What An-ski later called the "vigorous literary activity" of the Hebraist presses held especially for the Stybel publishing house, which continued its ever-expanding transla-tion program and published the first two massive issues of *Ha-Tekufah* in spring 1918 and the third well into summer, if the printed dates are accurate. At the same time, local Yiddishist efforts began to make some headway, though Yiddish culture in Moscow remained weak relative to He-braism. The circle of figures around Broderzon and Tsharni, which in this period formally became the "Moscow Circle of Jewish Writers and Artists," founded the Khaver publishing house and organized an impressive Jewish art exhibition that drew some one thousand visitors during July and Sep-tember.[23]

But beginning in April and May 1918, the situation began to change. In Russia proper, the regime began to exercise control on "the Jewish street" in the context of a larger move to suppress Russia's remaining islands of civil society. During March and April there was an expansion of the hith-erto negligible regime organs for Jewish affairs. In some places, such as Petrograd, these bodies aggressively suppressed Jewish political and civic life almost immediately.[24] Other regime organs like the Moscow EvKom initially displayed a relatively restrained attitude toward the organized Jew-ish public, including toward "bourgeois" (Zionist- and liberal-dominated) Jewish community and private institutions.[25] But such restraint gave way by mid-1918 to a more decisive policy of repression.[26]

The regime's policy toward Jewish cultural institutions (as distinct from civic organizations) was complicated. The first significant regime involve-ment in Jewish cultural life came only in mid-1918, and was marked by crossed purposes. As part of its general repression of Jewish public life, the Petrograd EvOtdel shut down the Jewish ethnographic museum that An-ski had recently created.[27] By contrast, the Moscow EvKom not only set up the journal *Kultur un bildung* and reached out to Yiddishists like Niger and Tsharni, but also proved open to requests for support from independent Yiddishist organizations.[28] A variety of other state and party organs not particularly concerned with Jewish affairs also found themselves exercising administrative power over aspects of Jewish culture, which made for a situ-ation characterized by even greater variation, contradiction, and accident.

Jewish schools in some locations received financial subsidies from local workers' councils, but in other cases, especially during the early months of Bolshevik rule in Ukraine in 1919, Jewish language schools were suppressed in the name of internationalism. In some places, even Hebrew schools received support briefly.[29]

Out of this initial incoherence, a two-pronged policy toward Jewish secular-national culture emerged between November 1918 and May 1919: Hebrew culture was to be suppressed, while Yiddish culture would perhaps receive state support. The suppression of Hebrew on the grounds that it was "reactionary" and "clerical" proceeded at the initiative of the party-state's Jewish organs, the EvKom and, increasingly, the Jewish section of the Communist party, or Evseksiia. These were staffed not by veteran Bolsheviks but by veterans of the specifically Jewish left, with their special hostility toward Zionism and Hebrew. In fact, many full-fledged Bolsheviks with no experience of the internecine conflicts within Jewish life were not terribly bothered to learn that some Jews continued to cultivate the "archaic-Jewish language." But in the absence of any countervailing force within the regime, who was to gainsay the charge that Hebrew culture was dangerous? Soviet authorities tended to defer to their "Jewish experts" like Semyon Dimanshtein, one of the only Old Bolsheviks with any knowledge of Jewish culture and head of the EvKom. Thus, Soviet authorities in Kiev forwarded a July 1919 appeal from Tarbut to Dimanshtein in Moscow with a comment on the numerous "Jewish Zionist, half-Zionist, and 'socialist'" organizations they were encountering and a request that he guide them in the intricacies of work on the "Jewish street."[30]

The first material attack by the new regime against Hebrew literary culture came in late 1918 or early 1919, when Jewish commissars seized Moscow's Hebrew publishing houses (destroying in the process several Hebrew translations set to print at Stybel). This move was taken in the context of the German evacuation of Vilna and the Soviet desire to recenter their Jewish work there.[31] By this time, actually, little remained of the 1916–1918 Hebrew flowering in Moscow. Most Hebraists had recognized even before the active repressions that the regime could not bode well for Hebrew culture. Already in April, An-ski had reported "no hope" among Moscow's Jewish activists. In summer 1918, most of Moscow's major Hebrew patrons, activists, and organizations had left for independent Ukraine. Zlatopolsky and Persits had transferred their Omanut publishing house and Tarbut's administration to Odessa and Kiev, and much of Moscow's

Zionist-Hebraist literary community seems have gone with them; the massive journal of literary and political writing *Masuot,* which brought together writings by Moscow's Hebraists, was published in Odessa during this period.[32]

But the emerging Bolshevik policy toward Hebrew culture caught up with these cultural refugees when the Bolsheviks took Ukraine in early 1919. Even before the formal policy was elaborated, Ukrainian Jewish Communists who had gained positions in the party-state cultural infrastructure denied paper to Hebrew publishers and put an end to journals like *Ha-Shiloah.* Tarbut struggled to sustain local activity, which was now reduced largely to educational efforts.[33]

The Evsektsiia activists and regime-affiliated Jewish Communists hoped to destroy Hebrew culture as such, without regard for its political affiliations. In this respect, they did not wholly succeed. In July, the Ukrainian Communist authority's National Commissariat for Internal Affairs decided on the decisive suppression only of all "Zionist and Jewish-clerical" activity. Given this, Hebrew cultural bodies could still slip through if they could convince the authorities that they were politically acceptable. A substantial number of Hebraists who genuinely sympathized with the Revolution sought to find a rapprochement.[34] In Odessa, a cooperative of young Hebrew writers led by the pro-Communist Shteynman and his friend Tsemah secured paper from local authorities for what would be one of the last significant Hebrew publications on Soviet soil, the 1919 literary anthology *Erets;* it was this collective too that published Shteynman's *Ha-komunist ha-ʿivri.* A similar drama would play out in 1920–1921 in Moscow as the Ha-Bimah Hebrew theater managed to outmaneuver outraged Evsektsiia activists by winning support on artistic grounds from luminaries like Gorky.[35]

The policy of suppressing Zionism was broad enough, however, that Hebrew culture as an organized venture essentially ceased to exist in Russia by the end of 1919. Tarbut was formally dissolved, Hebrew education was outlawed, and Hebrew publishing houses were expropriated.[36] Hebrew did have a strange afterlife of sorts in the years that followed. Even as the established Hebrew literary sphere was suppressed and its activists driven underground, a new cohort of Hebraists took up the ideal of "Soviet Hebrew (others called it Communist Hebrew)" while distancing themselves from Zionism.[37] This loosely affiliated cohort included students and teachers in Soviet schools, Red Army soldiers and veterans, even party members. But with a few paltry exceptions, Hebrew culture retreated into an ever narrower private sphere after 1919.

The suppression of Hebrew culture constituted the most significant Soviet intervention in the Jewish cultural sphere in the early revolutionary period. Within a year, the power of the new regime essentially erased a culture-in-the-making that in some ways dated back to the late eighteenth century; it also destroyed the movement that had been at the normative and institutional core of the cultural project since its inception in the 1880s. The regime's suppression of that other form of "reactionary" Jewish expression, Jewish religious life, meant that Yiddishists suddenly stood unopposed in their claim to represent Jewish culture. Even many of those Yiddishists who were uncomfortable with the new regime could not hide their glee.[38]

Yiddishist hopes were also buoyed by another emerging Soviet policy toward Jewish culture: a vague but serious promise of state support for a politically acceptable Jewish national culture, and a concomitant readiness on the part of most officials to view Yiddish secular culture as the rightful claimant to this status. From the first, there were positive signs for those who wished to see them. The new Soviet government immediately declared its commitment to "free development for the national minorities and ethnic groups among the population residing on Russian territory."[39] Leading figures in the new regime, including Lenin and Stalin, maintained that ethnonational minorities had a genuine right to national development and self-determination—albeit within the confines of the Revolution's dictates. Some Bolsheviks held that the new Soviet society should not only tolerate (and manage) ethnonational cultural expression, but even actively foster it.[40] Although Bolshevik theorists, including Stalin himself, had gone out of their way in the prewar era to "prove" that the Jews did not constitute a nation (as part of a bitter internecine conflict with the Bund), these principles were suspended after the Revolution in the face of Russian Jewry's self-evident distinctiveness.

As noted earlier, some Soviet officials even proved willing to extend these principles to Hebrew institutions initially, but it was the Yiddishist camp that viewed the evolution of Soviet nationalities' policy with rising interest. From mid-1918, Soviet Jewish organs in Moscow and Petrograd offered piecemeal support to Yiddishist initiatives. More intriguing was the policy of the regime during the brief period in early 1919 when Soviet forces held the prewar Jewish cultural center of Vilna, with its significant

Yiddishist intelligentsia. Presumably because of its large Jewish population—which might be won over to support for the Bolsheviks in light of the threatening prospects for Jews under White, Polish, or local nationalist rule—the Bolsheviks essentially dissolved Moscow's EvKom and sent its few staff to work in the newly declared LitBel (Lithuanian-Byelorussian) SSR. Tsharni, intimately familiar with Vilna's Jewish cultural scene, was sent to Vilna under a young commissar named Tomsinski to oversee state-supported Yiddish culture there; they came bearing the stolen libraries of Zlatopolsky and Persits for a "central [Soviet] Jewish library." By February, the Jewish section in Vilna (under Tsharni) was sponsoring the educational journal *Folksbildung* and the cultural journal *Di Naye Velt,* edited by the city's two leading Yiddishists, the linguist and editor Zalman Reyzen and none other than the former editor of *Kultur un Bildung,* Niger. A third journal for children was slated to appear under Tsharni's editorship. Moreover, the regime absorbed the local Yiddishist theater company (the soon-to-be-storied Vilna Troupe), creating a short-lived Soviet Yiddish state theater in Vilna.[41]

Initially, the Bolshevik victory in Ukraine in February 1919 bore no such grand implications for the Yiddishist cultural project. The new regime immediately dissolved the Jewish autonomous bodies that had survived 1918 or had reemerged under the short-lived Directory.[42] This included the reestablished Jewish Ministry, which in its brief existence had granted the Kultur-Lige de facto authority in all Yiddish cultural and educational matters and appointed leading Kultur-Lige activists to formal positions.[43] Bolshevik victory over the "reactionary" Directory rendered this agreement not only a dead letter but also a source of danger to the organization. Thereafter, the new regime did not initiate anything equivalent to its cultural policy in Vilna. Organs for Jewish affairs were established piecemeal in Kiev, Kharkov, and Odessa, but no encompassing system of Soviet support for Yiddish culture was established. This was in keeping with the larger policy of the first Bolshevik commissars in Ukraine, hard-line internationalists who balked at offering even the Ukrainian majority substantial national autonomy.[44]

These developments reinforced the longstanding fears of many Yiddishists that the old Bolshevik antinational line might determine the fate of their cultural project, fears that helped shape their emerging relationship with the Revolution and its executors through mid-1919.[45] Yet there were countervailing signs that the alternative attitudes on display in

Vilna and Moscow might also apply in Soviet Ukraine. From the first, the Kultur-Lige and even the "bourgeois-nationalist" Folks-Farlag turned to the newly established party-state Jewish organs for protection from dispossession by other local Soviet institutions; permission to send representatives to Kharkov, Moscow, Petrograd, and Vilna to sell and exchange books; and monetary support for old and new projects.[46] Their efforts were in part simply a matter of seeking succor wherever possible, but there was more to it than that. Some in the new administration recognized an obligation to "the cultural and social interests of the proletarian and worker masses of the national minorities," as the Kharkov EvKom put it. The most intriguing feature of Soviet rhetoric and policy toward Jewish culture in the eyes of Yiddishists was this tendency by the Soviets to frame Jewish ethnocultural self-determination (within limits) as a right.[47]

The initial cooperative attitude on the part of individual local authorities in Ukraine emboldened some Yiddishists to turn to the new regime not as supplicants but with grand plans for state-supported cultural formation. The Kultur-Ligist Mayzl, who had apparently been delegated to the Temporary EvKom by the Ukrainian Communist party's newly established Collegium for Education and Propaganda, drew up a request for 1.5 million rubles to publish "books for the folk" including eighteen "classics," and an additional one million for twenty-five original and twenty-five translated Yiddish children's books; in a second version, he requested an additional one million rubles for the publication of twenty translated classics.[48] Sometime in March or April 1919, Kiev's EvKom submitted a request to the Kiev soviet closely paralleling Mayzl's to cover the budget of Jewish educational institutions for past and coming months.[49]

Thus, by mid-1919, Yiddishists first in Russia and then in Ukraine had encountered two faces of Bolshevik policy toward secular Yiddish culture: a surprising readiness to pledge unprecedented support, and a view that claims on behalf of national cultural self-development were "objectively reactionary." This confusing, intriguing policy toward Jewish culture was certainly one important factor behind the emerging Yiddishist reconsideration of the meaning of October for the cultural project. But the Revolution was not simply a matter of a new administration and a new state with which Jewish culturists had to deal. Less institutionally tangible but arguably far more important was the emerging revolutionary discourse that framed all transactions between the state and the populace and defined the parameters of the new public life.

In other words, Yiddishists were compelled to grapple with not merely the offers and threats of the Soviet state (and the implications of events transpiring beyond its reach), but also the ideological demands of the Revolution. The meaning of the Revolution for the cultural project, as opposed merely to that of Soviet power, was not (yet) dictated by any one clear authority; this would be deferred, arguably, until the 1930s. But already, a rising chorus began to demand of the Yiddishist intelligentsia a revolutionary turn in Jewish culture.

First, many of those who staffed the Bolsheviks' Jewish policy apparatus took for granted that their assignment to carry the Revolution into Jewish life applied to the Jewish cultural sphere too. The EvKom official Agursky offers a case in point. By the time he returned to Russia to join the Bolsheviks in 1917, he had spent his whole adult life in the service of revolution. Born to a poor family in 1884 and made a tailor at age thirteen, he had joined the underground Jewish socialist Bund as a young man and had to flee Russia by age twenty-one. Thereafter he drifted into Yiddish-language anarchist circles first in Leeds, then in Chicago. Whatever relationship he had had to an emerging Yiddish high culture had been at a distance, and firmly subordinated to his revolutionary commitments. The Bolsheviks' choice to use him as a cultural worker bespoke no status on his part in culturist circles, only their own complete lack of activists literate in Yiddish as of early 1918.[50]

Agursky expressed his own relationship to the Jewish cultural project in 1918 in his first cultural initiative: a state-published edition of poems by a Yiddish revolutionary poet of the 1880s, Yoysef Bovshover, whose heartfelt but artless proclamatory poetry had been popular in the nascent Jewish workers' movement of England and America thirty years earlier. By 1918, no Yiddishist, whatever his or her politics, could take seriously this sort of "royt-broyt-noyt-toyt poezye" ("red-bread-need-dead poetry"). Agursky, however, insisted on its significance in a fiery thirty-page introduction, which marked the beginning of a long campaign to instate Bovshover and several other proclamation-poets of the 1890s as the new foundation of the Yiddish canon.[51]

Those who sought to impose the Revolution on the Jewish cultural project from without included not only Evsektsiia activists like Agursky but also a growing, variegated group of self-declared Jewish Communists linked to the old Jewish socialist parties. Some of these figures were far more significant in the life of the Jewish left than itinerants-turned-commissars like Agursky. Moyshe Rafes was a veteran Bundist leader who led the newly declared KomBund out of the Bund and quickly emerged as the most articulate and forceful spokesman for the emerging Jewish Communist camp. His attitude toward the meaning of the October Revolution for Jewish culture was summed up in a pithy warning, delivered sometime in mid-1919: "We Jewish Communists are the great broom that will sweep all your Mendeles, Peretzs, Sholem Aleichems, your whole petit bourgeois culture, off the Jewish workers' street."[52]

Both the Evsektsiia activists and figures like Rafes shared at least a sliver of common ground with Yiddishist circles: like the Yiddishists, they conceded or insisted that party-state support for Yiddish cultural work was necessary. But their conception of what that cultural work meant was decidedly at odds with many of the most basic principles of the cultural project. They rejected any firm distinction between culture and politics, art and propaganda, and brushed aside the Yiddishist effort to balance high-cultural creation and mass dissemination. Instead, they made a more straightforward demand for a propaganda-culture that spoke to the Jewish masses in an unambiguously revolutionary-political voice.

Figures like Agursky inspired nothing but contempt among culturists. Tsharni and Niger, the first Yiddishists to work with him in the EvKom, evidently regarded him as a hack. Across the border, in Ukraine, the critic Mayzl dismissed Agursky's efforts to promote Bovshover in terms that neatly capture the independence of culturists' aesthetic demands from their political commitments: despite Mayzl's own socialism, he simply could not find any cultural value in a 1880s poet who had not been "fated to lift himself from unmediated emotion to specific, considered feelings, from simple, tendentious revolutionary challenges to complicated, subjective artistic motifs." Mayzl reserved far more vitriol for Agursky himself: in his view, Agursky's introduction substituted an overwrought "proclamation tone" for a serious historical explanation of Bovshover's firmly secondary place in the history of Yiddish literature and offered "nothing" to the broad audience "for which the book was intended." Intrigued by the very fact of a Soviet publishing house publishing Yiddish literature, Mayzl lamented the choice of the EvKom—that is, Agursky—to publish literature without a "systematically based plan and more serious academic goals."[53]

Yet whatever they might think of such figures, Yiddishists could not ignore the looming implications of their attitudes for the Yiddishist endeavor. Agursky's attitudes were now reproduced in some of the state-based Jewish institutions emerging in Ukraine. In April, the Kharkov Commissariat for Jewish Affairs declared its plans to serve "the Jewish street and combat Jewish counter-Revolution" with works on "political (especially Communist) and scientific questions, and proletarian art."[54]

At the same time, the newly minted Jewish national Communists launched an increasingly aggressive attack on Kiev's Yiddishist circles—as embodied in the Kultur-Lige—as insufficiently revolutionary or even counter-revolutionary. These attacks not only transpired in the relatively free public life that persisted for a few months after the Bolshevik takeover, but also involved denunciations of the Kultur-Lige directly to the new regime.[55] The attacks on the Kultur-Lige reflected specific internecine conflicts within Ukraine's Jewish left regarding the character of the organization, the political commitments of some of its leading figures, and its relations with the Ukrainian nationalist movement in the waning days of the Directory. But they also illustrated a larger retrenchment on the nominally Yiddishist left regarding the proper policy toward the new Jewish culture now that the Bolsheviks had brought revolution to Ukraine (and seemed on the cusp of spreading it further).

Figures like Rafes not only demanded a new sort of revolutionary Yiddish culture at the level of content; they also envisioned full-fledged absorption of the Jewish cultural sphere by the party-state. After February, many Jewish socialist-nationalists who had previously supported a system of Jewish national autonomy renounced these longstanding demands. Those involved in this precipitous renunciation included figures directly involved in Kiev's Yiddishist cultural sphere, like Rafes and the Hebraist-turned-Bundist A. Tsheskis, who had been a member of the Kultur-Lige's central committee.[56] By May, Yiddishists who wanted robust cultural autonomy were charging openly that their former comrades on the Jewish left were to blame for the new regime's failure to set up such a system.[57]

Yiddishism at the Crossroads

It was in this fraught context that the first sustained, public Yiddishist debate on the meaning of Bolshevik rule and the October Revolution for the Yiddish cultural project took place. From May 19 to 22, 1919, the Kultur-Lige held its second national conference in Kiev.[58] Recorded in stenographic detail by a participant, apparently Litvakov, the proceedings of the conference offer a critical benchmark for reconstructing the Revolution's unfolding effects on the cultural project.

Scheduled months earlier, the conference took place at a moment when there was ample reason for both optimism and pessimism about the future of the Yiddishist endeavor. The mass murders of Jews in non-Bolshevik Ukraine continued to increase in frequency and scale. Yet the popular roots of the Yiddish cultural agenda seemed to run deep. One conference participant recalled that the unexpected arrival of delegates from the provinces despite the terrible dangers of travel made a tremendous impression on the Kiev leadership, inspiring optimism even in the perpetually despairing Dovid Bergelson.[59]

But it was the Revolution above all in its multiple and seemingly contradictory guises that set the agenda of debate at the conference. Participants, who represented most of Ukrainian and, arguably, world Yiddishism in their mix of left-wing politics and unyielding Yiddishist commitments, struggled to interpret and respond to October's seeming offer of support but also the inconstancy of that offer, its suppression of competitors to Yiddishism coupled with its assault on insufficiently revolutionary Yiddishists, and the rising chorus of demands to subordinate the prerogatives of culture to the needs of revolutionary sociopolitics, mass accessibility, and the disciplining and purification of the intelligentsia itself. Understandably, some of the fiercest discussion at the conference revolved around specific questions of the moment, above all the tense relationship between the Kultur-Lige and the Jewish Communist bloc hostile to it, and the ambiguous status of Jewish autonomy in newly Soviet Ukraine. But as they hashed out some immediate if tentative answers, delegates also reopened the fundamental questions that Jewish culturists had sought to answer definitively in the two years preceding Bolshevik hegemony: questions concerning the content of the new Jewish culture itself; the proper relationship between the formation of a high culture and mass dissemination; the proper relationship between culture, party politics, and the state; and the prerogatives of artistic and individual free expression in an ideological age.

On several of these issues, most of the delegates proved defiantly committed to their pre-Bolshevik stances. The question of Jewish culture's content and concerns about its dissemination had always been linked at some level, especially for culturists trying to balance their high-cultural commitments with a real populist or socialist agenda. Now, however, this linkage loomed especially large because of demands by Jewish Communists like Agursky or Rafes for a "Jewish proletarian culture"—meaning both a culture defined by revolutionary or "workers'" themes and a culture formally accessible to a mass audience. But regarding the imposition of revolutionary or workers' themes in Yiddish culture, the most vocal delegates at the conference were unyielding. In response to a modest call for the Kultur-Lige to join the Proletkult groups that had begun to emerge in Kiev and other Ukrainian cities in the previous few months, delegates from the cultural moderates Bergelson and Golomb to the cultural radical Litvakov sounded off, rejecting the call for an immediate and sweeping renunciation of all previous Jewish culture as incurably "petit-bourgeois" and defending the right of Jewish culturists to shape the new Jewish culture with one eye on their own religious-cum-national past. As Litvakov put it, the culturists needed to be able to "seek new paths and create new values, and also hold on to and use those values which have already been created."[60]

Delegates were also fairly unified and defiant in their defense of the continued legitimacy of the Kultur-Lige's efforts to cultivate Yiddish high culture as an end in itself; they wanted to support more than just those cultural expressions that were immediately accessible to a broad audience. At the close of a prolonged but abstract debate, the majority of delegates agreed that one of the Kultur-Lige's continuing missions was "to elevate the Jewish working class to all the achievements of human and national culture," although they also acknowledged its responsibility to help this Jewish working class "seek and find the paths and forms of proletarian-socialist cultural creation."[61]

The conference delegates displayed similar defiance regarding the relationship between private cultural initiative and the state. At one point, some group of representatives, presumably the emerging pro-Communist left wing of the Kultur-Lige, introduced the resolution that "one of the main tasks of the Kultur-Lige is to unify all Yiddish cultural activity as long as and to the degree that this is not done through state organs." The leading voices in the organization reacted sharply against this purely temporary justification, insisting, in the words of the editor and theater critic Moyshe Katz, that "the Kultur-Lige as a concentrated unified organ must exist even if the state concerns itself with Jewish cultural work." These champions of the Kultur-Lige's significance even after the establishment of the hoped-for state-level autonomy mobilized a discourse that counterposed the necessity of private, socially located "creative initiative" in cultural life to the threat of "bureaucratization." Litvakov insisted that "the Kultur-Lige does not pretend to any state-role; it wishes to remain a free association which can show more creative initiative than any state organ." Similarly, the sharply anti-Bolshevik but intensely pro-Revolutionary Bundist cultural theorist A. Litvak insisted that there were kinds of work "which the state cannot do," and that the "state itself" should be positively disposed toward such work because "without the activity of private organizations, state organs become entirely bureaucratized." From Moscow, the Fareynikte activist Dovid Hokhberg charged that the Soviet regime had "forgotten that culture without an environment is impossible; there must be private initiative in culture"—and that the Bolshevik regime needed the Kultur-Lige because "in Jewish life it is the only bearer of culture."[62]

Delegates displayed much less unity and defiant certainty, however, regarding the perennial question of what autonomy, if any, cultural activity should have from the zero-sum conflicts of the political sphere. On the agenda of the May conference was a proposal to limit membership in the Kultur-Lige to "members of socialist parties, professional associations, worker-cooperatives, and socialist cultural circles." This move would have undone a constitutional principle that the Kultur-Lige had upheld from its beginnings: openness to all of those whom the educator Khayim Kazdan now called "[socially] conscious democrats and Yiddishists."[63]

Now, despite the new conditions, the radicalizing proposal provoked strong and successful resistance. The educator Noyekh Lurie, though a good Bundist, insisted that membership in the Kultur-Lige should remain independent of whether "one belongs to this or that political stream; the main thing is to recognize the platform of the Kultur-Lige." Counterattacking, the Jewish Communist Kheyfets pushed a still more radical resolution declaring that membership in the Kultur-Lige should be limited to "members of political parties which are part of the Workers' Soviet"; simply limiting membership to "socialists" was not stringent enough. The majority, however, voted to support Lurie's counter-resolution that membership in the Kultur-Lige be open to anyone who recognized its fundamental principles. In response, Communist delegates at the conference announced a partial secession from the organization: declining to take part in the elections or send delegates into the Kiev central committee, they promised to strengthen their influence in individual committees and local chapters and fight the enactment of this looser membership principle—in other words, fight to bar or drive out the "petit-bourgeois elements" to whom this resolution "freely opened the doors."[64]

The debate had a certain practical significance. Like all national cultural movements, Yiddishism depended heavily on middle-class people who had

had the opportunity to pursue the sort of education and social trajectory that could allow them to become cultural producers of the "correct" sort. Stringent political tests for membership in the Kultur-Lige might not only "narrow its base" but also "take away many activists," as Litvak put it. But this was not really the chief issue, because it was matter of policy in the new regime that even "bourgeois" intellectual "specialists" could play a role in cultural production and dissemination. The leading figure in the Communist camp and proponent of the most radical resolution, Kheyfets himself, noted as much when he closed his resolution by remarking that "exceptions to the rule can be made, but this [political test for membership] must be the principle."[65]

Nor was the entire debate merely a fig leaf for a more naked struggle for dominance between the Jewish Communist parties and their opponents in the other Jewish socialist parties, though this element was no doubt at work. It is highly significant that this agenda was pushed not only by the Jewish Communist fraction led by Kheyfets and Khintshin, but also by the organization's chairman Litvakov, who was at that point still at odds with the Jewish Communists and a far more influential insider in the Kultur-Lige and Yiddish cultural sphere than they. Litvakov, in fact, was one of the most articulate champions of this position, pointing to the presence of nonsocialist Yiddishists like Niger and An-ski in Vilna's Kultur-Lige and Zionists like Ravnitsky in the Odessa branch as examples of the sort of people who had to be kept out of the organization.

Rather, the debate over the Kultur-Lige's membership policy signified a larger split within the Jewish socialist left over the proper relationship between politics and culture in institutional spheres. Lurie insisted that "nonparty, apolitical people" had a legitimate right to help shape the new Yiddish culture through the Kultur-Lige and that to deny them "their right would be an act of violence against freedom of thought." This formulation posited a sharp distinction between politics and culture. Culture, even one "socialist in spirit," could be created and disseminated even by those chose who were not engaged in socialist revolution; it was, furthermore, a realm where rules of "freedom of thought" applied in a way that they did not for party politics. Against this, Kheyfets insisted that "Jewish Communists, for example" could not be expected to work with members of parties excluded from the soviets because "against such parties, one can only fight." The party principle, in other words, was absolute: it did not stop at some imaginary border between "politics" and "culture." Litvakov stated this principle differently. He harshly criticized the admission of nonsocialist Yiddishists like Niger or Sh. An-ski into the Kultur-Lige. The Kultur-Lige could not open itself up to simply any "adherent of Yiddishism," he implied, because this would dilute the cultural revolution that it sought to carry out.[66]

The deliberations at the May 1919 conference attest simultaneously to the persistence of the culturists' convictions, the accelerating erosion of these convictions by the Revolution's very different imperatives, and the fateful intersection of these revolutionary imperatives with lines of tension within the cultural project itself, particularly on the Yiddishist left. If Yiddishists stood fast on their right to create a new Jewish high culture as they saw fit both in content and form, they proved less unwavering in their defense of culture's autonomy from direct political determinations. All the vocal participants agreed that the Kultur-Lige had to conduct its work in the service of "the working masses" and in "a socialist spirit," with that vague but potent slogan itself marking a significant politicization of the organization's stated goals. It is surely significant that Lurie's resistance to a stringent political test for membership won the majority, and that it did so, moreover, in a body composed almost entirely of avowed socialists who would not themselves have been affected by the limiting resolutions. It is, however, equally significant that even if this support reflected agreement with the conception of culture embodied in Lurie's argument and the Kultur-Lige's earlier history, Lurie's justification itself represented a substantial narrowing of the Kultur-Lige's previous anti-*parteyishkeyt* principle. Lurie defended only the membership rights of "apolitical" and nonparty elements; there was no mention of guaranteeing such rights for members of "bourgeois" parties like the Folks-Partey or the Zionist party. Indeed, attacks on "bourgeois" elements within the Yiddishist movement from all sides of the debate signaled the shared, deepening leftist radicalism of the Kultur-Lige's so-called right wing as well as its "left" and "center." Moreover, the stipulation that every member had to accept the Kultur-Lige's principles specified that the new Jewish culture had to be "for and through the working masses" and that the Kultur-Lige would devote special attention to guiding the Jewish working-class in a search for "proletarian-socialist" culture.

The May conference did not take place in a free environment. Indeed, representatives of the regime took part in the meeting. Kheyfets spoke not only as a member of the organization but also as an official in the new Ukrainian soviet government. More significant still, the central Bolshevik regime's chief authority over Jewish affairs, Dimanshtein, arrived from Moscow to take part as an "interested observer." With regard to the most concrete question taken up by the conference—the fate of the Kultur-Lige in the near future—both brought reassuring words. Dismissing the attacks by Jewish Communists like Rafes, both recognized that the Kultur-Lige was, for now, the only organization capable of actually carrying out substantial Yiddish cultural work.

But with regard to the more fundamental issues, both sounded a very different line. It was Kheyfets who authored the most radical resolution concerning political restrictions on membership and stated that Communists could not cooperate even in cultural work with members of other parties. Although he supported maintaining the Kultur-Lige's independence from Proletkult, he also insisted that the Kultur-Lige "must, of course, be reorganized and become closer to the worker-masses." Regarding the content of the new Soviet Yiddish culture, he shared the impatience of Rafes with activists working "to conserve the old culture."[67]

More important still, the trusted regime commissar Dimanshtein seconded these comments across the board. He coupled his support for the Kultur-Lige with a thinly veiled warning: "The Kultur-Lige must continue to exist, but one must not bring into it any politics which can interfere with its relations with Soviet power." He capped the debate about the organization's constituency with the vague but fraught comment that "the tone must be set by the working masses." And in response to arguments by Bergelson about the need to insulate Jewish culture from Russian culture's hegemony, he casually remarked that the Kultur-Lige would "before anything else" have to get rid of "those elements which fear that other, stronger cultures will harm them." This remark could be interpreted in two ways. On the one hand, Dimanshtein was perhaps insisting that in the new socialist society, weaker national cultures had nothing to fear from stronger ones because they would be nurtured—a stance that he and the Narkomnats administration seemed to take seriously. On the other hand, his condemnation served to put intellectuals like Bergelson on notice that "excessive" cultural nationalism—as defined by commissars like himself—would not be tolerated.[68]

Yet the retreat from some of the cultural project's principles cannot be attributed solely to outside pressure. The May conference attested not only to the effects of revolutionary pressure on basic culturist commitments, but also a fateful consonance between the Revolution's ideals and certain aspects of the culturist agenda that had hitherto been held in check by other counterbalancing commitments. First, while all the defiant talk of "private initiative" and "bureaucratization" seemed to indicate a robust commitment to the structural autonomy of the cultural sphere in relation to political authority, there lurked behind the delegates' bravado a deep ambivalence. The champions of private initiative in cultural life were pulled between their commitment to protect the cultural sphere's autonomy, and their equally strong desire to embody their national culture-in-the-making in the state and harness its unequaled capacities and authority. The tension between these two principles in the Kultur-Lige mainstream itself is evident in the "right-center" counter-resolution, which ultimately carried the day. Formulated by Litvak, it called for the centralization of all aspects of "Jewish cultural work among the working masses" in a state body.[69] Moreover, the arguments of the delegates reflected the limits imposed on them by their own Marxist principles: without a bourgeois-liberal conception of culture's intrinsic autonomy from the state (in its capacity as part of a civic sphere), the grounds for demanding such autonomy came down to merely empirical claims about efficiency—who was best suited to perform necessary cultural work—rather than claims based on principle.

The delegates no doubt were sincere in their advocacy regarding private initiative. But whereas the large Hebraist and small Yiddishist nonsocialist camps excluded from conference—and from the new revolutionary society—had a philosophical basis for holding such views, socialist Yiddishists clearly derived these views only from the experience of cultural practice and its complexities. In principle, they really could not disagree with the suggestions of Kheyfets or Dimanshtein that private organized cultural initiative should be phased out as the Commissariat of Enlightenment grew more competent in Yiddish cultural work.

This same philosophical affinity between the Yiddishist socialist left and the Bolshevik regime that they generally disliked left the door open to further rapprochement on other fronts—and to the abrogation by culturists themselves of other principles hitherto central to their cultural project. Thus even though the delegates loudly resisted demands for a radical "proletarian" turn in Jewish cultural expression, nobody could simply reject the notion tout court because no socialist could deny a fundamental relationship between culture and class structure. At most, delegates could posit that the time had not yet come—and this stance was of course subject to revision at any moment in an environment where the Revolution could always be declared to have leapt forward, entered another stage, or telescoped social development yet more drastically.

More to the point, not everyone in the Kultur-Lige or the Yiddishist movement shared the sophisticated sensibilities of Litvakov and Bergelson. At the conference, it became clear that demands for a "revolutionary" or "proletarian" Yiddish culture were not coming solely from outsiders like Agursky or Rafes. One of the most committed defenders of the Kultur-Lige's autonomy was the staunch anti-Bolshevik Litvak, as we have seen. Yet his vision for the new culture itself was altogether similar to that of the Communists he reviled. He bridled at the suggestion by the Communist delegate Kheyfets that the Kultur-Lige's vision of Yiddish culture itself was conservative: "Comrade Kheyfets' talk of activists who conserve the old culture bears no relation to the activists of the Kultur-Lige, in whom there is no conservatism." His counter-argument that Communist attacks on the Kultur-Lige were purely political hinged on the stance that there was little substantive difference in their plans for Yiddish culture itself. In the months that followed the meeting, Litvak would demonstrate the genuineness of his stance by mounting a harsh attack on Kiev's Yiddish literary establishment: uninterested in the debates of universalizers and indigenizers, modernists and classicists, he would demand art that directly represented and celebrated the Revolution and made itself part of "the struggle."[70]

At the same time, the conference also reflected the progress of a more subtle but also more encompassing retrenchment within the Yiddishist high culturist camp, represented not by Litvak but by the more sophisticated Litvakov. Even as he refrained from the crude reduction of art to politics represented by Litvak, Litvakov attacked the most paradoxical but also most fundamental constitutional principle of the cultural project: that a worthwhile new Jewish culture could only be built by individual creators freely pursuing their individual prerogatives. In the context of his demands for limiting Kultur-Lige membership to members of the socialist parties, soviets, or workers' cooperatives, Litvakov worried aloud that "art-people, free of all party discipline, can serve this ideal today and another tomorrow." Litvakov was not renouncing his longstanding conviction that at its heart, the new culture could only be created by artists. But he was giving notice that these artists had to be guided in turn by ideologists properly attuned to the needs of the Revolution.[71]

Rapprochement's Advocates and Discontents

Though Kiev's Yiddishists felt themselves under siege by May 1919, June and July brought an unlooked-for turn in their fortunes: the rapid development of a close cooperative relationship with Soviet power involving unprecedented levels of state funding and institutionalization. In mid-June a Jewish section of the All-Ukrainian Central Publishing House (VseIzdat) was created and charged with publishing "art-literature for adults and children in Yiddish" at state expense. On July 3, the Kultur-Lige's art section was put under the authority of the All-Ukrainian Committee for Plastic Arts. In the VseUkrLitKom of the Commissariat of Enlightenment, Jewish sections were created in the propaganda office and the literary publishing office. Astonishingly, positions of authority in these new bodies were given not to the clamorous supporters of the new regime like Rafes, but to the very Yiddishists with whom the Jewish Communists had been engaged in furious polemic: the Jewish sections in the Commissariat of Enlightenment were given over to Lurie and Litvak, two of the most uncompromising maximalists in the Kultur-Lige regarding organizational and ideological independence from the regime. Litvakov was made one of the three figures in charge of the LitKom.[72] At the same time, the Kultur-Lige itself not only escaped repression, but even began to receive extensive material support from state organs.[73]

Under these new circumstances, Yiddishists both inside the state and out enthusiastically renewed their cultural endeavors. In close consultation with the Kultur-Lige's literary section, the Jewish section of the VseIzdat developed plans to publish Yiddish classics, anthologies of Yiddish poetry in Russia and abroad, translations of major European writers, books on "the theory and history of art and literature," and, for children, collections of folk tales around the world, literary translations, and the biweekly illustrated journal *Shretelekh*.[74] The Kultur-Lige intensified efforts to solidify the connections between Jewish artists trained in the Russian and European academy and the emerging Yiddish literature and theater. The organization's long-planned music section now began to function under the leadership of the ethnomusicologist Moyshe Beregovsky and composer A. Dzimitrovsky. While supporting the private production of art and organizing an array of public concerts of European and Jewish classical music for "Jewish workers" and evenings dedicated to Sholem Aleichem and Peretz, the section also moved to institutionalize popular Jewish music education through courses for Jewish teachers and an "art-choir," laid the groundwork for a Jewish music studio, and planned a Jewish opera.[75]

For the most part, these initiatives represented a direct continuation, in both form and content, of the cultural program that Yiddishists had pursued in 1917–1918. In the summer of 1919, the Kultur-Lige published an anthology of literary work and essays on literature, art, and music entitled *Oyfgang* (Ascent) with direct funding support from the central bureau of the Evsektsiia in Moscow.[76] But by stark contrast with the previous year's *Kultur un bildung, Oyfgang* was indistinguishable from non- or pre-Bolshevik Yiddishist products. It was there that the critic Dobrushin published the essay that hailed Hofshteyn as the leading figure in the new Yiddish poetry on wholly formal grounds (and praised Bialik, an unrelenting opponent of the Bolshevik regime, in the process). *Oyfgang*'s literary contents included a symbolist tale by Nister, a piece by Bergelson concerned with the prerevolutionary era, an expressionist play by the newcomer Beynish Shteyman, and gentle lyric poetry by Hofshteyn and Shvartsman. All of this marked it as a direct successor to the previous year's *Eygns,* with its unabashed apoliticism and openness to any writer and style that helped cultivate the new Yiddish literature. An essay on Jewish art and another on contemporary Jewish music rounded out an anthology completely free of expressly political writing.

Yet the question of what the Revolution meant for the Jewish cultural project—or what the Revolution and the new society demanded of it—was by no means neutralized by the rapprochement of June and July. Demands for a properly revolutionary Jewish culture from Communist circles did not subside, and many of these figures themselves now began to attain substantial power in party and state organs. Unable to remake or unmake the Yiddishist cultural sphere as they saw fit, Jewish Communists began instead to plan direct cultural competition with the newly restored and incorporated Kultur-Lige. In July, as an important archival discovery by David Shneer reveals, Kheyfets and other Jewish Communists called for another regime-sponsored cultural journal to be named *Kamf* (Battle) that would express a more "purely party perspective" than the journals and anthologies being produced by the Yiddishist mainstream.[77]

More significant still were the first signs of ideological reorientation within the culturist milieu. The first aesthetically significant experiments in "revolutionary literature" among Yiddish writers occurred in 1919.

Among the most striking works in this vein were the expressionist dramas of the twenty-two-year-old playwright Beynish Shteyman. In his person, Shteyman represented the highest hopes of the Yiddishist movement, as noted in Chapter 4. All the more striking, then, was Shteyman's sharp trajectory toward a revolutionary aesthetics prior to his death in that year.

Shteyman's first published drama, "Baym Toyer" (At the Gate), which dramatized the reactions of the Christian populace of a medieval German town to the execution of Jews accused of defacing the Host, spoke to the present pogrom-ridden moment but also stood in clear continuity with pre-revolutionary Yiddish literary developments. Centering around a midnight dream-encounter between the silent Jews' Christian guard and Jesus Christ, and inhabited by figures (including speaking bells) that are less characters than types and symbolic functions, "Baym Toyer" can be said to have emerged directly out of the prewar symbolist dramas of the recently deceased Peretz.[78]

Shteyman's writing after "Baym Toyer," however, made a decisive shift away from this lineage, under the sign of the Revolution. In his drama "Meshiekh ben Yoysef" (The Messiah of the Line of Joseph), the Messiah comes to redeem a "frozen world" from "the thousand-year reign" of queen Lilith (a demoness of Jewish mystical and folk tradition). But the "people," reduced to an abject state of mental slavery, stone him to death when Lilith warns them that only their children but not they themselves will be redeemed (as was the case with the generation of Israelites who left Egypt). The play ends when in the Messiah's place there appears the Messiah of the line of Joseph, the figure who according to some Jewish messianic traditions was to set the redemption in motion through apocalyptic warfare. More formally innovative than "Baym Toyer," in that it presented its symbolist and expressionist setting and action without the psychologizing framework of a dream, "Meshiekh ben Yoysef" was nevertheless a simpler work of art. It mobilized Jewish mystical motifs and expressionist stagecraft in the service of a patricidal revolutionary morality tale—an apologia for the necessity of purifying violence.[79]

Literary experiments like Shteyman's did not necessarily connote the demand for a full-fledged transformation of the cultural project in accordance with the Revolution's imperatives. The enthusiasm with which Yiddishist aesthetes like Mayzl and Dobrushin welcomed both of the aforementioned plays by Shteyman—they were published in the culturist bastions *Oyfgang* and the second *Eygns*, respectively—suggested as much.

But at the same time, far less compromising demands for a revolutionary cultural shift began to issue from within the Yiddishist milieu.

In July, the Jewish section of the literary publishing office published the first (and last) issue of the journal *Baginen* (Dawn) under the editorship of the Bundist cultural critic Litvak. As scholars have noted, *Baginen* was an organic part of the Kiev Yiddishist cultural scene (see fig. 9). Its stable of authors overlapped closely with that of its predecessor *Eygns* and of its contemporaries *Bikher-velt* and *Oyfgang*. It shared the resolutely high-cultural focus of these other publications, eschewing any directly political writing. Above all, it proclaimed its commitment to the cultivation of a modern Yiddish culture as a legitimate and pressing end in itself.

Yet in both form and content, *Baginen* constituted a sharp rebuke to these journals and the cultural project itself. *Baginen* built its literary section primarily around mainstream local writers like Hofshteyn and Kvitko as well as the rising American Yiddish Romantic-Expressionist poet and former Bundist H. Leivick, the veteran novelist Sholem Ash, and the transplanted Polish Yiddish writer Y. Y. Singer. But the works it selected by these authors embodied a clear revolutionary political agenda. From Kvitko's works, it chose his frankly revolutionary "In Roytn Shturm." From Leivick's writings, it chose the poem cycle "In Shney," which depicted the poet's escape from Siberian exile in images of revolutionary and messianic martyrdom. In case the reader missed the point, the cycle was prefaced by an editorial statement about Leivick himself emphasizing that he was "a Jewish worker, a painter," a Bundist, and a poet who published in "anarchist" and "socialist" journals—and made no mention of his affiliation with Di Yunge, the loosely affiliated group of New York Yiddish poets who had pioneered the break with Yiddish social poetry in the name of art and irreducibly individual expression.

These pieces appeared alongside a translation of a play by John Galsworthy entitled "Struggle" and described as a "social drama." Singer, not generally a politically programmatic writer, was here represented by a story about lumbermen worked to exhaustion by overweight capitalists with golden pince-nez. Even Ash, generally regarded with suspicion on the left for both political and aesthetic reasons, appeared here with a story about an orphaned immigrant girl thrust with "thousands of others" into the life of the proletariat in "the strange big city." Finally, a story by the Russian left's patron saint Gorky rounded out this "social" focus while a piece about the life of a political exile in Siberia reaffirmed the Russian and

Jewish left's shared history of revolutionary martyrdom—a theme that the editor Litvak might have especially wanted to stress in light of his own resolute loyalty to the non-Bolshevik Bund. What defined this selection was a purely thematic unity: a shared radical politics cutting across eclectic aesthetics.

Baginen coupled this first stab at an anthology of revolutionary Yiddish literature with a barrage of critical articles demanding that Yiddish literature and Jewish art now harness themselves directly to revolutionary goals. The critic P. Reyland welcomed the formal and thematic innovations of the Kiev-Grupe poets Hofshteyn, Kvitko, and Markish but insisted that their aesthetic achievements and those of future Yiddish poets be assessed in relation to the Revolution.[80] An essay on theater by Moyshe Katz yoked together a sophisticated understanding of theater as *Gesamtkunstwerk* with an assertively Marxist analysis of the tasks incumbent on a new Yiddish theater of the "Jewish working class" in revolutionary Russia. Acknowledging the significance both of the indigenous Yiddish theater tradition and Europeanizing translations at this stage of the Yiddish theater's development, he nevertheless insisted on the importance of moving from a "petit-bourgeois" theater to a "proletarian" one that Yiddishist cultural producers needed "to fill with a new social content." The existing repertoire, whether Jewish or European, would have to be reinterpreted and subjected to selection according to whether it "allows itself . . . to be interpreted in a new, social fashion."[81]

Baginen's editor Litvak offered the most unvarnished formulation of the proper relationship between art and Revolution in an essay entitled "Literature and Life."[82] He attacked contemporary Yiddish writers for failing to produce a properly revolutionary literature that would give readers "the spirit of struggle, the interior world of the great many headed-personality called 'the masses,' and the interior world of the individual fighter." He focused particular ire on the leading force in Kiev's Yiddish letters, Bergelson. Here was a prose writer who used his tremendous descriptive abilities merely to chew over the same themes of shtetl decline and degeneration, petit-bourgeois sensibilities, and the provincial intelligentsia's assimilationism, careerism, defeatism, and moral-political rudderlessness.[83]

Litvak took great pains to emphasize that he did not wish to jettison the normative aesthetic considerations of the literary sphere: the point was not merely to write about revolutionary themes, but to embody them in compelling literature. But he also had no patience for any protests that the inherent character of art precluded representations of the Revolution in progress:

> It is said that elevating the life of a generation into art can only be done when that generation is passing and can be objectified and captured whole in cast, cooled forms. This is entirely incorrect. Art does not limp behind life. It goes with it; it often sweeps before it and shows new horizons.[84]

Most significant for how future revolutionary intellectuals would approach these questions was Litvak's practical conclusion. Given his claims, there was no excuse for contemporary writers to remain aloof from the Revolution and its Jewish cognates. The only explanation for such aloofness was political "inertia." And the only antidote was ideological guidance by the revolutionary intelligentsia:

> This inertia must be broken. One must take our young talents and weld their attention to the new, to their own generation. One must turn their eyes to the broad horizons, out of the old ghetto . . . It doesn't matter if in this regard one even exaggerates. The stick is bent to one side: if one wants to straighten it out, one has to bend it in the other direction.[85]

Litvak himself had made similar demands of Yiddish literature a decade earlier. But now, to demand a realism that dealt directly with revolution was to demand that Yiddish writers toss out two decades of literary development. To demand that writers harness themselves to a particular historical-literary task was to contravene a principle of aesthetic autonomy that had become a given. And now, most importantly, Litvak was not a voice in the wilderness, an outsider to the literary field watching impotently as Yiddish literature drifted away from the "banner" of the Bund. He was, rather, invested with cultural power by the victorious Revolution. As an anti-Bolshevik, his position was shaky, and he would soon be driven out by Jewish Communist political enemies. But he was nonetheless one of the first of an evolving breed in Soviet Jewish cultural life: the part-time or full-time Marxist cultural critic whose authority to criticize, badger, and instruct Jewish cultural producers stemmed not from the respect accorded him in the literary sphere but from the position accorded him by the Revolution.

The demands voiced and attacks mounted in *Baginen* were evidently not confined to print. In mid-1919 Kiev Yiddishist intelligentsia were convulsed by fierce debate, soul-searching, new convictions for some, and self-doubt for others.[86] It was in this context that Bergelson, Kiev's dominant Yiddish writer and the chief target of Litvak's critique, published his seminal essay "Dikhtung un Gezelshaftlekhkeyt" in the August issue of *Bikhervelt*. The essay, best translated as "Art-Literature and the Revolutionary Public" (for reasons that will become clear), was in part an elaboration of Bergelson's aesthetic program for Yiddish literature. In particular, the essay defended the work of Hofshteyn, Nister, and Bergelson himself against critics like Litvakov who accused Kiev's literati of failing to elaborate a literature appropriate to the revolutionary age. But the specific problem of Yiddish literary aesthetics was actually only one, and indeed the least significant, of the concerns underpinning Bergelson's short but complex essay.[87]

The central purpose of "Dikhtung un Gezelshaftlekhkeyt" was to argue—or prophesy, and indeed to lament—that a chasm was now opening between the revolutionary builders of the new society and the sphere of the arts, that this split was unavoidable for the foreseeable future, that it would be temporary but essentially total, and that it would be even worse for Yiddish high culture than for the Russian. The crux of the essay was Bergelson's elaboration of the objective and hence unavoidable causes of this division. "Dikhtung un Gezelshaftlekhkeyt" did not motivate this coming split in terms of a moral claim to aesthetic autonomy or in terms of ideological differences between the revolutionary movement and artists. On the contrary, Bergelson stressed to his readers that he meant nothing other than that art which is "in essence progressive and entirely on the side of the revolutionary movement," that is, art whose creators shared the Revolution's ideology and will to societal transformation. Rather, this split followed inexorably from the nature of the revolutionary process on the one hand and the artistic process on the other.[88]

The Revolution necessarily began with the negation of all existing social, cultural, and psychological forms, which it replaced in accordance with the "naked lines" of ideology and social experimentation. This fact bore very different implications for writers and artists as opposed to the revolutionary movement and the politically mobilized, radical society emerging around it (the *gezelshaftlekhkeyt* of the title). The movement and resulting society experienced the present liminal moment as one of unbridled possibility, because it was now free to follow its abstract sociopolitical ideas where ever they might lead.[89]

But quite the opposite obtained for artists, even those who embraced the Revolution, due to the nature of artistic creation and reception. True art, Bergelson argued, was "mostly a consequence of the lived-through; it is the impulse of lived-through impressions." The creative process, in this view, essentially entails a passive reception of phenomenal experiences, followed by an inner compulsion to communicate these experiences through art:

> Nothing defines the artist more than his unique mode of grasping impressions. The more impressions he has, the more he possesses impulses which do not allow him to rest but call him and awaken him; the more images the artist sucks in from childhood on, the more raw material he possesses, the more possibilities. Nobody is as alone as the artist, because the artist grasps in a unique fashion not only whole life-situations, but even their smallest subdivision. He receives every image differently from all around him . . . And he strains all of his powers to break out of this loneliness—he does not rest until he compels all those around him to see with the same eyes.

Dramatic social and political implications followed from these claims about the nature of artistic creation. The artist could only synthesize finished art out of some constellation of "bilderlekhkayt," by which Bergelson meant both the sensuous, experienced social world and established formal traditions of aesthetic representation. Consequently, true art about the Revolution's new society-in-the-making could not yet be created; any premature attempts would be mere abstraction.

In a further decisive move, Bergelson linked this account of the creative process to an account of art's reception in society. To be received properly, art needed a receiver who shared some part of the universe of forms and references that the artist had deployed. Moreover, it required receivers who shared the genuine need for art that drove the artistic process itself. In terms common to Jewish culturist discourse and self-conception, Bergelson described this need as an embodied history born of cultural education but experienced as a felt inner necessity: "art has for us even a certain physiological meaning," it satisfied "nerves" that craved such food. These "nerves," however, could function only in times of calm and only in cultivated readers. The revolutionary intelligentsia were not equipped to meet either of these requirements—not merely because of their ideological hostility to any art that mirrored the old social and cultural world, but again, due to their nature as revolutionary intelligentsia. Hence the essential cause of this objective parting of the ways: necessarily, the arts had to remain bound to the "old outlived *bilderlekhkayt*" even as the revolutionary movement abolished it and, in the process, created a reader—the revolutionary *inteligent*—who simply could not apprehend either the "old world" or its "imagistic traditions" and would thus find genuinely complex, richly referential art irrelevant.[90]

It was in the context of this general argument about politics and aesthetics that Bergelson took up the fate of Yiddish literature and culture. The predicament of Yiddish literature, he argued, would be exacerbated by the sociological abnormality of its audience. Other national literatures (obviously, he had in mind the Russian case) would be able to tide themselves over through the wilderness years given their educated middle stratum with an epigonic tie to the old forms and to the art traditions that expressed them. But Yiddish literature had no such middle-stratum reader. Bergelson insisted that Yiddish literature had always depended on two audiences: the uneducated folk reader and the Jewish national-revolutionary intelligentsia. Neither of these audiences, however, could relate properly to Yiddish literature at present: the uneducated folk reader lacked the cultural education to apprehend it formally, while the revolutionary intelligentsia could only apprehend its "naked lines" and could not understand or appreciate its "national-subjective" character. The proof of this latter claim, Bergelson argued, was the cold reception by the left-Yiddishist public of *Eygns,* the flagship of the new Yiddish word, and its contrasting warm embrace of Peretz Markish's "naked" Futurist lines, a mere abstraction that the revolutionary public had misread as Yiddish literature's breakthrough to the universal subject.

Eventually, Bergelson concluded, the successful Revolution would endow a new kind of human subject with an exponentially expanded capacity and craving for aesthetic "food, and the great regeneration of art will begin." But until then, art as such was condemned to incomprehension and isolation, if not outright persecution. Bergelson held out the hope that the Revolution's eventual deliverance of art would apply as well to Yiddish national culture, but the only certainty was that the intervening era would be especially severe for those who had hoped to create a modern Yiddish culture in Russia.

"Dikhtung un Gezelshaftlekhkeyt" was, on one level, a powerful defense of the Kiev Yiddish literati against both the accusations made by the Jewish Communists like Rafes and the argument pressed by fellow culturists like

Litvak. If artists simply could not successfully apprehend the Revolution because it was as yet pure abstraction, then their failure to try simply meant that they were remaining true to the nature of art itself. The Litvaks of the world could demand that literature capture the reality of the Revolution all they liked, but such a literature simply could not be produced, and any attempt to do so would inevitably produce bad art—something that Litvak himself insisted was not his intention. All the good will, ideological suasion, or pressure in the world could not change the nature of artistic creation and reception. The accusations of Jewish Communists like Rafes were even more incoherent because to this impossible demand, they added the requirement that Jewish aesthetic culture sever itself from the prerevolutionary Jewish past and divest itself of its accumulated tradition of aesthetic possibilities. Bergelson rejected this latter demand not on nationalist grounds but on aesthetic ones: art was impossible without materials, Jewish art had quite reasonably used Jewish materials among others, and there was no reason to forbid these in particular. By definition, the entirety of human experience and the forms it made possible were prerevolutionary; hence, to single out Jewish forms merely added ideological inconsistency to what was already aesthetic incoherence.

Yet although the polemical dimension of Bergelson's argument is clear, it would be wrong to read his argument solely as a commentary on Kiev's Yiddishist world or even as a defense of aesthetic autonomy in the framework of the Revolution. Significantly, Bergelson did not shy away from the dangerous and even shattering implications of his argument for himself, the Yiddish literary sphere, and the entire Jewish cultural project. Although Bergelson insisted on the political innocence of himself and his friends, he did not back down from a principled rejection of the "Communist culture" idea in general. The Revolution would ultimately succeed in building a new society, and concomitantly a new art would indeed emerge. But Bergelson insisted that even this new art would necessarily—and properly—draw its materials from the totality of human experience rather than beginning from nil. That is, a mature revolutionary (and revolutionary Jewish) art would rework the aesthetic achievements of prerevolutionary society in the same way that a stabilized Christian civilization had reworked the pagan achievements that it had first denounced. The Soviets would not necessarily have found this view suspicious—on the contrary, no less a figure than Trotsky insisted on much the same inheritance model in his contemptuous attacks on radically anticlassical "proletarian culture" trends in the Russian cultural sphere. But it was a direct challenge to the culturally extreme Jewish Communists. Though he sought to clear Kiev's Yiddish literary community of charges of political unreliability by casting the conflict between art and Revolution as essentially nonideological, Bergelson ultimately acknowledged that there was indeed an unbridgeable ideological gap between the part of that community that he represented and the emerging Jewish Communist cultural consensus.

More broadly, if "Dikhtung un Gezelshaftlekhkeyt" was a defense of one of the central terms of the Jewish cultural project—aesthetic autonomy—it marked a despairing renunciation of another central principle: the idea that a new Jewish art would play a leading role in the reconstitution of Jewish nationhood and the individuality of the modern Jewish person. Given Bergelson's analysis of the natures of aesthetic production and of the Revolution, it followed that artists could not provide revolutionary audiences with meaningful aesthetic syntheses and mediations of shared experiences. This was true not merely of Jewish artists but of artists in general in a revolutionary context: Bergelson contended that the most important Russian writers and poets had also fallen silent or been rendered irrelevant, which marked the proof of his thesis.

Bergelson's stance announced a death of faith in the Yiddishist cultural project no less profound than that of his Communist antagonists. The very essence of the Kultur-Lige's undertaking was the belief that it was possible to create a new Jewish aesthetic culture that would simultaneously serve art and regenerate the nation. "Dikhtung un Gezelshaftlekhkeyt" announced a loss of faith in these certainties by one of their staunchest and most talented proponents. Bergelson would now retreat into the literary field. He ended his essay not with a riposte to his attackers but with a warning to his fellow writers:

The revolutionary movement, too, will, after its decisive triumph, have to make concessions regarding the old forms of life in art, which will no longer be, incidentally, any danger to it by that point. But it will be a long time yet before that happens, and until then, true literature will be, if not fanatically persecuted by revolutionary society, then at any rate unrecognized. It will be alone, and because of the reasons already mentioned, Yiddish literature will come to find itself in more terrible isolation than the literature of any other people. And this isolation has already begun—it is happening now.[91]

Bergelson did not speak for all of his fellow literati. But other, non-polemical sources by contemporaries suggest that the objective tension he depicted between the imperatives of the Revolution and central imperatives of the Jewish cultural project was both deeply and widely felt. Far from Bergelson's Yiddishist circles, on the far left of Odessa's embattled Hebraist milieu, the self-declared Red Hebraist Shteynman confided to his diary sometime in 1919 a despairing argument that closely paralleled Bergelson's. In notes that he (perhaps later) dubbed "Revolution and Art," he articulated a similar—and given his own trajectory, heretical—opposition between the two. Asserting that "professional revolutionaries" hated art despite their protestations of support for it, Shteynman located the root of this hatred in the same sort of objective tension that Bergelson posited. Groping for terms, Shteynman called art a "mirror" and characterized it as the realm of "regime and order"; able only to reflect, he suggested, it was inherently pessimistic, and its essential power was not to transform but to offer consolation. By contrast, revolution was optimistic, believed deeply in its capacity to transform the nature of individuals and collectives, and embraced cruelty and chaos in its striving for the new.[92]

Shteynman also shared Bergelson's perception of an especially grave danger in the present moment for Jewish culture. Whereas in times of revolution the fundamentals of art were preserved in the "village"—in the spirit and practices of the folk—this would not be true in the Jewish case: the shtetl was ruined, Jewish society was destroyed, and the line was cut. Reflecting on the responsibilities and choices of himself and his friends in the Hebraist camp, he wrote that "we, the men of tradition and holders of the line" were now abandoning the larger nation. He offered a despairing, self-lacerating (and accurate) prophecy that whereas the other nations in Russia would continue their national traditions, the Jews would soon be "naked" of any "tradition or culture"—the only nation without its own culture in a country of nations.[93]

The coming year would deepen the predicament of Jewish culturists. The expanding suppression of Hebrew culture would, in a sense, short-circuit Shteynman's more rarified dilemma. But Bergelson and his fellow Yiddishists would face a different fate: unprecedented state support and recognition of Yiddish culture accompanied by the direct subordination of cultural life outside the arts to revolutionary authority, and for the arts themselves, a strange sort of double-entry bookkeeping: relative formal freedom coupled with demands for revolutionary expression that were, indeed, impossible to satisfy.

— 7 —

Making Jewish Culture Bolshevik

> I will speak briefly, perhaps you'll understand: the fact that [the
> Bolsheviks] are the only material basis for Yiddish cultural work
> makes this cultural work loathsome to me . . . And when the
> *gedoylim* [the Bolsheviks] are here, everything Jewish which is not
> on their side, just like every other aspect of culture, is buried.
>
> —ZELIG KALMANOVITSH TO SHMUEL NIGER, 1920

In August 1918, the first Soviet Yiddish journal, *Kultur un bildung,* opened
with a position statement by one Sh. Genrikh. Genrikh, apparently a pedagogue, rebuked his fellow Yiddishists for having devoted so much effort to
articulating the merits of their position to the Jewish public and for debat-
ing the countervailing views of the *"hern hebreistn,"* the "Hebraist sirs."
Not merely a de rigueur invocation of the era's pervasive suspicion of intelligentsia "moderation," Genrikh's article illustrates how the Revolution offered a powerful and seductive reconceptualization of the relationships
among social structure, authority, power, and persuasion in cultural life. In
Genrikh's view, Yiddishism no longer had to justify itself, as many diaspora
autonomists were wont to do, by arguing that the new Yiddish culture reflected East European Jewry's lived culture and changing character better
than the alternatives. Rather, its justification came from an essentially Leninist metaphysics that posited that even a tiny minority, if consecrated by
History itself, could represent the "real" (as opposed to actual) will of the
people, and that the naturally "progressive" classes, even if a numerical minority at present, represented the general will coming into being as society
itself metamorphosed under socialism. The metaphysics of Marxism-
Leninism magically resolved the tension between the fact that Yiddishism
represented a minority position within Jewish life and Yiddishism's own
claims to represent the Jewish masses.[1]

Yet even as he urged Yiddishists to take the cultural power offered them by the Bolsheviks, Genrikh also summoned Yiddishists to "the path of active revolutionary creation." Preaching an all-embracing program of "enlightenment" for the "newly born" Jewish laboring class and the cultivation of an exclusively secular and Yiddish-language culture for (and ultimately by) the Jewish masses, he presaged the logic that would come to govern the new Soviet Yiddish culture. Cultural policy was to be made by those embedded in the party and state, or at least sharing in the essential truth that the party-state possessed. Culture could not be for the elite alone, but had to serve the masses in as direct a fashion as possible. Cultural production and dissemination were state and Communist party concerns. Cultural revolution was an essential part of the Revolution itself.

Nothing about Genrikh can be found in either of the lexicons in which Yiddishism later enshrined its literati and publicists. Although he had moved in Yiddishist pedagogical circles before the war, he commanded no substantial authority in the Yiddishist milieu. Yet as a far more respected figure, Dovid Bergelson, prophesied in August 1919, it was Genrikh's vision that would redefine the Jewish cultural project in revolutionary Russia, beginning as early as 1920–1921.

At one level, 1920–1921 seemed like a moment of fulfillment for the Yiddishist vision. The emerging Soviet state had by this point consolidated its unprecedented support for secular-national Yiddish cultural institutions and publications, from literary journals and avant-garde theaters to Communist Yiddish newspapers to hundreds of elementary schools. A mere ten years earlier, Yiddishists in Warsaw and Odessa had struggled to create the first fledgling Yiddish "high art" theater troupe. Now Lunacharsky's Commissariat of Enlightenment sponsored an experimental Yiddish state theater in the heart of Moscow, state funds underpinned the Kultur-Lige theater studio in Kiev, and further state Yiddish theaters proliferated in other Soviet Jewish centers.[2]

Within these official Jewish cultural institutions, Yiddish enjoyed exclusive legitimacy. By 1920–1921, the Hebrew cultural sphere had been for all intents and purposes destroyed. In early 1921, the living symbol of Hebraism, Bialik, arrived in Moscow to beg Maxim Gorky to implore Lenin to allow Russia's silenced Hebrew writers leave the country (he did). Russian was excluded from Jewish culture as fully as Hebrew, at least on paper, realizing a longstanding goal of both Yiddishists and their erstwhile Hebraist counterparts. A few Russian-language Jewish journals persisted into the early 1920s, but it was clear that there was no sanction for such a hybrid phenomenon; tellingly, the literary historian Israel Tsinberg, a Russified man who had always reflexively used Russian for his scholarship on Hebrew and Yiddish writing, was compelled to write his magisterial history of Jewish literature in Yiddish after the first volume. Hence, even as Russian grew ever more central to Jewish life sociologically, it continued to lose its legitimacy as a language of Jewish culture. As individuals, Jews would flood into newly open Russian-language Soviet social spaces while official Jewish institutions shifted ever more completely to Yiddish with the support and even pressure of the Soviet state.

At another level, however, 1920–1921 marked a moment when the Jewish cultural project was reshaped root and branch by the dictates of the Revolution. Throughout 1920–1921 the cadres of revolutionary enthusiasts, builders, interpreters, and lawgivers who comprised the Bolshevik party, the Soviet state, and Russia's emerging revolutionary public tightened their hold on institutional and discursive power and accelerated their efforts to carry the Revolution into all corners of polity, culture, and consciousness. Although their grip would slacken with the end of War Communism and the beginnings of Russia's New Economic Policy in 1921, by that time new rules had been laid for all aspects of life—if not in the legal sense, then in the more informal but equally compelling imperatives and internalizations, mutual policing and self-monitoring that the Revolution enjoined on all Soviet citizens. These rules included new strictures governing the nature, bounds, and purposes of Jewish cultural production. The processes of institutional and ideological incorporation that had begun in earnest in early 1919 now accelerated, due to both the direct legal and administrative policies of multiple actors empowered by the state—most notably the official Jewish-affairs apparatus within the Communist party, to which I have been referring, for convenience, as "the Evsektsiia"—and due to ideological campaigns mounted by actors outside the party-state structure in the name of the Revolution.[3] New sociological underpinnings for this recasting of Jewish culture also took shape during 1920–1921 as a new generation of writers, teachers, and activists arrived who were attracted to the idea of Yiddish culture but fully committed to the Revolution.

In this context, notable Yiddish figures from the old world like Bergelson were not necessarily marginalized. On the contrary, if they were politically pliable, they were offered positions of prominence as cultural guides and leaders to their officially recognized folk. But they would have to learn to obey the rules implicit in Genrikh's essay—rules nowhere codified yet everywhere apparent, over which they had little if any power, because these rules emerged from the Revolution itself as articulated, enacted, and enforced by its numerous interpreters and executants, including growing numbers within the Soviet Yiddish intelligentsia itself.

Pressure from Without

In early 1920, as the smoke of Denikin's brief occupation of the Ukraine cleared and Soviet forces went on the offensive against Poland, demands for a properly revolutionary Jewish cultural sphere once again resounded both outside and within party and state institutions. These demands fell into three categories. First, Yiddish cultural producers were to serve the Revolution in their work, or at least acknowledge and support it. Second, and more radically, some demanded the direct oversight and absorption of Yiddish cultural organizations and producers by loyal party and state actors (commissars). Third, and most radically, a growing chorus of actors, drawing on the moral authority of Lenin, demanded that the category of "culture" itself be rethought and that prerevolutionary forms of cultural creativity be subsumed into an educative project, a radical *Bildung* imposed through new forms of agitation.

In Kiev, the elements that had split from the Kultur-Lige in May 1919 continued to function as a distinct Ukrainian Communist party fraction of the Kultur-Lige, and some time that year, a Yiddish branch of Proletkult appeared.[4] Throughout Soviet territory, the pro-Bolshevik but independent Jewish Communist Party (Poale Tsion)—the unloved stepchild of both the Jewish socialist and Zionist movements, now tolerated by the new regime—continued to work with both the independent Kultur-Lige and party-state institutions in cultural affairs. But it also aspired to the expansion of its own cultural policy and institutions. Its cultural initiatives, like those of Proletkult, were framed by a determined sociopolitical and cultural-ideological radicalism, which included a growing suspicion of the Kultur-Lige's supraparty stance and cultural "conservatism." Consider, for example, a 1920 letter sent to the Poale Tsion by a group of Kiev Jewish actors disgruntled with both the Kultur-Lige and with Soviet institutions more inclined to support the Kultur-Lige than good radicals like themselves. This actors' "collective" turned specifically to the party to request "moral" and material support for their efforts to create "a new Yiddish theater which should be in every respect appropriate to the new proletarian culture and which should stand on the appropriate height of proletarian art," because the Poale Tsion, unlike the politically and culturally compromised Kultur-Lige, was the right body to lead such genuinely revolutionary efforts.[5]

Meanwhile, Soviet and Communist party institutions undertook their own Yiddish cultural initiatives. Communist party Yiddish journals and newspapers like Kiev's *Komfon* increasingly made room for Yiddish literature and attempted to draw in appropriate established writers while also nurturing growing stables of politically engaged "movement" poets. In Vitebsk, the regional commissariat of the Russian Communist Youth Union published what was arguably the first official Communist party Yiddish cultural journal, *Khvalyes* (Waves) in August 1920. Dividing its contents between "Life and Struggle" and "Literature and Art," *Khvalyes* sought to mobilize Jewish workers and "youth"—two categories ever more closely conflated—for service on the Jewish street, and at the same time to provide an organ in which these workers and youth could "write [their] red history, their flaming life-story."[6]

The most notable of the efforts to articulate a revolutionary aesthetic culture in Jewish circles stemmed from the newly created State Jewish Chamber Theater, or GOSE(K)T. GOSET was born out of Granovsky's experimental St. Petersburg Yiddish theater studio (see Chapter 1), which had been nationalized by the Soviet authorities in January 1919 but then languished in Petrograd's materially and culturally inhospitable environment. In 1920, at Abram Efros's initiative, Granovsky moved what was left of his studio to Moscow where it was brought under the Commissariat of Enlightenment and became GOSET. Under these circumstances, Granovsky, caught up in the revolutionary fervor, broke with his symbolist tendencies and instead threw himself headlong into heady futurist experimentation and self-consciously revolutionary art. Starting with GOSET's official first performance January 1, 1921, Granovsky began to work out the theater studio's distinctive aesthetic. He wedded a fascinating and (for some) shocking stagecraft of antirealistic gymnastic movement based on various contemporary aesthetic or quasi-physiological theories to scripts drawn from classic Yiddish works on prerevolutionary Jewish life—creating a blistering, comical modernist representation of prerevolutionary Jewish spiritual and social deformity.[7]

Throughout 1920, these efforts to produce "revolutionary" Jewish culture through individual works, aesthetic practice, the making of journals, and the like were paralleled by a more general effort by Jewish Communists to subject the Yiddish cultural sphere as a whole to the Revolution's direct authority. The year 1920 was one of consolidation for the Evsektsiia. This consolidation was especially visible in Ukraine, where the Evsektsiia of the Russian Communist party—now ascendant over the rapidly fading state EvKom—was joined by a central Evsektsiia of the Ukrainian Communist party, which had been established in mid-1919 as Denikin's troops closed in on Kiev but had only really come together in Kiev in January 1920. Significantly for Ukraine's Yiddishist cultural sphere, the Ukrainian Evsektsiia Main Bureau was essentially a new, more powerful iteration of the Komfarband: Komfarband leaders like Rafes and Levitan became the new heads of Jewish work in the Ukraine, and the Komfarband's newspaper *KomFon* became the "official organ of the Main Bureau of the Jewish Sections of the Communist party in Ukraine."[8] Thus as of January 1920, Rafes, Kheyfets, Levitan, and the other former Bundists and Fareynikte members turned Jewish Communists now stood within reach of achieving the formal party-state authority they had lacked in 1919.

Evsektsiia consolidation in 1920 remained halting and partial. The group's mobilization into more pressing party work and the Russo-Polish War of 1920–1921 further disrupted Evsektsiia activity, especially in Ukraine, where Polish forces took Kiev briefly in May. As late as April 1921, a number of speakers at a conference of Kiev Evsektsiia activists complained that the work had barely gotten started due to these disruptions (and, more fatefully for the future of Jewish national Communist activity, because of the indifference of both the Jewish population and many nominally Jewish Communists).[9]

More generally, throughout the year, Jewish Communist activists in Russia and Ukraine continued to struggle to establish a sphere of competence and win support for "Jewish work" in various local, regional, and statewide bodies. This work included cultural efforts: in May 1920, the Ukrainian Evsektsiia complained that it was not receiving adequate support from Kiev's regional education authorities for substantial work in Jewish education.[10] Evsektsiia activists continued to bridle, too, at ideological hostility from party comrades toward its "nationalist" cultural work. As one activist in the Gomel region put it: "Russian comrades often failed to understand us in two ways: one couldn't understand why a Jewish culture has to be established at all, and everything which hinted at Jewish culture they [*sic*] called chauvinism, nationalism, and so forth. Others could under no circumstances understand our struggles with Hebraism and Zionist influence in the sphere of Jewish culture."[11] A November 1921 Evsektsiia report on "Jewish work" in Ukraine's regional cities lamented that while the "masses" continued to be "misled" by Zionist propaganda and attend illegal Hebrew courses and circles, the local workers' organizations and their Jewish members refused to make a place for Yiddish in cultural work.[12]

But if the Evsektsiia's status vis-à-vis other state and party institutions remained shaky, its monopolistic authority in Jewish affairs and its power to shape—or at least disrupt—organized Jewish life and Jewish culture grew ever more substantial. Thus, despite the apparent incomprehension of some other Communists as to why the extirpation of Hebrew culture was such a revolutionary necessity, Evsektsiia activists in the Ukraine were able to move quickly in early 1920 to suppress the Hebrew and Zionist cultural institutions that had reemerged under White rule (though with continued complaints about the indifference, leniency, or even financial support of these groups by some general Soviet authorities).[13]

In the Yiddish cultural sphere, the Evsektsiia continued the previous efforts of the EvKom, Narkompros, and other bodies to draw independent Yiddish cultural producers into cultural work sanctioned and dominated by the Communists. At party-state orchestrated conferences on Jewish culture like a Moscow meeting on "the question of Jewish culture" in May and the First All-Russian Congress of Jewish Activists in Education and Socialist Culture in July, non-Communist cultural activists were welcome, and at the latter, they outnumbered Communist party members and even declared "sympathizers": a plurality of eighty-three delegates declared themselves "nonparty," there were unreconstructed Bundists alongside Kombund members, and there were even two "Zionists" (presumably radical Tseire Tsion, as opposed to the Poale Tsion and "Communist Zionist" delegates).[14]

But during 1920 the Evsektsiia also moved more aggressively to suppress remaining legal large-scale independent cultural organizations, most notably the Kultur-Lige in Ukraine. Immediately upon its return to Kiev in January 1920, the leadership of the Ukrainian Evsektsiia under Rafes and the other former Komfarbandists declared its intention to finish what it had begun in 1919. The Ukrainian Evsektsiia leadership recognized that it would be compelled to work with the Kultur-Lige to some extent at least initially, "taking into account that there has not yet been organized a Jewish section in the Commissariat of Enlightenment which could take over the institutions of the Kultur-Lige." It registered the Kultur-Lige as a legal organization (unlike the popular Jewish sports association Makkabi, which was rejected outright because it used Hebrew and sported a Jewish star as its symbol), and even set up what must have been a chilly meeting between Rafes and the Kultur-Lige's Litvak and Moyshe Zilberfarb. But it also moved to gain control over Kultur-Lige policy and give its "activity a character in keeping with Soviet power" by appointing one of its own, Levitan, as special commissar over the entire Kultur-Lige organization.[15]

More broadly, the Evsektsiia made clear that its ultimate goal was the dissolution of the Kultur-Lige in favor of a Evsektsiia-run system of educational and cultural bodies. In March, Evsektsiia activists resolved that "the correct organization of cultural work among the Jewish working masses demands completely that this work should be concentrated in the Soviet institutions for Jewish educational work." Denouncing the Kultur-Lige as "a place where the pseudo-socialist Jewish intelligentsia endeavors to conserve its political standoffishness and its dying influence on the Jewish masses," they declared that the organization was "exclusively . . . a temporary evil which must disappear as soon as local and central Jewish educational sections begin to function well."[16]

Finally, during 1920 efforts intensified among those committed to the Communist, revolutionary, or proletarian Yiddish cultural projects to establish new ground rules regarding the relationship between the Revolution and "culture" as such. Some of these actors understood the Revolution as not overthrowing but consecrating the importance of "Art." But other champions of Communist culture sounded a very different note. Discussion of "cultural work" at the meeting of the Jewish Communist Party (Poale Tsion) in Kiev in April 1920 revolved exclusively around the provision of basic literacy and education, evening courses, and party reading rooms in the service of ideological goals: "culture" was purely a means to an end. This kind of cultural work offered a particular contribution toward the ground-up transformation of Jewish society; it would all serve a larger effort at ideological education and the formation of a new "consciousness" that would ready workers to perform "socially useful work . . . in the Soviet order." This construal of "culture" was dictated by the needs of the Revolution itself: "To a significant degree, [the Revolution's] victory is dependent on the character of [the proletarian masses'] consciousness, their ideology."[17]

Much the same attitude pervaded the discourse and work of the emerging Jewish Communist establishment within the party-state, that is, among the activists of the EvKom and the Evsektsiia. The ambitious publishing plans of the central Evsektsiia in the Ukraine included agitational literature aimed at various social groups (women, youth) and a "scientific journal," but nothing in the arts except a planned publication for children.[18] At the First All-Russian Congress of Jewish Activists in Education and Socialist Culture in July, questions of high culture were completely excluded in favor of educational questions—the one striking exception being a denunciation of Ha-Bimah and a demand for its suppression.[19]

These stances did not mean a complete break with the Yiddishist intelligentsia's emphasis on the importance of aesthetic culture. Elsewhere, both Communist Poale Tsion and Evsektsiia activists still included celebrations of Peretz in their cultural agenda.[20] But for many of these activists, the dominant trajectory in how they defined their "cultural" task was toward folding "high culture" into a general radical "education."

In this divide over the character of "cultural work," Jewish Communists were not alone. The same tensions were visible within the Communist party itself, where enthusiasts of "high culture" (some who envisioned a total revolution within culture, and others who, like Trotsky, championed the inheritance of classical culture) shared power with colleagues who did not see much value or significance in such rarefied pursuits. These tensions were rooted more generally in the overall Russian revolutionary tradition: since the mid-nineteenth century, valorization of high culture and especially literature had jostled with a violent iconoclasm that sought to tear down the old culture in the name of radical leveling (a stance associated with the nihilist Dobroliubov) and later, a populist tendency to see any culture created by the elite as unsuited to the masses. Starting around 1920, as many of this tradition's inheritors of all stripes began to work within the Bolshevik party-state, they brought with them these competing impulses. And although Bolshevik authorities were by no means ready to allow a wholesale dismantling of high culture, they too began to demand, in an increasingly impatient and categorical way, that cultural practices be integrated into the larger project of total revolution. As Michael David-Fox argues, 1920 marked a turning point for the party-state's relationship to culture: it started then to officially embrace "culture" as a policy concern and hence, too, "cultural revolution" as a practical policy.[21] Against this backdrop, the ideological pressure on Jewish culturists increased dramatically.

Pressure from Within

Given the double-edged sword of support from the state and demands from revolutionaries, Yiddishists renegotiated their cultural project throughout 1920 in a variety of ways. The dwindling population of nonsocialists in the Yiddishist camp followed complex and ambivalent paths. In Kiev, the major nonsocialist Yiddishist cultural institution, the Folks Farlag, remained within—and perhaps drew protection from—the Kultur-Lige. A high-quality publishing house that published not only its own list but also many materials for other houses, the Folks-Farlag remained independent, continued to sign new contracts, and felt secure enough to develop expansive new projects, including many of those discussed in previous chapters. Indeed, according to Shtif, one of its key editors, 1919 was the high-water mark of its work and it carried its ambitious plans well into 1920: as late as August 1920, Shtif wrote to the Yiddish activist Zalman Reyzen in Vilna inviting him to participate in the publishing house's planned cultural journal for a generous stipend. Enclosed with his letter was a thirty-eight-page prospectus of publications.[22]

On an individual level, the picture was more complicated for nonsocialist or ex-socialist Yiddishists. Publicly, figures like Shtif, the maverick populist Zionist Dinur, the pedagogue Kalmanovitsh, and the Yiddishist historian E. Tsherikover remained active in Kultur-Lige work while seeking to minimize connections to official Soviet Yiddishism. Some of these actors evidently perceived the cultural realm as one still relatively immune from political determinations. Significantly, this was true not only of nonsocialist Yiddishists now under pressure from the entire Jewish left, but also of Jewish socialists who found the new ideological environment inhospitable or repellent. Moyshe Zilberfarb, a founding member of the Fareynikte, openly retreated from political life due to the rise of "the Communist standpoint and tactics," as he put it, and immersed himself instead in Kultur-Lige work as the head of the Folks-Universitet.[23] Significantly, this sort of retreat was socially visible.[24] Militant left-wing elements would ultimately point to this "flight into culture" as proof to the regime that the Yiddish cultural sphere was actually a bastion of antirevolutionary elements and that the principle of cultural autonomy was merely a fig leaf for politically dangerous saboteurs.

Privately, these figures diverged in their assessment of the new regime. Shtif found himself increasingly sympathetic or at least "agnostic" toward the new regime despite his earlier uncompromising anti-Bolshevism.[25] His close friend Kalmanovitsh moved in the other direction, as the epigraph to this chapter testifies. By mid-1920, he was privately convinced that the Bolsheviks had "wrought greater destruction in the Jewish soul than all the pogroms."[26]

Zilberfarb's steadfastness and Kalmanovitsh's unyielding anti-Bolshevism were, however, exceptional. By late 1919, the general triumph of radical anti-Semitism in the White movement, as well as mounting evidence that the Bolsheviks were the only power in the region willing to prevent the mass murder of Jews, narrowed the political choices for Soviet Jews. The political differentiation and widespread radicalization that had marked the Jewish nationalist intelligentsia's relationship to the Revolution since 1918 accelerated after events of the winter of 1919–1920, especially the horrendous wave of pogroms unleashed by White troops in the south as Denikin's forces temporarily conquered Ukraine. Under the circumstances, growing numbers of Jewish nationalist intellectuals, including many cultural activists, embraced the Revolution. Many left-Yiddishist culturists continued their leftward trajectory. Nokhem Oyslender put aside his poetry and literary criticism to volunteer for the Red Army medical corps in August 1919; by early 1920, with Soviet power reestablished in Kiev and the Red Army on the march toward Warsaw, Dobrushin and Hofshteyn began to write for Bolshevik journals like the revived Moscow *Kultur un bildung* and *Komfon*.[27] The events of 1919–1920 brought about far more dramatic ideological conversions as well, turning the Folkist writer Moyshe Taytsh into a committed Bolshevik and driving the Zionist activist Shloyme-Yankev Niepomniashchi into the ranks of Ukraine's pro-Bolshevik *Borot'bisti* and then into the Red Army.[28]

By this point, even many of the Jewish nationalist intellectuals who remained opposed to the Revolution welcomed Bolshevik power as at least a guarantee of relative physical security. One budding Hebrew writer related that a feeling of relief swept "even the bourgeoisie" when the Bolsheviks reconquered Kharkov for the third and last time in the winter of 1920. The Hebrew poet Y. Karni, staunchly anti-Bolshevik, recalled the same relief in Odessa.[29]

By early 1920 most socialist Yiddishists and even some nonsocialists were ready to meet the October Revolution halfway at least. Leading culturists in Moscow, Kiev, and Odessa proved ready to write for state- and party-sponsored organs. In Kiev, the Evsektsiia planned a children's journal edited by the *Eygns* writers Hofshteyn and Der Nister, along with one Fanya Nirenberg (perhaps one of the Evsektsiia's own writers).[30] In Odessa, the Jewish section of the Gubnarobroz funded a commemorative anthology for Y. L. Peretz on the fifth anniversary of his death in April 1920, *Tsum ondenk fun Y. L. Peretz,* written largely by left-leaning but independent (in some cases Poale Tsion affiliated) culturists (see fig. 12). In Moscow, *Kultur un bildung* began to appear once again in early 1920 after the crises and mobilizations of 1919; published at this point by the Jewish section of the Central Commissariat of Education, it set itself the task of "illuminating the practice of cultural Communist creation by the Jewish worker-masses [and] organizing our cultural and educational activists on the Revolutionary platform."[31] Its pages, however, were filled with writings not only by minor Communist pedagogues, but also by leading Yiddishists like Litvakov, Dobrushin, and Shtif.

These more notable Yiddishist cultural actors who wrote for *Kultur un bildung* in early 1920 expressed there (and were allowed to express) views largely consonant with claims they had previously made in their own independent journals. Litvakov used an article on the death of A. Vayter, a Vilna Bundist-turned-Yiddish dramatist, to reiterate his long-standing call for "the dialectical task—to Judaize Jewish socialism with the aid of cultural universalism."[32] In an article on "Books, Readers, and Teachers," Dobrushin mobilized historical materialist rhetoric to defend radical artistic innovations. More boldly still, he defended the same "elitist" stance regarding the relationship between Yiddish literature and the currently existing Yiddish reader that the Kultur-Lige had long propounded. Happy to grant that popular consumption of quality Yiddish literature had risen to unprecedented levels, he nonetheless insisted that the new "average reader is spiritually, so to speak [insufficiently] developed" to respond to the "shaping power" of the aesthetic to the same degree as his intelligentsia forebears. Admitting that the nature of modern literature was partially to blame, Dobrushin nonetheless defended modernist experimentation as a historically necessary, productive development for literature. The implication was clear: the task of the Revolution was not to overthrow or reverse the course of literary development, but to raise both the reader and literature itself to the same higher level.[33]

At the same time, however, these writers began to make significant compromises with what they took to be the dictates of the Revolution. Shtif's "Literature and Culture" reiterated generally shared Yiddishist claims that secular Yiddish culture represented the spiritual liberation of the Jewish nation and the Jewish individual. But Shtif, a Folkist once committed to a supraclass nationalist politics, here referred to his national collective hero not as "the folk," the term he had previously employed in all his writings, but as the "*arbetsfolk*" or "the work-nation." Without actually embracing Marxist class analysis, this peculiar neologism signaled a readiness to make manual labor the test of national belonging and acceptability in the larger Soviet community of "work-nations."[34]

Yiddish literature itself registered both the weight of the demand for revolutionary reorientation and the tensions associated with it, both the demands of Litvak and the concerns of Bergelson. This state of tension was captured by the main Yiddish literary event of 1920, the publication of the second volume of the Kiev-Grupe's literary tribune, *Eygns*. Once again under the editorship of Bergelson, now published by the Kultur-Lige, and illustrated by the Jewish modernist Ryback, the new anthology was exclusively devoted to literature. In its very form, it asserted the importance of high literature: it eschewed any political or critical articles, offered no explicit acknowledgment of the controversy that had swirled around it, and avoided even an editorial statement. Volume two of *Eygns* also testified to the continuing literary authority of the old Kiev-Grupe and especially of Bergelson: despite all the critiques, the name *Eygns* could still attract Kiev's top literary talents regardless of their style, genre, or politics. Although figures like Hofshteyn, Kvitko, and Dobrushin were now writing for Bolshevik journals, they placed themselves under Bergelson's editorship and alongside the dominant presence of the suspiciously symbolist Nister. The journal made room for newcomers like the (deceased) dramatist Shteyman, the critic and poet Lipe Reznik, and the displaced Polish-Jewish teacher and budding poet Kadya Molodowsky; it even attracted Markish despite Bergelson's harsh critiques of his work. Bergelson remained a respected critical authority for young Yiddish writers even as his political star waned; Molodowsky regularly came to solicit Bergelson's literary guidance and later attributed her own understanding of the "essence of writ-ing" to these meetings.[35]

Yet if the publication of volume two of *Eygns* demonstrated its continu-ity with the pre-Bolshevik Yiddishist vision of a new Yiddish literature, its contents betrayed a more complicated situation. On the one hand, the an-thology was dominated by long prose works by Bergelson and Nister. It opened with the complete text of Bergelson's own masterwork, the novella *Opgang,* on which he had labored throughout the war years. His third major work, *Opgang* confirmed both Bergelson's literary greatness and his critics' charges: as I noted in the Introduction, *Opgang* presented Bergelson's most complete picture yet of total Jewish societal and social-psychological decay with no concession to leftist critics' demands for "pos-itive heroes." Bergelson's very title, "descent" or "decline," was an affront to those who demanded that writers celebrate the new.

On the other hand, many other works in the journal reflected the ideo-logical distance that many in the Yiddishist intelligentsia had traversed in the two years since the first anthology. Beynish Shteyman's symbolically freighted "dramatic poem" "Meshiekh Ben-Yoysef" (see Chapter 6) and Lipe Reznik's "Lider" (Poems), replete with night, dawn, walls, and the smashing of chains both iron and "golden," were barely veiled meditations on the Revolution and the Jews. Perhaps the most dramatic evolution was evident in the work of Dovid Hofshteyn. His established poetic voice of quiet lyrical celebration was now joined by a pogrom poetry of shattered, helpless mourning and an embryonic poetry of more nakedly revolution-ary zeal. His cycle *Tristia* or *Troyer,* dedicated to "all those cut down before their time," marked the first powerful example of the accelerating reorgani-zation of Yiddish literature around the horrors of the Ukrainian pogroms. The Hofshteyn of *Tristia* framed his poetry with citations from the Book of Job and the Jewish laws of mourning, meditated on the nature of post-traditional Jewish mourning, and openly invoked Bialik's great Hebrew pogrom poems of the prewar era.[36] Concomitantly, Hofshteyn's "In mit fun tog" (At Midday) recast his vision of individual and national trans-formation in a more active, violent, and self-immolating mode appropriate to the age:

> Hey, all of you, whoever of his own will
> with strong light hand
> raised up his young life and threw it high

against the dark wall
of human insignificance and superstition
threw it and forgot
and did not take it back . . .

Hey, all of you, whoever
in the ripeness of his years
with burning thresher
threshed himself down . . .
to you now my heart is bowed![37]

Furthermore, Hofshteyn's work in *Eygns* demonstrated that even those in the Jewish intelligentsia most unswervingly devoted to the ideal of a new Jewish high culture were now, in the context of the Revolution and the pogroms, beginning to rethink "culture" no less than were their Communist counterparts and rivals. Hofshteyn now expressed potent doubts about aestheticist conceptions of poetry and proclaimed the poet's inextricable connection to extraliterary human affairs like the pogroms and the Revolution:

I see in far wildernesses
burning simooms
I see caravans
coming and going—
where to and where from?
In abyssal crashing
in the spew of volcanoes
I hear the silence of human weeping,
in the play of early-year sunlight
on old rusted stones
I hear the pure clamor
of children,
of children, who can in the blink of an eye
both laugh and cry . . .

I have hung my consciousness on World—
a wedding canopy without corners and poles—
but I cannot for a moment sever myself
from earthly changes! . . .
I lift my eyes

to the dusts of the stars,
but the notes of the spheres
cannot drown out
the jubilee of human joys,
the wailing of human woes.[38]

Similar tendencies played out in Yiddishist organizational practice and public cultural life. After the return of Soviet power to Kiev in December 1919, the leading institutions of Kiev's Yiddishist intelligentsia reaffirmed their core conceptions of Yiddish culture, presumably in the hope that the new regime would once again support them. In January 1920, the Kultur-Lige reasserted its presence with a public mass meeting (apparently packed to overflowing), participation by its theater troupe in a city-wide New Year's celebrations for children, and the impressive 1920 exhibition of artworks by Kiev Jewish artists.[39]

But if these sorts of writings and public efforts asserted the continued legitimacy of Yiddishism's culturist vision, they were matched by intensified efforts to earn proper revolutionary credentials. The broad Yiddishist left displayed an increasingly unanimous and complete intolerance not only toward any Hebrew culture but also toward insufficiently "socialist" Yiddish culture. Within Yiddishism, the rhetorics of class warfare, which had been held partially in check by the countervailing principle of culture's autonomy from politics, now became the norm. Back in May 1919 at the Kultur-Lige's second conference, the Bundist educator and activist Kazdan, speaking for the central committee of the Kultur-Lige, had proclaimed: "Into the central committee came the best talents which Kiev had to offer, if one does not take into account a few representatives of the bourgeoisie, whose acceptance into the central committee was bound up with certain material hopes and who, incidentally, entirely did not justify these hopes." Now, in the first months of 1920, in a manner worthy of the Evsektsiia, the Kultur-Lige leadership attacked the remnants of Kiev's "bourgeois" OPE; repudiated the very idea of a broad front of Jewish "democratic elements," which it had once embraced; and engineered a purge of nonsocialist elements in Kharkov's Kultur-Lige chapter.[40] Whether Kultur-Lige activists acted out of tactical necessity or belief (and in what proportion) is perhaps irrelevant: such behavior still testifies to the reshaping of the cultural project according to revolutionary imperatives.

Moreover, the composition of the Yiddishist culturist camp itself was beginning to undergo a fateful change. By 1920, a new cohort of culturists with a much more robust faith in the Revolution began to emerge, making their views known in print and in Yiddishist centers like Kiev. Although they did not break fully with their forebears, the young men and women who now began to flow into Yiddish cultural life were impatient with the doubts of their elders and were reflexively committed to revolutionary modes of thought. They had come of age after 1917, and many of their views were molded by experiences in the Revolution's most central institutions, especially the Red Army. Many began their cultural life almost completely within the universe of Jewish Communist, Evsektsiia institutions and identified themselves as party poets ("poets from our ranks"). In some cases, Evsektsiia figures acted as mentors to these budding party-poets: the poet Moyshe Khashevatski, who served as literary editor of *KomFon,* took such poets under his wing.[41] By the time some of the more talented younger writers had gravitated to more significant poets like Hofshteyn, they already bore revolutionary credentials and ideals. Itsik Fefer, for example, was a Bundist-turned-Communist who fought in the Red Army, served in the Bolshevik underground during Denikin's control of Kiev, and debuted in 1919 in the *KomFon.* He went on to work with Hofshteyn and to publish in more specifically literary contexts. But regardless he maintained his bottomless faith in the Revolution and a cheerful readiness to use his poetry as a weapon: in the 1930s, he would distinguish himself for his odes to Stalin and answer criticisms of Soviet policy by the novelist Sholem Ash with the rhetorical death sentence: "A bullet in your head, Sholem Ash, Sholem Ash!"[42]

The Bolshevization of the Cultural Project

Neither the retrenchment of growing numbers of culturists nor the prospect of a demographic solution to the "problem" satisfied the authorities appointed to bring the Revolution into Jewish life. Throughout 1920, the Evsektsiia intensified its efforts to win more direct control over the Jewish cultural sphere—in particular, the Kultur-Lige.

Evsektsiia efforts to suppress the Kultur-Lige in early 1920 had been constrained not only by its own limited resources, but also by support for the organization from central Russian Communist authorities, including Dimanshtein. His decision to provide the Kultur-Lige with five million rubles in January and February 1920 infuriated the Ukrainian Evsektsiia, as a transcript of a telephone conversation between Dimanshtein and Moyshe Rafes in Kiev shows. Noting that the Evsektsiia could have used that five million in its own way, Rafes complained: "Your decision about the Kultur-Lige constitutes a great mistake. We here have tried to concentrate all matters of Jewish enlightenment in the hands of the sections of the Commissariat of Enlightenment . . . We have decided for the time being not to liquidate the Kultur-Lige, [instead] placing over it a commissar, but in general we are not interested in the expansion of its activity." Rafes also urged Dimanshtein to "drive [the Kultur-Lige activist Zelig] Melamed out of Moscow to Kiev," which suggested that the Kultur-Lige had been lobbying on the ground in Moscow.[43] It is not surprising that leaders of the Ukrainian Evsektsiia were feeling defensive; they also faced a lack of support for Jewish work by local Communist authorities in the Ukraine.[44]

The Kultur-Lige was indeed mounting an active self-defense both through direct lobbying of higher Soviet authorities (hence the complaint about Melamed) as well as making its case in the councils of Jewish Communist activists. The Kultur-Lige sent representatives to regime-sponsored meetings, like the March 1920 Evsektsiia conference in Kharkov.[45] The Kultur-Lige bulletins of November 1919 and May 1920 were evidently designed in large part to give evidence of the Kultur-Lige's success and continued utility. And in April 1920, when some Kultur-Lige activists fled Kiev for Moscow in advance of the Polish army, they created a bureau of the organization's central committee in the Soviet capital that was intended, in part, to be the "representative of the Kultur-Lige vis-à-vis the relevant organs of Soviet power."[46]

In these forums, the Kultur-Lige continued to insist that its continued existence was both necessary and appropriate. In April, the Central Committee resolved that even if a full-fledged Jewish cultural body sponsored by the state should come into being, the Kultur-Lige would remain vital for the sort of creative "experiments" that could only be fostered by "free organizations"—albeit organizations "with the support and under the overarching and control of the relevant state organs."[47] The essay that opened the Kultur-Lige's May bulletin, "We and the Regime," insisted that even after the Revolution, there would remain aspects of cultural life that should not come under the authority of the state.[48]

But the Kultur-Lige could not hold out forever against the Evsektsiia, the empowered agent of Soviet Ukraine's Jewish cultural policy. Even as it defended the Kultur-Lige's right to exist, the once-defiant Central Committee made increasingly conciliatory gestures. At the March 1920 Evsektsiia meeting, the Kultur-Lige representatives offered the Evsektsiia 50 percent of the seats on the Kultur-Lige Central Committee.[49] In the April resolutions, the same activists who had stood firm against the Communist elements in the Kultur-Lige itself a year earlier now displayed a more flexible attitude: "The Kultur-Lige seeks to unify in socialist-creative cultural work the cultural powers of all socialist and Communist groups. It strives to work in the closest contact with Soviet power and especially with its Jewish organs."[50]

The second half of 1920 brought the endgame. As the situation in Ukraine stabilized and the Kultur-Lige began halting efforts to reestablish ties with Jewish communities in the provinces, the Evsektsiia stepped up its attack.[51] In August, the Ukrainian Jewish Communists expanded their oversight of Kultur-Lige work. The Kultur-Lige was obliged to "submit the plan of its work to the Jewish Sections of the Commissariat of Enlightenment and Education." It was allowed to administer "only those institutions which the Jewish Section of the Commissariat of Education cannot yet take under its own authority for whatever reason." The Ukrainian Communists suggested to the "Central Bureau of the Evsektsiia in Moscow that it give funding to the Ukrainian Kultur-Lige only with the knowledge of the Jewish Department of the Central Committee of the Communist party of Ukraine and the Jewish Section of the Commissariat of Enlightenment."[52] And the Third All-Russia Conference of the Jewish Sections of the Russian Communist Party resolved that all Jewish "cultural-enlightenment" work must be carried out according to the "Communist world-view" and that therefore "Jewish educational organs must as soon as possible free themselves of their cultural traditions."[53]

How the Evsektsiia attack played out on the ground is suggested by the recollections of an outsider to the struggle, the anarchist Alexander Berkman, who was deported from the United States to Soviet Russia along with his partner Emma Goldman and some two hundred other radicals, and who traveled through Ukraine in 1920:

> Formerly the League was a powerful organization, with 230 branches throughout the South [that is, Ukraine], doing cultural work among its co-religionists. The institution had much to suffer through the various political changes, the Bolsheviki were tolerant at first, and even financially aided its educational efforts. But gradually the help was withdrawn

and obstacles began to be placed in the way of the League. The Communists frown upon the too nationalistic character of its work. The *Yovkom* [*sic*], Jewish branch of the Party, is particularly antagonistic. The League's teachers and older pupils have been mobilized into State service, and the field of its efforts narrowed down. In the provinces most of its branches have been compelled to close entirely, but in Kiev the devotion and persistence of its leading spirits still enable the League to continue.[54]

The Evsektsiia also worked to discredit the Kultur-Lige in the eyes of other Soviet bodies. In October, the Evsektsiia's official organ in Ukraine, *Komfon,* accused the Kultur-Lige of exploiting the still-unstable conditions to secure undeserved money from general state organs.[55] In November, Jewish Communist authorities announced that they were finally "getting down to the Communization [*kommunizirovania*] of the leading organs of the Kultur-Lige" and presented the Kultur-Lige with an ultimatum that "majorities in the Central Committee and the executive office be placed in the hands of Communists."[56]

The Kultur-Lige refused, continuing to defend its revolutionary credentials by insisting (in a third bulletin that was never published) that its provincial work was drawing in "all the active powers of the socialist and Communist groups."[57] But to no avail: in December, the central authorities in Moscow sided with the Ukrainian Evsektsiia. On December 17, the Central Committee and Executive Office of the Kultur-Lige "were dissolved 'because their activity does not reflect the educational line of Soviet power,'" and in their place seven "kosher but unknown Communists," in the bitter words of the Kultur-Lige's former leadership, were installed to oversee the organization.[58] The Kultur-Lige continued to exist in this "reorganized" form, nominally independent but party-run with a state subsidy, until November 1921, when, as David Shneer puts it, "it became an official Soviet organization and state publisher of Yiddish materials."[59]

What was the source of the animus that lay behind the Evsektsiia's campaign, and what does it tell us about the fate of culture in the new Soviet society? The Evsektsiia's attack on the Kultur-Lige was driven not merely by a simple desire for institutional monopoly, but also by deeply felt ideological imperatives. One of the charges leveled against the Kultur-Lige was that it was politically untrustworthy or even merely a front for recalcitrant "right-wing" socialist elements. Significantly, this was not merely a charge made for public consumption by other Communist party institutions, but a strongly held belief by Evsektsiia activists on all levels. Back in mid-1919, the EvKom in Petrograd had refused to legalize a Kultur-Lige chapter there because it constituted "a stronghold of counterrevolutionary elements" (its members included the Poale-Tsionist Shneur Zalman Rubashov, later Zalman Shazar, first president of Israel).[60] In Ukraine, the Evsektsiia made it a point to bar the politically hostile Zilberfarb from teaching the course on public law at the Kultur-Lige's Folks-Universitet (though it permitted the publication of his pamphlet *Nasha burzhuaziia,* or "Our Bourgeoisie") and decided that the course on "social questions" could only be entrusted to teachers who supported the party platform.[61] Equally scandalous was the Kultur-Lige's pretension of representing the Jewish workers. In a report to regional authorities from Poltava, one M. Kiper complained that "there are also groups of Bundists and Fareynikte activists in the nonparty Kultur-Lige, which lays claim to exclusive representation of the Jewish workers."[62]

Second, the Evsektsiia found fault with the Kultur-Lige's cultural policies, especially vis-à-vis education: as the Ukrainian Evsektsiia Main Bureau put it in its midyear report on "enlightenment work and the Kultur-Lige," it was concerned that cultural work "would not be conducted in the Kultur-Lige in the desirable Communist spirit."[63] In some respects, Evsektsiia activists were least concerned with the high-cultural work of the Kultur-Lige; in keeping with its own conception of what was truly important in Soviet Jewish cultural policy, the Evsektsiia was more worried about the Kultur-Lige's work as a mass-education organization. Thus in February, the Ukrainian Evsektsiia decided to defer the question of nationalizing the Kultur-Lige's art studio until after it had dealt with the question of education.[64] But this deferral did not mean that the Kultur-Lige's work in the realm of aesthetic culture could continue free and clear. Evsektsiia activists apparently attacked the Kultur-Lige for devoting too much of its (and the state's) resources to aesthetic culture rather than education, judging from the defensive tone of the Kultur-Lige's budgetary report in its May 1920 bulletin: "The opinion predominates that the Kultur-Lige is primarily an *art-league.* The expense totals demonstrate how false this accusation is."[65]

Third, and most fundamentally, the Evsektsiia's animus stemmed from a deeply held hostility to any separate cultural authority outside the Communist party regardless of that body's ideology. As the Evsektsiia stated apodictically in May: "In this question of state [enlightenment work], a private [and particular, as opposed to universal] society cannot substitute for a state organization."[66] Particularly telling were the comments of the Ukrainian Jewish Communist authorities to the Ukrainian Communist party fraction of the Kultur-Lige, which reminded these Yiddishist Proletkultists that the Kultur-Lige was merely a transitional organization regardless of its political stance. The radical elements within the Kultur-Lige who had seceded in the name of Communism and proletarian culture in May 1919 were thus also put on notice that they would not be allowed to create some kind of independent Jewish Communist institution modeled on Proletkult, no matter what its ideology.[67]

Why did the central authorities allow the Ukrainian Evsektsiia to win? Ex post facto, the Russian Central Bureau of the Evsektsiia, acknowledging the extensive support it had provided to the Kultur-Lige, summed up the reasons for its change of heart with the comment that the Kultur-Lige had increasingly become the provenance of "almost exclusively nonparty and Menshevik elements—and particularly those sort of Mensheviks who had a special odor . . . the work [of the Kultur-Lige] took on an ever more petty bourgeois nationalist content; thus, finally, the only path which remained was to reorganize the Central Committee of the Kultur-Lige."[68] But there was more to the process than political suspicion of the Kultur-Lige or even hostility to its version of Jewish culture. The central regime tolerated the Kultur-Lige while it remained useful. But as the Bolshevik suppression of Proletkult in 1921 was to demonstrate, it was not only members of the Evsektsiia who were constitutionally incapable of permitting large-scale private initiatives to remain active in the new Soviet order.

Against the backdrop of the Evsektsiia's triumph, the only sphere of relative freedom that remained was the one at the core of the cultural project: high literature. Literature was subject to direct censorship, of course, and it could be summary and indiscriminate. In a report to his superiors in Moscow, one Evsektsiia activist in charge of printing in Odessa spoke with contempt about the "piddling Hasidic stories" of some of the local Yiddish literati and reported that he himself had vetoed publication of one such "pious story."[69] Moreover, there was no shortage of critics in Jewish life both within and outside regime institutions who continued to demand a thoroughgoing transformation of literary practice into a tool of direct revolutionary education.

But by 1921, the legitimate status of high art in the Soviet Yiddish cultural sphere as in the larger Soviet Russian cultural sphere seemed essentially secure. Hofshteyn prefaced one of the works he published in 1921 with the credo: "And if I cannot give you repose / accept at least the sunlit world around [*nem zhe zikh likhtikn rum*]." He thus reserved for himself and his reader the right to return at least in part to his earlier poetry of quotidian, natural beauty. The same exaltation of art could be found among more wholehearted advocates of revolutionary culture as well. The doggerel poem that opened an anthology dedicated to the Kultur-Lige's Kiev Yiddish theater invoked the heroic revolutionary struggle and "the holy Temple of holy Art" in virtually the same breath (see fig. 13).[70] Even the Evsektsiia seemed ready to accord a more significant place to a high-cultural ideal in the wake of its conquest of the Kultur-Lige. In Odessa, the Evsektsiia took up the *echt*-Yiddishist practice of public celebrations of Peretz. In August 1921, the organ of the main bureau of the Evsektsiia construed the goals of the Evsektsiia's theater work as helping to develop "both a purely artistic and also a revolutionary original and translated repertoire" as well as "the creation of a traveling model-theater (artistic) and agitational-theater."[71]

Nevertheless, even loyal literati who disclaimed the tensions that Bergelson had described in 1919 wrestled with ways to square their art with revolutionary dictates. Even as they continued to assert their right to cultivate Yiddish literature as an end in itself, Hofshteyn and other elements of Kiev's Yiddish literary establishment moved to shore up their revolutionary credentials with the anthology *In fayerdikn doyer*. This anthology selected "revolutionary lyrics" by *Eygns* poets (as well as Broderzon, Kulbak, and other isolated talents), while the introduction both tendentiously presented the poetry of the Kiev-Grupe as born directly of "war and Revolution, Civil War and pogroms" and insisted on a seamless fit between formal innovativeness and properly revolutionary content.[72]

That this approach was not merely a tactical defense but, at least for some, the expression of an inner conflict between two opposing sets of commitments can be seen in the writings of Markish, a Yiddish writer who already had substantial revolutionary legitimacy. In 1921, Markish left the Soviet Union, but remained a strong supporter of the Revolution, eventually returning in 1925. Taking up residence in independent Poland, he published a book-length declaration of his aesthetic beliefs that, in intoxicated expressionist prose, reiterated the culturist principle that the imposition of any sort of ideological demands on art would inevitably ruin the artwork itself:

> The artist does not create out of a duty, with a program, thus must he do; no, thus does he wish to do, thus he feels like doing. If he is not satisfied,

he destroys it and—starts anew. An artist is not obliged to anyone—even the past. An artist cannot know in advance what he needs. If there are musts, if there are duties—he must be national, he must be proletarian, [then] he must be everything but "himself" . . .

If the artist knows in advance what must be received from him, because that's his duty—then he's nothing more than a craftsman.[73]

Markish defiantly directed these claims not only to those who demanded that the artist adhere to some Jewish nationalist program, but also to those "various apostles of the Revolution" who required, "with no less parading and tendentiousness," a revolutionary agenda. Slogans about "'masses,' 'collectivism,' 'proletarian-art'" were as senseless in the arts as slogans of "those 'high priests' about 'nation,' 'folk,' and the like" because both subjected poetry to "purely political-societal accounting"—which could only contravene the essence of poetry. Only through the poet's "individualized accounting of the soul" could he represent the "experiences . . . dreams . . . [and] hopes of his epoch, of his tribe."[74]

But Markish's *Farbaygeyendik* is also pervaded by an anxious desire to avoid Bergelson's despairing conclusions about the irreconcilable tension between art and revolution. Throughout the book, Markish proclaimed undiminished revolutionary enthusiasm and his desire to join the Revolution's other questing spirits in their effort to build "a tower . . . in the middle of the day." The Revolution meant redemption not only for world culture but for Yiddish culture too, because it expropriated everything in the name of the people and thus restored to Jews their "eygns"—their own culture. Having just left the Soviet Union, Markish declared his programmatic readiness to return and participate in "the great international culture" taking shape in Russia. Faced with the task of explaining how he could participate in the Revolution's tower-building without trammeling his own art, he gave up the very individuality he had earlier asserted. The poet as agent, who "rips off and smashes off and breaks off as much as is possible according to the power of his creative will and in the form dictated by his individual feeling, greatness, and beauty," sat uncomfortably next to Markish's other pervasive image of the poet as marching soldier, part of the new collective born of war and consummated in Revolution. Tellingly, Markish concluded by joining in the attack on those Yiddish writers (like Bergelson) who had so far avoided writing about the Revolution.[75]

In fayerdikn doyer and *Farbaygeyendik* both sought to protect aesthetic autonomy while claiming loyalty to the Revolution. But the ideological fervor and the historiosophical logic of the Revolution could only undercut such efforts, as Bergelson had foreseen. Back in February 1919, in an article in the Moscow *Kultur un bildung,* an unknown writer by the name of Kh. Malinin had put his finger on an essential feature of the Revolution's relationship to art. Malinin pilloried the tendency of "bourgeois publicists, art-theorists, and art practitioners . . . to unite the concept of 'class-art' with the notion of 'tendentious art.'" Instead, he propounded a striking double claim: "art is a great social power, and in *revolutionary* epochs, it must be used as a means of struggle by the rising class. From works of art we demand only one thing: they must have artistic truth."[76]

Faced with the evident tension between these two statements—that art must now be "used as a means of struggle" but that the new regime demanded nothing more than "artist truth"—we might be tempted to invoke Orwell's notion of doublespeak, as does the critic Tzvetan Todorov in personal reflections on growing up under Bulgarian Communism: "Faced with . . . two irreconcilable givens—contradictory utterances on the one hand and the requirement of non-contradiction on the other—the Party chooses to override the latter, not by accepting contradiction, but by conditioning reason not to notice it."[77] Yet there is good reason to imagine that Malinin saw no contradiction to be overcome. A good Marxist-Leninist could believe that the progress of the Revolution would perforce harmonize an artist's subjective truth with the objective, transcendent "social truth" of the new society. There were two implications of this notion, which would become a key tenet of Socialist Realism. First, an artist who refused to speak the Revolution's truth was essentially lying, and of course such a lie was a form of sabotage. And second, anyone who did not yet believe fully in the truth of the Revolution's claims had to continue working on his or her own belief system until it aligned with those claims—at which point there would be no tension between freedom and necessity. Artistic truth would be completely identical with the "truth" dictated by belief in the Revolution's infallibility.

Aftermath

The year 1921 was one of decision for the culturist intelligentsia. The Soviet order was firmly established, the Civil War was over, and outside Soviet borders, the postwar order in Eastern Europe had begun to stabilize. With Hebrew culture suppressed and the institutions of independent Yiddish culture dismantled, those committed to the Jewish cultural project faced a stark choice: continue cultural work within the strictures of the emerging Soviet Yiddish order or secede from it by going underground, abandoning cultural activism, or leaving revolutionary Russia. A fair number of Yiddishists and even a few Hebraists chose to stay. They did so because of their beliefs in Communist ideology and its promises in some cases; a sense of the cultural opportunities the Communist state might offer the Jewish nation, Jewish culture, and, not least, oneself; and, perhaps most generally, an excitement over the unfolding Soviet experiment.

By 1921, however, others had had enough. For Hebraists (apart from the few Communists among them), the choice was hardly a choice at all. A few hardy figures chose to continue some semblance of Hebrew cultural life underground. Most, however, had already reoriented their hopes to Palestine. In 1921 there began the famous exodus, in which Gorky had a hand, of Odessa's remaining great Hebraist figures to Palestine or to temporary sanctuary in Berlin.

Despite the far more attractive terms offered them by the new state, many Yiddishists also refused to accept the new dispensation. Some Yiddishists who might otherwise have been willing to work in the new order revolted against the Evsektsiia's political control over culture in an institutional sense and the reduction of cultural producers to obedient *spetsi*. Shtif later contrasted the "fanaticized party-men" of the Evsektsiia and their scant regard for "free civil and private initiative and energy" with the general Soviet regime's "honest relationship to Yiddish literature."[78] In the Kultur-Lige Central Committee's resignation announcement in December 1920, Zilberfarb, Litvak, Mayzl, Melamed, and Kazdan laid much of the blame on the "party politics" of the Jewish Communists and their principle of "everything for the state, no organized civil society for cultural work."[79] As the same activists noted in private correspondence, the takeover of the Kultur-Lige by the Communists was "tragic not only because the better, responsible activists were pushed aside, but because the entire tendency and direction is toward the gradual liquidation of an independent Kultur-Lige and its transformation into a party-state thing."[80]

Some Yiddishist cultural activists, like the leadership of the Kultur-Lige and writers like Bergelson, were also affronted by the tendency of Jewish Communists to downgrade the importance of high culture in favor of propagandistic and educational efforts. The Kultur-Lige leadership contrasted its commitment to "the development of eternal cultural values [and] the building up of new values which our cultural lacks" with the Communist commitment to "satisfying first and foremost the demands of the broad street." No less than its denial of culture's institutional autonomy from politics or its suppression of certain versions of Jewish culture itself, the Evsektsiia's dismissive attitude toward high culture represented an attack on the constituent principles of the Jewish cultural project.

Finally, some revolted against the very real truncation of what Jewish culture could be in the framework of the new Soviet cultural "freedom." Most cultural figures in the Hebraist camp, for whom the stark choice was flight or silence, took this stance. But even some left-wing Yiddishists who had been willing to treat with the Bolsheviks in the name of a new socialist Jewish culture felt increasingly stymied: thus the Kultur-Lige leadership identified as another reason for its inability to compromise with the Evsektsiia the Communist organization's skepticism as to whether there really were problems specific to national cultural spheres that demanded special policies and special sensitivities.[81]

Under these circumstances, many of revolutionary Russia's leading Yiddishists also left in 1921 (although many would later return). Some smuggled themselves illegally across the Ukrainian or Byelorussian border into Poland: Mayzl, Kazdan, Litvak, Melamed and the other members of the Kultur-Lige's former Central Committee did so in early 1921. Others, like Bergelson, Shtif, or Kalmanovitsh, left via independent Lithuania, the only neighboring state with which the Bolshevik regime had diplomatic relations. Why they did so given the attractions that convinced other Yiddishists to stay is hard to determine; ideological reasons were inextricably bound up with personal considerations and especially the material hardships of life in revolutionary Russia. But in articulating their reasons for leaving, they collectively gave a last account of the ideals of the Jewish cultural project that had reached maturity in the era of the Revolution, only to be suffocated by it.

Conclusion

Zionism is a struggle for Jewish individuality—a struggle not for
the preservation and fruitless conservation of this or that fixed
trait of this individuality, but for the establishment of a free background for its unceasing re-formation, for its free and (to use the
terminology of Bergson) "cinematic" development.

—HAIM GRINBERG, "BOR'BA ZA NATSIONAL'NUIU
INDIVIDUAL'NOST," 1917

Between 1917 and 1919, in the midst of chaos, hunger, war, and revolution,
numerous Russian-Jewish nationalist intellectuals, writers, artists, and activists devoted their best energies to what they called "Jewish" creativity in
literature, music, and the plastic arts; to the creation of literary journals,
theater companies, and publishing houses pledged to "Jewish renaissance";
and to the organization, institutionalization, and dissemination of what
they called "the new Jewish culture." This book is the first attempt to explore these efforts in a single history, with a special focus on Hebrew and
Yiddish culture—and to analyze this diverse body of creativity in relation
to the intellectual, aesthetic, and political problems of this tumultuous period and of East European Jewish modernity as a whole.

Many of these initiatives were stillborn or had to be abandoned in the
face of war and pogroms. Moreover, between 1919 and 1921, the Bolshevik
regime and Jewish revolutionaries affiliated with it began to destroy much
of what actually had been accomplished and to put a very different kind of
cultural system in its place. Looking back, one of the most thoughtful par-
ticipant-observers in this undertaking, the Israeli historian Dinaburg
(Dinur), was moved to sum up the era's dreams of Jewish renaissance with
one of the rabbinic tales of Rabbah bar Bar Hanah. At sea on a long journey, he and his friends mistake the back of a whale for an island. Building a
cooking fire there, they are thrown off by the enraged beast, to swim back
to their vessel and return to their peregrinations.[1]

As a history of failure and suppression, the history of the Jewish cultural project from 1917 to 1921 can teach us much about the nature of the Revolution, about the wages of powerlessness in a violent place, and of statelessness in the wake of empire. But this history may also tell us much about the character of modern Jewish cultural creativity, about intellectuals outside the metropolitan West, and about the workings of nationalism, socialism, and "high culture" as ideologies and institutions. Self-declared Jewish cultural life in 1917–1919 was defined by a distinct vision of culture that both shaped the creative practice and institutional endeavors of the Jewish national intelligentsia and operated as an independent power over and against its political engagements. As we have seen, this vision was not born ex nihilo; rather, the conditions of 1917 allowed for the fullest expression to date of ideals and dispositions that had begun to develop well before 1914. For this reason, the history of Jewish culture in revolutionary Russia and Ukraine lays bare the most important features of an East European Jewish search for a modern culture—a search that spanned the nineteenth and twentieth centuries—and clarifies the Jewish cultural nationalism that framed this search.

The Rules of Culture

The cultural producers and activists examined here were divided along many lines: by place, by divergent aesthetic visions, by competing political commitments that pitted Zionists against diasporists and liberal nationalists against socialist nationalists, and by mutually exclusive Hebraist or Yiddishist ideologies of national linguistic transformation. Yet all these cultural producers strove consciously to forge a "new Jewish culture." This culture was to be secular, "modern," and high. It was to be modeled on Europe's leading national cultural spheres, and seek to become their equal. It was supposed to serve as a wellspring of a more general revolution in Jewish identity, psychology, and social life. And it was also intended to be an end in itself, indeed the highest end for modern Jews: the locus of all further Jewish creativity in a postreligious age.

The Jewish cultural life of revolutionary Russia was a product not merely of disparate urges to Jewish self-expression, but also of a distinct Jewish cultural project that shaped the plans of intellectuals; the agendas of editors, publishers, and organizers; the works of artists; and the priorities of the Russian Jewish nationalist intelligentsia as a whole. Certainly, each of these artists and intellectuals had his or her own artistic vision, his or her own complex mix of motives. This complexity was compounded by the specificity of the questions, rules, and traditions that governed each artistic genre, and by the specificity of the circumstances that shaped cultural life in the very different locales of Moscow and Kiev, Odessa and Minsk. But for all these specificities, the Jewish cultural life of the era was decisively framed by a single project in two senses: its creators wrestled with a shared set of problems regarding what it meant to shape a new "Jewish" culture, and they acted on the basis of deeply shared assumptions about culture itself.

Thus, first, beneath the noise of particular aesthetic disagreements (such as between avant-gardists and aesthetic traditionalists), the Jewish cultural life of 1917–1919 was shaped by a pervasive tension over the relationship between Jewishness and the larger world of expressive possibilities. This was true, significantly, on both the Hebraist and Yiddishist sides (and the roughly parallel Zionist and diasporist sides) of the divided cultural sphere. Countering continued expressions of the view that the new Jewish culture had to deepen its roots in "authentic" Jewish tradition, there was a surprisingly widespread insistence in 1917–1919, both aggressive and anxious, that the most pressing need of Jewish cultural life was to free Hebrew and Yiddish culture, even Jewish art and music, from the imperative of any particular "Jewish" content. These two stances were by no means firmly held by two well-formed opposing camps; many, if not most, culturists felt pulled in both directions and even dreamed of reconciling these aspirations. But by 1917, the felt tension between these two drives was real, the desire to deparochialize Jewish culture had reached fever pitch, and this structure of tension had concrete implications for aesthetic and institutional choices. This portrait of acute and pervasive tension between Judaizing and universalizing tendencies runs counter to the enduring but simplistic assumption that the history of modern Jewish culture is merely one of attempts to attain some sort of synthesis between Judaic tradition and modernity.

Understanding this fuller history also means realizing that in the Jewish case, cultural nationalism was not synonymous with the embrace of cultural particularity. In their own eyes, in their patterns of organizational affiliation, and in their uncompromising Hebraism or Yiddishism, the figures who pressed the deparochializing agenda were no less nationalist than those who pressed the Judaizing agenda. Indeed, their Yiddishism or Hebraism was, if anything, more consistent and uncompromising. It is this linguistic dimension that may provide the key to understanding a different trajectory of cultural nationalism, in which the overriding goal is not to reconnect the nation to some premodern national essence but rather to win for the nation and its members the combination of complete expressive freedom and self-sustaining national continuity that contemporaries saw in Europe's metropolitan cultures and desired for themselves. Although the culturists described here may have continued to entertain Herderian notions of some folk essence bound up in Yiddish or Hebrew, many operated simultaneously with an anti-essentialist conception of national language. In practice, they conceived language as a kind of permeable membrane. A national language would allow a national culture not because it would limit national expression to something ostensibly authentic—one of the reasons for the intense Hebrew-Yiddish language war is that both sides wanted a national language capable of empowering all dimensions of thought and expression. Rather it would provide a boundary within which an open-ended dialectic of particularity and universality, tradition and openness might play out as individuals wished. Having a language community would mean possessing a distinct space of national dialogue in which all forms of expression might be assayed without fear of national disintegration through assimilation.

Perhaps more important still than the shared concerns that bound culturists was the powerful set of convictions they shared regarding culture as such: what it was, why it was important, how it worked, and its unwritten but very real rules. For all culturists, it was a given that the Jewish cultural sphere was to encompass all of the art forms, roles, and institutions common to modern European cultures. Most culturists accorded art and aesthetic experience unparalleled significance in modern culture, implicitly or explicitly deeming them more important than philosophical or scholarly inquiry. They believed that aesthetic culture was not merely an object of transcendent contemplation and inner experience, but also an unrivaled means of transforming consciousness. Yet they also evidently believed that aesthetic creation and experience were exalted ends in themselves—the highest available to secular persons—and, critically, that the transformative power of art could only flow from its specifically aesthetic quality rather than ideological prescription. Most believed that a worthwhile culture demanded a single, completely expressive language rather than a "mishmash" of languages deployed for different uses. They insisted, and seem actually to have believed, that a culture could be both high and widely accessible. In an age of political parties locked in fierce ideological conflict, they insisted that the cultural sphere had to have institutional and even ideological autonomy from party politics. They showed a concern, bordering on an obsession, for the fate of "the individual" in the new Jewish culture-in-the-making, and at times posited an expansive individuality rather than national collectivity as both the fundament and the highest end of this culture.

To hold these stances simultaneously meant to wrestle with tremendous objective tensions. Yet it would be simplistic to think that members of the nationalist intelligentsia were enmeshed in a set of iron-clad contradictions from which they could not escape and that this is the whole of the story. Those who held these various commitments did try to make them work simultaneously, in aesthetic practice and in institutions, and this effort had real effects. The conviction that "opposing" ideals could be realized together shaped the theatrical experiments of Ha-Bimah (which promoted the idea that Hebrew theater will be worthwhile national culture only insofar as it becomes good art) and the poetry of Dovid Hofshteyn (which embodied the idea that Yiddish poetry will be a national art only when it is reconceived, simply, as the site where a Yiddish-speaking modern person expresses himself). It shaped the grand programs of the Stybel publishing house (which advanced the view that Hebrew literature will be a great national literature only when it and its readers are Europeans and cosmopolitans), as well as the broad vision and daily operations of the Kultur-Lige (which claimed that the highest culture must be made accessible to all, and that true Jewish revolution demands a cultural sphere insulated from revolutionary politics).

Taken together, these phenomena suggest not only a shared ideology, but also a shared anthropology of culture at work in the Jewish nationalist intelligentsia. The culturists shared not only terms of debate and practical programs for cultural development, but also a substratum of deeply internalized dispositions that dictated their cultural tastes and shaped their experience of culture. These dispositions and their effects operated independently from the dictates of consciously espoused ideologies—and could even conflict with them. Such independence was especially true with regard to art, aesthetic experience, and individual self-cultivation, the values at the core of the intelligentsia's cultural project. Thus, both the critics and the champions of Europeanization in Jewish art recognized younger Jewish consumers' objective desire, even need, for a less narrowly Jewish art. Both Bialik and Litai averred that not even the most ideologically dedicated nationalists could talk themselves into being content with a Hebrew literature that did not allow them the full play of modern inquiry and experience. Similarly, both the critics and the anguished defenders of ideals of aesthetic autonomy and individual self-cultivation in Jewish culture recognized that such prerogatives sprang from inner need and could not simply be argued out of existence by appealing to ideological principles like "the good of the nation."

In other words, at the heart of the cultural project lay two different sets of givens: a culture was an invention that could be—indeed, needed to be—planned, built, and developed along certain lines, but art was something organic, natural, and immediate, and could only function as art if allowed to remain so. The obvious tension between these two assumptions made itself felt at every level of cultural life, especially in the arts themselves. Did the demonic Yiddish expressionism of an avant-garde poet like Peretz Markish help build the new culture because it was compelling and innovative art, or did it undermine it because it called into question every humanist hope and conviction? Yet for culturists, the felt truth of both propositions dictated symbiosis: cultural spheres needed to be structured so as to allow for the ongoing creation of such art. Indeed, much that seems strange in culturist activity may best be understood as enacting this felt imperative. The new Jewish cultural sphere had to make possible the perpetual growth and regrowth of art and aesthetic experience by securing appropriate institutional and sociological conditions: a generically complete culture independent of surrounding cultures, educated creators and educated audiences, and a creative process insulated from outside determinations like the demands of the market, the dictates of political ideologies, and even the perceived needs of the nation.

In 1917, But Not Of It

What went on in Jewish secular-national cultural life in 1917–1919 should not be understood primarily as a product of "the Revolution" or of the wartime experience. Rather, developments touched off by February 1917 allowed Jewish culturists to express and enact more fully than ever before a bundle of ideas and dispositions regarding art, "culture," nationhood, and modern individuality that had been several decades in the making for post-traditional East European Jews. There are many reasons to take this view, however perverse it may seem in light of the powerful scholarly tradition that finds in World War I and the Russian Revolution junctures of near-total rupture and new beginnings.

First, most of the actors surveyed here did not see their endeavor as born of 1914 or 1917. Instead they viewed 1917 as an unfettering and culmination. As the most revolutionary of the Yiddish poets, Peretz Markish, put it: "Many measure us with the measure of the current revolution. That's incorrect, an accidental happy meeting."[2]

Second, in practice, almost all of the actors who stood at the center of cultural life in 1917–1919, even those who did speak in terms of revolution, had begun to pursue manifestly similar visions before the war. Third, the depth and character of their assumptions about art and culture testify to prewar origins. And finally, as I noted in the Introduction, there is a clear kinship between the sorts of conceptions, institutions, and practices discussed here under the banner of "Jewish culture" and those revealed by numerous other investigations into various aspects of Hebrew and Yiddish cultural life across the whole sweep of the mid-1880s through the mid-twentieth century.

Tellingly, similar tendencies emerged simultaneously well beyond the borders of revolutionary Russia. By 1917, and indeed, a good decade earlier, Hebraists and Yiddishists in Poland, Romania, the United States, and Palestine were all converging on visions of Jewish cultural formation manifestly similar to those expounded by the culturists in revolutionary Russia and Ukraine, despite the very different social, cultural, and institutional contexts in which they found themselves. In Palestine, Hebraists proclaimed the critical importance of systematic translation for further cultural development just when their Russian Hebraist and Yiddishist counterparts did.[3] In the United States, the spokesmen of the first great Jewish modernist movement, In-zikh (the Introspectivists), insisted that a Jewish national culture properly understood had no predetermined boundaries of content, at exactly the time when their East European counterparts were groping toward this idea.[4] This view was echoed by other American Yiddishists well beyond avant-garde circles; a 1922 Yiddish literary journal by relative unknowns in Boston featured essays on "Walter Pater als estetiker" and the legend of Prometheus, and translations of Aeschylus and Petrarch.[5] In both Palestine and the United States, as in wartime Warsaw and Vilna, culturists had by then come to see some insulation of cultural

institutions from political movements (even their own political movements) as a precondition for worthwhile cultural creation.[6]

In short, the pursuit of a new Jewish culture in Russia after 1917 marked
a culmination of something born in the nineteenth century and carried
wherever post-traditional Hebrew- and Yiddish-using Jewish intellectuals
settled. Much of the cultural creativity of these Jewish moderns may be
usefully approached not only in individual biographical or generic terms,
but also as part of a project, a distinct ideology and vision of culture separate from individual goals and circumstances.[7] At the heart of this vision
was a recognizably "Western European" cultural ethos, in which priority is
given to expressive individuality and individual creative plenitude in a secular age.

Furthermore, this ethos was not mere lip service. This vision possessed
real normative power—the power to shape interests and actions. As we saw
in Chapter 5, by 1917, Jewish culturists found themselves compelled to
practice forms of aestheticism and expressive individualism that often
stood in painful tension with their desire to serve as guides to their posited
nation. When Max Weber penned his famous observations about aestheticism as a kind of anarchic religion, they applied just as well to the Jewish
cultural project as to the German or French cultural sphere he intended:

> [With] the development of intellectualism and the rationalization of life
> . . . art becomes a cosmos of more and more consciously grasped inde-
> pendent values which exist in their own right . . . Every rational religious
> ethic must turn against this inner-worldly, irrational salvation . . . To the
> creative artist, however, as well as to the aesthetically excited and recep-
> tive mind, the ethical norm as such may easily appear as a coercion of
> their genuine creativeness and innermost selves.[8]

In this sense, the history of the Jewish cultural project demonstrates both
the causal power of culture as an institution generally and the reach of that
power beyond dominant, metropolitan cultures.

More specifically, the history of the cultural project must be read in
tension with the history that has heretofore dominated the study of East
European Jewish modernity, namely the history of modern Jewish politics.
The world of values and institutions constituted by the cultural project beginning in the 1890s was intimately related to the world of intelligentsia
party politics in its nationalist and socialist forms. But even though they
were held by closely overlapping groups of people, these were two different

systems of values and norms—and hence they were always potentially in conflict.

Finally, the Jewish cultural project stood in a complex relationship to the larger ideology out of which it emerged (along with modern Jewish politics itself): Jewish nationalism as an organizing principle of the Jewish response to modernity. The bid for Jewish culture was in many important senses a product of Jewish nationalism, without which it had no stabilizing, motivating raison d'être. But over time, the ethos of culture reshaped that nationalism in its own image.

Nationalism, Revolution, Culture

This ideology of culture took shape not against a national movement, as a form of "resistance," but in the bosom of a national movement, on the part of self-proclaimed nationalists, and against the backdrop of nationalism as a given. Nationalism in this case was not a coherently collectivist, totalizing ideology utterly opposed to liberal conceptions and practices; instead, it allowed radically various and opposed conceptions of culture and selfhood. This is not to deny that certain formations of nationalism in Eastern Europe were inimical to modes of free self-expression and self-making that flourished (in certain times and contexts) further west. It is simply to say that the reactive origins of nationalism did not dictate a coherent and unchanging stance on such matters. Rather, nationalism in this context was a powerful yet underdetermining existential commitment that could be fused with all sorts of contradictory ideals and institutions.

It is easy to assume that nationalism has been inimical to cultural development among those unfortunate peoples afflicted by it because the nationalist division of the world into us and them would seem to limit the range of expressive possibilities by definition. But such an assumption freezes nationalism at a moment in time, focusing our interpretations on how the imposition of nationalist logic and discourse alters and deforms cultural spheres already in place.[9] What, then, would we make of the Jewish cultural project, which was born long after nationalism—or better, nationhood—had become an institutional fact, in a region with no supraethnic spheres of expression?

In the case of the Jewish cultural project, belatedness and reactivity cut two ways.[10] In regions where nationalism held sway as a principle of "vision and division" and all cultural choices were nationally charged (the

Russian-Polish borderlands between 1880 and 1945, for instance), those who embraced the pan-European ideal of "culture" and its related prerogatives of art and self did not face two choices, but three.[11] Some sought membership in the more metropolitan cultural spheres of other nations. Others did what the scholarly literature on cultural nationalism would suggest: they sought to particularize and nativize the institution of culture in accordance with posited "national values" (usually communitarian and antiliberal values that sat ill with the institution's basic principles). But others chose neither route. Having adopted and internalized the values and dispositions intrinsic to culture as an institution through sustained engagement in its cherished practices and roles—author, artist, reader, and self-cultivating individual—they were not willing to give up these values even for the sake of the nation. Yet for affective, linguistic, or moral reasons, they were also unwilling to abandon their community for greener pastures. Instead, they sought to carve out an autonomous space of culture within their nationalist political spheres and ethnic communities. Over time, they came to conceive such an autonomous culture as an essential end of nationalism itself, for what good nationalist would deny his national fellows the fulfillment that he himself enjoyed? And with time—in the Jewish case, by 1917—cultural nationalism could itself come to mean not only the search for "origins" and unalloyed native essence, but also the opposite: a very conscious attempt to attain the conditions for unrestricted cultural creativity and free self-formation for oneself and one's nation. The Jewish cultural project thus illustrates how nationalism itself could not only accept but also authorize—even compel—the enactment (however imperfect) of cosmopolitan ideals.[12]

The other organizing ideology of twentieth-century East European life, revolutionary socialism, was very different than nationalism in its implications for cultural practice. Such implications were evident from the first encounters between Jewish culturists and the Bolsheviks, and would become altogether clear in the decade of Soviet Jewish life that followed. On the one hand, the Soviet Union made Jewish culture a state obligation. Yiddishists who stayed (or came back) gained resources, sinecures, even real authority—benefits of which Yiddishists elsewhere, stateless and penniless, could only dream. Yet this glittering new cultural sphere was founded on principles profoundly different than those that had defined the cultural project—it was framed by the dynamic, encompassing religion of Revolution, not the static, law-bound religion of *Kultur*. Teachers, publishers, and editors were servants of the party-state charged to enact the party's vision. Writers and artists, nominally free, in fact had to serve "the revolutionary process." This process was evidently agonizing for many: in several of the finest works in the understandably small canon of compelling Soviet Yiddish literature, a central character identified with the cultural project is subjected to brutal suffering because his ideals are out of step with the demands of History.[13] Such works were partly expressions of pain by dedicated culturists who now had to renounce lifelong commitments like the view that freedom of expression was the essential ground of art. But they were also acts of renunciation, as these writers prepared to reconsecrate themselves to their rigorous new religion: "And I answered: 'Yes, I must have been sick, and I took illusions to be reality.'"[14] By the time official Soviet Yiddish culture was essentially dismantled in the 1930s due to shifting party-state policy and the massive Russification of Soviet Jews, it was an unrecognizable deformation of what "Jewish culture" had once meant.

It may be argued that this outcome was the product of something specific to Bolshevism rather than of revolutionary socialism. There is some truth to this claim. But as we have seen, identical demands for the revolutionary mobilization and servitude of culture flourished among Marxist Yiddishists well beyond Bolshevik circles. The Bundist cultural theorist Litvak was a staunch anti-Bolshevik—indeed, the leading figure of the least compromising Bundist fraction by 1919. But his vision of culture in service to revolution converged with that of the most radical supporters of the Revolution. For him no less than for his Leninist enemies, the Revolution meant an end to patience with any sort of defense of culture's autonomy.

However one chooses to subdivide revolutionary socialism, one cannot ignore the difference that revolutionary ideology and historiosophy made with regard to culturist claims. It is true that Jewish nationalists and more moderate socialists outside Soviet space made and continued to make all sorts of political-cum-moral demands on the cultural sphere. In 1922, for instance, the still nonsocialist Yiddishist Nokhem Shtif could attack Bergelson's work for failing to offer the nation moral and cultural guidance due to his "internal pessimism about the world," just as the socialists and Communists had attacked Bergelson for failing to serve the Revolution.[15] The burgeoning Hebrew cultural sphere of British Mandatory Palestine was marked by ever more intense ideological pressure on cultural producers to align themselves with one or another Zionist party. And more broadly, the principle that culture was a discreet realm of genres, practices, and values relevant to all realms of life but reducible to none stood in growing tension with visions of more encompassing political, socioeconomic, spatial, and psychic transformation that were flourishing on both the left and the right of Yishuv political culture.[16]

But it was only in the framework of revolutionary socialism's eschatological vision and the nearly complete subordination of all institutions and social spheres to a unitary party-state that the mobilizational inclinations common to nationalist and socialist intelligentsias became total programs. In Poland and Palestine, and later in the new Israeli society, cultural activity was conscripted by Zionist or Jewish socialist movements, scarred by ethnonational confrontation and the desire to justify its injustices, and deformed by the various anti-liberalisms and collectivisms that characterized interwar cultural life around the world. Consequently, culturist claims to autonomy were placed on the defensive, autonomous culturist institutions were forced to the margins, and some sorts of unprogrammatic self-expression were driven into the private sphere. But in the Soviet Union, within the space of total Revolution, there was no viable ideological defense, no autonomous institutions were allowed, and whether we can speak of a private sphere at all is debatable.

The Cultural Project and Jewish Modernity

Thus in the 1920s and 1930s, it was in the United States, in the new East European nation-states, and in Palestine that recognizable versions of the Jewish cultural project continued. Whether and how the Jewish cultural project persisted beyond the mid-twentieth century is a different matter. In Eastern Europe, its potential bearers were killed—though growing numbers were already in the process of embracing other East European languages and cultural projects even as they were made increasingly unwelcome. In main centers of Jewish life as disparate as the Soviet Union and the United States, whatever outposts of Jewish culturism were already present dissipated as Jews remade themselves as Russians or hyphenated Americans and, not coincidentally, as they put aside Jewish languages for the languages of the larger society. For Jews in those societies today who do not live with a distinct language of their own, what can "Jewish culture" mean other than a minority subculture defined by distinguishing marks of Jewishness, religious and otherwise? American (or French, or Russian)

Jews may maintain a vital Jewish subculture much as German Jews did in the 1920s and 1930s, but this is a very different project than that which the culturists of Eastern Europe pursued.

It is only in the nominally secular part of Israeli society that the cultural project can be said to exist today on a significant scale. Of course, as a project it may be dead in Israel too. The high rhetoric of *tarbut* and its mission, painfully old-fashioned and often insultingly Eurocentric to boot, is no doubt as irrelevant to most young secular Israeli Jews as is the rest of late Mandate and early statehood rhetoric.[17] Moreover, in Israel's intensely charged political environment, the very concept of "culture" as a distinct realm of values irreducible to political life can provoke angry criticism.[18] But if the ideology of *tarbut* has been abandoned, culture itself has at the same time become an institution, self-sustaining and self-renewing. Every day, without fanfare or planning, Israelis (and not only Israeli Jews) fulfill Natan Bistritsky's vision of a Hebrew culture created without "any goal . . . born of any sort of prior and special deliberation."[19]

This does not mean that the individual creators of culture in Israel do not think and agonize as much as cultural creators anywhere else. What it means is that the Israeli cultural system is becoming ever less like that of post-traditional Jewish cultural expression in Eastern Europe, and even less like that of contemporary diasporic Jewish expression in languages identified with a larger cultural community. To begin with, this contemporary Hebrew culture requires no particular ideological mobilization to maintain itself. For a large part of Israel's population, it is now simply a given that all expression regarding any human problem or possibility will be made in Hebrew; this givenness is maintained not by culturist ideology, but by a mix of market incentives, institutional rewards, and the socio-linguistic fact that Hebrew has become a default language.

Several consequences flow from this situation, a novum in Jewish history. One obvious one is that the distinction between Jewish and non-Jewish in culture (though not, certainly, in politics) grows increasingly meaningless for secular Israelis even as it grows ever more important to Jewishly involved diaspora Jews. Take for instance the well-loved Israeli collection of children's songs and nonsense stories "The Sixteenth Lamb." The book and the album of music derived from it treat themes familiar to many modern children: school, growing up, fear of thunder, chocolate, going to bed, the pleasures of incongruity and absurdity. Significantly, it does so with total lack of reference to any Jewish cultural tradition—even the titular "lamb" is not the *lemele* or *taleh katan* of Jewish children's songs but the sheep of Western culture that one counts in order to fall asleep. Regardless, these songs are now part of Hebrew culture no less than texts that explicitly manifest Jewishness—and are quite a bit more familiar and dear to many Israelis than many works of the latter sort.

By the same token, even the nonverbal arts in Israel are no longer necessarily defined by Jewishness or the question of Jewish identity. Enmeshed in a cultural system bound to a language community, possessed of its own self-sustaining institutions, Israeli art and music may grapple with the question of Jewishness (or mutatis mutandis, "Canaanism," or "Levantinism")—or they may choose not to. That language, territorialization, and statehood would paradoxically make possible this freedom was already clear years ago; Benjamin Harshav notes that when Chagall arrived in 1951 for a grand exhibition, his work already seemed "'too Jewish' and too thematic for the adherents of modernism and abstraction in Israeli art."[20]

Perhaps the most striking testament to the post-Jewish possibilities inscribed in Israeli Hebrew culture is to be found in the growing participation of Israeli Arabs in Hebrew-language cultural life. Such participation takes place within an extraordinarily fraught framework of ethnopolitical conflict, disinheritance, and discrimination. Yet this unchanging (perhaps, indeed, worsening) ideological tension coexists with a rapidly changing sociological reality, as growing numbers within Israel's Arab communities undergo sociologically typical processes of linguistic assimilation and acculturation to the dominant culture. The result that has most impressed many scholars and commentators is the accumulation of Hebrew-language texts that directly confront or "resist" Zionist and Jewish national narratives with countervailing articulations of Palestinian experience—not least by powerful appropriation of literary tropes and sources usually understood to be "Jewish." But perhaps even more striking, for our purposes, are the ways in which Israeli Arab cultural creators (and other non-Jewish citizens and denizens of Israel) lay claim to Hebrew as a language of individual voice and universal cultural experience. As the writer Sayed Kashua puts it in a recent interview: "Look, on the one hand [Hebrew] is the language of the enemy, the conqueror. And yet this is the language that means a kind of freedom for me, more freedom." His point is not, of course, that Hebrew is somehow intrinsically freer than Arabic or any other language, but that a variety of conditions, not least the efforts of several generations of culturists, have made Hebrew a supple language for the expression of modern selfhood and its dilemmas—not only the political dilemmas faced by Arab citizens of a Jewish state, but also other dimensions of modern selfhood and experience that, however interlaced with this one, are also distinct from it. Kashua's comments, echoed by those of many other Israeli Arab writers and intellectuals, mark another confirmation—perhaps the most dramatic of all—that regrounding Jewish cultural life in language and place might paradoxically allow it to develop beyond the bounds of Jewish identity.[21]

These cultural developments discomfit many. For much of Israel's growing traditionalist camp, the new Israeli culture can only be construed as an abomination. For those Jews, Israeli and non-Israeli, who remain invested in the ideal of self-conscious synthesis between Jewish tradition and European civilization, this trajectory threatens terrible failure. Some of the culturists encountered in this work might say that these critics underestimate the power of language: just as the givenness of Hebrew liberates individual cultural creators from any felt obligation to Jewishness, so too does it render traditional Jewish texts perpetually more accessible and culturally usable to educated Israelis than to their non-Hebrew-speaking counterparts. Conversely, other culturists, like Bialik, might take the current situation as evidence of their darkest fears: that the new culture would prove unable to salvage something of Judaism in modernity.

Regardless of how one feels about them, though, these trajectories in secular Israeli culture further delineate the lasting significance of the Jewish cultural endeavor in 1917–1919. First, they suggest that moment's historiographical and diagnostic significance. Nationalist, anti-nationalist, and even Orthodox accounts of modern Jewish history tend to fixate on the division between "assimilation" and "authenticity." In a more narrowly academic vein, much Jewish history-writing still explains the main outlines of contemporary Jewish life in terms of eighteenth- and nineteenth-century processes of Enlightenment and emancipation, conceiving modern Jewish culture in the broad sense as a response to Enlightenment and/or maintaining that the lasting divisions of Jewish modernity can be traced to the uneven distribution of emancipation and liberal possibilities in the nineteenth century. But for the purposes of contemporary and future Jewish cultural life, it may be that the essential distinctions are best explained not in terms of assimilation versus authenticity, the embrace of the Enlightenment or its rejection, or emancipation versus nonemancipation, but rather in terms of whether, in the "long twentieth century" of nations, one became modern in someone else's tongue or in one's own, on someone else's terms entirely or at least in part in an institutional order that belonged to no one else.

Second, contemporary trends suggest that culturist visions of how a nationalist project might give birth to something far less limited than the stereotypical nationalisms of their day were not mere wishful thinking—indeed, they contained a good deal of truth. This is most obvious with regard to the culturist conviction that the expansion of either Hebrew or Yiddish to cover all realms of modern expression, and the enthronement of one of these languages as the encompassing language of all aspects of Jewish life, would allow Jews to transcend the painful choice between full freedom of expression and national loyalty. A Jew writing in a language identified with a larger national community who nevertheless wishes to create something "Jewish" faces a limiting choice: to make something part of an ongoing Jewish conversation, he or she must explicitly differentiate it from that whole universe of things that are "not Jewish." If he or she writes in French about Buddhism, translates Milton into French, or simply writes love poetry in French, the resultant cultural products will naturally be received, canonized, and subject to further cultural activation as French culture. By contrast, an Israeli who does these exact same things in Hebrew has made these things available to future consumers and creators in Hebrew, to be brought into dialogue with other elements of the evolving Hebrew-language tradition (including the premodern Jewish tradition) as future creators and consumers see fit. The culturists of 1917–1919 would not be surprised by this divergence—they anticipated it; they saw its effects in the anemic, apologetic Jewish subcultures that had already developed in Russian, German, and Polish; and they strove desperately to attain the condition now enjoyed, at least in principle, by their Israeli inheritors.

It is worth noting in passing that the same logic holds for another aspect of culturist discourse: arguments about the cultural effects of territorialization largely specific but not limited to Zionist circles of Jewish culturists. Just as the culturist conception of language entertained two contradictory visions of how a separate Jewish language would shape Jewish culture—an essentializing "Herderian" vision versus an anti-essentializing, universalist one—so too could Zionist and territorialist culturists entertain two contradictory visions regarding the cultural implications of territory. Essays like those of Bistritsky and Grinberg, or those of Yishuv intellectuals such as Rachel Katznelson, or for that matter writings by the Yiddishist territorialist Latski-Bertoldi, resonated with a tension between the idea that territorialization would renew some native Jewish "ur"-culture and the idea that it would secure freedom from any such essentialism for cultural producers. In light of the many-sided de-Judaization of secular culture in Hebrew, coupled with the powerful critiques to which secular Israeli Jews have begun to subject their myths of place, we may say that these intuitions were even more accurate than culturists understood—although they did not anticipate the very different sorts of essentialist religious nationalism that would be awakened by (re)territorialization.[22]

Like contemporary Israeli cultural life, the Jewish cultural project of 1917–1919 was rife with conflicts that threatened to shatter its fragile framework of rules, ideals, refusals, and experiments. But for all its fragility, that cultural project represented the fullest expression up to that point of the desire—the felt necessity—among ever-growing numbers of East European Jews to participate in modernity without abandoning the human possibilities bound up in one's own communal and cultural inheritance. In this brief moment, the boldest Jewish culturists strove to imagine a new kind of Jewish culture that would leave past Jewish cultural experience accessible but not stifling. They sought, imperfectly but honestly, to do so not only for themselves but for other Jews catapulted into modernity. Finally, the best of them did so in the full awareness that they belonged to a community in cultural crisis and terrible political danger. Yet they looked beyond the needs of the moment and sought to lay the groundwork for a different kind of Jewish future—one in which Jews as individuals, liberated from inner crisis and outer siege, might engage the full range of creative possibilities, questions, and freedoms that modernity offers.

Notes

A complete bibliography can be found online at http://sites.google.com/site/kennethbmoss/jewish-renaissance—bibliography.

Abbreviations

Beit Bialik	Archive of Beit Bialik, Tel Aviv
CAHJP	Central Archive for the History of the Jewish People, Jerusalem
CZA	Central Zionist Archive, Jerusalem
DAKO	Derzhavnyi arkhiv kievskoi oblasti, Kyiv
GARF	Gosudarstvennyi arkhiv Rossiiskoi Federatsii, Moscow
Gnazim	Asher Barash "Gnazim" Institute, Tel Aviv
JNUL	Manuscript Collection, Jerusalem National and University Library, Jerusalem
RGALI	Rossiiskii gosudarstvennyi arkhiv literatury i isskustva, Moscow
RGASPI	Rossiiskii gosudarstvennyi arkhiv sotsial'no-politicheskoi istorii, Moscow
TsDAHOU	Tsentral'nyi derzhavnyi arkhiv hromads'kykh ob'iednan' Ukrainy, Kyiv
TsDAVO	Tsentral'nyi derzhavnyi arkhiv vyshchykh orhaniv vlady i upravlinnya, Kyiv
TsIAM	Tsentral'nyi istoricheskii arkhiv Moskvy, Moscow
Vernadsky	Vernadsky Library, Jewish Section MSS, Kyiv
YIVO	YIVO Institute for Jewish Research, New York

Introduction

Epigraph: "Vos iz di Kultur-Lige," *Kultur-Lige: Ershtes zamlheft* (Warsaw, 1921).

1. Ben-Tsion Katz, *Zikhronot* (Tel Aviv, 1964), 250–252.
2. For these options, see William G. Rosenberg, *Liberals in the Russian Revolution: The Constitutional Democratic Party, 1917–1921* (Princeton, 1972), 186;

Yosi Goldshtain, *Usishkin: Biografyah* (Jerusalem, 1999), 281–282; on Jewish refugees, see Peter Gatrell, *A Whole Empire Walking: Refugees in Russia during World War I* (Bloomington, 1999).

3. The defining study of this nationalist intelligentsia is Jonathan Frankel, *Prophecy and Politics: Socialism, Nationalism, and the Russian Jews, 1862–1917* (Cambridge, Eng., 1981); for a suggestive formulation of how the tsarist regime politicized ethnicity, see Charles Steinwedel, "To Make a Difference: The Category of Ethnicity in Late Imperial Russian Politics, 1861–1917" in *Russian Modernity,* ed. David L. Hoffmann and Yanni Kotsonis (New York, 2000), 69–70.

4. This political activity has received extensive attention, by contrast with other aspects of revolutionary-era Jewish life. See Yehudah Slutsky, "Yahadut Rusyiah bi-shnat ha-mahapekhah 1917," *He-'Avar* 15 (1968): 39–48; Zvi Y. Gitelman, *Jewish Nationality and Soviet Politics* (Princeton, 1972); Mordecai Altshuler, "Ha-kehilah ha-demokratit be-rusiyah," *Divre ha-kongres ha-'olami ha-shishi le-mada'e ha-yahadut* (Jerusalem, 1973): 229–235; Henry Abramson, *A Prayer for the Government: Ukrainians and Jews in Revolutionary Times, 1917–1920* (Cambridge, 1999); Mikhail Beizer, *Evrei Leningrada 1917–1939: Natsional'naia zhizn' i sovietizatsia* (Jerusalem, 1999); Tanja Penter, *Odessa 1917: Revolution an der Peripherie* (Cologne, Ger., 2000), 303–304.

5. Nokhem Shtif to Shmuel Niger, 13 June 1922, Shmuel Niger Collection, YIVO, record group 360, folder 442.

6. Paul Oskar Kristeller, "The Modern System of the Arts," *Journal of the History of Ideas* 12, no. 4 (1951): 496–527 and 13, no. 1 (1952): 17–46.

7. Recent research on revolutionary-era Jewish cultural production focuses primarily on theater and the arts. See Jeffrey Veidlinger, *The Moscow State Yiddish Theater* (Bloomington, 2000); Vladislav Ivanov, *Russkie sezony: Teatr Gabima* (Moscow, 1999); the articles and catalog in *Tradition and Revolution: The Jewish Renaissance in Russian Avant-Garde Art, 1912–1928,* ed. Ruth Apter-Gabriel (Jerusalem, 1988), esp. Seth Wolitz, "The Jewish National Art Renaissance in Russia" and John Bowlt, "From the Pale of Settlement to the Reconstruction of the World," 21–60; Hillel Kazovsky, *Khudozhniki Kultur-Ligi: The Artists of the Kultur-Lige* (Moscow, 2003). I am indebted to Wolitz's essay particularly for its pioneering account of the Russian-Jewish creative intelligentsia's concept of culture.

8. Like the Russian intelligentsia, the Jewish intelligentsia sometimes used the term "culture" to refer to all forms of human civilization, general education, and modernization; see David Joravsky, "Cultural Revolution and the Fortress Mentality" in *Bolshevik Culture: Experiment and Order in the Russian Revolution,* ed. Abbot Gleason et al. (Bloomington, 1985), 93–97. As I will show, however, a good part of the Jewish intelligentsia conceived "high culture" as

something distinct from all other aspects of human civilization—a stance that, however ideological, found very real expression in practice. For the Russian equivalent, see Katerina Clark, *Petersburg: Crucible of Cultural Revolution* (Cambridge, 1995). Throughout the text that follows, I refer to "high culture" or "the cultural sphere" not to suggest a stable separate sphere, but to capture the realities of differentiation in cultural practices, institutions, and mentalities that terms like "high" and "low" both reflected and shaped over time. This dimension is missing from work that seeks merely to "problematize" the distinction between high and low or assumes that the distinction is merely discursive. A much richer conception is Pierre Bourdieu's treatment of high culture in *The Rules of Art: Genesis and Structure of the Literary Field* (Stanford, 1996).

9. I borrow this term from Jeffrey Brooks, "Readers and Reading at the End of the Tsarist Era," in *Literature and Society in Imperial Russia,* ed. William Mills Todd (Stanford, 1978).

10. Shaul Tchernikhovsky, "La-shemesh," trans. Robert Alter as "To the Sun" in *Reading Hebrew Literature,* ed. Alan Mintz (Hanover, N.H., 2003).

11. "Partey-khronik: A forlezung fun Dovid Bergelson," *Unzer vort: Arbayter tsaytung farn dorem-gegend; organ fun odeser rayon-komitet (Fareynikte)* (Odessa), 4 July 1917.

12. A. Litvak, "Literatur un lebn," *Baginen* 1 (Kiev, 1919): 97–102; Shtif to Niger, 13 June 1922, YIVO, record group 360, folder 442.

13. See Chapter 6.

14. Cf. Boris I. Kolonitskii, "Antibourgeois Propaganda and Anti-'Burzhui' Consciousness in 1917," *Russian Review* 53, no. 2 (1994): 183–196.

15. Yaacov Fichman, "'Im Bialik: Zikhronot u-reshimot mi-pinkasi," *Keneset: Divre sofrim le-zekher H. N. Bialik* 2 (1937): 74; Nahman Mayzl et al. to Bialik, 8 January 1918, Beit Bialik, correspondence collection (collection organized alphabetically by correspondent). Emphasis added.

16. "Partey-khronik," *Unzer vort,* 4 July 1917.

17. Dan Pines, "Haganah 'atsmit be-Rusiyah (1919–1920)," Gnazim, Natan Goren Collection 102, doc. 9992/26.

18. David Shneer, *Yiddish and the Creation of Soviet Jewish Culture, 1918–1930* (Cambridge, Eng., 2004); Veidlinger, *Moscow State Yiddish Theater.* The two classic studies of the early Sovietization of Russian Jewish communal life contain much on the Jewish cultural sphere. Gitelman, *Jewish Nationality;* Mordecai Altshuler, *Ha-yevsektsiyah bi-vrit hamo'atsot, ben le'umiut le-komunizm* (Tel Aviv, 1981).

19. Gennady Estraikh, *In Harness: Yiddish Writers' Romance with Communism* (Syracuse, 2005).

20. Avner Holtsman, *Melekhet mahshevet tehiyat ha-umah: Ha-sifrut ha-'Ivrit le-*

nokhaḥ ha-omanut ha-plastit (Haifa, 1999). In so doing, they broke with a previous generation of reformers who had sought a limited renovation of Jewish religious and literary life wedded harmoniously and as a supplement to imperial Russian culture. See Ben-Avigdor, "Ha-'ivriut veha-klaliut ba-sifrut ha-'ivrit," *Ha-Melits,* 21 April 1895, 2.

21. David E. Fishman, *The Rise of Modern Yiddish Culture* (Pittsburgh, 2005), part 1; D. A. El'iashevich, *Pravitel'stvennaia politika i evreiskaia pechat' v Rossii, 1797–1917* (St. Petersburg, 1999), 454–455.

22. Histories of Jewish theater in this period attest to the spread of interest in Jewish culture among Russified Jewish youth and Jewish youth in provincial towns. See, for example, Nahma Sandrow, *Vagabond Stars: A World History of Yiddish Theater* (Syracuse, 1996), 206–207; Ivanov, *Russkie sezony,* 11. See also the organizational report of the Jewish Literary Society, *Evreiskoe Literaturnoe Obshchestvo* (St. Petersburg, 1910): 10–12, which notes with surprise the popular demand for branches in the provinces.

23. Given the robustness of the assumption that World War I caused a radical cultural rupture for all participants, it is worth stating up front that I have not found this to be the case for the majority of figures examined in this work, and have not found the war to be a radically transformative moment in the terms of their cultural vision. Certainly, some of the young men who served at the front would move toward the languages of disillusionment and rupture characteristic of "the Generation of 1914," but these were exceptions. They did not (yet) set the terms of Jewish culturist institutions, and even these figures tended not to arrive at such "rupture" positions until the early 1920s. See Dan Miron, "Uri Zvi Grinberg's War Poetry," in Yisrael Gutman, et al., eds. *The Jews of Poland between Two World Wars* (Hanover, N.H., 1989). For a larger argument about cultural continuities across the 1914–1918 "rupture," see Jay Winter, *Sites of Memory, Sites of Mourning* (Cambridge, Eng., 1995). Concomitantly, Robert Wohl argued forcefully many years ago that the war's "meaning" as a radical cultural rupture was in good measure constructed by a cohort of West European intellectuals who had been ideologically primed for such a break well before the war. See Robert Wohl, *The Generation of 1914* (Cambridge, 1979). The figures examined in this book seem not to have entered the war with such attitudes, for reasons that would have to be explained elsewhere but surely have to do with their very different sociology relative to Wohl's Western university–trained, middle-class cohort. On continuities, see especially Chapter 2.

24. Jacob Katz, *Out of the Ghetto: The Social Background of Jewish Emancipation, 1770–1870* (New York, 1973); Pierre Birnbaum and Ira Katznelson, eds., *Paths of Emancipation: Jews, States, and Citizenship* (Princeton, 1995).

25. Aron Rodrigue, *French Jews, Turkish Jews: The Alliance Israelite Universelle and the Politics of Jewish Schooling in Turkey, 1860–1925* (Bloomington, 1990);

Olga Borovaya, "Translation and Westernization: *Gulliver's Travels* in Ladino," *Jewish Social Studies,* n.s. 7, no. 2 (Winter 2001): 149–168.

26. Steven Zipperstein, *Imagining Russian Jewry* (Seattle, 1999), ch. 2. I draw this overarching model of three distinct trajectories of Jewish modernity from Aron Rodrigue, "From *Millet* to Minority: Turkish Jewry," in Birnbaum and Katznelson, *Paths,* 260–261. Of course, the geographical division is merely a rough catch-all. For exceptions, see Steven Zipperstein, *The Jews of Odessa: A Cultural History, 1794–1881* (Stanford, 1985) and Benjamin Nathans, *Beyond the Pale: The Jewish Encounter with Late Imperial Russia* (Berkeley, 2002).

27. The treatments of culture as a concept and institution that I have found most helpful include Geoffrey H. Hartman, *The Fateful Question of Culture* (New York, 1997); Raymond Williams, *Culture and Society, 1780–1950* (New York, 1983), xviii, 40–42, 62–64, 85–86; Daniel Bell, *The Cultural Contradictions of Capitalism* (New York, 1996), ch. 2; Hannah Arendt, "The Crisis in Culture," in Arendt, *Between Past and Future* (New York, 1961); Josef Chytry, *The Aesthetic State: A Quest in Modern German Thought* (Berkeley, 1989); Gyorgy Markus, "A Society of Culture: The Constitution of Modernity," in *Rethinking Imagination: Culture and Creativity,* ed. Gillian Robinson and John Rundell (London, 1994), 18–20; and Bourdieu, *Rules of Art.* Each of these is a critique of the concept of culture at some level, but nevertheless takes seriously its effective power.

28. See the suggestive discussion in Robert Pippin, *Modernism as a Philosophical Problem: On the Dissatisfactions of European High Culture,* 2nd ed. (Malden, Mass., 1999), xii-xix, ch. 2. My thanks to Eric Oberle and Marc Caplan for their valuable comments on the multiple skepticisms surrounding culture as a concept.

29. For example, David Lloyd and Paul Thomas, *Culture and the State* (New York, 1998); David Lloyd, "Arnold, Ferguson, Schiller: Aesthetic Culture and the Politics of Aesthetics," *Cultural Critique,* no. 2 (Winter, 1985–1986): 137–169; Abdul R. JanMohamed, "Humanism and Minority Literature: Toward a Definition of Counter-Hegemonic Discourse," *boundary 2,* 12, no. 3 (Spring–Autumn, 1984): 281–299.

30. My understanding of institutionality draws on essays in *The New Institutionalism in Organizational Analysis,* ed. Walter W. Powell and Paul J. DiMaggio (Chicago, 1991) and Bourdieu's more nuanced conceptions of the "field" in his later work, notably *Rules of Art.* For a further elaboration, see note 55 of this chapter.

31. Hartman, *Fateful Question,* 39–40.

32. Zygmunt Bauman, "Intellectuals in East-Central Europe: Continuity and Change," *Eastern European Politics and Societies* 1, no. 2 (Spring 1987): 168–169.

33. See on the one hand Ernest Gellner, *Nations and Nationalism* (Ithaca, 1983),

55–56, and Eric J. Hobsbawm, *Nations and Nationalism since 1780* (Cambridge, Eng., 1992); and on the other, Anthony D. Smith, *The Ethnic Origins of Nations* (Oxford, 1986), 169–208, and Charles Taylor, "Nationalism and Modernity," in *The Morality of Nationalism,* ed. Robert McKim and Jeff McMahan (Oxford, 1997), 31–55.

34. Yuri Slezkine, *The Jewish Century* (Princeton, 2004); Pieter M. Judson, *Guardians of the Nation* (Cambridge, 2006).

35. Jeffrey Brooks, *When Russia Learned to Read* (Evanston, 2003 [1985]), ch. 9; Louise McReynolds, *Russia at Play: Leisure Activities at the End of the Tsarist Era* (Ithaca, 2003); Mark D. Steinberg, *Proletarian Imagination: Self, Modernity, and the Sacred in Russia, 1910–1925* (Ithaca, 2002); Beth Holmgren, *Rewriting Capitalism: Literature and the Market in Late Tsarist Russia and the Kingdom of Poland* (Pittsburgh, 1998).

36. Robert Alter, *The Invention of Hebrew Prose* (Seattle, 1988), 12–13; Joshua A. Fishman, "The Sociology of Yiddish: A Foreword" in *Never Say Die! A Thousand Years of Yiddish in Jewish Life and Letters,* ed. Fishman (The Hague, 1981), 12–14, esp. n. 6; Slezkine, *Jewish Century,* 101.

37. Frankel, *Prophecy.* Cf. Craig Calhoun, *Nationalism* (Minneapolis, 1997), 11: "the development and spread of nationalist discourse is not reducible to state formation or political manipulation; it has autonomous significance, [and] appears in cultural arenas not directly defined by state-making projects . . . Nationalism is not just a doctrine . . . but a more basic way of talking, thinking, and acting." On the pervasiveness of ethnonationalist self-identity beyond nationalist movements in late imperial Russian Jewry, see Zipperstein, *Imagining Russian Jewry,* ch. 2; Ben Nathans, "The Other Modern Jewish Politics," in *The Emergence of Modern Jewish Politics,* ed. Zvi Gitelman (Pittsburgh, 2003), 29–32.

38. Rashid Iangirov, "Jewish Life on the Screen in Russia, 1908–1919," in *Jews and Jewish Topics in the Soviet Union and Eastern Europe* 1 (Spring 1990): 20–21.

39. Gennady Estraikh, "On the Acculturation of Jews in Late Imperial Russia," *Rassegna Mensile di Israel* 62, nos. 1–2 (1996): 217–226; Shaul Stampfer, "Patterns of Internal Jewish Migration in the Russian Empire," *Jews and Jewish Life in Russia and the Soviet Union,* ed. Yaacov Ro'i (Portland, 1995), 28–47; Stampfer, "Gender Differentiation and Education of the Jewish Woman in Nineteenth-Century Eastern Europe," *Polin* 7 (1992): 63–87; Sarah Abrevaya Stein, *Making Jews Modern* (Bloomington, 2004); Yehuda Slutsky, *Ha-'itonut ha-yehudit-rusit ba-me'ah ha-'esrim, 1900–1918* (Tel Aviv, 1978), ch. 1.

40. Chone Shmeruk, "Le-toldot sifrut ha-'shund' be-Yidish," *Tarbits* 52, no. 2 (1983): 325–354; Clark, *Petersburg.*

41. Olga Litvak, *Conscription and the Search for Modern Russian Jewry* (Bloomington, 2006), 156.

42. In fact, it seems that there was a genuine popular hunger for such cultural products, judging from the reception of the period's most famous Jewish drama, Sh. An-ski's *Between Two Worlds (the Dybbuk)*. A tragedy about a young woman possessed by the soul of the deceased youth to whom she should have been married, the play drew much of its symbolic vocabulary from its author's long-standing study of East European Jewish folk culture. By all accounts, it was experienced by rapturous audiences as a mythic work about wartime Jewish national suffering. Some nationalists hailed it in these terms, not as art but as a ritual of collective mourning and national identity formation; see the essays in *The Worlds of S. An-sky: A Russian Jewish Intellectual at the Turn of the Century*, ed. Gabriella Safran and Steven J. Zipperstein (Stanford, 2006). The reaction of many culturists, however, was notably cool, and that demands explanation.

43. Peter Holquist, "What's So Revolutionary about the Russian Revolution?" in *Russian Modernity*, ed. Kotsonis and Hoffmann, and Holquist, *Making War, Forging Revolution: Russia's Continuum of Crisis, 1914–1921* (Cambridge, 2002); Geoff Eley, "Remapping the Nation: War, Revolutionary Upheaval, and State Formation in Eastern Europe, 1914–1923," in *Ukrainian-Jewish Relations in Historical Perspective*, ed. Peter J. Potichnyj and Howard Astor (Edmonton, 1988), 205–246.

44. Moyshe Litvakov, "Di sistem fun iberzetsungen II," *Bikher-velt* (Kiev) 4–5 (August 1919): 37.

45. *Kultur-lige* (Kiev) 1 (November 1919): 5.

46. See the Conclusion.

47. It would be temptingly simple to locate the sources of these conceptions and practices of Jewish culture in some general "Zeitgeist": the liberating effect of the February Revolution or maybe the influence of pan-European modernist sensibilities. It would be equally simple to attribute these modes of Jewish culture to the influence of the larger Russian cultural sphere in 1917–1918, where such assertions of culture's sovereign prerogatives could be found not only in liberal quarters but also on the political left, from Gorky's nonaligned leftist paper *Novaia zhizn'* to the organs of the anarchically inclined Futurists under Mayakovsky. See Charles Rougle, "The Intelligentsia Debate in Russia, 1917–1918," in *Art, Society, Revolution: Russia, 1917–1921*, ed. Nils Ake Nilsson (Stockholm, 1979), 60–67, 95–96. But neither strategy could constitute an adequate explanation of why the actors on whom I focus adopted and enacted these institutions of culture. Revolutionary rupture may have liberated them to make whatever cultural choices they wished, but why these particularly? And the direct influence of a stronger, metropolitan cultural sphere may explain why they parroted slogans about cultural autonomy, but it does not explain why they internalized these slogans and sought to actually institutional-

ize and enact them. Empirically, a great many of the Jewish culturists who asserted and practiced similar principles were in no way modernists; many, especially those outside Moscow and Petrograd, had little or nothing to do with the Russian cultural sphere in 1917. More important is the larger point to which this note is appended: all of these elements of cultural sensibility were to be found in the prerevolutionary Jewish cultural milieu, and all were in the process of gaining ground in that cultural milieu well before 1917.

48. As Dan Miron has demonstrated, a whole generation of Hebrew writers defined themselves at the turn of the century in part by their distance from organized Zionist politics; see Miron, *Bodedim be-mo'adam* (Tel Aviv, 1987). Recent work suggests similar patterns in the Yiddish cultural sphere. See David Fishman, "The Bund and Modern Yiddish Culture" in Gitelman, *Emergence of Modern Jewish Politics,* 115; Kenneth B. Moss, "Between Renaissance and Decadence: *Literarishe Monatsshriften* and Its Critical Reception," *Jewish Social Studies* 8, no. 1 (Fall 2001): 153–198; Moss, "1905 as a Jewish Cultural Revolution?" in *The Revolution of 1905: A Turning Point in Jewish History?* ed. Stefani Hoffman and Ezra Mendelsohn (Philadelphia, 2008).

49. See Miron's encompassing account of the relations between Hebrew literature as an institution and Zionism as a movement over the course of a century in "Mi-yotsrim u-vonim li-vne beli bayit," in Miron, *Im lo tihiyeh Yerushalayim: Masot 'al ha-sifrut ha-'ivrit be-heksher tarbuti-politi* (Tel Aviv, 1987); there is nothing equivalent for Yiddish, but see Chone Shmeruk, *Peretses yiesh-vizye* (New York, 1971), ch. 1.

50. Seth Wolitz, "Between Folk and Freedom: The Failure of the Yiddishist Modernist Movement in Poland," *Yiddish* 8, no. 1 (1991): 26–42; Yaacov Shavit, *Athens in Jerusalem* (London, 1997), ch. 8; Iris Parush, *Kanon sifruti ve-ideologyah le'umit* (Jerusalem, 1992).

51. Marcus Moseley, *Being for Myself Alone: Origins of Jewish Autobiography* (Stanford, 2006), ch. 4. Many of the figures examined in this book owed a deep intellectual debt to Berdichevsky.

52. This was by no means a unidirectional process. Tellingly, the dominant literary figures of the early twentieth-century Jewish cultural sphere, the poet Haim Nahman Bialik and the Yiddish-Hebrew neo-Romantic writer Y. L. Peretz, both assumed an increasingly critical stance regarding these developments and demanded that their younger colleagues rededicate themselves to the education of the nation, the task of creating a deeply "Jewish" modern culture, and so forth. But what is interesting about their demands, articulated in essays and speeches in the decade before 1917, is precisely that they propounded them *defensively* in the face of what they perceived as a general shift away from such conceptions of Jewish culture in the Hebrew and Yiddish cultural spheres. See Chapter 5.

53. Benjamin Harshav's treatment of Jewish culture as a formal "system of systems" possessing its own structural rules suggests that line of analysis. See his *Language in Time of Revolution* (Berkeley, 1993), chs. 6–7. I approach the question from a more institutionalist perspective, stressing less the structural features of cultural practice than the power of culture both as idea and interest.

54. Lynn Mally, *Culture of the Future: the Proletkult Movement in Revolutionary Russia* (Berkeley, 1990), xvi–xvii.

55. A note on my theoretical and methodological assumptions: I do not intend to suggest an idealist account of "ideas in history." Certainly the Jewish intelligentsia's embrace and internalization of culture, though it evolved over a long period in myriad contexts that defy any crude interest-based account, did take place within a fairly narrow group with quite definite social characteristics: most were male, young, and autodidacts with traditional education (at least in the 1880s–1890s). An adequate explanation of why Jewish culturists in Eastern Europe adopted these principles of practice with increasing commitment over thirty to forty years would require detailed sociologies of the East European Jewish intelligentsia, nationalist movement, and cultural sphere that we do not yet possess. A *Begriffsgeschichte* would reveal the particular micropolitical conflicts and ideologies that shaped the concept of "Jewish culture." More traditional Marxian and Weberian sociologies of the intelligentsia would help to reveal the interests that this concept served. Finally, we would want to ask how this cultural endeavor related to concerns around a changing gender order, a question that has already been broached in promising fashion in Litvak, *Conscription*, ch. 3, and Iris Parush, *Reading Jewish Women: Marginality and Modernization in Nineteenth-Century Eastern European Jewish Society* (Waltham, Mass., 2004). My study does not assay these kinds of sociology systematically, but it is informed by an account of human intention and institutions that sits ill with the assumptions often embedded in the forms of analysis described earlier. Empirically, my study counterposes an account of how Jewish culture had come to function ideationally and institutionally by 1917 to any claims about what interests it served in earlier stages. In that respect, my analysis accords with the work of institutionalist sociologists in that it posits interests as emergent and substantially defined by embeddedness in particular institutional realms or fields. Jewish culturists may have embraced the concept of culture sometime before 1917 because it suited their interests and desires, but in so doing, they came to have a distinct interest or investment in specifically cultural concerns. See Dimaggio and Powell, "Introduction," in Powell and Dimaggio, *The New Institutionalism;* and Bourdieu, *Rules of Art,* part 2, especially regarding the concept of field-specific capital. Such approaches to culture in Eastern Europe have been the province of literary

scholars. For the Russian case, see William Mills Todd III, *Fiction and Society in the Age of Pushkin* (Cambridge, 1986); for the Jewish case, the starting point is Miron, *Bodedim*.

56. Natan Grinblat, "Reshimot sifrutiyot: *'Olamenu,*" *Ha-Tekufah* 1 (Tevet-Adar, 1918): 670, 672.

1. The Time for Words Has Passed

Epigraph: Moshe Kleinman, "Shalosh ve'idot," *Ha-Shiloah* 32, nos. 4–6 (April–June 1917): 468.

1. Persits to Bialik, 24 Adar [18 March] 1917, Beit Bialik, correspondence collection (collection organized alphabetically by correspondent).

2. "Zlatopolsky, Hillel" in David Tidhar, *Entsiklopedyah le-halutse ha-yishuv u-vonav,* vol. 18 (Tel Aviv, 1947–1971), 5331; A. Litai, "Ha-'yarid' ha-sifruti-ha-'ivri ha-gadol be-Moskvah," *He-'Avar* 3 (1956): 55–59; Shmuel Ayzenshtadt, "Moskvah ha-'ivrit bi-yeme milhemet ha-'olam ha-rishonah," *Katsir: Kovets le-korot ha-tenu'ah ha-tsiyonit be-rusiyah* (Tel Aviv, 1960), 145–147. The quotation is from "Ha-ve'idah ha-rishonah shel Hoveve Sfat 'Ever," *Ha-'Am,* 17 April 1917.

3. "Persits, Shoshana" in Tidhar, *Entsiklopedyah,* vol. 7, 2824–2825.

4. Quote from ibid.; Uriel Ofek, *Gumot He"N: Po'alo shel Bialik be-sifrut ha-yeladim* (Tel Aviv, 1984), 73–74.

5. These resurgent national movements claimed to speak for ethnic groups that were themselves riven by social divisions and whose members were often drawn to the discourse of class identity and the emerging transethnic institutions of the revolutionary left. Yet until 1919, the logic of class intersected with nationalist claims as much as it interfered with them, and in many places, like Ukraine, movements advocating a mixed socialist-nationalist revolutionary platform were a powerful force on the left. See Ronald Grigor Suny, "Nationalism and Class in the Russian Revolution," in *Revolution in Russia: Reassessments of 1917,* ed. Edith Rogovin Frankel, Jonathan Frankel, and Baruch Knei-Paz (Cambridge, Eng., 1992), 219–246; and Geoff Eley, "Remapping the Nation: War, Revolutionary Upheaval, and State Formation in Eastern Europe, 1914–1923," in *Ukrainian-Jewish Relations in Historical Perspective,* ed. Peter J. Potichnyj and Howard Astor (Edmonton, Alb., 1988), 205–246. Such parties flourished in Jewish life as well: the Bund, the Fareynikte, and the Poale Tsion were committed to not only internal social revolution, but also intensive cultivation of Jewish national institutions and extensive national self-determination.

6. Yehudah Slutsky, "Yahadut Rusiyah bi-shnat ha-mahapekhah 1917," *He-'Avar* 15 (1968): 39–48; Tanja Penter, *Odessa, 1917: Revolution an der Peripherie*

(Cologne, 2000), 303–305 and fn. 95; Jonathan Frankel, "The Dilemmas of Jewish Autonomism: The Case of Ukraine, 1917–1920," in *Ukrainian-Jewish Relations,* ed. Potichnyj and Astor, 263–279; Henry Abramson, *A Prayer for the Government: Ukrainians and Jews in Revolutionary Times, 1917–1920* (Cambridge, 1999), ch. 3.

7. Peter Gatrell, *A Whole Empire Walking: Refugees in Russia during World War I* (Bloomington, 1999); Eric Lohr, *Nationalizing the Russian Empire* (Cambridge, 2003); Salo W. Baron, *The Russian Jew under Tsars and Soviets,* 2d ed. (New York, 1987), 156–167; David G. Roskies, *Against the Apocalypse: Responses to Catastrophe in Modern Jewish Culture* (Cambridge, 1984), 115–117; Steven J. Zipperstein, "The Politics of Relief: The Transformation of Russian Jewish Communal Life during the First World War," *Studies in Contemporary Jewry,* vol. 4 (1988): 22–40; Ben-Tsion Dinur, "Me-Februar 'ad Oktober," *He-'Avar* 15 (1968): 9.

8. Slutsky, "Yahadut Rusiyah," 32; Leyb Jaffe, opening statement, *Sborniki "Safrut"* (Moscow), 1 (1918).

9. Bialik, "Halakhah ve-aggadah," in *Kol kitve Ḥ. N. Bialik* (Tel Aviv, 1955), 213.

10. "Ne'umo shel Ḥ. N. Bialik," *Ha-'Am,* 17 April 1917; collected as "Umah ve-lashon" in *Kol kitve Bialik.*

11. Hillel Zlatopolsky, "'Al ha-perek," *Ha-'Am,* 17 March 1917.

12. Ben-Zion Dinur, *Bi-yeme milḥamah u-mahapekhah: Zikhronot u-reshumot mi-derekh ḥayim* (Jerusalem, 1960), 404.

13. Bialik, editorial statement, *Kneset* (Odessa, 1917). Those familiar with Bialik's 1915 philosophical meditation on language and silence, "Gilui ve-kisui be-lashon" (Revealment and concealment in language), which itself appeared in *Kneset,* will hear the intriguing resonances between this introduction and that essay's ideas about the existential terror of silence and the Janus-faced character of speech.

14. Alec Nove, *An Economic History of the USSR,* 2d ed. (London, 1989), 22–23; Dinur, "Me-Februar," 14.

15. Kenneth B. Moss, "Between Renaissance and Decadence: *Literarishe Monatsshriften* and Its Critical Reception," *Jewish Social Studies,* 8, no. 1 (Fall 2001): 153–198. To explore more than these proximate causes would take us far beyond the scope of this chapter. Deeper factors that drove Hebraist-Yiddishist conflict both in 1917 and well before include the very real pre-ideological love of Hebrew retained by some (but not all) traditionally educated literati even after their break with tradition; the deep contempt felt toward Yiddish among many proud Jewish nationalists (no less than among the Polonized or Russified haute-bourgeoisies of Warsaw and Petersburg); the idealization of Yiddish as part of a powerful myth of "the masses" among some (but not all) Russian Jewish leftists; the genuinely exciting (re)discovery

of the linguistic possibilities of one's own mother tongue during the nineteenth century; and the very real convictions of both sides regarding the question of which Jewish language—"vital," "young" Yiddish or "rich," "resonant" Hebrew—offered the best resources for meeting the challenges of creating a compelling modern Jewish culture. Perhaps the fundamental structuring factor behind the consolidation of militant Hebraist and Yiddishist visions of cultural dissemination was, ironically, a conviction that both sides shared—namely, that Jews could not become full-fledged, autonomous modern subjects unless they possessed a single "whole" language adequate to all domains of experience and to the expression and constitution of an integrated selfhood. This question demands further investigation. For fruitful initial formulations, see Israel Bartal, "From Traditional Bilingualism to National Monolingualism" in *Hebrew in Ashkenaz: A Language in Exile,* ed. Lewis Glinert (New York, 1993); Joshua A. Fishman, "The Sociology of Yiddish: A Foreword" in *Never Say Die! A Thousand Years of Yiddish in Jewish Life and Letters,* ed. Fishman (The Hague, 1981); and Robert Alter, *The Invention of Hebrew Prose* (Seattle, 1988), 12–13.

16. Yosef Klausner, "Koḥo shel Mendeli," *Ha-Shiloaḥ* 34, no. 1 (January 1918): 31; Yosi Sofer, "Le-toldotav shel Mendeli," *Ha-Shiloaḥ* 34, no. 1 (January 1918): 29; Moshe Kleinman, "Shloshet ha-Mendelim," *Ha-Shiloaḥ* 34, no. 1 (January 1918): 78; Moyshe Litvakov, "Mendele Moykher Sforim," in Litvakov, *In Umruh* (Kiev, 1918), 76–87.

17. Baal-Makhshoves, "Tsvey shprakhn—eyneyntsike literatur," reprinted in Fishman, *Never Say Die!,* 463–478, esp. 463–475; this article was published in the *Petrograder togblat* in 1918, but the first part was written in late 1908 or 1909. See also Y. H. Ravnitsky, "Tsi bin ikh a 'yudishist,'" *Untervegs* (Odessa, 1916/1917), 171–181.

18. On the prewar OPE, see Brian Horowitz, "The Society for the Promotion of Enlightenment among the Jews of Russia and the Evolution of the St. Petersburg Russian Jewish Intelligentsia, 1893–1905," *Studies in Contemporary Jewry* 19 (2003): 195–213. On the internal conflicts that split the organization during World War I, see Mazeh, Marek, et al. ("group of non-party members"), undated leaflet, OPE Collection, TsIAM, file 2309, op. 1, d. 44; Dinur, *Bi-yeme,* 88–113; Y. A. Gilboa, *A Language Silenced* (New York, 1982), 16–18. On the post-revolutionary collapse, see A. Zaidman, "Ha-otonomiyah ha-le'umit ha-yehudit ba-Ukrainah ha-'atsma'it ba-shanim 1917–1919," Ph.D. diss., Tel Aviv University, 1980, 159; OPE letters to provincial libraries, 1917, in TsIAM, record group 2309, finding aid 1, folder 167, docs. 97a–97f.

19. Dinur, *Bi-yeme,* 312–320.

20. Kalman Zingman to Niger, letterhead of "Ferlag 'Idish,'" 15 June 1917 or possibly earlier, YIVO, record group 360, folder 871; A. Golomb, *A halber*

yorhundert yidishe dertsiung (Rio de Janeiro, 1957); Z. Anoykhi to Baal Makhshoves, Isidor Eliashiv collection, Gnazim, record group 142, doc. 18513.

21. Yehuda Slutsky, "Ha-pirsumim ha-'ivriyim be-Vrit ha-Mo'atsot ba-shanim 1917–1960," in *Pirsumim yehudiyim be-Vrit ha-Mo'atsot, 1917–1960,* ed. Yitshak Yosef Kohen (Jerusalem, 1961), 32–34.

22. Yosi Goldshtain, *Usishkin: Biografyah* (Jerusalem, 1999), 276–277.

23. Dinur, *Bi-yeme*, 239–304; Eliyahu Meitus, *Bi-meḥitsatam shel sofrim* (Tel Aviv, 1977), 95–99. On the conferences, the best source is *Novyi Put',* a diaspora autonomist paper committed to liberal notions of Jewish civil society that covered the whole range of Jewish organizations; see the issues for April and May 1917. Regarding the *Petrograder Togblat,* see inaugural announcement, 18 October 1915; the paper published work by An-ski, the Yiddish literary critic Baal Makhshoves, Bialik, and others. On the growing hostility to it among Yiddishists, see Bal-Dimyen, "Gedanken," *Di yidishe folksblat* (Petrograd) 3 (October 1917).

24. Because of the primacy of political mobilization, Kiev did have a *Yiddish*-language Zionist newspaper, *Af der vakh.* On beginning largely from scratch in 1918, see H. Grinberg for Central Council of Tarbut: Ukrainian Section to Dovid Shimonovits, undated (mid-1918), David Shimoni collection, Gnazim, record group 165, doc. 75735; Persits to Bialik, 3 June 1918, Beit Bailik, correspondence collection; Hillel Zlatopolsky, cited in G. Kohelet, "'Avodat ha-Tarbut ba-'avar uve-'atid" in *Ha-Toren* 23 (22 August 1919): 13. In the city census of September 1917, 18.7 percent of the civilian population identified itself as nationally Jewish, 49.5 percent as Russian (a complex category that may have included a fair number of Jews), and 16.4 percent as Ukrainian. See Steven Guthier, "The Popular Base of Ukrainian Nationalism in 1917," *Slavic Review* 38, no. 1 (1979): 41, n. 43. The population statistic is from Abramson, *Prayer,* 184, n. 34, which also notes (p. 13) that between 1897 and 1917 the Jewish population grew at 1.5 times the rate of the Russian population and nearly twice the rate of the Ukrainian population.

25. N. Mayzl, "Dos yidishe bukh in Ukrayne," *Bikher-velt* 1 (January 1919): 5.

26. "Vserossiiskaia konferentsiia Bunda," *Novyi Put',* 23 April 1917, 51. Even the Zionist movement, the most popular and best-funded Jewish party, could not easily meet the practical demands of the moment. In June 1917 the Central Committee of the Russian Zionist organization in Petrograd informed its regional office in Kiev that it had few resources and had not yet been able to produce any political literature. Central Committee of the Zionist Organization in Russia to the Kiev Regional Office, 14 June 1917, Jewish Political Parties and Organizations Collection, TsDAHOU, record group 41, finding aid 1, folder 240.

27. Sh. A. Ayzenshtadt, "Le-harḥavat ha-gvulin," *Ha-'Am,* 17 March 1917.

28. Shmuel Niger, "A shmues," *Di yidishe folksblat,* 3 October 1917; Mayzl, "Dos yidishe bukh," 5–8.

29. Mayzl to Niger, 29 September 1910, YIVO, record group 360, folder 283; Broderzon to Niger, 17 July 1917, YIVO, record group 360, folder 98.

30. Sholem, "Dray Veteranen fun Bund," *Unzer tsayt* (1979): 24.

31. Jewish Folks-Partey faction in Petrograd Kehillah to Niger, 10 January 1918, YIVO, record group 360, folder 690; Tsharni to Niger et al., 1 January 1918, YIVO, record group 360, folder 16.

32. Zalmen Ahronson (Anoykhi) to Y. H. Brenner, undated but probably ca. 1907, Brenner Collection, Gnazim, record group 20, doc. 18120.

33. "Me-et Tarbut," *Ha-'Am,* April 1917; M. Zerubavel, "Ha-ve'idah ha-rishonah shel Ḥoveve Sfat 'Ever," *Ha-'Am,* 17 April 1917; see also articles under the same byline in subsequent issues.

34. Gabriele Freitag, *Naechstes Jahr in Moskau!* (Goettingen, 2004), 70–73, 77 n. 5; Ayzenshtadt, "Moskvah ha-'ivrit," 143. By mid-1917, municipal sources put the number of Jewish adults in Moscow around 57,000; this population continued to increase until the political and economic shocks that began at the end of the year and intensified throughout 1918.

35. Shmuel Ayzenshtadt, "Le-toldot ha-tsiburiut veha-tarbut ha-'ivrit be-rusiyah bi-tḥilat ha-me'ah ha-'esrim," *He-'Avar* 15 (1968): 141–148; Ayzenshtadt, "Moskvah ha-'ivrit"; Ben-Tsion Katz, *Zikhronot* (Tel Aviv, 1964), 243; A. Z. Ben-Yishai, "Sifrut ve-'itonut 'ivrit be-rusiyah bi-tkufat ha-mahapekhah ve-aḥarehah," *He-'Avar* 15 (1968): 170–172. Other leading patrons of Hebraist and Zionist causes in wartime and early revolutionary Moscow included Zalman Epshteyn of Kolomea, Avrom Podlishevsky of Warsaw, Yitshok Leyb Goldberg of Vilna, and the locally settled Y. Nayditsh. Litai, "Ha-'yarid'," 56.

36. Ayzenshtadt, "Le-toldot ha-tsiburiut," 136–137. Ayzenshtat also cofounded a society for the development of a Jewish national legal system through the secular reconstrual of traditional Jewish law, a precursor of the modern *mishpat 'ivri* idea in Israeli jurisprudence.

37. *Ustav evreiskago dramaticheskago obshchestva "Gabima"* (Moscow, 1916), 1–2; copy in TsIAM, record group 2309, finding aid 1, folder 313. Cf. Vladislav Ivanov, *Russkie sezony: Teatr Gabima* (Moscow, 1999); and Emanuel Levy, *The Habima—Israel's National Theater, 1917–1977: A Study of Cultural Nationalism* (New York, 1979).

38. On the popularity of the exhibition in Jewish circles, see Ben-Yishai, "Sifrut ve-'itonut," 169; on the organization, see *Otchet evreiskago obshchestva pooshchreniia khudozhestv za 1916 god* (Petrograd, 1916).

39. Ayzenshtadt, "Moskvah ha-'ivrit," 147; Stybel to Niger, 18 March 1921, YIVO, record group 360, folder 930.

40. Nils Ake Nilsson, "Spring 1918: The Arts and the Commissars," in Nilsson, *Art, Society, Revolution: Russia, 1917–1921* (Stockholm, 1979), 23; M. Gnesin, *Darki 'im ha-teatron ha-'ivri* (Tel Aviv, 1946), 115–119.

41. Litai, "Ha-'yarid'," 56–57.

42. Niger, "A shmues."

43. Litvakov, *In Umruh,* 3; *Peretz mit unz* (Kiev, 1917); Hirshkan to Niger, 21 October 1917, YIVO, record group 360, folder 167.

44. "Partey-khronik: A forlezung fun Dovid Bergelson," *Unzer vort,* 4 July 1917; "Mit vemen zaynen mir?" *Di naye tsayt,* 1 September 1917; Dobrushin to Niger 14 November 1918, YIVO, record group 360, folder 145; Zelig Melamed for the Temporary Executive Committee of the Kultur Lige to Niger, 1 January 1918, YIVO, record group 360, folder 817.

45. Joseph Sherman, "Leyb Kvitko," in *Dictionary of Literary Biography,* vol. 333: *Writers in Yiddish,* ed. Joseph Sherman (Detroit, 2007).

46. "Tsu di fraynt-lezer," *Di yidishe folksblat,* 1 December 1917.

47. Yosef Klausner, "Mi-ma'amakim: Ḥazon ha-yamim," *'Olamenu* (Petrograd, 1917), 34–36.

48. Richard Pipes, *The Formation of the Soviet Union: Communism and Nationalism, 1917–1923* (Cambridge, Eng., 1964). On culturist hopes for state support from the Provisional Government, see Moshe Kleinman, "Ripublikah federativit," *Ha-'Am,* 5 May 1917. Apparently, the Provisional Government founded a Jewish Commission for Matters of Enlightenment and Education in close cooperation with the OPE; see memoirs, undated, Aryeh Tsentsiper(-Rafaeli) Collection, CZA, record group F-30, folder 98/1. On the borderlands, see Frankel, "Dilemmas of Jewish Autonomism," 263–265.

49. Dinur, *Bi-yeme,* 332–333. This was part of a broader phenomenon of de-Russification in the successor states that remains to be studied; see Shmuel Kassow, "Zalman Reyzen un zayn gezelshaftlekh-politishe arbet, 1915–1922" in *YIVO bleter: Naye seriye* 2 (1994): 67–98.

50. Agudat ha-tsionim bne ḥorin Pishtshanke, 19 June 1917, TsDAHOU, record group 41, finding aid 1, folder 242; Pinhas Govrin, *Hayinu ke-ḥolmim: Megilat mishpaḥah* (Jerusalem, 2005), 156–157. Poltava Society for Jewish Art (Ha-zamir) to An-ski, 25 October 1917, Vernadsky, An-ski Collection, RGALI, record group 339, folder 864.

51. On the prewar shift, see Hirsz Abramowicz, *Profiles of a Lost World,* ed. Dina Abramowicz and Jeffrey Shandler (Detroit, 1999); David Fishman, "Language and Revolution" in Fishman, *The Rise of Modern Yiddish Culture* (Pittsburgh, 2005), 33–47.

52. A. Levinson, *Ha-Tenu'ah ha-'ivrit ba-golah* (Warsaw, 1935), 38–39; Ayzenshtadt, "Moskvah ha-'ivrit," 143–144; *Obzor deiatel'nosti "ORPME" za vremia voiny* (Petrograd, 1916), 3–20; Zosa Szajkowski, "The Struggle for Yid-

dish during World War I," in *Never Say Die!*, ed. Fishman; *Di grunt-oyfgabn fun der Kultur-Lige* (Kiev, 1918), 5.

53. Yosef Klausner, "Le-sha'ah ule-dorot," *Ha-Shiloah* 32, nos. 4–6 (April–June 1917): 293–294.

54. Yehoshua Margolin, cited in "Ha-ve'idah ha-rishonah shel Hoveve Sfat Ever: Hemshekh," *Ha-'Am*, 5 May 1917; Nokhem Shtif, *Yidn un yidish* (Kiev, 1919), citing from the partial reprint *An entfer di gegners fun yidish* (Tshernovits, 1922), 16.

55. "Vserossiiskaia konferentsiia Bunda," *Novyi Put'*, 23 April 1917. For the history of this division see Jonathan Frankel, *Prophecy and Politics: Socialism, Nationalism, and the Russian Jews, 1862–1917* (Cambridge, 1981); for its consequences in the early Soviet years see Zvi Y. Gitelman, *Jewish Nationality and Soviet Politics* (Princeton, 1972).

56. D. S. Pasmanik, *Chto takoe evreiskaia natsional'naia kul'tura?* (Odessa, 1917–1918), 6, 12, 15, 17, 22–23.

57. A partial list includes Ester Frumkina and Vladimir Medem (Bund), Yitshok Gruenbaum (Russian Zionists), Litvakov (Fareynikte).

58. Izd. Kinneret to bur. Zi. Org. Kiev obl, 19 Dec 1917, TsDAHOU, record group 41, finding aid 1, folder 242, doc. 114.

59. See, for example, Kh. Grinberg, "Gabimah" [Ha-Bimah], *Evreiskaia Zhizn'*, 15 January 1917; the translation of a story by Zalman Shneur in *Evreiskaia Zhizn'*, 5 February 1917; A. Efros, "Fel'eton: Evreiskie khudozhniki; Marc Chagall," *Evreiskaia Zhizn'*, 12 March 1917.

60. The key exception was the Bund, which rejected, on Marxist grounds, formal autonomy beyond the cultural realm. Significantly, all of the other Jewish parties, including the other two socialist-autonomist parties, attacked the Bund for this approach, in a standoff reminiscent of 1903–1906, when these alternatives to the Bund had initially emerged; see Frankel, *Prophecy,* chs. 4–6.

61. "Di platform fun der tsionistisher organizatsye tsu der tsaytvayliger natsionaler farzamlung" undated, CZA, record group F-30, folder 111.

62. Y. Sh. Herts, "Di tsveyte ruslender revolutsye (1917 un vaytere yorn)," in *Di geshikhte fun Bund,* ed. Grigori Aronson et al., vol. 3 (New York, 1966), 98; Levinson, *Ha-Tenu'ah,* 36–37; Moskovskii raionnii komitet narodnoi fraktsii sionistskoi-org. Ts. Ts., circular no. 2, Tseire Tsion Collection, GARF, record group R-647, finding aid 1, folder 1, doc. 81; Moshe Kleinman, "Shalosh ve'idot" *Ha-Shiloah* 32, nos. 4–6 (April–June 1917): 461–477; Sholem Shvarts, "Keren-zavit," *Ha-Shiloah* 33, no. 1 (July 1917): 100–102; "Ha-knesiah ha-tsionit ha-shevi'it be-Petrograd" *Ha-'Am*, 16 June 1917.

63. Benyamin Lukin, "'An Academy Where Folklore Will Be Studied': An-sky and the Jewish Museum," in *The Worlds of S. An-sky: A Russian Jewish Intellectual at the Turn of the Century,* ed. Gabriella Safran and Steven J. Zipperstein

(Stanford, 2006), 303, notes that An-ski gave a speech to the delegates of the All-Russian Jewish Congress; Moshe Ungerfeld comments on the reading of *The Dybbuk* in Kiev sometime in 1917 to early 1918 in *Bialik ve-sofre doro,* ed. Ungerfeld (Tel Aviv, 1974), 25. On Bialik, see A. Z. Ben-Yishai, "Pirke Ukrainah ('al pi yoman)," *He-'Avar* 18 (1971): 169–173.

64. Saul Borovoi, cited in Penter, *Odessa, 1917,* 310.

65. Avigdor Ha-Meiri, *Be-gehenom shel matah* (Tel Aviv, 1989), 422–423.

66. Dovid Hofshteyn to Shmuel Niger, 6 October [1917], YIVO, record group 360, folder 160; the poem "Der plonter fun shteynerne hayzer" has been reprinted in Hofshteyn, *Lider un poemes,* vol. 1 (Tel Aviv: Farlag 'Yisroel-Bukh', 1977).

67. Moyshe Kulbak, "Di shtot," in *Vayter-bukh,* ed. Zalman Rejzen (Vilne, 1920). Parts of the poem were published in 1919: see Volf Yunin, "Moyshe Kulbak," *Di goldene keyt* 5 (Winter 1950): 166–168.

68. Avraham Shlionsky, "Bi-dmi-yeush," *Ha-Shiloah* 35, nos. 3–4 (September–October 1918): 274. A copy of *Shevivim,* containing several pieces by the young Shlonsky—including a translation of Gorky, a long narrative poem "Yirmiyahu," and a series of poems "On the Shore of the Dnieper"—can be found in Tchernikhowsky Collection, Gnazim, folder 1: "other material."

69. Why this was so has yet to be investigated fully. An important beginning can be found in Iris Parush, *Reading Jewish Women: Marginality and Modernization in Nineteenth-Century Eastern European Jewish Society* (Waltham, Mass., 2004).

70. E. Lisheva, *Tainyia piesni: Stikhotvoreniia* (Moscow, 1919); Dinur, *Bi-yeme,* 332; Ayzenshtadt, "Moskvah ha-'ivrit," 150; Menahem Gnesin to Elisheva, 10 December 1918, Elisheva Collection, Gnazim, record group 7, doc. 7657; Carole Balin, *To Reveal Our Hearts: Jewish Women Writers in Tsarist Russia* (Cincinnati, 2000), 138.

71. Music Societies Collection, YIVO, record group 37, folder 1.

72. See Jeffrey Veidlinger, *The Moscow State Yiddish Theater* (Bloomington, 2000); Protocols of the Jewish Theater Society, December 1916–1917 and related letters, GOSET Collection, RGALI, record group 2307, finding aid 2, folder 530.

73. M. Broderzon to Sh. Niger, postscript by Lissitzky, 1 April 1918, YIVO, record group 360, folder 98. Key articles on this development include Seth Wolitz, "The Jewish National Art Renaissance in Russia" and John Bowlt, "From the Pale of Settlement to the Reconstruction of the World," which both appear in *Tradition and Revolution: The Jewish Renaissance in Russian Avant-Garde Art, 1912–1928,* ed. Ruth Apter-Gabriel (Jerusalem, 1988).

74. Litai, "Ha-'yarid,'"; N. Mayzl, "Tsum idishn artistn tsuzamenfor," *Di naye tsayt,* 14 September 1917.

75. See, for example, Leonid Pasternak, "Ha-omanut ha-'ivrit," *Tarbut: Yedi'ot ha-va'ad ha-merkazi* 2 (28 August 1918): 12–13.

76. Gnesin, *Darki,* 119.

77. Natan Goren, *Demuyot be-sifrutenu* (Tel Aviv, 1953), 71.

78. Iris Parush, *Kanon sifruti ve-ideologyah le'umit* (Jerusalem, 1992), part 1.

79. Dania Amichay-Michlin, *Ahavat I"sh: Avraham Yosef Stybel* (Jerusalem, 2000), 37–65; Slutsky, "Ha-pirsumim," 25–30.

80. Ben-Yishai, "Sifrut ve-'itonut," 172.

81. Zaidman, "Ha-otonomiyah," 181–182.

82. Zerubavel, "Ha-ve'idah," *Ha-'Am,* 17 April 1917, with additional material in subsequent issues.

83. "Me-et Tarbut."

84. Zerubavel, "Ha-ve'idah ha-rishonah," *Ha-'Am,* 28 April 1917.

85. Zerubavel, "Ha-ve'idah ha-rishonah," *Ha-'Am,* 5 May 1917.

86. Y. Saaruni, "Rehifim (Perakim me-ma'avak ha-sifrut ha-'ivrit be-Vrit ha-Mo'atsot)," *He-'Avar* 21 (1975): 119.

87. A. Strashun to Niger (postscript, Shimen), 29 December 1917, YIVO, record group 360, folder 598; Strashun to Niger, Kalmanovitsh, and Dinaburg, 30 March, 12 April 1918, YIVO, record group 3, folder 3089. On the autonomy, see Abramson, *Prayer;* on its cultural dimensions, Zaidman, "Ha-otonomiyah," 162–178. In 1918, Hebraists also reacted to the promise of autonomy in Ukraine with guarded excitement, though by that time, they were already watching their grand endeavor in central Russia crumble under Bolshevik repressions. A Tarbut circular from 1918 hailed the moment as "unprecedentedly well-suited to cultural work . . . There is reason to hope that many of the external factors that have hitherto interfered with our organized effort will no longer place obstacles in our path, and we will be able, with a certain breadth and security, to devote our public powers to building the Hebrew culture." Ha-va'ad ha-merkazi shel hevrat "Tarbut," Kiev, hozer aleph, 1918, Ussishkin Collection, CZA, record group A-24, folder 145/1(7). Hebraist hopes in Ukraine were probably fed more by the clear success of Zionism on the local level and in local Jewish communal institutions than by any hopes for support from the central government.

88. Moyshe Katz, "Di Kultur Lige in Ukrayne," *Di tsukunft* 3 (March 1921): 183; "Takones fun der Kultur Lige," TsDAVO, record group 3304, finding aid 1, folder 2, doc. 1.

89. *Kultur Lige (a sakh-akl): Zamlung* (November 1919): 7–34; Kalmanovitsh to Vayter, 3 September 1918, YIVO, record group 360, folder 34.

90. *Kultur Lige (a sakh-akl),* 34–40; *Kultur Lige: byuleten num. 2* (June–July 1920): 50–59; Wolitz, "Jewish National Art Renaissance," 35.

91. *Kultur Lige (a sakh-akl),* 41–42; *Grunt-oyfgabn,* 17–18; Katz, "Di Kultur Lige," 185; Kalmanovitsh to Vayter, 3 September 1918, YIVO, record group 360,

folder 34; Kultur Lige to Ministry of Jewish Affairs of Ukrainian People's Republic, undated [probably January 1919], Collection of the Ministry of Jewish Affairs, Ukrainian State, TsDAVO, record group 2060, finding aid 1, folder 4.

92. Kalmanovitsh to Vayter, 6 September 1918, YIVO, record group 360, folder 34.

93. Kalmanovitsh to Vayter, 3 September 1918, YIVO, record group 360, folder 34; Dinur, *Bi-yeme*, 404–405.

94. Shtif to Zalman Reyzen, 9 August 1920, YIVO, record group 3, folder 3035; Shtif to Niger, 13 June 1922, YIVO, record group 360, folder 442; Dinur, *Bi-yeme*, 404–405; announcement, *Vilna leben* 3–4 (June 1920): 53; Kalmanovitsh to Vayter, 6 September 1918, YIVO, record group 360, folder 34.

95. Tellingly, the Folks Farlag sought to gain support directly from the newly restored Jewish Ministry (rather than through the Kultur-Lige) in early 1919. See Folks-Farlag to Jewish Ministry, 31 January 1919, TsDAVO, record group 3304, finding aid 1, folder 18; Shtif to Niger, 28 August 1918, YIVO, record group 360, folder 442; announcement, *Vilna leben* 3–4 (June 1920): 53.

96. Peretz Markish, "[Hey, vos handelt ir dort—umet?]," reprinted in *Shpigl af a shteyn*, ed. Chone Shmeruk (Tel Aviv, 1964), 382. The translation is a modified version of Etta Blum's incomplete translation in *A Treasury of Yiddish Poetry*, ed. Irving Howe and Eliezer Greenberg (New York, 1969), 183–184.

97. Hillel Kazovsky, *Khudozhniki Kultur-Ligi: The Artists of the Kultur-Lige* (Moscow, 2003); Seth Wolitz, "The Kiev-Grupe (1918–1920) Debate: The Function of Literature," *Yiddish* 3, no. 3 (1978).

98. Statement of Purpose, *Bikher-velt* 1 (January 1919): back cover; Nahman Mayzl, "Batlonishe kuriozn," *Bikher-velt* 1 (January 1919): 44; Z. Elin, "L. Boymvol (Buf), 'Khatzkele Kol-boynik': Operetta in 4 aktn," and "Afn ganef brent dos hitl: Komedye in 1 akt," both in *Bikher-velt* 2–3 (March 1919): 50–51.

99. Dinur, *Bi-yeme*, 321–332, 389–390.

100. Ibid., 332; Y. Sh. Hertz, ed., *Doyres Bundistn*, vol. 1 (New York, 1956), 470–473.

101. Kalmanovitsh to Vayter, 3 September 1918 and 13 November 1918, YIVO, record group 360, folder 34 (notably, Kalmanovitsh began with a jaundiced view, but his opinion improved quickly); Mayzl, "Dos yidishe bukh," 6–8.

102. *Peretz mit unz* (Kiev, 1917).

103. "Oyb ikh bin yung," repr. in Moyshe Broderzon, *Oysgeklibene shriftn*, ed. Shmuel Rozhanski (Buenos Aires, 1959).

104. Cited in Wolitz, "Jewish National Art Renaissance," 31.

105. Broderzon to Niger, 25 May 1917, 17 July 1917, 14 October 1917, and Broderzon with Lissitzky, 1 April 1918, YIVO, record group 360, folder 98; Gilles Rozier, *Moyshe Broderzon: Un ecrivain yiddish d'avant-garde* (Saint Denis, 1999), 52–54.

2. The Constitution of Culture

Epigraphs: Di Grunt-oyfgabn fun der Kultur-Lige (Kiev, 1918); Haim Nahman Bialik, "Tarbut ve-'politikah,'" *Ha-Ginah* 6 (July–August 1918): 5.

1. Ben-Yankev [Kalman Zingman], *In der tsukunft-shtot "Edenyah": Roman*, republished in *Be-'ir he-'atid 'Edenyah*, ed. A. Zimrani (Tel Aviv, 1996). Thanks to Vicki Ash and Gennady Estraikh for bringing this invaluable source to my attention. Estraikh describes some aspects of the utopia and situates it in Zingman's biography in "Utopias and Cities of Kalman Zingman, an Uprooted Yiddishist Dreamer," *East European Jewish Affairs* 36, no. 1 (2006): 31–42.

2. Ben-Yankev, *Tsukunft-shtot*, esp. 12–22.

3. Ibid., 18, 42.

4. Zalman Reyzen, "Zingman, Kalman," in *Leksikon fun der yidisher literatur, prese un filologye* (Vilna, 1929).

5. Ben-Yankev, *Tsukunft-shtot*, 36.

6. Estraikh, "Utopias." Zingman's shift from the nationalist, nonsocialist Folks-Partey (if in fact he was a Folkist) to Communism was by no means unique. Other Folkists who made the same journey included Zingman's Kharkov colleague Moyshe Taytsh; see Chapter 7.

7. Zingman to Shmuel Niger, 1 Kislev TaR'Akh [15 November 1917] and 6 December 1917, YIVO, record group 360, folder 203.

8. Cited in A. Levinson, *Ha-Tenu'ah ha-'ivrit ba-golah* (Warsaw, 1935), 36.

9. Shoshana Persits to Yosef Klausner, 2 June (?) 1918, Joseph Klausner Collection, JNUL, collection 4–1086, folder 201.

10. Ben-Avigdor, "Ha-'ivriut veha-klaliut be-sifrut ha-'ivrit," *Ha-Melits*, 21 April 1895; Avner Holtzman, *Sifrut ve-omanut plastit* (Tel Aviv, 1997), chs. 1–2.

11. Iulian Krein, "Kompozitory Grigori i Aleksandr Krein," *Vestnik Evreiskogo Universiteta* 1, no. 5 (1994): 218.

12. See *Sborniki "Safrut"* (Moscow), 1 (1918) and the publications cited therein, which also list illustrators; Brian Horowitz, ed., "Pis'ma L. B. Yaffe k M. Gershenzonu," *Vestnik Evreiskogo Universiteta* 2, no. 18 (1998): 216–217; Vladislav Khodasevich, *Iz evreiskikh poetov* (Moscow, 1998), 15–22.

13. *Ustav evreiskago dramaticheskago obshchestva "Gabima,"* TsIAM, record group 2309, finding aid 1, folder 313; M. Gnesin, *Darki 'im ha-teatron ha-'ivri* (Tel Aviv, 1946).

14. *Kultur-Lige* 1 (1919): 35; Hillel Kazovsky, *Khudozhniki Kultur-Ligi: The Artists of the Kultur-Lige* (Moscow, 2003).

15. "Kunst-khronik: Teater," *Baginen* (1919): 89; quote from *Kultur-Lige* 1 (1919): 35. Significantly, none of this applied in the literary realm. Thus, while all of

this was taking place, the Russian-language avant-garde literary community in Kiev published a literary anthology *Germes*. Judging by names like Vengrov, Evreinov, Makkaveiskii, and Rabinovich, more than half of the participants were of Jewish descent; the journal published such Jewish-born young lions of the avant-garde as Mandel'shtam and Benedikt Livshits. Perhaps these Jewish aspirants to Russian literary legitimacy had special reason to ignore the local Yiddish culture, and vice versa. See *Germes: Sbornik* 1 (Kiev, April 1919).

16. See the relevant sections in *Kultur-Lige* 1 (1919) and 2 (1920).

17. It is difficult to know what language these organizations used for their administration, because so little internal documentation can be found. The Kultur-Lige's music section, the archive of which has survived, used Russian for internal memos, presumably because composers as a group were highly Russified; see Music Societies Collection, YIVO, record group 37, folder 3. But all other official Kultur-Lige documents I have seen used Yiddish; see, e.g., A. Strashun for Central Committee to Niger, 30 July 1918, YIVO, record group 360, folder 913. Similarly, all business communication between the Folks-Farlag and Ben-Tsion Dinur was in Yiddish, including the formal contract; see contract with Dinur and Zelig Kalmanovitsh 1 July 1919, Dinur Collection, CAHJP. Among many courtesies extended to me in my brief time at the CAHJP in 1999 was access to the Dinur Collection before it was fully processed. I am, consequently, not certain about the collection's final organization and numbering.

18. See V. Kel'ner and D. El'iashevich, eds., *Literatura o evreiiakh na russkom iazike, 1890–1947* (St. Petersburg, 1995), 336–339. Kinneret's cultural publications devoted to educating the Russian-Jewish reader about Hebrew culture and Zionism included Y. Klausner, *Saul Tchernikhovsky—Poet vozrozhdenie* (1918) and Y. Fichman, *Pevets liubvi sionskoi (A. Mapu)* (1918). On Safrut see A. Z. Ben-Yishai, "Sifrut ve-'itonut 'ivrit be-rusiyah bi-tkufat ha-mahapekhah ve-aharehah," *He-'Avar* 15 (1968): 170; Leyb Jaffe, opening statement to *Sborniki "Safrut"* 1; and "Pechautsiia," *Sborniki "Safrut"* 1: back cover, which lists forthcoming works like *Ieguda Galevi: Literaturnii-psikhologicheskii etyud'*, by the Zionist-Hebraist activist Haim Grinberg.

19. Donyel Tsharni to Niger and family, 8 March 1918, YIVO, record group 360, folder 16.

20. For instance, the Leningrad *Evreiskaia mysl': Nauchno-literaturnyi sbornik* (1923) or the Moscow *Evreiskii vestnik* (1922).

21. Khevre "mefitsey haskole" in Ukraine, Temporary Central Committee, 19 January 1919, TsDAVO, record group 2060, finding aid 1, folder 41.

22. Seth Wolitz, "The Jewish National Art Renaissance in Russia," in *Tradition and Revolution: The Jewish Renaissance in Russian Avant-Garde Art, 1912–1928,* ed.

Ruth Apter-Gabriel (Jerusalem, 1988); Broderzon to Niger, 25 May 1917, 17 July 1917, YIVO, record group 360, folder 98.

23. Broderzon and Lissitzky to Niger, 1 April 1918, YIVO, record group 360, folder 98.

24. See Ha-Bimah to S. An-ski, 11 July 1917, Vernadsky, collection 339, folder 431; Stybel to Niger, 18 March 1921, YIVO, record group 360, folder 930; An-ski to Bialik, undated, but clearly 1917, in Moshe Ungerfeld, *Bialik ve-sofre doro,* ed. Ungerfeld (Tel Aviv, 1974), 24–25; Kh. Lunski, "A halb yor zikhroynes vegn An-ski" in *Pinkes far der forshung fun der yiddisher literatur un prese,* ed. Hyman Bass (New York, 1975), 492–498.

25. Benjamin Harshav, *Marc Chagall and His Times: A Documentary Narrative* (Stanford, 2004), part 3; Peretz Markish, "In droysn," *Pust un pas* (Katerinoslav, 1919), 7, 10.

26. Here I am indebted to Harshav, *Language in Time of Revolution* (Berkeley, 1993), chs. 6–7.

27. On Proletkult, see Lynn Mally, *Culture of the Future: The Proletkult Movement in Revolutionary Russia* (Berkeley, 1990); a much closer parallel is the short-lived organization Kul'tura i svoboda, founded in April 1918 by Gorky and other figures associated with the non-Bolshevik but left-leaning Russian cultural intelligentsia. See Charles Rougle, "The Intelligentsia Debate in Russia, 1917–1918," in *Art, Society, Revolution: Russia, 1917–1921,* ed. Nils Ake Nilsson (Stockholm, 1979), 95–97.

28. L. Kvitko and Y. Ryback, *Foyglen* (Berlin, 1922); this is a reprint of a version published in Kiev in 1919.

29. Bar-Tuviah, "Be-ulam ha-temunot," *Ha-Shiloah* 34, no. 2 (February 1918): 218–219.

30. Shmuel Feiner, *Haskalah and History* (Portland, 2002); David N. Myers, *Re-Inventing the Jewish Past: European Jewish Intellectuals and the Zionist Return to History* (Oxford, 1995); Cecile Kuznitz, "The Origins of Yiddish Scholarship and the YIVO Institute for Jewish Research," Ph.D. diss., Stanford University, 2000.

31. See the essays in *The Worlds of S. An-sky: A Russian Jewish Intellectual at the Turn of the Century,* ed. Gabriella Safran and Steven J. Zipperstein (Stanford, 2006); Semyon An-ski, "Sholom-Aleichem, Perets, i Frug," discovered by Irina Sergeeva and published in *Egupets: Khudozhn'o-publitsistichnii almanakh* 1 (Kiev, 1995): 83, 85–86.

32. Abram Efros, "Aladdin's Lamp." Efros's essay was first published in the 1918 *Evreiskii mir;* the English translation can be found in Semyon An-sky, *The Jewish Artistic Heritage: An Album,* ed. Alexander Kantsedikas (Moscow, 1994), 7–15.

33. Sh. Niger, "Folks-shafung [continuation]," *Kultur un bildung* (Moscow) (26 August 1918): 9.

34. Based on earlier versions of *Between Two Worlds*, Anne Eakin Moss suggests that Niger is referring to an earlier version, which makes sense given that Niger was in Petrograd with An-ski in 1916–1917.

35. Moyshe Kulbak, "Dos yidishe vort," *Der veker* (1918); reprinted in *Di goldene keyt* 43 (1962): 238–242.

36. *Kultur-Lige* 1 (1919): 38.

37. Bialik, "Halakhah ve-aggadah," in *Kol kitve H. N. Bialik* (Tel Aviv, 1955), 213.

38. Dania Amichay-Michlin, *Ahavat I"sh: Avraham Yosef Stybel* (Jerusalem, 2000), 190.

39. Steven J. Zipperstein, *Elusive Prophet: Ahad Ha'am and the Origins of Zionism* (Berkeley, 1993), 262–265.

40. Persits to Klausner, June(?) 2, 1918, Joseph Klausner Collection, JNUL, collection 4–1086, folder 201; *Kultur-Lige* 1 (1919): 1. Several of the figures encountered in these pages (Litvak, Shtif, Tchernikhovsky) practiced linguistic and literary-historical scholarship. But surprisingly few Hebraists or Yiddishists in this period put scholarship at the center of their culturist agenda. This general disinterest or neglect is especially unexpected given the explosion of Hebraist and Yiddishist scholarship in the interwar period. It may be that some culturists shifted to scholarship precisely insofar as they despaired of grand culturist hopes.

41. Menahem Ribalov, "Ha-mahapekhah ha-medinit ve-sifrutenu," *Ha-'Am*, 17 April 1917.

42. Yosef Klausner, "Keren-zavit," *Ha-Shiloah*, 32, nos. 4–6 (April–June 1917): 415–421; M. Kitai, "Di revolutsye un dos bukh," *Unzer vort* (Odessa), 4 July 1917; Shmuel Niger, "A shmues," *Di yidishe folksblat*, 3 October 1917.

43. "Me-et Tarbut," *Ha-'Am*, 28 April 1917; "Ha-ve'idah ha-rishonah shel hoveve sfat 'ever (hemshekh)," *Ha-'Am*, 5 May 1917.

44. "Tsu di fraynt-lezer," *Yidishe folksblat*, 1 December 1917.

45. Ibid.

46. Undated document (ca. 1918) cited in Dori Parnas, *80 lailah ve-lailah: "Ha-Bimah," 1918–1998* (Tel Aviv, 1998), 8. My thanks to Livia Parnes for providing me with this source.

47. Bialik, "Tarbut ve-'politikah,'" *Ha-Ginah* 6 (July–August 1918): 1–6. The reprinted version in *Kol kitve Bialik* omits the quotes around "politikah," thus obscuring the depth of Bialik's antagonism toward the concept.

48. Ibid., 1.

49. Ibid. Shaped by complicated internecine debates, the essay was further overdetermined by the fact that the two principals enjoyed notoriously dif-

ficult personal relations. But these difficult relations do not explain the logic of Bialik's argument.

50. In his essay "Mi-yotsrim u-vonim li-vne beli bayit," Dan Miron has suggested that competition for national authority was the chief structuring principle of relations between the Hebrew literary sphere and the Zionist movement in Russia. In Miron, *Im lo tihiyeh Yerushalayim: Masot 'al ha-sifrut ha-'ivrit be-heksher tarbuti-politi* (Tel Aviv, 1987). His more detailed analysis of this relationship in *Bodedim be-mo'adam* (Tel Aviv, 1987), however, suggests a considerably more complicated set of concerns at work in Hebraist discourse about "culture and politics." My analysis here seeks to develop this second intuition.

51. Bialik, "Tarbut ve-'politikah.'"

52. "Le-memshelet ha-marsh," *Kol kitve Bialik,* 182; cf. Hamutal Bar-Yosef, "Bialik and the Russian Revolutions," *Jews in Eastern Europe* n.s. 1, no. 29 (1996): 5–31.

53. This also rules out any easy assumption that these formulations were a direct imitation of the parallel discourse in Russian cultural life. Prerevolutionary development of these ideas in Jewish culturist circles was no doubt shaped by the successive articulations of similar ideas in Russian cultural circles; see Jeffrey Brooks, "Literature, Liberalism, and the Idea of Culture: Russia, 1900–1910," Ph.D. diss., Stanford University, 1972.

54. All investigations of the relationship between socialism and nationalism in modern Jewish politics must begin with the late Jonathan Frankel's *Prophecy and Politics: Socialism, Nationalism, and the Russian Jews, 1862–1917* (Cambridge, Eng., 1981), a work to which I am greatly indebted.

55. "Tsu di lezer," *Literarishe monatsshriften* 1 (February 1908).

56. Kenneth B. Moss, "Between Renaissance and Decadence: *Literarishe Monatsshriften* and Its Critical Reception," *Jewish Social Studies,* 8, no. 1 (Fall 2001): 153–198.

57. See translation of "Fun partey-leben: Berikht fun der ershter vilner rayoner konferents" in *Folksshtime* 6 (1907): 76–79 in *Tenu'at "ha-Tehiyah" ("Vozrozhdenie") u-mifleget ha-po'alim ha-yehudit-sotsyalistit (M.P.Y.S.): Mivhar ketavim,* ed. Avraham Greenbaum (Jerusalem, 1988). More generally, see Kenneth Moss, "1905 as a Jewish Cultural Revolution?" in *The Revolution of 1905: A Turning Point in Jewish History?* ed. Stefani Hoffman and Ezra Mendelsohn (Philadelphia, 2008).

58. Miron, *Bodedim,* esp. 335–336; Yosef Klausner, "Megamatenu: Davar me-et ha-'orekh ha-hadash," *Ha-Shiloah* 11 (1902): 6–7; Jaffe to Yaacov Fichman, 5 November 1908, Fichman Collection, Gnazim, record group 8, doc. 4815.

59. Yosef Klausner, "Sifrutenu: Kvutsah shniah," 5; G. Shofman," *Ha-Shiloah* 33, no. 1 (July 1917): 75, 77–78; Klausner, "Ha-hidah 'Tchernikhovsky,'" *Ha-Shiloah* 35, no. 2 (August 1918): 104–105.

60. A. A. Goldenveizer, "Iz kievskikh vospominanii," *Arkhiv russkoi revoliutsii* 6 (Berlin, 1922): 184.

61. "Der kandidaten-tsetl fun der tsionistisher organizatsye," *Oyf der vakh* 9 (12 June 1918); A. Z. Ben-Yishai, "Pirke Ukrainah ('al pi yoman)," *He-'Avar* 18 (1971): 169–173. But see Chapter 5 for further discussion of the Yiddishist left's unfinished relationship with Bialik.

62. Nahman Mayzl, "M. N. Sirkin" (obituary), *Bikher-velt* 1 (January 1919): 43.

63. List of participants, *Yidishe folksblat,* 4 October 1917. In so doing, the journal's editors sought not to innovate but to sustain a tradition of party-independent Yiddishist writing that had flourished in the interrevolutionary years, particularly in the Vilna journal *Di yudishe velt;* but now they did so in the face of a robust, reemergent party politics, and were hence compelled to articulate and enact the principle in a more programmatic fashion.

64. Ibid.; Dinur, *Bi-yeme milḥamah u-mahapekhah: Zikhronot u-reshumot mi-derekh ḥayim* (Jerusalem, 1960), 404–406; Announcement, *Vilna leben* 3–4 (June 1920): 53; Kalmanovitsh to Vayter, 6 September 1918, YIVO, record group 360, folder 34.

65. Ravnitsky to Niger, Tishrei 1917 (17 September–17 October) and 3 Tevet TaRAKh (18 December 1917), YIVO, record group 360, folder 410.

66. Donyel Tsharni to Niger, 22 January 1918, YIVO, record group 360, folder 16.

67. Suggested by Donyel Tsharni to Niger, 13 December 1917, YIVO, record group 360, folder 16.

68. Tsharni to Niger, 13 December and 25 December 1917, YIVO, record group 360, folder 16.

69. Protocol of the Culture Commission of the Ts.-K., 14 March 1918, Collection of the Kievskoi ispolnitel'noe byuro Ts. K. Obedinennoi Evreiskoi Sotsialisticheskoi Rabochei Partii (Fareynikte), DAKO, record group 1786, finding aid 1, folder 16.

70. Protocols of Poale-Tsion meeting, undated (first two pages missing), All-Russian Jewish Workers' Bund Collection, GARF, record group R-8417, finding aid 1, folder 70, docs. 204–206.

71. Protocol, Culture Commission of the Ts.-K., 14 March 1918, DAKO, record group 1786, finding aid 1, folder 16.

72. Protocol of Poale-Tsion meeting, GARF, record group R-8417, finding aid 1, folder 70. Note that although record group R-8417 is supposed to house the papers of the Bund, the final folders (largely Yiddish and even Hebrew materials) are stuffed with largely unrelated documents, many pertaining to the competing Poale Tsion party and its Communist successor, the JCP.

73. Yankev Lestshinsky, "Di yidishe entsiklopedye" *Bikher-velt* 2–3 (March 1919). Lestshinsky's rhetoric is itself telling: to use "yidishe demokratye" rather than

a class-defined term as late as 1919, and in Bolshevik Kiev to boot, was to assert cultural nationalism and culture's autonomy from revolutionary politics.

74. *Di Grunt-oyfgabn fun der Kultur-Lige* (Kiev, 1918), 2–4.

75. Kh. Sh. Kazdan, "Der lebns-veg fun A. Litvak" in A. Litvak, *Geklibene shriftn* (New York, 1945), 112.

76. Kh. Sh. Kazdan, "Di shul- un kultur-tetikeyt," *Geshikhte fun Bund,* vol. 4 (New York, 1972), 333.

77. Moyshe Katz, "Di Kultur Lige in Ukrayne," *Di tsukunft* 3 (March 1921): 185.

78. Zelig Melamed for Temporary Executive of the Kultur-Lige to Niger, 1 January 1918, YIVO, record group 360, folder 817.

79. "Statut tovaristva 'Kulturna liga'," doc. 1 in *Pravda istorii: Dialnist' evreiskoi kulturno-prosviytnits'koi organizatsii "Kulturna Liga" u Kievi (1918–1925),* ed. M. O. Ribakov (Kiev, 1995), 16.

80. Natan Cohen, "Igud ha-soferim veha-'itonaim ha-yehudim be-varshah be-
ḥayav uve-yetsirotav shel Yitsḥok Bashevis-Singer" in *Ben shte milḥamot 'olam: Peraḳim me-ḥaye ha-tarbut shel Yehude Polin li-leshonotehem,* ed. Chone Shmeruk and Shmuel Verses (Jerusalem, 1997), 255.

81. Katz, "Di Kultur Lige," 185.

82. Kalmanovitsh to Niger, 13 November 1918, YIVO, record group 360, folder 34; M. L., "Tsuzamenfor," May 1919, TsDAVO, record group 3304, finding aid 1, folder 2.

83. Protocols of the Novgorod-Seversk Kultur-Lige Group meeting, 5/18 November 1918, TsDAHOU, record group 41, finding aid 1, folder 21.

84. "Der kandidaten-tsetl fun der tsionistisher organizatsye," *Oyf der vakh* 9 (12 June 1918); M. L. "Tsuzamenfor," TsDAVO, record group 3304, finding aid 1, folder 2, docs. 5a–9.

85. Nirenberg's comments are reprinted in "Vserossiiskaia konferentsiia Bunda," *Novyi Put'* (23 April 1917); on the respect accorded him, see Kalmanovitsh to Niger, 13 November 1918, YIVO, record group 360, folder 34.

86. Dinur, *Bi-yeme* 316; L. Brovarnik, Executive Bureau, Kultur-Lige Central Committee to Dinur, 9 July 1919, Dinur Collection, CAHJP.

87. Kalmanovitsh to Niger, 13 November 1918, YIVO, record group 360, folder 34.

88. See *Kultur-lige* 1 (1919): 1; M. L. "Tsuzamenfor," 12–13. The politics sur-
rounding the Kultur-Lige and Yiddish culture in the framework of Bolshevik rule in Ukraine in 1919 will be dealt with extensively in Chapter 6.

89. L. E. Motyliev, *Osnovy evreiskago obshchinnago ustroistva* (Moscow, 1918), 43.

90. Kazdan, "Di shul- un kultur-tetikeyt," 333–334.

91. Bialik, "Tarbut ve-'politikah.'"

92. Kulbak, "Dos yidishe vort," 242.

93. A. Golomb, *A halber yorhundert yidishe dertsiung* (Rio de Janeiro, 1957), 101.

94. *Grunt-oyfgabn,* 16.

3. Unfettering Hebrew and Yiddish Culture

Epigraphs: Moyshe Litvakov, "Di sistem fun iberzetsungen II," *Bikher-velt* 4–5 (August 1919): 42; A. Ben-Moshe [Litai], "Sifrut ha-'olam," *Ha-Shiloaḥ* 34, nos. 5–6 (April 1918): 540.

1. "Hofshteyn, Dovid," in Zalman Reyzen, *Leksikon fun der yidisher literatur* (Vilna, 1928).
2. Y. Dobrushin, "Dray dikhter," *Oyfgang* (Kiev, 1919), 95.
3. Ibid.
4. Hofshteyn, "Nemen," cited in full in ibid. My translation.
5. Translation by Chana Kronfeld in Kronfeld, *On the Margins of Modernism: Decentering Literary Dynamics* (Berkeley, 1996), 214. See also her close analysis immediately following.
6. Dobrushin, "Dray dikhter," 94–95. Many critics, including recent readers of Hofshteyn, have found a very different relationship between his poetry and Jewish tradition, finding many of his poems replete with Jewish intertexts. For the purposes of the cultural historian, however, this fact makes Dobrushin's insistence that Hofshteyn had transcended this practice all the more interesting and significant.
7. Ibid.
8. Ibid.
9. See important recent accounts in Roskies, *A Bridge of Longing: The Lost Art of Yiddish Storytelling* (Cambridge, Mass., 1995); Mark Kiel, "A Twice Lost Legacy: Ideology, Culture, and the Pursuit of Jewish Folklore in Russian until Stalinization (1930–1931)," Ph.D. diss., Jewish Theological Seminary, 1991; and Adam Rubin, "From Torah to Tarbut: Hayim Nahman Bialik and the Nationalization of Judaism," Ph.D. diss., UCLA, 2000.
10. Bialik, "Ha-sefer ha-'ivri," in *Kol kitve Ḥ. N. Bialik* (Tel Aviv, 1955), 196.
11. Ibid., 194.
12. Bialik, "Tse'irut o yaldut?" in *Kol kitve Bialik,* 203; ibid., 201.
13. Mark Kiel, "Vox Populi, Vox Dei: The Centrality of Peretz in Jewish Folkloristics," *Polin* 7 (1992): 88–120.
14. An-ski, "Der yudisher folks-gayst un zayn shafn," in *Gezamlte shriftn,* vol. 5 (Vilna, 1920), 15–18, 21–26.
15. Pinhas Schiffman, "Aḥdut ha-lashon," *Ha-Shiloaḥ* 35, no. 1 (July 1918): 65. For those who sought to create a modern Jewish culture in the spirit of indigenous sources, 1917–1919 was a watershed in another respect as well. Figures like Bialik and Peretz had privileged one line of tradition without negating the other entirely; Peretz had placed the Bible at the center of his Jewish cultural canon and Bialik had made an important place for folklore. But the sundering of the Jewish cultural project into two opposing monolingualist Yiddishist

and Hebraist camps at the 1917–1919 juncture divided the indigenizing approach largely along Zionist-Hebraist-classicist versus Yiddishist-Diasporist-folkist lines. See Kenneth B. Moss, "'A Time to Tear Down and a Time to Build Up': Recasting Jewish Culture in Eastern Europe, 1917–1921," Ph.D. diss., Stanford University, 2003, chs. 2–3. The resulting division, however, did not alter the basic cultural logic of the indigenizing strategy for its champions in each camp.

16. See the discussion in John Hutchinson, *Modern Nationalism* (London, 1994), ch. 2. Hutchinson's detailed discussion of Irish nationalist strategies of cultural formation in the nineteenth century is considerably more complex; see Hutchinson, *Dynamics of Cultural Nationalism* (London, 2003).

17. David Frishman, "'Al ha-sifrut ha-yafah," *Kol kitve David Frishman,* vol. 8 (Warsaw, 1932), 57–58; Iris Parush, *Kanon sifruti ve-ideologyah le'umit* (Jerusalem, 1992).

18. A. Litai, "Perishut sikhlit o hitbollelut," *Ha-'Am,* 10 March 1917.

19. Moyshe Litvakov, "Di sistem fun iberzetsungen II," *Bikher-velt* (Kiev) 4–5 (August 1919): 37.

20. A. Ben-Moshe [Litai], "Sifrut ha-'olam," *Ha-Shiloah* 34, nos. 5–6 (April 1918): 540–546.

21. Ben-Eliezer, "'Al ha-targumim," *Kneset* (Odessa, 1917), 319. The contents of the anthology were evidently written well before February 1917, and publication was delayed by old regime censorship. See ch. 1.

22. Moyshe Litvakov, "Di sistem fun iberzetsungen I," *Bikher-velt* 1 (January 1919): 9–12; Litvakov, "Di sistem II," 37, 41.

23. "'Hotsa'at Stybel' be-'arikhat David Frishman," *Ha-Tekufah* 2 (March–May 1918): back matter.

24. Yosef Klausner, "Keren-zavit: Nitsahon," *Ha-Shiloah* 35, nos. 3–4 (September–October 1918): 344.

25. Litvakov, "Di sistem II," 42–43.

26. L. Gomlen, "Kritik un bibliografye: Poezye un beletristik: *Himel un erd,*" *Bikher-velt* 2–3 (March 1919): 42.

27. E. Shteynman, "Hotsa'at Stybel" in "Ma'amarim u-reshimot," in *Erets: Ma'asef le-sifrut yafah ule-vikoret* (Odessa, 1919), 29–30. On *Erets,* see Yehoshua A. Gilboa, *Oktobra'im 'ivriim: Toldotehah shel ashlayah* (Tel Aviv, 1974), 17–19.

28. Ben-Moshe, "Sifrut ha-'olam," 543.

29. On the Vsemirnaia Literatura project, see Ol'ga D. Golubeva, *Gorkii—Izdatel'* (Moscow, 1968), 96–99, 100, 110; A. D. Zaidman, "Literaturnye studii 'Vsemirnoi Literatury' i 'Doma Iskusstv' (1919–1921 gody)," *Russkaia literatura* 16, no. 1 (1973): 141–142. For a comparison with the Jewish case during 1917–1919, see Kenneth B. Moss, "Not *The Dybbuk* but *Don Quixote:* Translation, Deparochialization, and Nationalism in Jewish Culture, 1917–

1919" in *Culture Front,* ed. Benjamin Nathans and Gabriella Safran (Philadelphia, 2008).

30. Litvakov, "Di sistem I," 10 and "Di sistem II," 37, 41. For a direct comparison (and contrast) with the patterns of intention visible in prewar translations, especially into Yiddish, see Moss, "Not *The Dybbuk* but *Don Quixote.*"

31. Litvakov, "Di sistem II," 37–38, 43.

32. Ben-Moshe, "Sifrut ha-'olam," 541.

33. Parush, *Kanon sifruti,* ch. 12.

34. Litvakov, "Di sistem II," 38.

35. A. B. M. [Aharon Ben-Moshe; Aharon Litai], "*Ha-Tekufah* [review]" *Masuot* 1 (1919): 605.

36. Frishman to Bialik, 15/28 April and May 11/24 1918, *Keneset: Divre soferim le-zekher Ḥ. N. Bialik,* 5 (1940): 34–35; Stybel to Bialik, 27 April 1918, Beit Bialik, correspondence collection.

37. Writing in the Yishuv in 1919, Yaacov Steinberg voiced a similar notion of "gaps" in a putative universal literary structure. See Zohar and Yaacov Shavit, "Lemale' et ha-arets sefarim: Sifrut mekorit le'umat sifrut meturgemet be-tahalikh yetsirato shel ha-merkaz ha-sifruti be-erets yisrael," *Ha-Sifrut* 25 (1977): 55.

38. E. Korman, "*Fremds,*" *Bikher-velt* 4–5 (December 1919): 56.

39. See, e.g., Nister's negotiation of Andersen or Ha-Meiri's relationship to Hungarian Decadent Endre Ady; see, respectively, Roskies, *Bridge of Longing,* 202, and the translations of Endre Ady by Avigdor Feuerstein (Ha-Meiri) in *Erets: Ma'asef le-sifrut yafah ule-vikoret* (Odessa, 1919), 149–156.

40. David Frishman, *Mikhtavim ḥadashim 'al devar ha-sifrut* (Berlin, 1922–1923), 6–7.

41. Ben-Eliezer, "'Al ha-targumim," 319.

42. Tellingly, the logic of their stance echoed that voiced a century earlier by the German Romantic Friedrich Schleiermacher: "An inner necessity, in which a peculiar calling of our people expresses itself clearly enough, has driven us to translating en masse; we cannot go back and we must go on. Just as our soil itself has no doubt become richer and more fertile and our climate milder and more pleasant only after much transplantation of foreign flora, just so we sense that our language, because we exercise it less owing to our Nordic sluggishness, can thrive in all its freshness and completely develop its own power only through the most many-sided contacts with what is foreign." Friedrich Schleiermacher, "On the Different Methods of Translation," in *German Romantic Criticism,* ed. A. Leslie Willson (New York, 1982), 28–29.

43. Shteynman, "Hotsa'at Stybel," 30.

44. Klausner, "Keren-zavit: Nitsaḥon," 343; Ben-Eliezer, "'Al ha-targumim," 319–320.

45. Shteynman, "Hotsa'at Stybel," 30.

46. Litvakov, "Di sistem II," 42.

47. Ibid., 37; Lit, "Kritik un bibliografye: *Eygns*," 25.

48. Yosef Klausner, "Sifrutenu 4: 'Al Bialik," *Ha-Shiloah* 32, no. 4 (April–June 1917): 453.

49. Marcus Moseley, *Being for Myself Alone: Origins of Jewish Autobiography* (Stanford, 2006), 212–234.

50. Yosef Klausner, "Ha-ḥidah 'Tshernihovski,'" *Ha-Shiloah* 35, no. 2 (August 1918): 104–105.

51. Aleph, "Genizah ve-ḥatimah," in "Ma'amarim u-reshimot," a section of *Erets: Ma'asef le-sifrut yafah ule-vikoret* (Odessa, 1919), 28–29.

52. Bialik, "Ha-sefer ha-'ivri," 195–196; Rubin, "From Torah to Tarbut."

53. Aleph, "Genizah," 28.

54. *Kultur-Lige* 1 (1919): 38.

55. Ravnitsky to Bialik, 20 August 1918, Beit Bialik, correspondence collection.

56. "Shoshana Persits" in David Tidhar, *Entsiklopedyah le-ḥalutse ha-yishuv u-vonav*, vol. 17 (Tel Aviv, 1947–1971), 2825.

57. See, for example, "Mi-sipure Korea," *Shetilim* 3 (2 August 1917): 40–44.

58. Uriel Ofek, *Gumot Ḥe"N: Po'alo shel Bialik be-sifrut ha-yeladim* (Tel Aviv, 1984), 71.

59. Dobrushin, "Universal-bibliotek"; "Literarishe nayes," *Bikher-velt* 1 (January 1919): 39.

60. M. D., "K. Zingman: *Motl der shnayder*," *Bikher-velt* 4–5 (December 1919): 53.

61. Donyel Tsharni, *A yortsendlik aza, 1914–1924: Memuarn* (New York, 1943), 227–228; *Shriften: Fremds; Eyropeishe poezye* (Moscow, 19[18?]), inner cover.

62. Ben-Zion Dinur, *Bi-yeme milḥamah u-mahapekhah: Zikhronot u-reshumot mi-derekh ḥayim* (Jerusalem, 1960), 405; *Idisher Folks-farlag* (Kiev, 1920), 8; *Kultur-Lige* 1 (1919): 41–42.

63. See my "Not *The Dybbuk* but *Don Quixote*" for a consideration of the mixed motives of the various publishers.

64. Persits, Stybel, and a founder of the Yiddishist Folks-Farlag were all donors. Subscription list, 1917–1918, S. An-ski collection, RGALI, record group 2583, finding aid 1, folder 8.

65. Nokhem Shtif, *Humanizm in der elterer yidisher literatur* (Berlin, 1922), 63–64, which is the second edition of a work published in 1919 by the Kiev Kultur-Lige.

66. Shaul Tchernikhovsky, preface to *Shire Anakreon* (Varshah, 1920), 3.

67. Citing from first lines of *Iliad*, book 9. I am citing from Tchernikhovsky's translation as it appeared later in book form, *Sefer Ilias*, vol. 1 (Vilna, 1930). Here, I am trying to approximate Tchernikhovsky's Ashkenazi pronunciation.

68. Aminadav Dykman, "Homeros shel Tsherniḥovski," in Boaz Arpali, ed. *Shaul Tsherniḥovski: Ma'amarim u-te'udot* (Jerusalem, 1994), 429.

69. Of course, avoidance of Jewish intertexts could only be relative. Dykman notes many structures and forms reminiscent of Biblical, rabbinic, and liturgical corpi in Tchernikhovsky's translation. The key point here, however, is the attempt to avoid such influences and the product it yielded: a translation in which what Dykman calls Hebraization was "immeasurably less than that in the translations of his predecessors and was not a guiding foundational principle in the translation." Dykman, "Homeros," 456, 447–455. Ironically, Dykman suggests that Tchernikhovsky believed—or came to believe—that his translations recovered a historically real "Canaanite" affinity between the cultures of ancient Greece and ancient Israel (463). But this does not alter the fact of ideological affinity between his translation technique and the larger non-Judaizing agenda examined here.

70. Boaz Arpali, "Tom ve-yedi'ah be-khlil ha-sonitot 'La-shemesh,'" in *La-shemesh: Masot 'al kelil-sonitot le-Shaul Tsherniḥovski,* ed. Zvi Luz (Ramat-Gan, 1996).

71. Quotations are from Robert Alter's extraordinary translation of this poem, "To the Sun" in *Reading Hebrew Literature,* ed. Alan Mintz (Hanover, N.H., 2003), 64–72. All other translations from Tchernikhovsky are my own.

72. Ibid.

73. Ibid.

74. "Song of gold" or *shir zahav* is a Hebrew term for the sonnet that plays on the fact that the numerical value of the Hebrew letters in "gold" *(zahav)* is fourteen. Thanks to Marcus Moseley for pointing this out.

75. "El ha-sonetah ha-'ivrit" and "Ba-shi'amum ha-rav," dated Odessa 1920 and Odessa 1919, respectively, *Kol kitve Shaul Tsherniḥovski* (Tel Aviv, 1990 and 2004): 230, 202.

76. Sh. Tsemah, "Shaul Tsherniḥovski," *Masuot* 1 (1919): 583, 593.

77. See the essays in *Ha-Shiloaḥ (Ḥoveret-Tsherniḥovski)* 35, no. 2 (August 1918).

78. Eliyahu Meitus, "Ha-'ahavah' be-shiratenu ha-tse'irah," *Ha-Shiloaḥ* 33, nos. 2–3 (August–September 1917): 271.

79. M. Gershenzon, "Predislovie," *Evreiskaia antologiia* (Moscow, 1918), viii.

80. Meitus, "Ha-'ahavah,'" 264.

81. Natan Grinblat, "Reshimot sifrutiyot: 'Olamenu," *Ha-Tekufah* 1 (December 1917–February 1918): 673.

82. Seth Wolitz, "The Kiev-Grupe (1918–1920) Debate: The Function of Literature," *Yiddish* 3, no. 3 (1978); P. Reyland, "Bibliografye: Yung treyst," *Baginen* 1 (1919): 115–117; Lit, "Kritik un bibliografye: *Eygns,*" 24.

83. This translation by Chana Kronfeld and Bluma Goldstein appears in Kronfeld, *On the Margins of Modernism,* 204. See also Kronfeld's analysis, 204–208. For

original, see Peretz Markish, "[Veys ikh nit, tsi kh'bin in dr'heym]," in *Shpigl af a shteyn*, ed. Chone Shmeruk (Tel Aviv, 1964), 375–376.

84. Lit, "Kritik un bibliografye: *Eygns*," 24.

85. M. Gnesin, *Darki 'im ha-teatron ha-'ivri* (Tel Aviv, 1946), 132.

86. Aleksander Granovskii, "Our Goals and Objectives," and M. Rivesman, "The Past and Future of Yiddish Theater," both in Benjamin Harshav, *The Moscow Yiddish Theater* (New Haven, 2008), 85, 89.

87. Abram Efros, "Aladdin's Lamp," reprinted in Semyon An-sky, *The Jewish Artistic Heritage*, Alexander Kantsedikas, trans. and ed. (Moscow, 1994), 15.

88. Cited in Hillel Kazovsky, *Khudozhniki Kultur-Ligi: The Artists of the Kultur-Lige* (Moscow, 2003), 66.

89. Y. Ryback and B. Aronson, "Di vegn fun der yidisher moleray," in *Oyfgang* (Kiev, 1919), 99–124.

90. Kazovsky, *Khudozhniki*, 121, n. 68. Kazovsky's selection of artists by institutional affiliation (that is, by dint of their choice to affiliate with the Kultur-Lige) rather than content makes his book an invaluable illustration of the range of what "Jewish art" could mean to its practitioners. His own analysis is alive to the tensions at work in Jewish artists' work, though he does not systematically develop this argument; cf. 100.

91. Verses, "'Bein shne 'olamot'"; Sh. Tshernovits to Ḥ. N. Bialik, 3 November (?) 1917, Beit Bialik, correspondence collection; A. B. M, "*Ha-Tekufah*," 604.

92. Litai, "Perishut sikhlit," 9.

93. Frishman, "'Al ha-sifrut ha-yafah," 57.

94. Ibid.

95. Zeev Livneh (Lerman), "Lifne yovel shanim be-Kiuv [Kiev]: Kit'e zikhronot," *He-'Avar* 16 (1968–1969): 106.

96. Sh. An-ski to Bialik, 10/23 April 1918 in *Bialik ve-sofre doro*, ed. Moshe Ungerfeld (Tel Aviv, 1974).

97. Avigdor Ha-meiri, *Be-gehenom shel matah* (Tel Aviv, 1989), 422–423; Tsharni, *Yortsendlik*, 160–161.

98. For Bialik's speech, see Zerubavel, "Ha-ve'idah ha-rishonah," *Ha-'Am*, 17 April 1917 (reprinted as "Umah ve-lashon" in *Kol kitve Bialik*); on Turgeman, see Ofek, *Gumot He"N*, 65–69.

99. Latski-Bertoldi, "*In Umruh* [review]," *Bikher-velt* 2–3 (March 1919): 27.

100. Litvakov, "Di sistem II," 37.

101. Marcus Moseley argues that this very tension could itself become the key "hermeneutical principle" and generative ground of the new Jewish culture. He identifies this idea with the late Berdichevsky especially. See Moseley, *Being for Myself Alone* and personal communication. Without denying the significance of this essential insight, which could no doubt be extended to other leading figures of twentieth-century Jewish culture from Peretz to Agnon, I do however see powerful tendencies toward more unilateral and total "anti-

parochialism" or "Europeanism" operative in the Jewish cultural sphere from the 1890s on; as I argue later, I also believe this approach had a special relationship to radically monolingualist Hebraism and Yiddishism.

102. A key instance of the former is Nokhem Oyslender; see Mordkhe-Volf Kiel, "Folklor un veltlekhkayt: Nokhem Oyslenders *Grunt-shtrikhn fun yidishn realizm*," *YIVO-Bleter* n.s. 4 (2003): 259–262. On Tsemah, see also Shlomo Tsemah, *Sipur ḥayai* (Jerusalem, 1983), 102–103.

103. Judith Bar-El, "The National Poet: The Emergence of a Concept in Hebrew Literary Criticism (1885–1905)," *Prooftexts* 6 (1986): 214–215; Chone Shmeruk, *Peretses yiesh-vizye* (New York, 1971), 7–8, esp. n. 9; Yaacov Shavit, *Athens in Jerusalem* (London, 1997), 245.

104. Dan Miron, *Bodedim be-mo'adam* (Tel Aviv, 1987), 35–38; Bertoldi (Zeev Latski), "Yudishkayt un yuden, oder, vegen yudisher apikorsus," *Di yudishe velt* 1, no. 2 (February 1914): 228–246; David Fishman, *The Rise of Modern Yiddish Culture* (Pittsburgh, 2005), 101–102.

105. Bertoldi, "Yudishkayt un yuden," 237.

106. Yosef Klausner, "Ha-ḥidah 'Tshernihovski,'" *Ha-Shiloaḥ* 35, no. 2 (August 1918): 104–105.

107. Grinberg, "Bor'ba za natsional'nuiu individual'nost," *Sborniki "Safrut"* 1 (Moscow, 1917): 67.

108. Ibid., 64–69, 90.

109. Natan Bistritski, "Shiḥrur ha-prat," *Tarbut: Yediot ha-va'ad ha-merkazi* (Kiev) 2 (28 August 1918): 5–7.

110. Latski-Bertoldi, *"In Umruh,"* 30.

111. Translator's comment to Endre, "Shirim," in *Erets: Ma'asef le-sifrut yafah ule-vikoret* (Odessa, 1919), 149.

112. Klausner, "Keren-zavit: Nitsaḥon," 344.

113. Charles Taylor, *Sources of the Self* (Cambridge, Eng., 1989), 415.

4. To Make Our Masses Intellectual

Epigraph: Kultur-Lige 1 (1919): 1.

1. Executive Committee, Tarbut branch in Zvinihorodkah to Klausner, 14 Nisan (27 March) 1918 and Tarbut branch in Zvinihorodkah to *Ha-Shiloaḥ*, Klausner Collection, JNUL, collection 4–1086, folder 211; see Chapter 3.

2. Bistritsky to Klausner, 31 July 1918, and Bistritsky to Klausner, undated (postmarked 18 September 1918), JNUL, collection 4–1086, folder 211.

3. Steven J. Zipperstein, *Elusive Prophet: Ahad Ha'am and the Origins of Zionism* (Berkeley, 1993), 262–265, ch. 2.

4. Steven Guthier, "The Popular Base of Ukrainian Nationalism in 1917," *Slavic Review* 38, no. 1 (1979).

5. The genealogy of this loaded association among women, education, and as-

similation dates back to well before the national movement itself, and played an important role in the anti-assimilationist (and in some formulations "proto-nationalist") turn of certain Jewish enlighteners in the 1860s and 1870s. See Shmuel Feiner, "Ha-ishah ha-yehudiah ha-modernit: Mikreh-mivḥan be-yaḥase ha-haskalah veha-modernah," *Zion* 58, no. 4 (1992–1993): 453–499. Yet however ideologically loaded, this image also captured a fascinating sociological reality. Many Hebrew and Yiddish cultural producers seem to have had Russified sisters, some more accomplished than their brothers in many respects (e.g., Ester Eliasheva, who was sister of the literary critic Baal-Makhshoves, holder of a German doctorate, and author of a 1922 essay entitled, in Yiddish, "The Third Sex"). I am currently investigating the complex social and representational structures of relations between the sexes as part of research on relations between nationalists and non-nationalists within Russian Jewish society.

6. Ben-Yankev [Kalman Zingman], *In der tsukunft-shtot "Edenyah": Roman,* republished in A. Zimrani, ed., *Be-'ir he-'atid 'Edenyah* (Tel Aviv, 1996), 40–41.

7. Charles Rougle, "The Intelligentsia Debate in Russia, 1917–1918," in *Art, Society, Revolution: Russia, 1917–1921,* ed. Nils Ake Nilsson (Stockholm, 1979), 57, 96–98; Lynn Mally, *Culture of the Future: The Proletkult Movement in Revolutionary Russia* (Berkeley, 1990), xvi; Paul Robert Magosci, *A History of Ukraine* (Toronto, 1996), 491; D. Rozovyk, *Ukraïns'ke kul'turne vidrodzhennia v roky natsional'no-demokratychnoï revoliutsiï, 1917–1920* (Kiev, 2002).

8. Rougle, "Intelligentsia Debate," 69; Boris I. Kolonitskii, "Antibourgeois Propaganda and Anti-'Burzhui' Consciousness in 1917," *Russian Review* 53, no. 2 (1994): 183–196.

9. Yaakov Leshtshinsky, *Ha-yehudim ba-rusiyah ha-sovietit* (Tel Aviv, 1943), 209–220; Nahman Mayzl and Zelig Melamed to Shmuel Niger, undated [1921], YIVO, record group 360, folder 283.

10. Yitshok Zelig mi-Sokolov, *Ma'amarim u-mikhtavim miha-rav ha-kadosh morenu ve-rabenu Yitshok Zelig shalit"a mi-Sokolov: Ḥoveret aleph* (Warsaw, 1926–1927), 5.

11. Gershon Bacon, *The Politics of Tradition* (Jerusalem, 1996), ch. 2; Mendel Piekarz, *Ḥasidut Polin* (Jerusalem, 1990), esp. 21–22.

12. Matthew Arnold, *Culture and Anarchy, 1867–69,* ed. Stefan Collini (Cambridge, Eng., 1993), 79; *Kultur-Lige* 1 (1919): 1; "Me-et Tarbut," *Ha-'Am,* 28 April 1917.

13. Ben-Yankev, *Tsukunft-shtot,* 18–19.

14. "Protokol-zased. Bibliot. Komissii," 3 September 1915, TsIAM, record group 2309, finding aid 1, folder 141, doc. 36. On the 1916 "Tambov decision," see A. Levinson, *Ha-Ten'uah ha-'ivrit ba-golah* (Warsaw, 1935), 38–39.

15. Ben-Tsion Dinur, "Ba-merkaz ha-Kiuvi," *He-'Avar* 7 (1960): 15.

16. Sh. Tshernovits to H. N. Bialik, 3 November (?) 1917, Beit Bialik, correspondence collection; Sfog (Tshernovits), "Ha-Bimah" in *Ha-'Am,* 27 January 1917.

17. *Kultur-lige* 2 (June–July 1920): 50–59; Carole Balin, *To Reveal Our Hearts: Jewish Women Writers in Tsarist Russia* (Cincinnati, 2000), 138.

18. "Ha-ve'idah ha-rishonah shel Hoveve Sfat 'Ever: hemshekh," *Ha-'Am,* 5 May 1917, 16.

19. "Ishurah shel ḥevrat 'Tarbut,'" *Tarbut* 2 (28 August 1918): 17; Melamed to Niger, 1 January 1918, YIVO, record group 360, folder 817.

20. Central Committee of Tarbut, Ukraine Branch, circular 3, Menaḥem Av [10 July–9 August 1918], TsDAHOU, record group 41, finding aid 1, folder 255. *Tarbut* 2 was dedicated to the "Week of the Land of Israel."

21. *Kultur-Lige* 1 (1919): 43; *Kultur-Lige: Ershtes zamlheft* (Warsaw, 1921), 22.

22. "Khronik," *Shul un lebn* (Kiev) 1 (December 1918): 71–72; Kultur-Lige Central Committee Executive Bureau, circular 5, Kiev, April 1919, GARF, record group R-8417, finding aid 1, folder 72, doc. 133.

23. "Obshchii obzor deiatel'nosti o-va 'Tarbut' za period ot VI-XI 1917 goda," CZA, record group F-30, folder 98/1; G. Kohelet, "'Avodat ha-Tarbut ba-'avar uve-'atid," *Ha-Toren* 23 (22 August 1919): 12; Kalmanovitsh to Niger, 13[?] November 1918, YIVO, record group 360, folder 34; Kalmanovitsh to Vayter, 3 September [1918], YIVO, record group 360, folder 34; Central Council of Tarbut, circular 7, and [?] to M. Ussishkin, 25 August 1918, Ussishkin Collection, CZA, record group A24, folder 145/1(7); Benyamin Lukin, "'An Academy Where Folklore Will Be Studied': An-sky and the Jewish Museum," in *The Worlds of S. An-sky: A Russian Jewish Intellectual at the Turn of the Century,* ed. Gabriella Safran and Steven J. Zipperstein (Stanford, 2006), 303–304. On prewar *farraynen,* see Michael Steinlauf, "Fear of Purim: Y. L. Peretz and the Canonization of Yiddish Theater," *Jewish Social Studies,* n.s. 3 (1995): 47.

24. "Me-et Tarbut," 23.

25. *Idisher Folks-Farlag* (Kiev, 1920), 3.

26. "Shetilim" (Advertisement), *Ha-'Am,* 16 July 1917.

27. *Ustav evreiskago dramaticheskago obshchestva "Gabima,"* TsIAM, record group 2309, finding aid 1, folder 313.

28. Brovarnik to Dinur, 9 July 1919, Dinur Collection, CAHJP; *Di Grunt-oyfgabn fun der Kultur-Lige* (1918), 16.

29. *Kultur-Lige* 2 (1920): 55; and Seth Wolitz, "The Jewish National Art Renaissance in Russia," in *Tradition and Revolution: The Jewish Renaissance in Russian Avant-Garde Art, 1912–1928,* ed. Ruth Apter-Gabriel (Jerusalem, 1988), 38–39.

30. "A por verter," foreword to Reb Mordkhele, *Mesholim* (Katerinoslav, 1919).

31. Miriam Katchansky, "Hibat-Zion and Yiddish: The Multidimensional En-

counter between Movement, Language, and Culture," Ph.D. diss., Jewish
Theological Seminary, 2002; Moyshe Olgin, "Di yidishe shprakh in undzer
privat-lebn," reprinted in *Never Say Die! A Thousand Years of Yiddish in Jewish
Life and Letters,* ed. Joshua A. Fishman (The Hague, 1981), 551–563; on the
Russian case, see Jeffrey Brooks, *When Russia Learned to Read* (Evanston, 2003
[1985]), ch. 9. This chapter owes much to insights by my colleague Jeff Brooks
regarding the very different and even opposing ways of pursuing an ideal of
cultural fusion between intelligentsia and "folk."

32. *Shul un lebn* 1 (December 1918): 79.

33. *Kultur-Lige* 1 (1919): 5.

34. *Shul un lebn* 1 (December 1918): 72.

35. "Beynish Shteyman," obituary, *Oyfgang* (Kiev, 1919), 131–132; "Shteyman, Beynish," in *Leksikon fun der nayer Yidisher literatur* (New York, 1981).

36. This formulation was first suggested to me by David Myers of UCLA.

37. "Tsu di lezer," *Literarishe monatsshriften* 1 (February 1908): 1–3.

38. Levinson, *Ha-Tenu'ah ha-'ivrit,* 11–15, 35–37; Shmuel Ayzenshtadt, "Le-toldot ha-tsiburiut veha-tarbut ha-'ivrit be-rusiyah bi-thilat ha-me'ah ha-'esrim," *He-'Avar* 15 (1968): 138.

39. Kenneth B. Moss, "Between Renaissance and Decadence: *Literarishe Monatsshriften* and Its Critical Reception," *Jewish Social Studies,* 8, no. 1 (Fall 2001): 153–198.

40. Kenneth Moss, "Bringing Culture to the Nation: Hebraism, Yiddishism, and the Dilemmas of Dissemination, 1917–1919," in *Jewish History* 22, no. 3 (September 2008) investigates the actual reception of the new culture beyond intelligentsia circles.

41. Ben-Zion Dinur, *Bi-yeme milhamah u-mahapekhah: Zikhronot u-reshumot mi-derekh hayim* (Jerusalem, 1960), 389; Zeev Livneh (Lerman), "Lifne yovel shanim be-Kiuv: Kit'e zikhronot," *He-'Avar* 16 (1968–1969): 106.

42. *Kultur-Lige* 1 (1919): 22.

43. For suggestive comments on this generation of Hebrew cultural creators' being at home more in Russian culture than in Jewish tradition, see Dan Miron, *Imahot meyasdot, ahayot horgot* (Tel Aviv, 1991), 88–89.

44. "Excerpt from a letter," 21 November 1921, Jewish Section of the Central Committee of the Ukrainian Communist Party Collection, TsDAHOU, record group 1, finding aid 20, folder 782, doc. 128.

45. Thus, the Kultur-Lige school in Medzhibozh reported 84 girls and 13 boys in 1919. Report, Medzhib. Id. Folks-shul "Mendele Mokher Sforim," TsDAVO, record group 2060, finding aid 1, folder 41, doc. 18. That this imbalance was not accidental can be seen from that fact that throughout the interwar period, the Yiddishist schools of interwar Lithuania recorded a 75–25 percent imbalance in favor of girls; Eliyohu Shulman: "Di yidish-veltlekhe shuln in Lite" in *Lite,* vol. 2, ed. Ch. Leikowicz (Tel Aviv, 1965), 339.

46. "Me-et Tarbut," 22. On recruiting in the synagogue, see Agudat ha-Tsionim bene ḥorin Pishtshanke to Zionist bureau, Kiev region 29 Sivan 1917 [19 June 1917], TsDAHOU, record group 41, finding aid 1, folder 242.

47. Pinḥas Govrin, *Hayinu ke-ḥolmim: Megilat mishpaḥah* (Jerusalem, 2005), 161.

48. This composite portrait is based on handbills and programs from 1917–1918 in TsDAHOU, record group 41, folder 266.

49. "Tshemerinsky, Baruch: Kavim le-toldot ḥayav, reshumim be-yade ʿatsmo," Gnazim, collection of questionnaires.

50. "Tokhnit le-haskalat ʿam ba-kehillah ha-ʿivrit ha-Kiuvit," manuscript, GARF, record group R-8417, finding aid 1, folder 72, doc. 168, part 3. The quoted material is in a footnote, and marked with a question mark.

51. *Shul un lebn* 1 (December 1918): 55–56, 76.

52. A. Zaidman, "Ha-otonomiyah ha-leʾumit ha-yehudit ba-Ukrainah ha-ʿatsmait ba-shanim, 1917–1919," Ph.D. diss., Tel Aviv University, 1980, 180.

53. *Shul un lebn* 1 (December 1918): 55–56. Thanks to Anne Eakin Moss for clarifying the *klassnyi nastavnik* reference.

54. Inspector of Kremenets Jewish upper-level elementary school to Ministry of Education, 15 January 1919, TsDAVO, record group 2060, finding aid 1, folder 41 regarding zemstvo support from April 1918; *Shul un lebn* 1 (December 1918): 72–76.

55. *Shul un Lebn* 2 (January 1919): 95.

56. Daniel Orlovsky, "The Provisional Government and Its Cultural Work," in *Bolshevik Culture: Experiment and Order in the Russian Revolution,* ed. Abbot Gleason, Peter Kenez, and Richard Stites (Bloomington, 1985), 48–49.

57. On the idea of the consecratory power of the state and its role in the consolidation and institutionalization of national culture, see Pierre Bourdieu, "Rethinking the State: Genesis and Structure of the Bureaucratic Field," *Sociological Theory* 12, no.1 (March 1994): 4–9.

58. G. Gurevitsh, chairman, Jewish Society for the Encouragement of Art to Ministry for Jewish Affairs, Department of National Education, 22 April 1918, TsDAVO, record group 1748, finding aid 1, folder 100.

59. Zaidman, "Ha-otonomiyah," 164.

60. N. Mayzl, "Dos yidishe bukh in Ukraine," *Bikher-velt* 1 (January 1919): 6–8; Kalmanovitsh to Vayter, 3 September 1918 and 13 November 1918, YIVO, record group 360, folder 34.

61. A. Z. Ben-Yishai, "Sifrut ve-ʿitonut ʿivrit be-rusiyah bi-tkufat ha-mahapekhah ve-aḥareihah," *He-ʿAvar* 15 (1968): 163–166; Dan Miron, *Bodedim be-moʾadam* (Tel Aviv, 1987), 44–47.

62. Miron, *Bodedim,* 97–99.

63. A. Litai, "Perishut sikhlit o hitbollelut," *Ha-ʿAm,* 10 March 1917, 10.

64. Gennady Estraikh, *In Harness: Yiddish Writers' Romance with Communism*

(Syracuse, 2005), 25; Zalman Reyzen, "Melamed, Zelig" in *Leksikon fun der nayer Yidisher literatur* (New York, 1981), 434–435.

65. Estraikh offers a richly informative portrait of the material and social dimensions of prewar Yiddish literary life in *In Harness,* 6–26. See also Chone Shmeruk, *Peretses yiesh-vizye* (New York, 1971), 16–17.

66. At least some of Omanut's publications for children were beautiful books with lush color illustrations, in sharp contrast to the chapbook format of the Yiddish children's books produced by Odessa's Farlag Blimelekh or the Kiever Farlag. See Yehuda Slutsky, "Ha-pirsumim ha-'ivriyim be-vrit ha-mo'atsot ba-shanim 1917–1960," in *Pirsumim yehudiyim be-Vrit ha-Mo'atsot, 1917–1960,* ed. Yitshak Yosef Kohen (Jerusalem, 1961), 32–34. According to one observer, Stybel's books were more beautiful than any contemporary Russian publishing efforts. Ben-Tsion Katz, "Ka-avor tekufah," *Ha-Tsefirah* (Warsaw), 4 March 1927. On Berlin, see David Roskies, *A Bridge of Longing: The Lost Art of Yiddish Storytelling* (Cambridge, Mass., 1995), 192–193.

67. I have not yet been able to find sources generated by the presses themselves that shed much light on their financial and organizational structure. With regard to Omanut in particular, I rely on descriptions in various memoirs and the unreferenced summation in Shavit, *Ha-ḥayim ha-sifrutiim be-erets Yisrael, 1910–1933* (Tel Aviv, 1982), 221–222, which notes that it was founded "on a patronage basis." Shavit's statement that the press did not expect profits and that its patrons could cover its losses refers specifically to its activities in Palestine after 1926, but it seems that the same situation obtained in revolutionary Russia.

68. Calculation based on information available at http://www.measuringworth .com.

69. [Aryeh Rafaeli?], "Zikhronot mehe-'avar ha-karov," CZA, record group F-30, folder 98/1; Adam Rubin, "From Torah to Tarbut: Hayim Nahman Bialik and the Nationalization of Judaism," Ph.D. diss., UCLA, 2000, 175–176.

70. Ben-Yishai, "Sifrut," 168.

71. Citing from Natan Goren, *Demuyot bi-sifrutenu* (Tel Aviv, 1953), 71.

72. Bergelson to An-ski, 14 August 1916, An-ski Collection, Vernadsky, collection 339, folder 551, where Bergelson describes Kletskin's generosity and invites An-ski to join them.

73. It did receive the support of a wealthy patron for its art section.

74. M. Katz, "Di Kultur-Lige in Ukrayne," 185; and Kalmanovitsh to Vayter, 3 September [1918], YIVO, record group 360, folder 34. As of early 1919, the publishing houses in question included the Kiever Farlag, Kletskin's Vilna Farlag Ukraine branch, the Folks Farlag, Di Velt, Onhoyb, Der Hamer, and Odessa's Blimelakh. By November 1919, the list had changed slightly: Kiever Farlag, the Folks Farlag, Di Velt, Onhoyb, Dos Nay-Lebn and the Kultur-Lige's own pub-

lishing imprint. See Kultur-Lige to the Ministry of Jewish Affairs of Ukrainian People's Republic, undated [probably January 1919], TsDAVO, record group 2060, finding aid 1, folder 4; *Kultur-Lige* 1 (1919): 42.

75. "Tsentraler bikher-lager' fun 'kultur-lige,'" *Bikher-velt* 1 (January 1919): 44; Kultur-Lige to the Ministry of Jewish Affairs of the Ukrainian People's Republic, 9 January 1919, TsDAVO, record group 2060, finding aid 1, folder 41; Kalmanovitsh to Niger, 13 (?) November 1918, YIVO, record group 360, folder 34. Book costs are based on Kiever-Farlag listings in *Eygns* 1 (1918) and *Bikher-velt* 1 (January 1919); prices remained roughly the same across this span of time.

76. *Grunt-oyfgabn,* 32; *Kultur-Lige* 1 (1919): 39–42. Kultur-Lige to the Ministry of Jewish Affairs of Ukrainian People's Republic, undated [probably January 1919], TsDAVO, record group 2060, finding aid 1, folder 41, docs. 13–14.

77. Moyshe Katz, "Di Kultur Lige in Ukrayne," *Di tsukunft* 3 (March 1921): 185. Details on these presses are few. Farlag "Rampe" in Kharkov and "Yunge Harpe" in Ekaterinoslav published lowbrow comedies, including the then-famous "Khatzkele"; Z. Elin, "Kritik un bibliografye: Poezye un beletristik," *Bikher-velt* 2–3 (March 1919): 50–51.

78. [The editors], "Tsu di lezer," in *Literarishe Monatsshriften* (Vilna) 1 (February 1908): 2.

79. *Shul un lebn* 1 (December 1918): 71, 79.

80. Ibid.; Bialik, "Ha-omanut ha-tehorah," in *Kol kitve H̦. N. Bialik* (Tel Aviv, 1955), 255.

5. The Liberation of the Jewish Individual

Epigraphs: Nokhem Shtif, Humanizm in der elterer yidisher literatur (Kiev, 1919), 7; Natan Bistritsky, "Shiḥrur ha-prat" Tarbut 2 (August 1918): 6.

1. On the lecture in Odessa, see Natan Goren, *Pirke Bialik* (Tel Aviv, 1949), 66; on Moscow, see Haim Grinberg, "Halokhe un agode" in *Yid un velt* (Buenos-Aires, 1960), 140. The essay subsequently appeared in *Kneset* (1917) and *Sborniki "Safrut"* 1 (1918).

2. H. N. Bialik, "Halakhah ve-aggadah," in *Kol kitve H̦. N. Bialik* (Tel Aviv, 1955), 212.

3. Ibid., 207.

4. Ibid., 213.

5. Ibid.

6. Ibid.

7. Grinberg, "Halokhe un agode"; Pinḥas Ginossar, "Bialik, Berl, ve-Brener: 'Halakhah ve-Aggadah' u-shte teguvot," in *Ha-sifrut ha-ʿivrit u-tenuʿat ha-ʿavodah,* ed. Ginossar (Beer-Sheva, 1989).

8. In this regard, one of the key moves early in the essay is its attribution of agency and action not to *aggadah* but to *halakhah:* "The dream is drawn to its interpretation, the desire to the deed, the thought to the word, the flower to the fruit—and the *aggadah* to the *halakhah.*" Bialik, "Halakhah ve-aggadah," 207.

9. This was the fundamental claim of Bialik's 1918 "Tarbut ve-'politikah'"; see Chapter 2.

10. It should be noted that "Halakhah and Aggadah" may be read in a more properly philosophical way as a groping expression of the view that it might simply be impossible to create a law-giving culture in a secular age. Thus, although Bialik can give many examples of modern forms of "aggadah" (art, most obviously), he does not (because he cannot?) adduce a modern, secular equivalent of *halakhah.* For our purposes, however, it suffices to claim that Bialik, whatever his private doubts (or the ultimate thrust of his thought), evidently wished the essay to be read as a corrective for the cultural project rather than a renunciation of it.

11. Menahem Ribalov, "*Kneset:* Bikoret (sof)," *Ha-Shiloah* 33, no. 5 (December 1917), 511–513; Yaacov Fichman, "Ba'ale ha-aggadah," *Ha-Ginah* 1 (September–October 1917); Fichman, "'Im Bialik: Zikhronot u-reshimot mi-pinkasi," *Keneset: Divre sofrim le-zekher H. N. Bialik* 2 (1937): 73.

12. D. A. Fridman, "Ba-mish'olim II," *Ha-Tekufah* 1 (December 1917–February 1918): 640.

13. Bialik, "Halakhah ve-aggadah," 213.

14. Bialik, "Ha-omanut ha-tehorah," *Kol kitve H. N. Bialik* (Tel Aviv, 1955), 255.

15. Moshe Kleinman, "Shloshet ha-Mendelim," *Ha-Shiloah* 34, no. 1 (January 1918): 70.

16. Ibid, 71.

17. Nokhem Shtif, *Humanizm in der elterer yidisher literatur* (Berlin, 1922) [Kiev, 1919], 4.

18. Ibid., 3.

19. Grinblat, "Reshimot sifrutiyot: *Olamenu,*" *Ha-Tekufah* 1 (December 1917–February 1918): 670.

20. Niger, "Yung-amerike," *Yidishe folksblat,* 21 November 1917.

21. Natan Bistritsky, "Shihrur ha-prat," *Tarbut: Yedi'ot ha-va'ad ha-merkazi* (Kiev) 2 (28 August 1918): 6.

22. M. H. Abrams, *The Mirror and the Lamp: Romantic Theory and the Critical Tradition* (London, 1953), 88–90.

23. Shtif, *Humanizm,* 7.

24. Y. Dobrushin, "Di yidishe literatur un di lerer-yugnt," *Shul un lebn* 2–3 (January–February 1919): 52–53.

25. Nahman Mayzl to H. N. Bialik, 8 January 1918, Beit Bialik, correspondence collection.

26. L. Podriachik, "Leil hitgalut shel Dovid Hofshteyn," in *Shvut* 2 (1974): 180; Dovid Hofshteyn, "Osher Shvartsman," obituary, *Oyfgang* (Kiev, 1919), 129.

27. Nahman Mayzl, *Kh. N. Bialik: Vegen un shafung* (Kiev, 1917).

28. *Eygns* 1 (1918): front matter.

29. Mayzl, *Bialik*, 45–46.

30. Ibid., 16.

31. Y. Dobrushin, "Dray dikhter," *Oyfgang* (Kiev, 1919), 94–95.

32. Mayzl, *Bialik*, 46.

33. Ibid., 24.

34. Dovid Bergelson to Bialik, 22 December 1912; Yehiel Mayzil to Bialik, undated [1910–1914] and Nahman Mayzl to H. N. Bialik, undated [but prewar] and 8 January 1918, Beit Bialik, correspondence collection.

35. Hofshteyn to Bialik, undated [1923], Beit Bialik, correspondence collection.

36. Moyshe Litvakov, "Sofn un onheybn," in Litvakov, *In Umruh* (Kiev, 1918), 105–106. Here Litvakov cruelly appropriated Bialik's own image from his searing 1910 poem "Lifne aron ha-sefarim" (Before the Bookshelf), which has the poet-persona facing a bookshelf of traditional Judaic texts that had once spoken deeply to him yet now seem dead and powerless to revive his own flagging creativity. See Dan Miron, *Bo'ah, lailah: Ha-sifrut ha-'Ivrit ben higayon le-i-gayon be-mifneh ha-me'ah ha-'esrim* (Tel Aviv, 1987).

37. A. Z. Ben-Yishai, "Pirke Ukraina ('al pi yoman)," *He-'Avar* 18 (1971): 176.

38. Natan Bistritsky, "Li-dmuto ha-piutit shel Y. L. Peretz," *Ha-'Am*, 15 April 1918; Bistritsky, "David Shimonovits," *Ha-Shiloah* 34, no. 2 (February 1918): 221–236; Bistritsky, "Shetikato shel Bialik," *Ha-Shiloah* 34, nos. 5–6 (April 1918): 511–518; Bistritsky, "Shihrur."

39. Bistritsky, "Shimonovits," 221; Bistritsky, "Shihrur," 6.

40. Bistritsky, "Shimonovits," 221–223, 228.

41. On this non-involvement, see Dan Miron, *Bodedim be-mo'adam* (Tel Aviv, 1987), 425–429; see also his suggestive comments on "the authors of the generation of the war and Revolution," 400–401, which Bistritsky's case supports.

42. Bistritsky, "Li-dmuto."

43. Ibid.

44. Bistritsky, "Shihrur," 7.

45. Bistritsky's "Shetikato" seeks to explain Bialik's poetic trajectory in terms of an inner psychic division or insufficiency that, significantly, Bistritsky sees as typical of the Jewish intelligentsia.

46. Bistritsky, "Shimonovits," 221.

47. Bistritsky, "Shihrur," 7.

48. M. Z. Valpovsky, "Bat Lita," *Ha-Tekufah* 1 (December 1917–February 1918): 463–466; cf. Kressel, "Valpovsky, M. Z." in *Leksikon ha-sifrut ha-'ivrit ba-dorot ha-aharonim* (Merhavyah, 1965) and Eliyahu Meitus, *Bi-mehitsatam shel sofrim* (Tel Aviv, 1977), 100.

49. David Shimonovits, "Nedudim," *Ha-Tekufah* 1 (December 1917–February 1918): 421–442, dated 1917; Kressel, "Shimoni, David" in *Leksikon ha-sifrut ha-'ivrit*. Thanks to Marcus Moseley, Neta Stahl, and Shachar Pinsker for their comments on this text and my interpretation.

50. Shimonovits, "Nedudim," 428.

51. Ibid., 439.

52. Charles Taylor, *Sources of the Self* (Cambridge, Eng., 1989), 419, 390. Taylor himself is a trenchant critic of the implications of this stance, and would no doubt find Bialik's thought congenial.

53. Bistritsky, "Shiḥrur," 5.

54. Bistritsky, "Shetikato," 517.

55. On the anarchic implications of ideals of self-formation through culture, see Daniel Bell, *The Cultural Contradictions of Capitalism* (New York, 1996).

56. Thanks to Ofer Nur for clarifying this part of Bistritsky-Agmon's life.

57. Bertoldi (Zeev Latski), "Yudishkayt un yuden, oder, vegen yudisher apikorsus," *Di yudishe velt* 1, no. 2 (February 1914): 228.

58. Litvakov, *In Umruh,* 76, 98.

59. On the "Caucuses" poems, see Mikhail Krutikov, "1919 god—Revolutsiia v evreiskoi poezii," in *Mirovoi krizis, 1914–1920 godov i sud'ba vostochnoevropeiskogo evreistva,* ed. O. Budnitskii (Moscow, 2005), 320–327.

60. See, e.g., "In vinter farnakhtn" or the 1914 "Nayyor," which compares the speaker's own scientifically mediated relationship to celestial beauty with the messianic meanings that his grandfather read in the stars. *Lider un poemes,* vol. 1 (Tel Aviv, 1977).

61. Dovid Hofshteyn, "A gantsn tog," in *Lider un poems,* vol. 1, 15.

62. Podriachik, "Leil hitgalut."

63. Dovid Hofshteyn, "Ovnt," in *Lider un poemes,* vol. 1, 56.

64. Dovid Hofshteyn, "In gas," in *Lider un poemes,* vol. 1, 66.

65. Pieter M. Judson, *Guardians of the Nation* (Cambridge, 2006), ch. 1; Tara Zahra, *Kidnapped Souls: National Indifference and the Battle for Children in the Bohemian Lands, 1900–1948* (Ithaca, 2008).

66. "Obshchii obzor deiatel'nosti o-va 'Tarbut,'" CZA, record group F-30, folder 98/1; A. Levinson, *Ha-Tenu'ah ha-'ivrit ba-golah* (Warsaw, 1935), 38; A. Zaidman, "Ha-otonomiyah ha-le'umit ha-yehudit ba-Ukrainah ha-'atsmait ba-shanim, 1917–1919," Ph.D. diss., Tel Aviv University, 1980, 181; *Kultur-Lige* 1: 4–24.

67. See, e.g., Avraham Epstein's "Himnon le-gananot," *Ha-Ginah* 1 (September–October 1917): 1.

68. Education also seems to have been one of the few realms within the Jewish national movement where women could attain real authority.

69. "Kurtsterminige kursn far gertnerins," *Shul un lebn* 2–3 (January 1919): 103.

70. Dobrushin, "Di yidishe literatur," 53.

71. Yehiel Heilprin, "Yesodot gan-ha-yeladim ha-'ivri," *Ha-Ginah* 1 (September–October 1917): 2.

72. Ibid., 3.

73. Quoting from Sh. D., "Di normale shul," *Shul un lebn* 6–7 (November–December 1919): 68; see also *Di Grunt-oyfgabn fun der Kultur-Lige* (Kiev, 1918), 14–15; for the Hebraist equivalent, see M. A. Beygel, "'Al ha-hinukh ha-esteti," *Ha-Ginah* 2 (November–December 1917): 12–17.

74. Ben-Zion Dinur, *Bi-yeme milḥamah u-mahpekhah: Zikhronot u-reshumot mi-derekh ḥayim* (Jerusalem, 1960), 322, 332.

75. Beygel, "Al ha-hinukh ha-esteti," 12.

76. Heilprin, "Yesodot," 4. On the heavily Judaizing anthologies of the preeminent pre-1914 Hebraist publisher Moriah, see Adam Rubin, "From Torah to Tarbut: Hayim Nahman Bialik and the Nationalization of Judaism," Ph.D. diss., UCLA, 2000.

77. A. Sokalov, "Funem tog-bukh fun a lerer," *Shul un lebn* 6–7 (November–December 1919): 33.

78. Yaakov Fichman, "Reshimot bibliografiyot," *Ha-Ginah* 1 (September–October 1917): 42; David Roskies, *A Bridge of Longing: The Lost Art of Yiddish Storytelling* (Cambridge, 1995), 202.

79. Noyekh Lurie, "Far yidishe kinder," *Shul un Lebn* 1 (December 1918): 65.

80. Yohanan Pograbinsky, "Le-toldot ha-mol"ut," *Jewish Book Annual* 9 (New York, 1950–1951): liv.

81. "Shetilim" (advertisement), *Ha-'Am,* 16 July 1917.

82. Indeed, some experienced the Revolution as having quite the opposite effect. In December 1917, the Hebrew writer Hava Shapira confided to her diary: "Public, collective life has perhaps attained greater content, become more interesting. But private, individual life has become so impoverished, impoverished and empty! Life, the whole inner, private 'I,' is contracting, dissolving into the mixed multitude of the collective, of collective work. And there is no internal development or internal fulfilment." "Me-yomanah shel Ḥava Shapira hi Em Kol Ḥai,'" *Gnazim* 1 (1961): 57.

83. This is attested in the essays cited earlier by Bistritsky, Litvakov, and Latski-Bertoldi.

84. Cited in Fishl Lahover, *Bialik: Ḥayav ve-yetsirotav* (Jerusalem, 1956), 243, 245.

85. Ibid., 244–245, 247.

86. Compounding the irony, the letter was in Hebrew. Peretz to Sholem Rabinovich, repr. in *Kol kitve Y. L. Peretz,* vol. 10, part 2 (Tel Aviv, 1962), 211–213.

87. Nahman Mayzl, "Tsen yor," in *Noente un vayte,* vol. 1 (Vilna, 1927), 14–15. The essay was written in 1922.

88. Michael Steinlauf, "Fear of Purim: Y. L. Peretz and the Canonization of Yiddish Theater," *Jewish Social Studies*, n.s. 3 (1995); Miron, *Bodedim.*

89. Shlomo Tsemah, "Be-'avotot ha-havay," in *Erets: Ma'asef le-sifrut yafah ulevikoret* (Odessa, 1919), 129.

90. Fichman, "Baale ha-aggadah"; Fridman, "Ba-mish'olim II."

91. A. Litai, "Perishut sikhlit o hitbollelut," *Ha-'Am,* 10 March 1917.

92. Natan Grinblat, "Reshimot sifrutiyot: *Olamenu,*" *Ha-Tekufah* 1 (December 1917–February 1918): 670, 672.

93. Fridman, "Ba-mish'olim II," 650. See also Ribalov, "*Kneset:* Bikoret," 505: "His most perfect and beautiful poem in *Kneset,* "Artzi" [my land], tells of his love for 'his land.' His land—this is our land, the land of the entire people, the Land of Israel. But in this poem there is no hint of the Land as we understand or feel it to be. It is not a land of ancestors or prophets."

94. Fridman, "Ba-mish'olim II," 651.

95. David Frishman, "'Al ha-sifrut ha-yafah," *Kol kitve David Frishman,* vol. 8 (Warsaw, 1932) [originally 1913], 58.

96. Fridman was active in the Zionist organizations of Russian Jewish university students and in Tseire-Tsion, among others. Kressel, "Fridman, David Aryeh" in *Leksikon ha-sifrut ha-'ivrit.*

97. Aleph, "Genizah ve-ḥatimah," in "Ma'amarim u-reshimot," in *Erets* (1919): 28.

98. Each move in the syllogism I impute to Shteynman was explicitly attested in other writings of his milieu, as we have seen: the first by figures like Grinblat and Bistritsky (see earlier in this chapter), the second by Bistritsky, Haim Grinberg, the Yiddishist Zeev Latski-Bertoldi, and others (see Chapter 3).

99. Latski-Bertoldi, "*In Umruh*" (review), *Bikher-velt* 2–3 (March 1919): 30.

6. The Imperatives of Revolution

Epigraph: Shmuel Niger, November 1918, in *Fun mayn togbukh,* ed. Haim Bez (New York, 1973), 169–170.

1. Avraham Stybel to Niger, YIVO, record group 360, folder 930; Shmuel Niger, *Fun mayn togbukh,* ed. Haim Bez (New York, 1973), 167.

2. Niger, *Fun mayn togbukh,* 169.

3. For a typology of intelligentsia responses, see Jane Burbank, *Intelligentsia and Revolution: Russian Views of Bolshevism, 1917–1922* (Oxford, 1989).

4. Jeremy Smith, *The Bolsheviks and the National Question, 1917–23* (New York, 1999); Mordecai Altshuler, *Ha-yevsektsiyah be-vrit ha-mo'atsot, bein leumiut le-komunizm* (Tel Aviv, 1981), 24–25.

5. Sh. Niger, "Folks-shafung [continuation]," *Kultur un bildung* 2 (26 August 1918): 9.

6. Shmuel Agurski, *Der idisher arbeter in der komunistisher bavegung, 1917–1921* (Minsk, 1925), 29, 30, note.

7. Sh. Niger, "Di revolutsye—Un der poet," *Di naye velt* 1–2 (January–February 1919): 27.

8. Donyel Tsharni, *A yortsendlik aza, 1914–1924: Memuarn* (New York, 1943), 212; Agurski, *Idisher arbeter,* 29, 30, note.

9. See the reaction to this development in Donyel Tsharni to Niger, 20 or 28 January [probably 1921], YIVO, record group 360, folder 16.

10. Evan Mawdsley, *The Russian Civil War* (Boston, 1987), 116–120; James E. Mace, *Communism and the Dilemmas of National Liberation: National Communism in Soviet Ukraine, 1918–1933* (Cambridge, 1983), 30–34.

11. Oleg Budnitskii, *Rossiiskie evrei mezhdu krasnymi i belymi (1917–1920)* (Moscow, 2006); Peter Kenez, "Pogroms and White Ideology in the Russian Civil War," in *Pogroms: Anti-Jewish Violence in Modern Russian History,* ed. John Klier and Shlomo Lambroza (Cambridge, Eng., 1992); Henry Abramson, *A Prayer for the Government: Ukrainians and Jews in Revolutionary Times, 1917–1920* (Cambridge, 1999), 150–151.

12. On the disillusionment, see *Di idishe avtonomye un der natsionaler sekretariat in Ukraine* (Kiev, 1920), 255–257; "In Kultur-Lige," *Shul un lebn* 2–3 (January–February 1919): 95; on rising Jewish support for the Bolsheviks in the wake of the pogroms "even [among] the bourgeoisie," see Y. Sa'aruni, "Reḥifim (Perakim me-ma'avak ha-sifrut ha-'ivrit be-Vrit ha-Mo'atsot)," *He-'Avar* 21 (1975): 118; Yehuda Karni, "Ma'avar ha-Dnister," *He-'Avar* 16 (1968–1969): 52.

13. Tsviah Balshan, "Ma'avakam shel yehude Lita al zekhuyoteihem ha-le'umiot 1917–1918," *Shvut* 10 (1984): 62–82.

14. Zvi Y. Gitelman provides a detailed analysis in his *Jewish Nationality and Soviet Politics* (Princeton, 1972), 151–217.

15. Eliezer Shteynman, "Hed ha-yamim: Ha-milḥamah veha-revolutsiyah," *Ha-Tekufah* 1 (December 1917–February 1918): 683; "Iber poshete zakhn," *Di vokh* (Odessa) 2 (March 1919): 8–9; Yehoshua A. Gilboa, *Oktobraim ivriim: Toldotehah shel ashlayah* (Tel Aviv, 1974), 10–16.

16. Eliezer Shteynman, "Bi-reshuti: Reshimot noshanot (Daf mi-pinkasi al rusiyah)," *Ketuvim* 43 (13 July 1927): 2–3.

17. Mayzl, "Der Kiever period in der yidisher literatur" in *Tsurikblikn un perspektivn* (Tel Aviv, 1962), 505.

18. "Shul-khronik," *Shul un Lebn* 2–3 (January–February 1919): 98.

19. Joseph Sherman, "Leyb Kvitko," in *Dictionary of Literary Biography,* vol. 333: *Writers in Yiddish,* ed. Joseph Sherman (Detroit, 2007).

20. Dubnov to Bialik and Ravnitsky, 11 December 1917, Ravnitsky Collection, JNUL, collection 4–1185, folder 147.

21. Peter Kenez, "Lenin and the Freedom of the Press," in *Bolshevik Culture: Experiment and Order in the Russian Revolution*, ed. Abbott Gleason, Peter Kenez, and Richard Stites (Bloomington, 1989), 140; Ben-Tsion Katz, *Zikhronot* (Tel Aviv, 1964), 254.

22. Sheila Fitzpatrick, *The Commissariat of Enlightenment: Soviet Organization of Education and the Arts under Lunacharsky, October 1917–1921* (Cambridge, Eng., 1970), introduction.

23. An-ski to Monoszon (Ettinger), 8/21 March 1918, in "Pis'ma S. An-skogo," *Novyi Zhurnal* (New York) 89 (1967): 125; An-ski to Bialik, 10/23 April 1918, in *Bialik ve-sofre doro*, ed. Moshe Ungerfeld (Tel Aviv, 1974), 29; Ben-Tsion Katz, "Ka-'avor tekufah," *Ha-Tsefirah* (Warsaw), 4 March 1927; Tsharni, *Yortsendlik*, 227–228; see also Tsharni to Niger, 27 January 1918, YIVO, record group 360, folder 16, though on the halting and thin character of Yiddish cultural life in Moscow in this period, see Tsharni to Niger, 6 April 1918, YIVO, record group 360, folder 16; Gennady Estraikh, "Yiddish Literary Life in Soviet Moscow, 1918–1924," *Jews in Eastern Europe* 2, no. 42 (2000): 25–55. On the art exhibit, see "Khronik," *Kultur un bildung* 3–4 (6 September 1918): 21–22.

24. N. Romanova, "Evreiskii otdel petrogradskogo komissariata po delam natsional'nostei (1918–1923 gg.)," *Vestnik evreiskogo universiteta v Moskve* 3, no. 10 (1995): 56.

25. *Bam likht fun komunistishn ideal* (Moscow, 1919), 281–282; Altshuler, *Ha-yevsektsiyah*, 23–24.

26. Gabriele Freitag, *Naechstes Jahr in Moskau!* (Goettingen, 2004), 188–189.

27. Romanova, "Evreiskii otdel," 56.

28. Note that the EvKom's own journal reported an appeal to the EvKom by the Moscow Peretz society for a subvention to support a Yiddish theater; *Kultur un bildung*, no. 3–4 (6 September 1918): 23.

29. "Brif," *Kultur un bildung* 2 (26 August 1918): 12–13; "Khronik," *Shul un lebn* 4–5 (March–April 1919): 93; Zvi Halevy, *Jewish Schools under Czarism and Communism* (New York, 1976), 128–129.

30. St. sekretar' Narkoma Inodel to S. Dimanshtein, RGASPI, record group 445, finding aid 1, folder 22, doc. 56.

31. Katz, "Ka-'avor tekufah," 4; Eliezer Shteynman, "Ba-ḥazit ha-'ivrit" in *(Hed) Ketuvim*, 20 August 1926.

32. An-ski to Bialik, 10/23 April 1918, in Ungerfeld, *Bialik*, 29; interview with Zlatopolsky in Kohelet, "'Avodat ha-Tarbut ba-'avar uve-'atid," *Ha-Toren* 23 (22 August 1919): 11–13; Katz, "Ka-'avor tekufah," 4.

33. "Plani i namereniia Sionistov," July 1919, TsDAHOU, record group 1, finding aid 20, folder 93, docs. 4–6 (3–4 in original).

34. Gilboa, *Oktobraim*, 8–9, 22–23.

35. Shlomo Tsemah, *Sipur ḥayai* (Jerusalem, 1983), 102–103; Vladislav Ivanov, ed., "Manifesti: Teatral'nie Skrizhali Nauma Tsemakha," *Teatr* 1 (1997): 109–127. I owe this source to Gabriella Safran.

36. E. Tsherikover, "Di yidishe komunistn un di gezelshaftn in Ukraine 1919," in *In der tkufe fun revolutsye (memuarn, materyaln, dokumentn)*, ed. Tsherikover (Berlin, 1924), 318–331.

37. Gershon Hanovits, "'Tsiltsele-Shema'—shenat 1923,'" *He-'Avar* 17 (1970): 152.

38. Ben-Zion Dinur, *Bi-yeme milḥamah u-mahapekhah: Zikhronot u-reshumot mi-derekh ḥayim* (Jerusalem, 1960), 345–347; L. Brovarnik, Executive Bureau, Kultur-Lige Central Committee to Ben-Tsion Dinur, 9 July 1919, Dinur Collection, CAHJP.

39. Benjamin Pinkus, *The Jews of the Soviet Union* (Cambridge, Eng., 1988), 54.

40. Yuri Slezkine, "The USSR as a Communal Apartment, or How a Socialist State Promoted Ethnic Particularism," *Slavic Review* 53, no. 2 (1994): 414–452; Smith, *Bolsheviks and the National Question;* Terry Martin, *The Affirmative Action Empire: Nations and Nationalism in the Soviet Union, 1923–1939* (Ithaca, 2001).

41. Tsharni, *Yortsendlik,* 214–215, 237–238, 241–242; N.a., "Kul'tura i prosveshchenie: V Litve," in *Zhizn' natsional'nostei,* 30 March 1919, 4; N.a., "Farn khoydesh (kultur-khronik)," *Di naye velt* (Vilna) 1–2 (January–February 1919): 117.

42. Anonymous, undated report on the history of the Jewish Commissariat in Kiev, mid-1919, TsDAVO, record group 3304, finding aid 1, folder 5; Tsherikover, "Yidishe komunistn," 315.

43. "Shul-khronik," *Shul un lebn* 2–3 (January–February 1919): 98.

44. Mace, *Communism,* 34; George S. N. Luckyj, *Literary Politics in the Soviet Ukraine, 1917–1934,* rev. ed. (Durham, 1990), 37.

45. Y. Kantor, "Kultur un lebn," *Shul un Lebn* 4–5 (March–April 1919): 63.

46. Folks-Farlag to Bumazhnyi Otdel Sovnarkhoza, 23 February 1919, and Folks-Farlag attestation for Z. Segalovitsh, 19 February 1919, TsDAVO, record group 3304, finding aid 1, folder 4; general request to all Soviet institutions regarding Kultur-Lige book transport, UCP Komissariat po Evreis. Delam, 20 February 1919, TsDAVO, record group 3304, finding aid 1, folder 4; Kultur-Lige TsK to Temporary Commissars of Ministry of Jewish Affairs, 26 February and 3 March 1919, TsDAVO, record group 3304, finding aid 1, folder 10; Kultur-Lige Adult Education Section to Jewish Commissariat, 14 February 1919, TsDAVO, record group 3304, finding aid 1, folder 18; "Education for Adults in Kiev and Provinces," undated, TsDAVO, record group 3304, finding aid 1, folder 17; Kollegia Osviti ta Propaganda to Komm-a po Evr. Sprava, 14 March 1919 and Protocol, "Conference on the organization in Kiev of a Department of the Central Publishing Office," 16 March 1919, TsDAVO, record group 3304, find-

ing aid 1, folder 4; Mayzl, undated requests (somewhat different in the Yiddish and Ukrainian versions), TsDAVO, record group 2060, finding aid 1, folder 43 and record group 3304, finding aid 1, folder 17.

47. Report, Komisar far yidishe inyonim V. Segalovitsh, Komissariat po evreiskim natsional'nym delam (Kharkov) to *Folkstsaytung,* April 1919, TsDAHOU, record group 41, finding aid 1, folder 34; Kharkov EvKom financial report for April 1919, TsDAHOU, record group 41, finding aid 1, folder 34; Temporary Commissars of the Ministry of Jewish Affairs to the Kiev Arbeter-Rat, undated, TsDAVO, record group 2060, finding aid 1, folder 43. Amir Weiner of Stanford University has emphasized this point to me.

48. Kollegia Osviti ta Propaganda to Komm-a po Evr. Sprava, 14 March 1919, TsDAVO, record group 3304, finding aid 1, folder 4; Mayzl, undated requests, TsDAVO, record group 2060, finding aid 1, folder 43 and record group 3304, finding aid 1, folder 17.

49. Temporary Commissars of the Ministry of Jewish Affairs to the Kiev Arbeter-Rat, undated, TsDAVO, record group 2060, finding aid 1, folder 43.

50. "Agursky, Shmuel," in *Leksikon fun der nayer Yidisher literatur* (New York, 1981).

51. See N. M. [Nahman Mayzl], "72. Idish-sotyalistishe bibliotek n. 2," *Bikher-velt* 2–3 (March 1919): 36–38.

52. Cited with slight variation in *Kultur-Lige* 1 (1919): 4; A. Litvak, "Literatur un lebn," *Baginen* 1 (1919): 99; Litvak, "Proletarishe kultur," in *Literatur un kamf* (New York, 1933), 243; Kazdan, "Der lebns-veg fun A. Litvak: Kemfer, shriftshteler, lerer," in A. Litvak, *Geklibene shriftn* (New York, 1945), 114. The statement, probably delivered either at the Kultur-Lige's second all-Ukraine conference or at a Kiev meeting of the Ukrainian Proletkult, evidently made an impression on those who were its targets.

53. N. M., "72. Idish-sotyalistishe bibliotek n. 2."

54. Report to *Folkstsaytung,* April 1919, TsDAHOU, record group 41, finding aid 1, folder 34.

55. It was perhaps in this context that the regime nationalized the Kultur-Lige's Folks-Universitet in April. See *Kultur-lige* 1 (1919): 23.

56. Dinur, *Bi-yeme,* 349.

57. Kantor, "Kultur un lebn," 62–63.

58. Report in *Bor'ba* (Kiev), 29 May 1919, doc. 14, reprinted in *Pravda istorii: dialnist' evreiskoi kulturno-prosviytnits'koi organizatsii "Kulturna Liga" u Kievi (1918–1925),* ed. M. O. Ribakov (Kiev, 1995), 44.

59. Katz, "Kultur-Lige," 188.

60. M. L., "Tsuzamenfor," TsDAVO, record group 3304, finding aid 1, folder 2, docs. 5a–9. On Proletkult in Ukraine, see Luckyj, *Literary Politics,* 36–37.

61. M. L., "Tsuzamenfor"; Ribakov, *Pravda istorii,* 44, doc. 14.

62. M. L., "Tsuzamenfor."
63. Ibid.
64. Ibid.
65. Ibid.
66. Ibid.
67. Ibid.
68. Ibid.
69. Ribakov, *Pravda istorii*, 44, doc. 14.
70. M. L., "Tsuzamenfor."
71. Ibid.
72. Kunst-khronik: Plastishe kunst" and "Kunst-khronik: Literatur," *Baginen* 1 (1919): 85, 95.
73. Moyshe Katz, "Di Kultur Lige in Ukrayne," *Di tsukunft* 3 (March 1921): 183; *Kultur-Lige* 1 (1919): 45.
74. "Kunst-khronik: Literatur," 86.
75. *Kultur-Lige* 2 (1920): 57; "Muzikal'naia studiia Kul't.-Ligi," August 1, 1919, YIVO, record group 37, folder 3.
76. David Shneer, *Yiddish and the Creation of Soviet Jewish Culture, 1918–1930* (Cambridge, Eng., 2004), 226. The actual publication date of the journal seems to have been late summer. It contains obituaries from August 1919, but some of the polemical content seems to have been written at any earlier stage in the rapidly shifting history of Yiddishist Kiev.
77. Ibid., 227.
78. Beynish Shteyman, "Baym toyer," *Oyfgang* (1919).
79. Beynish Shteyman, "Meshiekh ben-Yoysef," *Eygns* (1920).
80. P. Reyland, "Bibliografye: Yung treyst," *Baginen* (1919): 115–117.
81. Moyshe Katz, "Di vegn fun der yidishn teater," *Baginen* (1919): 79.
82. Litvak, "Literatur un lebn," *Baginen* (1919).
83. Ibid., 98–99.
84. Ibid., 99.
85. Ibid., 102.
86. Consider, for example, that Litvak's essay answers arguments by Bergelson that appeared in print only later.
87. Dovid Bergelson, "Dikhtung un gezelshaftlekhkeyt," *Bikher-velt* 4–5 (August 1919). To the degree that "Dikhtung un gezelshaftlekhkayt" has been addressed by scholars, it has been almost exclusively situated in aesthetic debates around Jewish modernism and the place of the "Jewish" element in the new Jewish culture (the question taken up in Chapter 3). See Seth Wolitz, "The Kiev-Grupe (1918–1920) Debate: The Function of Literature," *Yiddish* 3, no. 3 (1978). Both of these concerns are, certainly, present in the essay, but I would argue that the discussion of Yiddish modernism is clearly embedded in a

larger argument about the nature of art as such and the aesthetic demands of revolution, while any concern to define the Jewishness of the new Yiddish culture is actually only implicit.

88. Bergelson, "Dikhtung un gezelshaftlekhkeyt," 6.

89. Ibid., 5–6.

90. Ibid., 7–8.

91. Ibid., 16.

92. Shteynman, "Bi-reshuti," 2.

93. Ibid.

7. Making Jewish Culture Bolshevik

Epigraph: Zelig Kalmanovitsh to Shmuel Niger, 25 May 1920, YIVO, record group 360, folder 34.

1. Sh. Genrikh, "Unzer shul-arbet," *Kultur un bildung* 1 (19 August 1918): 2–3.

2. Mordechai Altshuler, ed., *Ha-Te'atron ha-yehudi be-Vrit ha-Mo'atsot* (Jerusalem, 1996).

3. The term "the Evsektsiia" is something of an abstraction; it refers to an ensemble of Jewish sections in party institutions at all levels coordinated by central bureaus at the republic level (a central bureau of the Evsektsiia of the Russian communist party, a central bureau of the Evsektsiia of the Ukrainian Communist party, and so forth).

4. Protocol, EvOtdel of the Central Committee of the CPU, 14 June [possibly January] 1920, TsDAHOU, record group 1, finding aid 20, folder 794; A. Abtshuk, *Etyudn un materyaln: Tsu der geshikhte fun der yidisher literatur bavegung in F.S.R.R.* (Kharkov, 1934), 17.

5. Collective of Jewish Actors to the Culture-Commission of the Kiev City Committee of the Jewish Communist party (Poale-Tsion), GARF, record group R-8417, finding aid 1, folder 70, docs. 167–169.

6. See David Shneer, *Yiddish and the Creation of Soviet Jewish Culture, 1918–1930* (Cambridge, Eng., 2004), 227–228. Another leading Soviet Yiddish poet of the 1920s, Izi Kharik, got his literary start in *Khvalyes* under the pseudonym Izi Zembin. For an account of Kharik's striking trajectory, which took him from the Tseire Tsion into the Red Army and then to the forefront of Soviet Yiddish literature, see Shneer, *Yiddish*, ch. 6.

7. Jeffrey Veidlinger, *The Moscow State Yiddish Theater* (Bloomington, 2000), 30–38.

8. V. I. Gusev, *Bund, Komfarband, Evsektsii KP(b)U: Mistse v politichnomu zhittu Ukraini (1917–1921)* (Kiev, 1996), 71–72.

9. "Protocol fun der algemeyner farzamlung fun idn komunistn," 16 April 1921, TsDAHOU, record group 1, finding aid 20, folder 794, doc. 14b.

10. "Otchet o deiatel'nosti Glavbyuro Evsektsii pri TsKKPY za 8 Dekabria 1919–9

Maia 1920 g.," TsDAHOU, record group 1, finding aid 20, folder 338, docs. 208–212.

11. "K predstoiashchei konferentsii deiatelei evreiskoi sotsialisticheskoi kul'tury," *Zhizn' natsional'nostei* 11 July 1920, p. 4.

12. "Excerpt from a Letter," 21 November 1921, TsDAHOU, record group 1, finding aid 20, folder 782, doc. 128.

13. "Report on Activity of Liquidation Committee for Jewish Affairs," May–June 1920, TsDAHOU, record group 1, finding aid 20, folder 340, docs. 17–19; Report, F. Frenkel for Main Bureau of the Evsektsiia of the Ukrainian Communist Party to Central Committee of the Ukrainian Communist Party, undated, TsDAHOU, record group 1, finding aid 20, folder 338, doc. 6.

14. "Soveshchanie po voprosam evreiskoi kul'tury v Moskve," *Zhizn' natsional'nostei*, 29 June 1920, p. 4; "Pervii vserossiiskii s"ezd evreiskikh deiatelei prosveshchenii i sotsialisticheskoi kul'tury," *Zhizn' natsional'nostei*, 10 August 1920, p. 4.

15. Report, Main Bureau of the Jewish Sections of the Communist Party in Ukraine, undated, TsDAHOU, record group 1, finding aid 20, folder 90, doc. 5; Protocols, meetings of Main Bureau of the Jewish Sections of the Communist Party in Ukraine, Kiev, 11 January, 16 January, 20 January, 23 January, 8 February 1920, TsDAHOU, record group 1, finding aid 20, folder 338, docs. 69, 83, 89, 99, 117–118.

16. Resolutions reprinted in "Di batsihung tsu der Kultur-Lige," *Kultur-Lige* 2 (1920): 32; "Soveshchanie Evreiskiikh Kommunisticheskikh Sektsii R.K.P.," *Zhizn' natsional'nostei* 9 (April 1920): 3.

17. "Cultural Work," Resolutions of First Kiev Region Conference of the JCP (P-Ts), 13–14 April 1920, GARF, record group R-8417, finding aid 1, folder 69, docs. 63–64.

18. Report, Main Bureau of the Jewish Sections of the Communist Party in Ukraine [probably November 1919], TsDAHOU, record group 1, finding aid 20, folder 90, doc. 3; Protocol, Main Bureau of the Jewish Sections of the Communist Party in Ukraine, 12 January 1920, TsDAHOU, record group 1, finding aid 20, folder 338, doc.75.

19. "Pervii vserossiiskii s"ezd" *Zhizn' natsional'nostei*, 10 August 1920, p. 4.

20. Protocol No. 1, Cultural Committee of the Kiev Committee of the JCP (P-Ts), 23 March [most likely 1920], GARF, record group R-8417, finding aid 1, folder 70, doc. 164; protocol, [Odessa regional Evsektsiia], 27 January [1921?], RGASPI, record group 445, finding aid 1, folder 43, doc. 189.

21. Michael David-Fox, "What Is Cultural Revolution?" *Russian Review* 58, no. 2 (April 1999): 181–201.

22. See contract between Folks-Farlag and Ben-Tsion Dinur and Zelig Kalmanovitsh, 1 July 1919, Dinur Collection, CAHJP; Nokhem Shtif to Zalman Reyzen, 9 August 1920, YIVO, record group 3, folder 3035; Bal-

Dimyen (Shtif), "Der idisher komunist, di Kultur-lige, un dos idishe bukh," *Tsukunft* 28, no. 1 (January 1923): 32.

23. Zilberfarb, autobiography, YIVO, record group 3, folder 2164.

24. Ben-Zion Dinur, *Bi-yeme milḥamah u-mahapekhah: Zikhronot u-reshumot mi-derekh ḥayim* (Jerusalem, 1960), 341.

25. This is evident in Shtif's "Der idisher komunist," 32; but for his persistent "agnosticism" regarding Bolshevism into the early 1920s, see Shtif to Niger, 31 August 1922, YIVO, record group 360, folder 442.

26. Kalmanovitsh to Niger, 25 May 1920, YIVO, record group 360, folder 34.

27. Mordechai Altshuler, ed., *Briv fun yidishe sovetishe shraybers* (Jerusalem, 1980), 7; Y. Dobrushin, "Bikher, lezer, lerer," *Kultur un bildung* nos. 4–5 (27–28) (1920): 52–58; Abtshuk, *Etyudn,* 16–17.

28. Altshuler, *Briv fun yidishe sovetishe shraybers,* 194, 370.

29. Y. Saaruni, "Reḥifim (Perakim mi-ma'avak ha-sifrut ha-'ivrit be-Vrit ha-Mo'atsot)" *He-'Avar* 21 (1975): 118; Yehuda Karni, "Ma'avar ha-Dnister" *He-'Avar* 16 (1968–1969): 52.

30. Protocol, Main Bureau of the Jewish Sections of the Communist Party in Ukraine, 12 January 1920, TsDAHOU, record group 1, finding aid 20, folder 338, doc.75.

31. "Fun der redaktsye," *Kultur un bildung* no. 1 (24) (1920): 2.

32. M. Litvakov, "Tsvey doyres," *Kultur un bildung* no. 1 (24) (1920): 22.

33. Dobrushin, "Bikher, lezer, lerer," 52–58.

34. Bal-Dimyen [Shtif], "Literatur un kultur," *Kultur un bildung* nos. 2–3 (25–26) (1920): 41–44.

35. Kadya Molodowsky, "Dovid Bergelson drukt op mayne ershte lider in zamlbukh 'Eygns,'" *Svive* (New York) 33 (January 1971): 56–57. Molodowsky recalls that at one such meeting, Bergelson explained to her the nature of a strong poetic line with an example from the Bible that lay on his reading desk. This act was a striking testament to the continued presence of Hebrew-language culture for Yiddish writers like Bergelson, who had received a strong traditional education, and Molodowsky, who had studied to be a Hebrew teacher. See Kathryn Hellerstein, introduction, *Paper Bridges: Selected Poems of Kadya Molodowsky* (Detroit, 1999), 19–21.

36. Dovid Hofshteyn, "Tristia," *Eygns* 2 (1920): 44.

37. Dovid Hofshteyn, "In mit fun tog," *Eygns* 2 (1920): 52–53, repr. in Hofshteyn, *Lider un poemes,* vol. 1 (Tel Aviv: Farlag 'Yisroel-Bukh', 1977), 120–121.

38. Dovid Hofshteyn, "Derze ikh af vayte midbaries," *Eygns* 2 (1920): 51, repr. in Hofshteyn, *Lider un poemes* vol. 1, 118.

39. *Pravda istorii: dialnist' evreiskoi kulturno-prosviytnits'koi organizatsii "Kultur-na Liga" u Kievi (1918–1925),* ed. M. O. Ribakov (Kiev, 1995), docs. 29–31; *Kultur-Lige* 2 (1920): 55.

40. A. Bibliofil, "A toyter kapital," and "A grus fun droysn," *Kultur-Lige* 2 (1920): 23–24, 65–66.

41. Hersh Smoliar, *Toḥelet ve-shivrah: Zikhronot shel 'yevsek' lishe-'avar* (Tel Aviv, 1979), esp. 44.

42. Abtshuk, *Etyudn,* 14, 26. "Fefer, Itsik" in *Shpigl af a shteyn,* ed. Chone Shmeruk (Tel Aviv, 1964), 764.

43. Rafes to Dimanshtein, transcript of telephone conversation, 10 February 1920, TsDAHOU, record group 1, finding aid 20, folder 339, docs. 10–11.

44. "Otchet o deiatel'nosti Glavbyuro Evsektsii pri TsKKPY za 8 Dekabria 1919–9 Maia 1920 g." TsDAHOU, record group 1, finding aid 20, folder 338, docs. 208–212.

45. Kh. Sh. Kazdan, *Mayn dor* (New York, 1977), 118.

46. "A grus fun droysn," *Kultur-Lige* 2 (1920): 64.

47. "Rezolutsye vegn kharakter un vayterdiker arbet fun Kultur-Lige," *Kultur-Lige* 2 (1920): 33.

48. "Mir un di melukhe," *Kultur-Lige* 2 (1920): 2–3.

49. Kazdan, *Mayn dor,* 118.

50. "Rezolutsye vegn kharakter," *Kultur-Lige* 2 (1920): 34.

51. "Di Kultur-Lige in Ukraine," in *Kultur-Lige: Ershtes zamlheft* (Warsaw, 1921), 23–24.

52. Protocol 6, EvOtdel of CPU Central Committee, 25 August 1920, TsDAHOU, record group 1, finding aid 20, folder 338, doc. 180.

53. "3-ia vserossiiskaia konferentsiia Evsektsii R.K.P.," *Zhizn' natsional'nostei,* 10 October 1920, 4.

54. Alexander Berkman, *The Bolshevik Myth (Diary 1920–1922)* (London, 1990 [1925]), 229. My thanks to Steven Zipperstein for directing me to this source. Berkman goes on to note that the Kultur-Lige remained "the only oasis in the city of non-partisan intellectual and social life" and that although "now limited in its activities, it still enjoys great popularity among the Jewish youth." Especially impressive were the organization's art classes and its theatrical studio; he found the studio's rehearsals of one of Beynish Shteyman's expressionist works "unique in artistic conception and powerful in expression." Berkman also makes the surprising but intriguing claim that the "younger elements that frequent the Kulturliga [*sic*] dream of Zion and look to the aid of England in securing to the Jewish nation its traditional home." Given the outright suppression of all Hebraist and Zionist institutions, and given what we now know about the upswell of Zionism among Ukrainian Jewish young people in the early 1920s, this makes sense; for an example of such participation, see Zeev Livneh (Lerman), "Lifne yovel shanim be-Kiuv [Kiev]: kit'e zikhronot," *He-'Avar* 16 (1968–1969): 106.

55. Kultur-Lige Central Committee to Main Bureau of the Jewish Sections of the

Communist Party, 13 October 1920, RGASPI, record group 445, finding aid 1, folder 22, doc. 72.

56. Report, EvOtdel, 11 November 1920, TsDAHOU, record group 1, finding aid 20, folder 339, docs. 112–113.

57. *Kultur-Lige: Ershtes zamlheft* (1921): 25.

58. Zilberfarb et al. to Niger, 10 April 1921, YIVO, record group 360, folder 283. See the document cited in Kazovsky, "The Art Section of the Kultur-Lige," *Jews in Eastern Europe* 3, no. 22 (Winter 1993): 11.

59. Shneer, *Yiddish,* 168.

60. V. Lebedeva-Kaplan, "Tri pis'ma iz 1919 g. (Iz istorii evreiskoi kul'tury Petrograda)," in *Istoriia evreev v Rossii,* ed. D. El'iashevich (St. Petersburg, 1993), 136.

61. Levitan, report, 16 February 1920 and protocol 32, 7 April 1920, TsDAHOU, record group 1, finding aid 20, folder 338, docs. 125–126, 165.

62. Report by M. Kiper, Poltava Gubkom meeting, 12 January 1920, TsDAHOU, record group 1, finding aid 20, folder 339, docs. 4–5.

63. "Otchet o deiatel'nosti," Dec. 1919–May 1920, TsDAHOU.

64. Levitan, report, 16 February 1920.

65. "Unzer byudzhet," *Kultur-Lige* 2 (1920): 26–27.

66. "Otchet o deiatel'nosti."

67. Protocol of EvOtdel of the CPU CC, 14 June [or possibly January] 1920.

68. "Barikht fun der Tsentral Byuro fun di Idsektsies bam Tsentral Komitet fun R.K.P. (far der tsayt fun ershtn Yuli 1920 biz ershtn Yuli 1921)," *Partey-materyaln* (Moscow) 5 (August 1921): 37.

69. F. Shprakh, Odessa Evsektsiia to Ts. K. Evsektsii, 15 December [1920 or 1921], RGASPI, record group 445, finding aid 1, folder 43, doc. 7.

70. Kazakevitsh, "*Tsu di, vos hobn gevogt!*" *Tsu der erefnung fun teater-studye Kultur-Lige* (Kiev, 1921), 6.

71. "Barikht vegn der tetikeyt fun der Tsentraler Idisher Byuro bam Felker-Rat in Folks-Komisariat far Bildung: teater-arbet," *Partey-materyaln* 6 (September 1921): 8.

72. Ezra Korman, "Tsu der ershter uflage" in *Brenendike brikn* [expanded version of *In fayerdikn doyer*], ed. Korman (Berlin, 1922), 5–11. Hofshteyn's own investment in this anthology and what it represented is suggested by the fact that he presented a signed version to the pro-Communist cultural activist and Moscow Literary Circle member Shakhne Epshteyn ("To the respected comrade Shakhne Epshteyn, with greetings, D. Hofshteyn, Moscow 10 October [?] 1921"). Harvard University has a microfilm copy of this inscribed version of *In fayerdikn doyer.*

73. Peretz Markish, *Farbaygeyendik* (Vilna, 1921), 18–19.

74. Ibid., 17–19, 42–43.

75. Ibid., 31, 49.

76. Kh. Malinin, "Klasn-kunst oder tendentsieze kunst," *Kultur un bildung* nos. 3–4 (20–21) (10 February 1919): 13–16.

77. Tzvetan Todorov, "Dialogism and Schizophrenia," in Alfred Arteaga, ed., *An Other Tongue: Nation and Ethnicity in the Linguistic Borderlands* (Durham, N.C., 1994), 205.

78. Bal-Dimyen [Shtif], "Der idisher komunist," 32–33.

79. "Di Kultur-Lige in Ukraine," 19.

80. Zilberfarb et al. to Niger, 10 April 1921.

81. "Di Kultur-Lige in Ukraine," 20.

Conclusion

Epigraph: Haim Grinberg, "Bor'ba za natsional'nuiu individual'nost," *Sborniki "Safrut,"* ed. Leib Jaffe (Moscow, 1917): 90.

1. Ben-Zion Dinur, *Bi-yeme milḥamah u-mahpekhah: Zikhronot u-reshumot mi-derekh ḥayim* (Jerusalem, 1960), 324.

2. Peretz Markish, *Farbaygeyendik* (Vilna, 1921), 19.

3. Zohar Shavit and Yaacov Shavit, "Lemale' et ha-arets sefarim: Sifrut mekorit le'umat sifrut meturgemet be-tahalikh yetsirato shel ha-merkaz ha-sifruti be-erets yisrael," *Ha-Sifrut* 25 (1977): 48–51.

4. See the In-zikh texts translated in *American Yiddish Poetry*, ed. Benjamin and Barbara Harshav (Berkeley, 1986).

5. *Eygns un fremds* (Boston, 1922); note that the title (Our Own and Foreign) did not denote a distinction between Jewish and European culture, but rather the difference between the authors' own work (including the pieces on Pater and Prometheus) and their translations.

6. In the Jewish cultural sphere of late Ottoman Palestine, this was inscribed in the system-changing insistence of Y. H. Brenner on a complicated but real editorial independence vis-à-vis the Ha-poel ha-tsair movement, even in the movement-affiliated *Ha-adamah;* see Dan Miron, "Mi-yotsrim u-vonim li-vne beli bayit," in Miron, *Im lo tihiyeh Yerushalayim: Masot 'al ha-sifrut ha-'ivrit be-heksher tarbuti-politi* (Tel Aviv, 1987), 37; Zohar Shavit, *Ha-ḥayim ha-sifrutiim be-erets Yisrael, 1910–1933* (Tel Aviv, 1982), 66–68. In the United States, the *Inzikhistn* were preceded in their demonstrative nonparty stance by a previous poetic movement, Di yunge, which had insisted on the same institutional distance from the American Yiddish socialist movement ten years earlier. See Ruth Wisse, "*Di Yunge* and the Problem of Jewish Aestheticism," *Jewish Social Studies* 38, nos. 3–4 (1976): 265, 273; on conflicting conceptions of nation and culture in the American Yiddish socialist movement, see Tony Michels, *A Fire in Their Hearts: Yiddish Socialists in New York* (Cambridge,

2005), chs. 3–4. In both wartime Warsaw and wartime Vilna, local Jewish nationalist intellectuals founded cultural organizations (writers' unions, an ethnographic society) that pledged themselves to political neutrality in the name of the nation, and were even initially open to both Hebraists and Yiddishists. See Natan Cohen, *Sefer, sofer, ve-ʻiton* (Jerusalem, 2003), 17–25; "Ufruf," Vilner Yidishe Historish-Etnografishe Gezelshaft, 1 January 1920, Vilna Collection, YIVO, record group 29, folder 345.

7. I will reiterate here that I certainly do not mean to suggest that all individual artistic and intellectual endeavors by Hebrew or Yiddish cultural producers should be seen *primarily* as expressions of this shared project. Alongside the obvious point that individual producers and individual works were distinct and demand wholly individualized interpretive attention, it is also true that Hebrew and Yiddish literatures as institutions were themselves never simply cogs in the cultural project. Both literatures began to emerge well before the beginnings of the national cultural project analyzed here; arguably, both literatures have outlived the ideals that animated the cultural project, albeit in very different ways; and both literatures as institutions allowed and even perhaps compelled writers to operate in tension with the cultural project. We might say that this was true generally insofar as one of literature's intrinsic briefs is to disrupt or unsettle all verities. More specifically, there were figures in both literatures, especially in Hebrew literature, who considered talk of "Jewish culture" as a kind of anemic, self-congratulatory substitute for genuinely meaningful efforts to confront the political, social, cultural, and psychological problems of Jewish society. This suspicion resonated most famously in the turn-of-the-century writings of Brenner, who extended his acid skepticism about all aspects of contemporary Jewish life to talk of "culture" as well. Yet even Brenner combined this rebellious skepticism with clear-eyed adherence to the basic culturist blueprint (as evidenced in his concern for programmatic translation and his unwavering commitment to Hebrew-language creativity). The seemingly contradictory embrace by such a figure of unremitting contempt for all ideological verities and a robust Hebraist and culturist agenda is no less interesting and historically important than his rebellious literary stance as such, and demands to be explained.

8. Max Weber, "Zwischenbetrachtung," translated as "Religious Rejections of the World and Their Directions" in *From Max Weber,* ed. Hans Gerth and C. Wright Mills (New York, 1946), 342.

9. See, e.g., David Lloyd, *Nationalism and Minor Literature* (Berkeley, 1987).

10. This argument is indebted to Rogers Brubaker, *Nationalism Reframed: Nationhood and the National Question in the New Europe* (Cambridge, Eng., 1996), though that work focuses exclusively on political nationalism. Gregory Jusdanis, in his *Belated Modernity and Aesthetic Culture* (Minneapolis, 1991)

starts toward this argument with his titular notion of the cultural realm as something that could be perceived belatedly by non-Western intellectuals as a modular whole.

11. The phrase "principle of vision and division" is Bourdieu's.

12. Some readers will be quick to point out that the nationalism surveyed in this book was a stateless and deterritorialized one, and may assume that the conclusions cease to apply insofar as such a cultural project is institutionalized in a particular state and place. But this does not seem to be the case either generally or in the Jewish case—instead, statehood and territorialization, like language, generate multiple and even contradictory effects in the cultural sphere. Thus on the one hand, statehood for Jews in the State of Israel meant greatly expanded powers to shape cultural life from above, and territorialization fed various sorts of nativisms and essentialisms in the Yishuv's and later Israel's Hebrew cultural sphere. See Yael Zerubavel, *Recovered Roots: Collective Memory and the Making of the Israeli National Tradition* (Chicago, 1998); Eric Zakim, *To Build and Be Built: Landscape, Literature, and the Construction of Zionist Identity* (Philadelphia, 2005). But on the other hand, the emergence of a Hebrew-language public and a Hebrew-language economy, fostered and secured not least by the nation-state, laid the groundwork for an Israeli contemporary Hebrew-language cultural life that over time has drifted ever further from meaningful state control.

13. See, e.g., Der Nister's "Unter a ployt (revyu)" and Moyshe Kulbak's *Montik*. These works are available in English. See Der Nister, "Behind a Fence," trans. Seymour Levitan in *A Treasury of Yiddish Stories*, ed. Irving Howe and Eliezer Greenberg (New York, 1990), 574–596; and Kulbak, "Monday," in *The Shtetl*, ed. and trans. Joachim Neugroschel (New York, 1989), 485–550.

14. Quoting from Nister, "Behind a Fence," 594. See also David Roskies, *A Bridge of Longing: The Lost Art of Yiddish Storytelling* (Cambridge, 1995), 222–229; Chone Shmeruk, "Yiddish Literature in the U.S.S.R," in *The Jews in Soviet Russia since 1917*, ed. Lionel Kochan (Oxford, 1978).

15. Shtif to Niger, 13 June 1922, YIVO, record group 360, folder 442.

16. In the vast literature on Yishuv political culture and its norms in general, works that deal directly with the connection between this political culture and the high cultural sphere particularly include Nurit Gertz, *Sifrut ve-ideologyah be-Erets-Yisrael bi-shenot ha-sheloshim* (Ramat-Aviv, 1988); Miron, "Miyotsrim," 41–67; and Oz Almog, *The Sabra: The Creation of the New Jew* (Berkeley, 2000), 143–159. Almog's study simultaneously suggests the degree to which culturist ideals were trammeled by intensifying demands for social and psychic reinvention and the very substantial sociological limits to any full-fledged rejection of classical European notions of self-cultivation and the sovereign significance of literature, even in the self-selecting circles where

ideas of Zionist revolution were most intense. Concomitantly, other sources suggest that despite nativizing emphases among many Yishuv educators, many Jews in the Yishuv, especially young people, remained individually committed to a more cosmopolitan mode of self-cultivation. Yishuv publishers produced so many translations that the Hebraist Ben-Yishai was moved to complain in 1929 that "Japheth has swallowed up Shem." Dania Amichay-Michlin, *Ahavat ish: Avraham Yosef Stybel* (Jerusalem, 2000), 291, 296. Beyond the empirical debate to which such claims are subject, a growing body of work contends that these very conceptions of aesthetic autonomy and individual self-expression were themselves mechanisms through which collectivist myth and statist and nativist ideologies were activated in the Yishuv; see, e.g., Zakim, *To Build;* Uri S. Kohen, *Hisardut: Tefisat ha-mavet ben milḥamot ha-'olam be-Erets Yisrael uve-Italyah* (Tel Aviv, 2007), ch. 4. Conversely, other recent work suggests the degree to which the actual cultural life in the immigrant society of the Yishuv was actually a congeries of disparate visions, practices, and commitments to which ideological unity can only be ascribed with a certain degree of interpretive violence. See Yisrael Bartal, "Mavo': 'Tarbut Yisrael' o 'tarbuyot Yisrael'?" in *Ha-'Agalah ha-mele'ah: meah ve-esrim shenot tarbut Yisrael* (Jerusalem, 2002). Yael Chaver's recent study of the fate of Yiddish-language literary culture in the Yishuv offers an interesting perspective on all these questions; see *What Must Be Forgotten: The Survival of Yiddish in Zionist Palestine* (Syracuse, 2004), esp. xix–xx, 37–44, 120–130, 148–149.

17. On the reflexive Eurocentrism, see Derek J. Penslar, "Transmitting Jewish Culture: Radio in Israel," in Penslar, *Israel in History* (London, 2007); for an example, see Rachel Katznelson-Shazar, "Binyan tarbut" (1934), in *'Al admat ha-'ivrit* (Tel Aviv, 1966), 251–252.

18. See, e.g., Aharon Shabtai, "Tarbut," in *Artsenu: Shirim 1987–2000* (Tel Aviv: 2002), 335.

19. Natan Bistritsky, "Shiḥrur ha-prat" *Tarbut* 2 (August 1918): 5.

20. Benjamin Harshav, *Marc Chagall and His Times* (Stanford, 2004), 745.

21. Kashua quoted in Bernard Avishai, *The Hebrew Republic* (Orlando, 2008), 226. For an analysis that focuses on forms of subversion and resistance within the works of select Israeli Arab writers, but also contains suggestive comments pointing toward this arguably more complicated process, see Rachel Feldhay Brenner, "'Hidden Transcripts' Made Public: Israeli Arab Fiction and Its Reception," in *Critical Inquiry* 26, no. 1 (Autumn 1999): 87, esp. fn. 8.

22. We might also adduce a different point about territorialization arising out of the contrasting fate of Yiddish and Hebrew culture in the interwar era. As growing numbers of Yiddishists began to realize with alarm in the late 1930s, territorial concentration (or lack thereof) was clearly the key causal factor in the divergent fates of Hebrew and Yiddish secular culture. See "Tsum farshteyendikn

kongres fun der yidisher kultur," in *Der oyfshtayg: Sotsialistisher-teritorialistisher yugnt organ* (Vilna, March 1937), 7: "The Jewish masses in their dispersion, always a minority, cannot compete with the powerful, rich cultures and languages of the peoples among whom they live. Clearly, only the concentration of the Jewish masses in one geographic point under the sun will provide the basis for the Yiddish language, will serve as the solid fundament for the future of the modern Yiddish school and culture." What neither the victorious Hebraists nor the despairing Yiddishists may have understood is that this divergence in the fortunes of the two languages had as much to do with economics as with ideology: territorialization began to make Hebrew an economic value and even a necessity in everyday life, and thus, unlike Yiddish, increasingly the default language of all forms of individual aspiration.

Acknowledgments

It is a great pleasure to thank the many people who made this work possible.

First, my teachers: Steven Zipperstein has overseen this project from its beginnings, and this book has been shaped above all in dialogue with his broad learning, his deep knowledge of Jewish history, and his critical imagination. I am deeply grateful for his teaching and his mentoring, his rigor and his generosity. Steve exemplifies the wisdom of the Mishnaic dictum: "Provide thyself a teacher, get thee a companion." This project began under the tutelage of two other supportive teachers, demanding critics, and friends, Aron Rodrigue and Amir Weiner, and I hope it shows some traces of their formidable analytical acuity. I wish to acknowledge two others who shaped this study more than they could know and passed away while I was completing it: Jonathan Frankel, to whose masterpiece *Prophecy and Politics* this work is deeply indebted; and Mordkhe Schaechter, who gave me the keys to Yiddish.

My colleagues in the History Department of the Johns Hopkins University offered helpful counsel on a very rough draft of this manuscript; for that, and for the demanding but warm environment they have created, I thank them. I owe special thanks in this regard to David Bell, Jeff Brooks, Gabrielle Spiegel, and my former colleague David Nirenberg, who put so much effort into this book and its author. Omer Bartov helped set me on the historian's path many years ago. Marci Shore gave terrifically helpful advice on how to bring this book to publication. Olga Borovaya, Marc Caplan, Olga Litvak, Marcus Moseley, and Ben Nathans offered rich critiques of various parts of my argument, and I apologize for having met their challenges only in part. The mutually opposed but equally friendly skepticisms of my friends Eran Shalev and Marc Caplan regarding, respectively, my actors' obsessions with preserving Jewishness and their aspiration to cultural universality helped me understand the dialectic of modern Jewish culture. Shikl and Gella Fishman provided warmth, standards, and a vital question at an early juncture, when they wondered skeptically why someone had bothered to translate the modern French poetic canon into Yiddish. Eric Oberle and Christine Holbo have influenced this project far more than they imagine with their stunning breadth of knowledge and unfailingly apt questions. Cecile Kuznitz and Tony Michels have shared my fascination with the history of Jewish culture and politics from the beginning, and it has been a privilege to learn from them and think with them for many years.

Among the many other scholars who contributed to the making of this book, warm thanks to Zachary Baker, Hamutal Bar-Yosef, Israel Bartal, Elissa Bemporad, Svetlana Boym, Nicholas Breyfogle, Gennady Estraikh, David Fishman, Gregory Freidin, Amelia Glaser, Francois Guesnet, Brian Horowitz, Elke Kellman, Misha Krutikov, Eli Lederhendler, Benyamin Lukin, Terry Martin, Caitlin Murdock, David Myers, Avrom Novershtern, Ofer Nur, Jess Olson, Derek Penslar, Shachar Pinsker, Simon Rabinovitch, Gabriella Safran, David Shneer, Marcos Silber, Neta Stahl, Sarah Stein, Adam Teller, Scott Ury, Jeff Veidlinger, Ruth Wisse, Seth Wolitz, and the readers for Harvard University Press. Misgav Har-Peled, Yitzhak Melamed, Neta Stahl, and Nira Stahl saved me from some dumb errors of transliteration. So many friends and fellow scholars have helped shape this book that I have surely omitted a few, and I beg their pardon.

I am grateful to the Center for Advanced Judaic Studies at the University of Pennsylvania and the Davis Center for Russian and Eurasian Studies at Harvard for two years of research and writing in wonderfully stimulating settings and at just the right moments. Special thanks to David Ruderman and Liz Tarlow, respectively. I also owe a debt of appreciation to the deans at Johns Hopkins who allowed me to take those opportunities, and to Felix Posen for generously sponsoring the chair that makes possible my presence at Johns Hopkins itself. Finally, it has been a pleasure to work with Harvard University Press. I thank Kathleen McDermott for her confidence and guidance, and Julie Carlson for her sharp editorial eye.

The research for this project involved more than a dozen archives and libraries on three continents. Warm thanks are due the archivists and staff of the YIVO Archive and the Center for Jewish Research in New York; the research libraries at Stanford, Johns Hopkins, the Center for Advanced Judaic Studies at the University of Pennsylvania, and the Jewish National and University Library in Jerusalem; RGASPI, GARF, RGALI, and TsIAM in Moscow; TsDAHOU, TsDAVO, DAKO, and the Manuscript Section of the Vernadsky Library in Kiev (where the warm hospitality of Anna Abramovna Rivkina deserves special mention); the Manuscript Section of the Jewish National and University Library, the Central Archive for the History of the Jewish People, and the Central Zionist Archives in Jerusalem; and in Tel Aviv, Beit Bialik and the Gnazim Institute (which as of this writing is closed due to lack of funds, a fact that would appall the subjects of this book and should horrify their inheritors).

Some material in Chapter 3 was adapted from my essay "Not *The Dybbuk* but *Don Quixote*: Translation, Deparochialization, and Nationalism in Jewish Culture, 1917–1919" in *Culture Front*, ed. Benjamin Nathans and Gabriella Safran (Philadelphia, 2008). Parts of Chapter 4 were adapted from my article "Bringing Culture to the Nation" in *Jewish History* 22, no. 3 (September 2008). Some of the arguments presented here concerning the workings of culture and the problem of the individual within nationalism are further elaborated in my article "Arnold in Eishyshok, Schiller in Shnipishok: Imperatives of Culture in Russian Jewish Nationalism and Revolutionary Socialism" to appear in the September 2009 issue of *Journal of Modern History.*

Finally, I would like to thank my family. My parents, Robert and Sandra Moss, imbued me with a love of learning and with respect for what matters. They exemplify for me what it means to be, as one of the subjects of this book put it, "honest and whole everywhere, on the street and in the home." My brother Dan, scholar of the actual Renaissance, has been unfailingly supportive and a great reader. My parents-in-law David and Tess Eakin have made their home my home as well for many years now. My children Itsik and Arn-Volf have not read any of this book (though they've enjoyed some of the children's literature examined in it), but I have written it for them too. Finally, *akhren akhren khoviv:* my wife, Anne, has been my most important intellectual companion for nearly two decades. Many of the ideas that this work explores are as much hers as mine, born of mutual intellectual enthusiasms. That Anne has done so much to transform these enthusiasms into real, everyday commitments in our life together demands thanks that far exceed the bounds of scholarly acknowledgments.

Index

Abramovitsh, Sh. Y. (Mendele Moykher Sforim): as cultural symbol, 45, 61, 152; Hebraists vs. Yiddishists over, 29, 88; national-cultural influence of, 96; nationalist assessment of, 181, 186, 210; as "petit-bourgeois," 231; politics of commemoration of, 88

Agnon, Sh. Y., 330n101

Agursky, Shmuel, 219, 230–231

Ahad Ha-'Am: and cultural debates of 1890s, 136, 207; culturist rejection of, 73, 76, 119, 136, 139; on Jewish culture, 73, 136, 142; in Russian, 69

Aḥinoar, 50, 120, *fig. 2*

Akhdes (Aḥdut), 162

Aleph: on individual, 197, 214; against tradition, 118–120, 138. *See also* Shteynman

All-Russian Jewish Congress, 44–45

Almog, Oz, 355n16

Alt'man, Natan, 36, 48, 50, 73, 91

Alterman, Natan, 206

Alterman, Yitzhak, 35–36, 202, 206

Anarchists, Jewish, 230, 244, 271–272

An-ski, Sh.: attacks on, by Jewish socialists, 94–95, 224, 236–237; cultural views of, rejected by some Jewish culturists, 74–75, 131; ethnographic museum of, 224; folk-art album of, 121, 167; and Jewish culture, 73–74, 107; and Moscow Jewish circles, 225; popular interest in, 40, 131, 305n42; and Russian-language Jewish culture, 70; transcends political divisions, 45, 85; and Yiddishism, 70, 236, 336n72; and Zionists, 70, 311n23. *See also* "Dybbuk, The"

Anoykhi (Zalman Ahronson), 33

Anticapitalism. *See* Class; Market; Marxism; Socialism

Anti-Jewish violence, 2, 25, 233; and cultural project, 221–222, 266, 275; impact on political views, 220–221, 263–264; as literary theme, 222, 243, 266–268; pogroms in Ukraine, 8, 220–222, 233, 263. *See also* Anti-Semitism; White movement

Anti-Semitism, 25–26, 220–221, 263. *See also* Anti-Jewish violence; White movement

Antokolski, Mark, 50

Apter, Yankev, 131, *fig. 12*

Arab community, Israeli, 293–294, 356n21

Arabic, 35

Arnold, Matthew, 148

Aronson, Boris, 130, *fig. 3*

Arpali, Boaz, 124

Art (aesthetic culture and aesthetic experience): "the arts" in culturist ideology, 2–3, 9, 36, 44, 48, 50–53, 62, 66–68, 283; autonomy of, as experiential and institutional fact, 179–180, 184–188, 210–212, 284–285, 287; autonomy of, as idea, 5, 17, 19, 21–22, 82–85, 96–97, 118, 179–180, 182–183, 189, 201–219; central to Jewish cultural project, 3–5, 62–63, 71–77, 283–285; Communists and, 231–232, 260–261, 273–274; culture as institution distinct from, 11–12, 99–100, 285; culture as institution in tension with, 354n7; culturist aestheticism attacked, 76, 173–182, 189, 210; culturist aestheticism defended, 177, 179–180, 182–183, 210; culturist conception of, as key to other convictions, 210–212;